# THE WORKS
# AND CORRESPONDENCE OF
# DAVID RICARDO

## VOLUME VIII

# PLAN OF THE EDITION

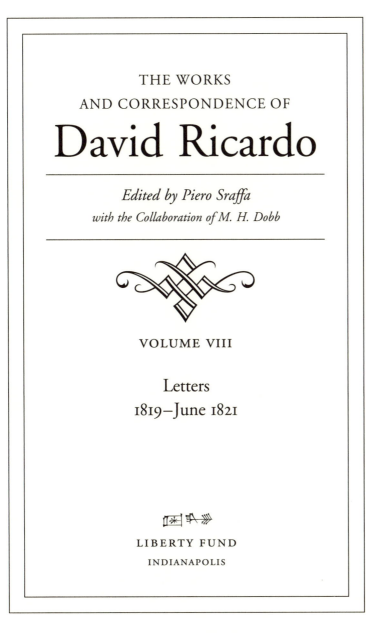

# THE WORKS
# AND CORRESPONDENCE OF
# David Ricardo

*Edited by Piero Sraffa*
*with the Collaboration of M. H. Dobb*

## VOLUME VIII

## Letters
## 1819–June 1821

LIBERTY FUND

INDIANAPOLIS

First published by Cambridge University Press in 1951.
© 1951, 1952, 1955, 1973 by the Royal Economic Society
Typographical design © 2004 by Liberty Fund, Inc.

This edition of *The Works and Correspondence of David Ricardo* is published by
Liberty Fund, Inc., under license from the Royal Economic Society.

10 09 08 07 06 05 04 P 5 4 3 2 1

Library of Congress Cataloging-in-Publication Data

Ricardo, David, 1772–1823.
[Works. 2004]
The works and correspondence of David Ricardo / edited
by Piero Sraffa; with the collaboration of M. H. Dobb.
p.    cm.
Originally published: Cambridge: At the University Press
for the Royal Economic Society, 1951–1973.
Includes bibliographical references and index.
Contents: v. 1. On the principles of political economy and taxation—
ISBN 0-86597-965-0 (pbk.: alk. paper)
1. Economics.   2. Taxation.   I. Sraffa, Piero.
II. Dobb, M. H.   III. Title.

HB161.R4812 2004
330.15′13′092—dc21        2002016222
ISBN 0-86597-972-3 (vol. 8: pbk.: alk. paper)
ISBN 0-86597-976-6 (set: pbk.: alk. paper)

Liberty Fund, Inc.
8335 Allison Pointe Trail, Suite 300
Indianapolis, IN 46250-1684

Text and cover design by Erin Kirk New, Watkinsville, Georgia
Typography by Impressions Book and Journal Services, Inc.,
Madison, Wisconsin
Printed and bound by Edwards Brothers, Inc., Ann Arbor, Michigan

# CONTENTS OF VOLUME VIII

PLATE

David Ricardo, 1820, from the miniature by Thomas Heaphy
(reproduced by permission of the late Lt.-Col. H. G.
Ricardo)       *facing p.* 1

# CALENDARS for 1819, 1820 and 1821 (Jan.–June)

## 1819

| | JAN. | FEB. | MAR. | APRIL | MAY | JUNE |
|---|---|---|---|---|---|---|
| Su | – 3 10 17 24 31 | – 7 14 21 28 | – 7 14 21 28 | – 4 11 18 25 | – 2 9 16 23 30 | – 6 13 20 27 |
| M | – 4 11 18 25 | 1 8 15 22 – | 1 8 15 22 29 | – 5 12 19 26 | – 3 10 17 24 31 | – 7 14 21 28 |
| Tu | – 5 12 19 26 | 2 9 16 23 – | 2 9 16 23 30 | – 6 13 20 27 | – 4 11 18 25 | 1 8 15 22 29 |
| W | – 6 13 20 27 | 3 10 17 24 31 | 3 10 17 24 31 | – 7 14 21 28 | – 5 12 19 26 | 2 9 16 23 30 |
| Th | – 7 14 21 28 | 4 11 18 25 | 4 11 18 25 | 1 8 15 22 29 | – 6 13 20 27 | 3 10 17 24 – |
| F | 1 8 15 22 29 | 5 12 19 26 | 5 12 19 26 | 2 9 16 23 30 | – 7 14 21 28 | 4 11 18 25 – |
| S | 2 9 16 23 30 | 6 13 20 27 | 6 13 20 27 | 3 10 17 24 | 1 8 15 22 29 | 5 12 19 26 – |

| | JULY | AUG. | SEPT. | OCT. | NOV. | DEC. |
|---|---|---|---|---|---|---|
| Su | – 4 11 18 25 | 1 8 15 22 29 | – 5 12 19 26 | – 3 10 17 24 31 | – 7 14 21 28 | – 5 12 19 26 |
| M | – 5 12 19 26 | 2 9 16 23 30 | – 6 13 20 27 | – 4 11 18 25 | 1 8 15 22 29 | – 6 13 20 27 |
| Tu | – 6 13 20 27 | 3 10 17 24 31 | – 7 14 21 28 | – 5 12 19 26 | 2 9 16 23 30 | – 7 14 21 28 |
| W | – 7 14 21 28 | 4 11 18 25 – | 1 8 15 22 29 | – 6 13 20 27 | 3 10 17 24 – | 1 8 15 22 29 |
| Th | 1 8 15 22 29 | 5 12 19 26 – | 2 9 16 23 30 | – 7 14 21 28 | 4 11 18 25 – | 2 9 16 23 30 |
| F | 2 9 16 23 30 | 6 13 20 27 – | 3 10 17 24 – | 1 8 15 22 29 | 5 12 19 26 – | 3 10 17 24 31 |
| S | 3 10 17 24 31 | 7 14 21 28 – | 4 11 18 25 – | 2 9 16 23 30 | 6 13 20 27 – | 4 11 18 25 – |

## 1820

| | JAN. | FEB. | MAR. | APRIL | MAY | JUNE |
|---|---|---|---|---|---|---|
| Su | – 2 9 16 23 30 | – 6 13 20 27 | – 5 12 19 26 | – 2 9 16 23 30 | – 7 14 21 28 | – 4 11 18 25 |
| M | – 3 10 17 24 31 | – 7 14 21 28 | – 6 13 20 27 | – 3 10 17 24 | 1 8 15 22 29 | – 5 12 19 26 |
| Tu | – 4 11 18 25 | 1 8 15 22 29 | – 7 14 21 28 | – 4 11 18 25 | 2 9 16 23 30 | – 6 13 20 27 |
| W | – 5 12 19 26 | 2 9 16 23 – | 1 8 15 22 29 | – 5 12 19 26 | 3 10 17 24 31 | – 7 14 21 28 |
| Th | – 6 13 20 27 | 3 10 17 24 – | 2 9 16 23 30 | – 6 13 20 27 | 4 11 18 25 – | 1 8 15 22 29 |
| F | – 7 14 21 28 | 4 11 18 25 | 3 10 17 24 31 | – 7 14 21 28 | 5 12 19 26 – | 2 9 16 23 30 |
| S | 1 8 15 22 29 | 5 12 19 26 – | 4 11 18 25 – | 1 8 15 22 29 | 6 13 20 27 – | 3 10 17 24 – |

| | JULY | AUG. | SEPT. | OCT. | NOV. | DEC. |
|---|---|---|---|---|---|---|
| Su | – 2 9 16 23 30 | – 6 13 20 27 | – 3 10 17 24 | 1 8 15 22 29 | – 5 12 19 26 | – 3 10 17 24 31 |
| M | – 3 10 17 24 31 | – 7 14 21 28 | – 4 11 18 25 | 2 9 16 23 30 | – 6 13 20 27 | – 4 11 18 25 – |
| Tu | – 4 11 18 25 | 1 8 15 22 29 | – 5 12 19 26 | 3 10 17 24 31 | – 7 14 21 28 | – 5 12 19 26 – |
| W | – 5 12 19 26 | 2 9 16 23 30 | – 6 13 20 27 | 4 11 18 25 | 1 8 15 22 29 | – 6 13 20 27 – |
| Th | – 6 13 20 27 | 3 10 17 24 31 | – 7 14 21 28 | 5 12 19 26 – | 2 9 16 23 30 | – 7 14 21 28 – |
| F | – 7 14 21 28 | 4 11 18 25 – | 1 8 15 22 29 | 6 13 20 27 – | 3 10 17 24 – | 1 8 15 22 29 – |
| S | 1 8 15 22 29 | 5 12 19 26 – | 2 9 16 23 30 | 7 14 21 28 – | 4 11 18 25 – | 2 9 16 23 30 – |

## 1821

| | JAN. | FEB. | MAR. | APRIL | MAY | JUNE |
|---|---|---|---|---|---|---|
| Su | – 7 14 21 28 | – 4 11 18 25 | – 4 11 18 25 | 1 8 15 22 29 | – 6 13 20 27 | – 3 10 17 24 |
| M | 1 8 15 22 29 | – 5 12 19 26 | – 5 12 19 26 | 2 9 16 23 30 | – 7 14 21 28 | – 4 11 18 25 |
| Tu | 2 9 16 23 30 | – 6 13 20 27 | – 6 13 20 27 | 3 10 17 24 – | 1 8 15 22 29 | – 5 12 19 26 |
| W | 3 10 17 24 31 | – 7 14 21 28 | – 7 14 21 28 | 4 11 18 25 – | 2 9 16 23 30 | – 6 13 20 27 |
| Th | 4 11 18 25 – | 1 8 15 22 – | 1 8 15 22 29 | 5 12 19 26 – | 3 10 17 24 31 | – 7 14 21 28 |
| F | 5 12 19 26 – | 2 9 16 23 – | 2 9 16 23 30 | 6 13 20 27 – | 4 11 18 25 – | 1 8 15 22 29 |
| S | 6 13 20 27 – | 3 10 17 24 – | 3 10 17 24 31 | 7 14 21 28 – | 5 12 19 26 – | 2 9 16 23 30 |

# ABBREVIATIONS

| | |
|---|---|
| *R.P.* | Ricardo Papers (consisting of letters received by Ricardo, and other of his papers, in the possession of Mr Frank Ricardo). |
| Mill-Ricardo papers | The letters and papers of Ricardo that belonged to James Mill, and which passed into the possession of the Cairnes family and Mr C. K. Mill. |
| 'at Albury' | Papers in the possession of Mr Robert Malthus, of The Cottage, Albury, Surrey. |

The following abbreviations are used by Malthus, Mill and Bentham, respectively, in their letters:

E.I. Coll., for East India College, Haileybury.
E.I. House, for East India House, London.
Q.S.P., for Queen Square Place, Westminster.

*David Ricardo 1820*

*from the miniature by Thomas Heaphy*

## 300. RICARDO TO McCULLOCH [1]
[Reply to 290 & 299]

Gatcomb Park
3 Jan.y 1819

My dear Sir

I have read with great pleasure the article on currency, for the next Edinburgh Review, which you have been so kind as to send me. It appears to me so able, so clear, so convincing, that I shall be puzzled to account for the obstinate prejudices of those who no doubt will continue to refuse their assent to doctrines so mathematically demonstrated.

3 Jan. 1819

Your kindness has again led you to bestow unmerited praise on me. I assure you that I feel very proud of the favourable opinion which you have formed of my speculations.

I have read the article with an endeavour to discover blemishes in it, but excepting on one or two trifling points, not in the least affecting the reasoning, I cannot discover any. Those points are as follows. In page 56 a few lines from the bottom, you say "and if one half the usual supply were brought to market, it (the price of commodities) would be increased one half." It is evident that you meant they would be doubled in price. [2]

In page 64 you give your readers reason to infer that the Bank advance the paper issued on occasion of the payment of the interest of the National Debt; now I believe that this

[1] Addressed: 'J. R. MCullock Esq.re / College Street / Edinburgh'. MS in British Museum.—*Letters to McCulloch*, V.

[2] Cp. below, p. 85, on McCulloch's making the opposite mistake.

never really happens. Certain taxes are pledged to the national creditor, they are paid into the Exchequer, and from
the Exchequer to the Bank, and are never for one moment at
the disposal of ministers. Your argument however is not
affected by this fact; because by means of direct loans, and
by the purchase of Exchequer bills in the market with their
notes, the Bank and Government together can issue any
amount of paper they please besides that which is issued
through the means of discounts.—

In page 66 you say "that all the difference that can take
place in the *value* of gold and silver currencies, among nations
trading together, will generally be limited to the expense of
the transfer of bullion from the one to the other." This
observation is true of the exchange—that can never differ
more than this expense, but I do not think that it is equally
so of the *value* of the precious metals. The value or price[1]
of cloth or of hats may in France be not only so much higher
than in England as will pay the expenses and profits of the
clothier and hatter who export them, but also the additional
expense of conveying the money for which they are sold from
France to England. Gold being a commodity is subject to
the same rule. I have endeavoured to explain this in my book
from Page 174[2] to the end of the chapter. It is of little importance in your essay but I am more induced to mention it
to you now, as you should guard against a misapprehension
in the article on Exchanges which you have it in contemplation to write. And here my observations end. I see no other
expression that I can cavil at.

In your quotation from me page 74 you end it by the word
"*performed*", on referring to my pamphlet page 25[3] I find,
in my copy which is one of the second edition, the words

---

[1] 'or price' is ins.
[2] Above, I, 144.

[3] Above, IV, 65. M^cCulloch had
quoted from ed. 1.

"they had been so advantageously applied" the first is inaccurate though I may inadvertently have used it.

The subject, of which metal to chuse for the standard, is I think of little importance. On the whole I am quite contented with the present mint regulations, 1^st, because I do not like a change without there is a very manifest advantage in it and 2^dly because it is confidently expected that the introduction of the most perfect machinery known into the silver mines may very considerably lower the value of that metal. If so it is unfit for a standard. The same objections cannot be made to gold.

Lord Lauderdale in his speeches and several writers in the Times have endeavored to shew that if the Bank paid in gold it would all leave the country in consequence of the mint regulations, notwithstanding that g[old] only is a legal tender in payments above 40/-. [1] This is very absurd and if you had shown it to be so, I should have been glad, for that is now the plea on which the continuance of the restriction is defended.

If you think I can be of any use to you in looking over the proof sheets of your article on exchanges I shall have great pleasure in doing it, but from what I have already seen you will make it all that it should be. To the best of my recollection Mushet did correct his tables in a subsequent edition. [2] I have not his book here.—

[1] On Lauderdale see above, I, 371, n. The argument had been advanced in a letter to *The Times* signed 'Daniel Hardcastle', and dated 12 Dec. 1818; this and subsequent letters were reprinted with the writer's real name in pamphlet form: *The Letters of Daniel Hardcastle to the Editor of 'The Times' Journal, on the subject of the Bank Restriction, the Regulations of the Mint, &c., With* *Notes and Additions,* By Richard Page, London, for the Author, 1819.

[2] Mushet had not made the corrections referred to by M^cCulloch; see above, III, 169, n. Ricardo's 'recollection' was probably of the earlier, and distinct, corrections made by Mushet, which are described above, III, 166–7.

I have attended to some of your suggestions for the improvement of my book. I cannot agree with you in thinking so lightly of the extinction of our national debt. I should agree to no other means of getting rid of it, but by paying it, which would relieve us from many of the evils you enumerate, such as the encouragement to gambling &c[a] We agree as to the evil, but not as to the remedy. Having noticed Buchanan in the former edition I cannot now omit making the same references to him, particularly as his objections are popular objections and such as I would wish to answer. I will consult with Murray about introducing a few pages from the pamphlet which you have honoured with your approbation.

Murray sent me for a few days the only copy that was in London of a French translation of my book, with notes by M. Say.[1] He speaks very respectfully and kindly of me, but does not agree with my doctrine. He does not appear to me to have seized my meaning. He attempts to shew that there is no land which does not pay rent, and then thinks that I am confuted—never noticing the other point on which I lay the most stress, that there is in every country a portion of capital employed on land already in cultivation for which no rent is paid,—or rather that no additional rent is paid in consequence of the employment of such additional capital.[2] Believe me My dear Sir

Faithfully Yours

DAVID RICARDO

This is a very confused letter, but I have written it in haste, and cannot undertake to write it over again.—

[1] See above, VII, 361, n. 1.      [2] See above, I, 412–3.

## 301. RICARDO TO MURRAY [1]

Gatcomb Park
Minchinhampton
3 Jan.ʸ 1819

Dear Sir

In the next Edinb. Review my pamphlet on "An 3 Jan. 1819
Economical Currency" will be noticed, and the plan I recommended in it will be favourably spoken of. It was that
plan that I wished, or rather Mr. M Culloch wished, [2] to see
inserted in the present edition of my work. I wrote to you
on the subject sometime ago, [3] mentioning the pages which
might be inserted if you thought it advisable. I think it
right to let you know that the subject will be noticed, and
recommended in the Review, which will of course tend to
give it publicity at a time when it might be advantageously
adopted on the Bank's resuming cash paymᵗˢ, in order that
you may be better able to judge whether to insert or omit
the pages referred to in the former pamphlet.—

Mr. Mill writes to me [4] that he was much obliged to you
for the loan of M. Say's notes—he is very far from being
pleased with them.

I am
Dear Sir
Faithfully Yʳˢ
D. RICARDO

[1] MS in the possession of Sir    [3] This letter is wanting.
John Murray.    [4] Letter 297.
[2] See above, VII, 353.

## 302. RICARDO TO MILL [1]
*[Answered by 303]*

Gatcomb Park.   13 Jan 1819

My dear Sir

I send you herewith a few reflections on Lord Grey's speech at Newcastle.[2] The Courier, or the Times, I forget which, appears to think that it is a declaration of the sentiments of the whig party;—if so, I do not think that it will increase their weight and influence in the country, for to me it appears hollow, weak, and insincere; and holds out no hope that the party will join heartily in recommending a reasonable reform, which from some observations in the papers I was in hopes they would.

What a poor figure Cobbett makes in his correspondence with Sir F. Burdett. The letter of Sir Francis to him pleased me very much.[3]

Mr. MCulloch has sent me the printed copy of an article, which will appear in the next Edinb$^{gh}$ Review, on my proposals for an economical currency. He speaks of me with his usual kindness, and has written a very able essay on the whole subject of currency, strongly recommending my proposals. He dwells with due force on the quantity of currency regulating its value, and vice versa; and there are not above one or two propositions, incidentally introduced, against which the slightest objection can be made. On this subject nothing very new can be said but to arrange it skilfully is a work of merit.—

I hope that you are quite reinstated in the possession of

---

[1] Addressed: 'James Mill Esq$^r$ / 1 Queen Square / Westminster'.

   MS in Mill-Ricardo papers.

[2] A speech at the Fox dinner at Newcastle, denouncing the radical reformers; reported in *The Times,*

7 Jan. 1819. Ricardo's paper has not been found.

[3] The correspondence, which concerned Cobbett's unpaid debts, was published in *The Times,* 4 Jan. 1819.

health, and that I shall find you able and willing to resume your walks with me the week after next, when I expect to have the pleasure of seeing you in London.

In correcting the sheets which Murray sends to me, I was struck with a passage which I have quoted from Say, Page 352 of the first edition,[1] pray look at it—I think you will agree with me that it is very much at variance with the spirit of some of his notes to the French translation.—

I have been reading pretty steadily since I last wrote to you, but I fear with little more profit than usual. I can find no remedy for the worst of memories. Writing is as distasteful as ever, I go to it reluctantly, and all my ideas appear to vanish the moment that I place the paper before me. As for speaking that I shall never do.

The time is now fast approaching when I shall know whether I am to be in the House, or not. If I am not, the party with whom I have agreed will have broken their engagement, a circumstance I suppose not very rare. I have been educated in a religious respect for engagements, and therefore it will not be my fault if the one in question is not fulfilled.

Truly Y$^{rs}$

DAVID RICARDO

## 303. MILL TO RICARDO[2]
### [*Reply to* 298 *&* 302]

Westminster 14 Jan.$^y$ 1819

My Dear Sir

I am roused by your talk of being in town the week after next, and must not let you arrive without another letter from

---

[1] Above, I, 256.
[2] Addressed: 'David Ricardo Esq / Gatcomb Park / Minchinhampton / Glo'stershire'.—MS in *R.P.*

me. As Hume sent me word he would probably call here to day, I shall also have a chance of a frank for you.

I have received all your communications; and congratulate you upon them most sincerely. The points cannot but be regarded as of unusual difficulty; because there are so few persons whom it is possible to bring to have clear conceptions upon them, and to reason consistently. And yet you both see to the bottom of them, and state the reasons upon which your own opinions are founded, and the objections which are made to them, with the utmost clearness; and give the last a conclusive answer. This is the general character of the whole. We shall go over them one by one; and they will afford us interesting subjects for a variety of our walks.—As you gave me no directions to do any thing with your answer to Torrens, I concluded you had sent a copy to the Magazine, and so keep this waiting your arrival.[1]

I am much gratified with your remarks upon Lord Greys speech, because they so exactly correspond with my own. You see through it completely, and describe most exactly the whole purport and temper of it, as well as the artifice, the flimsy varnish with which it is covered. You have been most struck with the *morality* of it: As my mind has been long made up about Whig morality, I am more surprised at the *intellectuality.* To be sure it is a pretty bold stretch in Ethics, to make all political morality consist in supporting the Whigs, and turning out the ministry; as you so well describe him as doing. This, however, I am not so much surprised at Lord Greys thinking; as at the weakness of the intellect which supposes that *other* people can be brought to think the same thing. You well describe the speech as a tissue of inconsistencies and contradictions: which of necessity happens when a man wishes what he is unwilling directly to say: and

---

[1] Ricardo's answer has never been published and the MS is missing.

thinks himself obliged to say something which he does not really wish: As when his lordship wishes people to believe that all political morality consists in hoisting the Whigs into place, which he does not dare to say in plain words; and thinks himself obliged to say at the beginning of his speech that he is for reform; though the whole of the remainder of it tends only to shew that he is for no reform.

Another of their artifices is the cry about *retrenchment.* They turn aside from parliamentary reform, and substitute the cry of *retrenchment.* They think that this will make them popular; and that the people fondly hoping for an abatement of taxes, will join in a cry to put out the present *expending* ministers and bring them, *retrenching* ditto, in! Now what is surprising is, the *intellect* of this. This is neither more nor less than the intellectual cry, Do, pray, exert yourselves, with us, to alter the *effect* without altering the *cause!* Get a different effect, by all possible means; but get it by the same cause! What has been the *cause* of that profligate expenditure, which has existed since the revolution, and of which they now cry that we have such unspeakable need of retrenchment? Of course, it has had a cause. And of course that cause has not been the wish of the people *to be* plundered. The cause has been the interest of the parliament to concur in plundering. Shall we put an end to that interest, the cause of the plunderage, by an effectual reform? Oh, no! By no means! For God's sake, think of nothing like that! It is wild! Immoderate! Ungenteel! Never think of altering the cause: only think of altering the effect, without altering the cause! —Is not *this* logic! Would it not be incredible that any men, above the rank of idiots, should impose upon themselves so far, as to yield up their understanding, to this irrationality, and to expect the same effects from it with regard to others; if we had not so much experience, that when men herd

together who have the same interests, and when they are
accustomed almost wholly to talk only with one another
about these interests, there is hardly any conclusion, favourable to their interests, which they are not capable of embracing,
however absurd.

I am well pleased to hear that Macculloch is again dealing
with you in the Edin.ʳ Review. I, too, I believe, am to be in
the next Nº.[1] I have looked at the passage you point out
where Say is quoted, and about his inconsistency there can be
no doubt. He is but a poor creature, I fear. This, with the new
edition of your book, will do for you, all that is necessary.
You are now, beyond all dispute at the head of Political
Economy. Does not that gratify your ambition? And who
prophesied all this? Tell me that! And scolded you on,
coward that you are? Tell me that!

I dined at Bow with Mr. Moses Ricardo on monday—and
was very happy, and very merry. All this may prove to you
that I am in no small degree better: so that there is no fear
of the walks—they will complete the cure.

I have no idea that there will, or can be any doubt about
the seat. And they must keep to their bargain, too. The
matter I understand rests till Sir H. Parnell comes, which will
be near—and then it will be concluded. Mr. Ralph, I think,
told me, that your solicitors have not yet got the extra copy
of the title-deeds; but this, I conclude, is only the usual delay
of d—d attorneys.

About your deriving profit from your reading, I have no
doubt at all. Bad memory! Why every body has a bad
memory. I have a bad memory, as well as you. But I can
remember what I take sufficient pains to remember; and so

[1] Dec. 1818: Art. I is a review
of Mill's *British India* (by W.
Coulson); Art. III a review of
Ricardo's *Economical and Secure
Currency* (by McCulloch).

can you. Memory is an effect; and you cannot have it without the cause; though lord Grey thinks otherwise of retrenchment. And as for speaking, you *must* speak—so there is no
more to be said about that matter.

I beg to offer my best respects to Mrs. Ricardo, and who-
ever else is of your party—in particular to my friend, Mrs.
Osman, for whom, since she likes Rousseau, I mean to send
his very beautiful, and in many respects very instructive work
on Education.

Most truly yours

J. MILL

304. TROWER TO RICARDO [1]
[Reply to 295.—Answered by 307]

Unsted Wood—Godalming.<br>Jan: 17—1819.

My Dear Ricardo,

Many thanks for your last kind letter, by which I am
glad to find, that a second edition of your Book is in the press.
When will it come out? If there were time I would look over
some notes I made when I read it, to see if there is any to
which it is worth while to call your attention. Not, that I
mean confidently to rely upon any observations I have made,
but, as a paragraph or an argument will some times strike
a reader differently from which it does the writer I would
point out any such to you.—By the by I have been engaged
in a controversy in support of your doctrine that Rent is not
a component part of Price. You have made it so clear, that
I am astonished there should now be any difference of opinion
upon the subject, nor have the arguments of my opponent
had any other effect than that of making me see more clearly

---

[1] Addressed: 'To / David Ricardo Esq / Upper Brook Street / Grosvenor Square'.—MS in *R.P.*

the truth of the opinions I entertain. I should be glad to find, that you approved the view I have taken of the question.—

I can however afford no more room for other matters, as I am anxious to reply to the arguments contained in your letter. You will recollect, my good friend, that in the origin of this discussion I observed, that there was a previous question to be considered before we could enter upon *that of reform,* and that was what form of Government was most conducive to the interests of the people? and it was *agreed* between us, "that a mixed Government such as ours, con-sisting of King, Lords and Commons, is the best form of Government," these are your words, and you add, "let us examine the question of reform in Parliament *on that sup-position.*"[1] How then can you say, as you do, in your last letter, "that in an enquiry into measures, which are likely to produce good Government, we *must not confine ourselves* to the question whether parliamentary reform would or *would not, endanger the establishment of Kings, Lords and Commons.*" How can you say, that "this establishment must be considered only *as means to an end.*" The moment that we agreed, that it *was the best form* of Government, *that* moment we made it the *end,* for which we were contending. Whether it *is* the best means of securing the objects in view, may be a fair question for discussion; but it is a *distinct question,* and cannot be entertained by those, who have already agreed, that it *is the best form of Government.* I apprehend, that it necessarily follows from this state of the question, that, in entertaining the subject of reform, we are bound constantly to bear in mind the effects, which the proposed reform are calculated to produce upon the established Government; and that *if* it be found to endanger the security of that form of Govern-ment, which has been *declared the best,* we are also bound,

---

[1] Above, VII, 320.

consistently with our opinions, to renounce *even on that*
*account only* the reform, which might have been in contemplation. These opinions appear to me, I confess, self evident; and if so, I do not see how I can be "guilty of a species of intollerance" in refusing to admit any reform which, in my conscience, I believe would subvert the Constitution. Any reform *consistent with the preservation of the constitution,* and of the principles upon which it is established, I would readily entertain; but any reform, which, under the notion of improving the condition of the people, should *endanger* this constitution, I cannot, consistently admit, as long as I continue of opinion, that *that constitution is the best.* I contend, then, if I can *shew,* that the proposed reform in Parliament would have the effect of endangering the constitution, (by destroying that balance of its powers, which is essential to its existence), *I* am bound, (and those, who agree with me, that that constitution is the best, *are bound*) to oppose it.—

How then can you say, that "I appear to have *changed* the subject of discussion"—"It is no longer (you say) an enquiry into the best means of making the people happy, but into the best means of preserving the monarchical and aristocratical branches." The *only question* before us is the *effect,* that a reform in Parliament would produce upon the Constitution.

It appears to me, that the preservation of that Constitution depends upon the powers of the different branches of which it is composed being properly balanced. These branches are the King, the Lords, and the Commons. The influence of each of these powers, respectively, must depend upon the general circumstances of the Country. It is obvious, that these must have a constant tendency to change—and that the popular part of the Constitution, *especially,* must encrease in force with the growth of wealth and the diffusion of knowledge. What ever additional influence this power may have received by the progress of society, must necessarily diminish the relative force of the other two branches—It follows therefore, that that distribution of the power, which was originally allotted to each branch, and which was what was required to preserve the due balance, under the *then* existing circumstances, may, under a different state of circumstances, be inadequate to produce the desired effect, and may render a different distribution necessary.—That such circumstances *have* occurred, and *have* given to the popular part of our constitution, an additional weight, which was not in contemplation when it was originally formed, I cannot entertain any doubt. And, that that additional weight requires to be met by a counteracting force in order to preserve the relative strength of the different powers, I am strongly persuaded. If it were not so met; if the whole of the seats in the House of Commons were thrown open to the people their influence would necessarily be predominant, and the voice of the other branches would be virtually annihilated.

Such an alteration might be deemed by many persons very desireable, but surely it cannot be contended for by those, who are desirous of preserving our mixed Government. The Government would then be essentially republican, and the House of Lords, and the Crown, would become mere nullities.—As I believe I remarked in my last letter, the influence of which you complain, is *necessary* to preserve that balance and secure to the Crown and to the Lords, that share in the Constitution, which is essential to its security, and which could not be obtained so advantageously to the public, in the manner pointed out by the theory of the Constitution. Unless the popular part of the Constitution is to be all in all, the other branches must have the right of exercising their judgment and their power on the various questions that may arise. If they do so exercise them, they must frequently differ from the judgments formed by the Commons. If in consequence, they openly oppose the measures of that House, and throw out their Bills, it is obvious, that a state of circumstances must soon arise, which no friend to the Constitution could desire. To remedy this evil, to supply this defect in the theory of the Constitution, practice which is the true test of the correctness of theory, has suggested a means by which the influence of these branches of the Constitution may be exercised without the evils I have enumerated. No doubt there must always be a question as to the *extent* to which this influence may be wholesomely exercised; which must be determined by the circumstances of the case. But it is nothing more than the question, which must always arise in a mixed Government like ours; how far the balance of the different branches is properly preserved; how far any one predominates. And it is a question, which must arise with respect to the extent of the force of the *popular part,* as well as of the other branches of the Constitution. And, I confess I think, that attentive observation of the progress of events must satisfy one, that it is to the *popular branch,* that we must continue to look for the time to come for any undue preponderance of power. *Undue* in reference to the preservation of our mixed Government.

You say that "if you cannot obtain a good choise of representatives without limiting the election franchise to the very narrowest bounds, you *would so limit it.*" Is it in human nature to expect it? Do not let us deceive ourselves with respect to the real state of mankind. Wisdom and virtue are not instinctive, they are the growth of education—and you might as well expect to gather good crops from an uncultivated field, as to meet with the qualifications requisite to secure good representatives in an uneducated and dependent people.—If mankind were what they ought to be, (what they might have been before the fall!) you might look with safety for the necessary requisites. But, that they do not exist in fact; that they are not to be found even where the freeest constitution would call them forth, look to the state of America, and to the very interesting account given of its political institutions and its feelings, in the recent work of Mr. Fearon.[1] But I must conclude, and must appologise for the unusual and I fear unwarrantable length of this letter. I shall direct this Letter to London, where I think you probably are, and where I shall hope to have the pleasure of seeing you ere long, as we shall be in Nottingham place for a *short time* in the beginning of March.

Mrs. Trower joins with me in kind remembrances to Mrs. R and family and I remain Dear Ricardo

Ys very truly

HUTCHES TROWER

## 305. RICARDO TO PLACE [2]

Dear Sir

Mr. Davies[3] mentioned to me the project of a review, wherein might be freely discussed those principles of reform which are so much out of favour with our other reviews. Of Mr. Mill's talents for managing such a concern no one has a higher opinion than myself, and I should be

---

[1] H. B. Fearon, *A Narrative of a Journey of Five Thousand Miles through the Eastern and Western States of America; contained in Eight Reports, addressed to the Thirty-nine English Families by whom the Author was deputed, in June 1817, to ascertain whether any, and what part of the United* *States would be suitable for their Residence. With Remarks on Mr. Birkbeck's 'Notes' and 'Letters'*, London, Longman, 1818.

[2] MS in British Museum (Place Papers), Add. 37,949, fol. 74.

[3] Not identified: possibly Col. T. H. Davies, M.P. for Worcester.

glad to contribute by my subscription towards such an     17 Feb. 1819
undertaking.[1]

I am Dear Sir

Yours very truly

DAVID RICARDO

Upper Brook Street
17 Feb 1819

306. SHARP TO RICARDO[2]

Brooks's
Thursday Morning
[25 Feb. 1819]

Dear Ricardo

I am this moment told by Sir Henry Parnell that the     25 Feb. 1819
Writ left Dublin on the 22$^{d}$, and of course must have arrived
in London, at the Crown Office this morning—

Tomorrow is the day on which the Usury Law will be
discussed—[3]

I advise you to send down in the morning to the Crown
Office (near the Rolls) in Chancery Lane, to ascertain it's
arrival, but whether this be ascertained or not, you should
go down to the House by $\frac{1}{2}$ past 3 and find some Deputy to
take your out of door oath and you must then give in your

---

[1] 'The need of a Radical organ to make head against the Edinburgh and Quarterly (then in the period of their greatest reputation and influence), had been a topic of conversation between him [James Mill] and Mr. Bentham many years earlier [before the foundation of the *Westminster Review* in 1824], and it had been a part of their *Château en Espagne* that my father should be the editor; but the idea had never assumed any practical shape.' (J. S. Mill, *Autobiography*, p. 91.)

[2] MS in *R.P.*—Ricardo was returned as M.P. for Portarlington on 20 Feb. 1819, after Sharp, who had been returned for that borough at the General Election in July 1818, had accepted the Chiltern Hundreds; the date of the letter is inferred from this.

[3] On 26 February the report stage of Sergeant Onslow's Usury Laws Repeal Bill was postponed till 26 April. (Report in *The Times*, 27 Feb. 1819.)

qualification in writing—Before 4. oClock you must take the oaths and your Seat *in* the House itself

Yours ever

R. Sharp

As soon as you have taken the Seat, I suppose I am to pay the 1050£—

I see that your dinner on the 6.<sup>th</sup> March[1] is a disloyal opposition to his Majesty the King of Clubs—which always meets on the first Saturday in the month

Mr Grenfell wishes you to call on him in Charles Street at eleven oClock (11 oClock) tomorrow respecting your Seat

## 307. RICARDO TO TROWER[2]
*[Reply to 304]*

London 28 Feb 1819

My dear Trower

Your last kind letter ought not to have remained so long unanswered—but my natural indolence conspired with a multiplicity of occupations to induce me to defer writing to you. Besides, the information you gave me that you would be in London, in March, made my negligence appear less unfavourable in my own eyes. Before March actually begins

---

[1] '6 March 1819.—Evening at Mr. Ricardo's. Every one full of Mr. Baring's evidence before the Lord's Committee. Admirable as to principles; but letting out all sorts of difficulties as to the practicability of resuming Cash payments; and hinting that it cannot be done in less than four or five years. Every one agrees that it is knocking the thing on the head; and that such an extension of time is tantamount to doing nothing. Sharpe [*i.e.* Richard Sharp] declares that he intends having 2 hours conversation with Alex: Baring to morrow, and leaves you to understand that he will teach him better principles. But my good friend Mr Sharpe is not up to that—. Ricardo looks very blank—.' (J. L. Mallet's MS Diary.)

[2] Addressed: 'Hutches Trower Esq<sup>r</sup> / Unsted Wood / Godalming' and franked 'London March one 1819 David Ricardo'.

MS at University College, London.—*Letters to Trower*, XXIV.

however I must assure you of the pleasure which I shall have 28 Feb. 1819 in seeing you in London, and I hope you will, on the earliest day you can, announce your arrival to me by presenting yourself in Brook Street at our breakfast hour at half past nine. At that time I am sure to be found, but at any other I may be engaged from home in some of the many objects which now draw my attention.

My efforts have at last been crowned with success, and I am now a seated member of the House of Commons. My introduction there was nowise disagreeable as the ceremony of taking the oaths is not very formidable, and the kind expressions of welcome given to me by my friends set me quite at my ease. I fear that I shall never become a very useful member.—

The inquiry into the state of our currency, and exchanges, is proceeding in both houses very satisfactorily. I have had many conversations with several of the Committees of both Houses—with Lord Grenville, Marquis of Lansdown, Lord King, Mr. Huskisson, Mr. F. Lewis, Mr. Grenfell and others.[1] All have a very perfect knowledge of the subject, and all agree that the progress of the public in comprehending the question has been very great. The Bank Directors themselves have improved, and they are far behind every other person. I confidently rely on measures being taken to place our currency in a satisfactory state. I am told that I shall be examined.

Believe me
My dear Trower
Very truly Y$^{rs}$
DAVID RICARDO

[1] 'Mr Ricardo...had been closeted in the morning with Lord Grenville and Mr Grenfell, discussing various parts of that important subject.' (13 Feb. 1819, entry in J. L. Mallet's MS Diary about a dinner at the Marcets with Ricardo.)

## 308. RICARDO TO McCULLOCH [1]
[*Answered by* 309]

Upper Brook Street, London
7 april 1819

Dear Sir

7 April 1819 It is a long time since I had the pleasure of hearing from you, and as I am not willing that our correspondence shall wholly cease, I write now without having any thing to say that you may think worthy of a letter. To put you in good humor with me I will begin with telling you that your essay on money in the last Edinburgh Review[2] is universally admired. It is acknowledged by all the competent judges on that subject, to be a sound, and able view of that department of Political Economy. You have I am sure been the means of affording the most useful instruction, to many members of the Committees of both houses,[3] and as for myself, I am under great obligations to you, for my plan might have slumbered, or have been forgotten, if you had not rescued it from oblivion, and said more in its favour than I had been able to do. You will be pleased to know that an investigation into the probable results of adopting that plan, or some modification of it, has formed one of the leading subjects of examination, by both committees, and from the speech of Mr. Peel, as well as from those of Mr. Canning, and the Marquis of Lansdown,[4] I have very little doubt but that it will be recommended, as a temporary, if not a permanent measure, in both reports. If so, we shall have the merit of having at least accelerated the return to a sound unfluctuating system of currency, for it is impossible to describe to you

[1] MS in British Museum.—*Letters to McCulloch,* VI.

[2] See above, VII, 354, n. 1.

[3] On the Resumption of Cash Payments.

[4] On 5 April, when the First Reports of the Committees were presented to Parliament (*Hansard,* XXXIX, 1399–1401, 1411–12 and 1397.)

the alarm of the Bank Directors at the thoughts of providing coin for that purpose—they have officially declared that not less than 30 millions would be necessary, besides the usual reserve; and yet they have opposed every obstacle to a scheme which will render such a provision unnecessary. The Bank Directors, alone, with two or three very distinguished exceptions, and they young men,[1] have made no progress in correct ideas on the subject of money since the last committee sat[2]—they still maintain as a Court of Directors, though not individually, that they cannot believe that the rise or fall of the exchange has any connection with the amount of their notes—they still maintain that the high price of bullion in their depreciated medium, means the same thing as a high exchangeable value of bullion in all other things—and they still maintain that their issues have rather been too moderate than excessive.[3] Happily the committees are better informed, and I think we may anticipate a report which will recognise all the important principles of the science, as far as it regards money.

You will have seen that I have taken my seat in the House of Commons—I fear that I shall be of little use there. I have twice attempted to speak, but I proceeded in the most embarrassed manner, and I have no hope of conquering the alarm with which I am assailed the moment I hear the sound of my own voice.—

[1] 'Young men have generally been found enlisted of late, among the friends of reasonable and enlightened views. Haldimand and Ward the two Bank Directors whose Evidence is favourable to cash payments, are among the youngest of that Body.' (J. L. Mallet's MS Diary, entry headed 'Session of 1819'.)

[2] The Bullion Committee of 1810.

[3] See the resolution of the Court of Directors of the Bank, 25 March 1819, printed in the 'Second Report of the (Commons) Committee on the Resumption of Cash Payments', 1819, 'Minutes of Evidence,' pp. 262–4.

We are promised two works on Political Economy, one from the pen of Mr. Malthus—the other from that of Major Torrens.[1] I am well acquainted with the opinions of both these gentlemen, and though I think they will assist in disseminating many sound principles, yet I think they adhere too firmly to their old associations to make a very decided progress in the science. You are the person who ought to give us a complete system of Political Economy, written in so popular a way as to be easily understood by the generality of readers:—nobody could do it better, as all will testify who have read your two articles in the Review and your essay on the Corn Trade.

I was introduced yesterday by Sir James Mackintosh, in the House of Lords, to Monsr. Sismondi, who is on a very short visit to this Country. He has just published a book on Political Economy,[2] in which he has endeavoured to shew the fallacies of my opinions. He told me that he differed from Say also. I have great curiosity to see his book, as by the few words which passed between us he does not appear to agree with any of our known writers.—

You may perhaps have heard that my brother Ralph is married, and has relinquished his travelling scheme. He has long been thinking of matrimony, but deferred it so long that all his friends thought it would be his fate to die a bachelor. He has a young and an agreeable wife, and is comfortably settled at the moderate distance of 10 miles from London.[3]

I hope I shall soon have the pleasure of hearing from you—

---

[1] Malthus's *Principles of Political Economy*, 1820, and Torrens's *Essay on the Production of Wealth*, 1821.

[2] *Nouveaux principes d'économie politique, ou de la richesse dans ses rapports avec la population*, 2 vols., Paris, Delaunay, 1819.

[3] Ralph Ricardo had married Charlotte Lobb on 30 March and was living at Chingford.

I suppose that I must not expect to see you for the present in 7 April 1819
this country, I wish I might—your visit would give me great
satisfaction.—

Believe me Dear Sir
Very truly Y<sup>rs</sup>
DAVID RICARDO

### 309. McCULLOCH TO RICARDO [1]
[*Reply to 308.—Answered by* 310]

Edinburgh 18<sup>th</sup> April 1819

My Dear Sir
    The kind and flattering manner in which you have been 18 April 1819
pleased to notice, in your letter of the 7<sup>th</sup> inst, my efforts to
contribute to the improvement of that science of which you
are so great a master, is peculiarly gratifying to me, and far
outweighs every other testimony that I could possibly
receive. I was also much pleased to learn that the Committees had been occupied in discussing the merits of your
plan for rendering bank notes exchangeable for bullion—
However ignorant the Bank Directors may be, they cannot
surely be so blind to their own interests as not to perceive
what an immense advantage the adoption of your scheme
would be to them, compared with being obliged to resume
specie payments—The adoption of your plan will be the
greatest triumph ever obtained by the science of Political
Economy: And you will have the undoubted merit of having
been the means of conferring a greater direct benefit on the
country, than was ever conferred by any other private
individual—
    In writing the article in the Review[2] I found myself at a

---

[1] MS in *R.P.*

[2] The article on money in the *Edinburgh Review*, Dec. 1818.

great loss to give any proper account of the expence of the coinage; and I am convinced that if any impression has been made by that article it would have been rendered much stronger, had I been able to state the precise sum which had been expended on the gold and silver currency since the great recoinage in the reign of William III—Perhaps you could make a motion in Parliament for the production of an account of all the expences incurred on account of the mint establishment from 1695 to the present era, distinguishing of course the expence on account of the gold coin from that of silver, &c—Such a motion would I presume be readily assented to; and it would by helping to shew the enormous expence of a gold currency, not only assist in recommending your scheme, but would also be extremely useful in other enquiries—Since I have taken the liberty to suggest one motion to you, I think I may as well trespass on your patience with another—I observe that an account of the issues of the Bank of Ireland from 1797 down to 1819 has been laid on the table of the House; but by way of completing this account, it is necessary that an account of the course of exchange between London and Dublin, London and Belfast, and Dublin and Belfast should also be presented—You know the effect produced by the great relative issue of Irish bank paper in depressing the exchange of Dublin on London, and you are also aware how, after the Bank of Ireland ceased extending its issues, the exchange became favourable to Ireland according as Bank of England paper was increased—All this however would be better made out from an official return, which I presume could be procured without difficulty—

I have seen the work of Sismondis to which you refer, and I confess that I feel astonished that a person of his acknowledged talents should have published such a work—He adopts all those parts of Dr. Smiths theory which your great work has shewn to be erroneous, and he attempts to subvert his conclusions in cases where they are universally acknow-ledged to be correct—Sismondi is too much of a senti-mentalist to make a good political economist—It is really not a little farcical to have a grave philosopher recommending *all classes* to marry, and at the same time telling them that it is their duty after having got two or three children to live in a state of celibacy!—I do not know whether this doctrine will conciliate Sismondi the favour of the dames of London, but I feel confident it will have no such tendency here—[1]

I was particularly delighted with your observations on Mr Sturges Bournes pauper education bill[2]—They com-pletely exposed the pernicious tendency of that measure; and if the House had been able properly to appreciate what you so ably stated, they would no longer have encouraged so absurd a scheme—

I beg you will offer my congratulations to your brother on the auspicious event of his marriage—You may say to him that I understand there is a work in the press in which some of his friends will appear rather ridiculous—The publication will, I daresay, be clever—It is by the Editor of Blackwoods Magazine and will be a compound of quizzing, ribaldry, and toryism[3]—

I regret exceedingly that it is not in my power to visit London, or rather I should say to visit you, for to me the one would be infinitely more attractive than the other, this season—that is a pleasure which however reluctantly I must

[1] The following day (19 April 1819) Sismondi married in London Jessie Allen, sister-in-law of Mackintosh.
[2] See above, V, 1.
[3] *Peter's Letters to his Kinsfolk*, 2nd ed., 3 vols., Edinburgh, Blackwood, 1819 (by J. G. Lockhart, under the assumed name of 'Dr. Morris'). A review in the *Scotsman*, 17 July 1819, describes it as 'little else than a republication of the dullest, most prosing, and malignant articles in Blackwood's Magazine.'

keep in reserve for another opportunity—I hope you will
have the goodness to let me hear from you as soon as any
thing decisive has transpired relative to the Bank—I trust
the success of your efforts to improve and perfect our
monetary system will be as complete as it deserves to be; and
I am sure that none of your friends will more cordially and
sincerely sympathise with your triumph on this occasion than
I shall do—

I am

With great respect

My Dear Sir

Yours faithfully

J. R. MᶜCULLOCH

### 310. RICARDO TO MᶜCULLOCH [1]
[*Reply to* 309.—*Answered by* 314]

London 8 May 1819

My dear Sir

The public papers will have informed you, better than
I could have done, of the substance of the Report from the
Bank Committee, which was read in the House of Commons
on wednesday last.[2] As I knew you would get correct information from that source, I did not write immediately after
I became authentically informed of the plan which the Committee recommended. The Committee have deviated in two
points from the plan as originally suggested—they think that
the bars of bullion delivered by the Bank, in exchange for
notes, should be assayed, and stamped, at the Mint; and they
have advised that after 1823, at the latest, we should revert
to the old system of specie payments. Perhaps, in both

---

[1] MS in British Museum.—*Letters
to MᶜCulloch,* VII.

[2] The Report was read on
Thursday, 6 May, according to
*Hansard,* XL, 152.

instances, they have done right, for the Bank persisting in the most determined opposition to them, they were under the necessity of having the bullion stamped that it might be legally called money of a large denomination, and that the Bank might not raise a clamour against them for having imposed upon that corporation the obligation of paying in Bullion, from which they said their charter protected them. In the second place they had to contend with public prejudice, and perhaps too with prepossessions which they themselves felt in favour of coin. If no inconvenience is suffered from the working of this plan for the next 5 years, the Bank will be amongst the foremost in contending that it should be adopted as a permanent system.

I have been very much surprised that with the opportunities for making large profits, which the monopoly of the Bank has given them, their surplus capital does not exceed 5 millions. How very much they must have mismanaged their affairs. With good management they ought to have been possessed of double that sum.

The Bank have uniformly contended that they have not issued too much paper. It will hardly be believed that in Aug. 1814 their loans to Government, alone, amounted to the enormous sum of 35 millions. In Feb. 1816 they sank to about 20 millions, were seldom less after that time than 27 to 28 millions, till the present year, when they again fell to 23 millions.

An account will be published in Appendix to the Lords' report of the quantity of silver and gold coined at the mint since 56 Geo 3 (1816) to Jan.^y 1819, also an account of the expence attending such coinage[1] from which a tolerably accurate estimate may be made of the expence attending the

[1] The first account was published in *Appendix,* D. 1 and 2; the second was not published.

coinage for any particular year, or any number of years. I fear that Ministers would not give me so particular an account as that which you suggest.

I thank you for making me acquainted with Mr. Leslie[1]— I have as yet only seen him for a few minutes.

I have so little information to give you that it is hardly worth troubling you to read my letter but it is the best I have, and therefore you must not complain.

I thank you for the various numbers of the Scotsman which you have sent me, but I beg you will not trouble yourself to do so in future, as I never miss reading them at Brookes'[2], where they are taken in. I had read, before I received it from you, the paper of the 17th of April, and was highly pleased with it. I am sure that it cannot be answered.[3]—I am doomed every now and then to hear the grossest absurdities on the subject of the agricultural interest and the necessity of up-holding it by further restrictions on the importation of corn, in the House of Commons, and wish that I had the talent of repelling these foolish arguments with my tongue as ably as you do with your pen—they should not then go without an answer.

Believe me with great esteem
Y.rs very sincerely
DAVID RICARDO

[1] John Leslie (1776–1832), Professor of Mathematics and later of Natural Philosophy at the University of Edinburgh, a contributor to the *Edinburgh Review* and the *Supplement to the Encyclopaedia Britannica*. His invention of a machine for artificial congelation is referred to above, IV, 249.

[2] The opposition club, of which Ricardo had been elected a member on 13 March 1818, being proposed by Lord Essex and seconded by Lord Holland. (*Memorials of Brooks's*, London, 1907, p. 92.)
[3] Leading article 'On the Importation of Foreign Corn'.

## 311. TROWER TO RICARDO [1]
[*Answered by* 312]

Unsted Wood.
May 21—1819

Dear Ricardo.

21 May 1819

Although a long time has elapsed since I have had the pleasure of hearing from you, yet, I have been frequently *reminded* of you by observing the active part you are taking in the great Councils of the nation.—I must congratulate you on the success, which appears to attend your exertions in Parliament, and I am desirous of hearing, from yourself, how far they have satisfied your own expectations. One thing at least is certain, that whatever reluctance you have felt to hear the sound of your own voice in that awful assembly, you have not suffered it to stand in the way of expressing your sentiments when you have felt disposed to deliver them. And, practice will ultimately insure facility. I rejoice with you in the compleat victory your opinions have at length obtained on Bank and Bullion affairs. It is very gratifying to hear your opinions not merely sanctioned but adopted by such high authorities. And, I hope and trust, that Parliament will act upon the recommendation of its Committees—The opposition attempted in the City is equally impertinent and contemptible; and I doubt not will end in the disgrace and confusion of those with whom it originated [2] —What a pittiful figure does the Chancellor of the Exchequer cut in his intercourse with the Bank; I wonder Ministers do

---

[1] Addressed: 'To / David Ricardo Esqr / M.P. / Upper Brook Street / Grosvenor Square'.
  MS in *R.P.*
[2] A meeting of merchants had been held at the London Tavern on 18 May, with Sir Robert Peel (the elder) in the chair, and Major Torrens one of the speakers, to protest against the Reports of the Committees on the Bank; a petition to Parliament had been drawn up and it was presented to the House of Lords by Lauderdale on 21 May (*The New Times*, 19, 21 and 22 May 1819).

not cast from them a Man, who has done them so much discredit, and who has so essentially injured their cause—

I am very impatient to see the Committees Reports themselves, and if you could obtain copies for me I should be much obliged—

I think you Gentlemen have used poor Sturges Bourne very ill, in treating his Bill so cavalierly.[1] No doubt it had faults, and perhaps great ones, but surely it was capable of improvement, there was some good in it, and it might have been made more perfect in the Committee. However you afford but little encouragement for labor, exertion and anxiety in so good a cause, by the example you have set in the case of Bournes Bill.—

So we are to have another loan![2] If Ministers had proper firmness and resolution they would raise the money by *taxes,* and if they had the confidence of the Country they would be supported.—If the People wont bear an *income tax,* let *necessaries* be taxed, and thus the money might be easily raised. It is a folly to attempt raising any considerable sum by taxing Luxuries, and yet, the cry of the day *in Parliament* is that *necessaries must not be taxed,* because they fall on the poor; and so they would deprive us of the few productive taxes we have left. As to economy, do all you can, cut down expences as much as you will (and *you ought as far as possible*) yet what will it amount to; perhaps not 1 million a year! If, by touching the sinking Fund, Ministers are affraid of affecting the prices of the funds, they might try the experiment of a *conditional* encroachment upon that sacred deposit!

---

[1] Sturges Bourne's Settlement of the Poor Bill, to enact that Settlement should be acquired only by residence for three or five years, had been thrown out by the House of Commons at the report stage on 10 May.

[2] A loan of £12,000,000 was contracted for on 9 June; Ricardo was the unsuccessful bidder against Rothschild.

Let it be understood, that no stock shall be purchased by the 21 May 1819 Commissioners *above a certain price,* and let the surplus remaining uninvested at the end of the year, be carried to the account of supplies. But I must cease my speculations. By the by, as I observe you still have a list for the Loan I shall hope for the Honor of having my name in it. I think you Gentlemen have *pretty well,* what is called *prepared* for the Loan this time, by the violent shake you have given the prices of the funds.

Pray make our united regards to Mrs. Ricardo and family and believe me My Dear Ricardo

Yours very sincerely,

HUTCHES TROWER

## 312. RICARDO TO TROWER [1]
*[Reply to 311]*

London 28 May 1819

My dear Trower

I take advantage of a little respite in the business of the 28 May 1819 House to acknowledge the receipt of your kind letter, and to inform you that I am every day rejoicing with increased satisfaction at the triumph of science, and truth, over prejudice, and error. You will perceive by the Newspapers that Parliament has at length decided that we should revert to a sound currency.[2] The feeble resistance, in point of argument, of the Bank Directors, was easily overcome. I had the courage to set myself foremost in the battle, and was amply rewarded by the support of the House, which enabled me to get to the end of my speech without any great degree of fear or trepidation. I hope that during the next fortnight we shall give the

---

[1] Addressed: 'Hutches Trower Esq' / Unsted Wood / Godalming'. MS at University College, London.— *Letters to Trower,* XXV.

[2] Peel's Resolutions for the Resumption of Cash Payments had been agreed to by the House of Commons on 26 May.

death blow to the theory of an abstract pound sterling. The alarm that prevailed in the City is incomprehensible:[1]—it must have been occasioned by the imprudent remonstrance of the Bank to Government setting forth the great danger which would attend the reduction of the currency.[2] I regret that the Committees have not adopted the measure of obliging the Bank to buy gold at £3 17. 6, whenever it is offered to them at that price—the reverting to specie payments appears to me unnecessary, and not likely to be attended with any advantage.

I sent you by the coach the Lords Report, as I had two, one from the Lords as a witness who had given evidence before them, the other as a member of the House of Commons, but I have only one copy of the report from the Commons' Committee which I will lend you with pleasure, but which I must keep as a valuable document. Tell me whether I shall send it to you.

There were I think very serious objections against the Poor Law settlement bill.—It would have borne very heavy on the towns, particularly on some that are in the neighbourhood of the mines. Why is not a more efficient measure proposed? The fact I believe is that no party in the House dare take upon themselves to propose or support any plan which may make them unpopular. This is one of the ill effects of party; the public interest is neglected.

I agree with you that we ought not to add to our debt by

---

[1] 'No sooner was it known that the Resolutions in favour of Mr Ricardo's novel and visionary scheme had passed the House [of Lords] without a division that an actual panic took place on the Stock Exchange.' (*The New Times,* 24 May 1819.)
[2] The Representation laid before the Chancellor of the Exchequer by the Directors of the Bank, expressing their concern at the measures proposed by the Committees, 'which they cannot but consider fraught with very great uncertainty and risk'; it was presented to the House of Lords on 21 May. (*Hansard,* XL, 600 ff.)

loans, we should have the firmness to raise taxes for any deficiency that may now be wanted. Our sinking fund is gone, and I am not disposed to raise a new one, for the purpose of placing it again at the disposal of ministers. Do what you will, they will not respect it, and after a few years we should be as much in debt as ever. I am for a vigorous system of taxation, if it is for the purpose of paying off debt once for all, but I am sure that ministers will never respect any fund, which is to accumulate at compound interest. With the slightest pressure on the finances such a fund would be diverted from the employment to which it had been destined.

28 May 1819

Mr. Elwin is in London—I saw him for a moment on tuesday—he is looking very well.

Mrs. Ricardo unites with me in kind regards to Mrs. Trower.

Believe me ever

My dear Trower

Very truly Y$^{rs}$

DAVID RICARDO

I have omitted saying that your name will be remembered when we prepare our list.—I have not sold any stock against the loan for I have been thinking the price low ever since they were 74—[1]

## 313. RICARDO TO TROWER [2]

My dear Trower

London June 1—1819

I write to you without delay to give you my opinion respecting an investment of money in Bank Stock at the present price. The fall has been great,[3] but I think not so great

1 June 1819

---

[1] Consols, which had been at 80 in Dec. 1818, had gradually fallen and were now at 66$\frac{1}{2}$.
[2] Addressed: 'Hutches Trower Esq$^r$ / Unsted Wood / Godalming'.

MS at University College, London.—*Letters to Trower,* XXVI.
[3] Bank of England Stock had fallen from 272 in Jan. 1819 to 210 in May.

as the facts with which we are now acquainted warrant and justify. I calculated on the Bank having a much greater surplus Capital than the reports of the Committees inform us they have. That Capital is stated to be 5 millions, I thought it more than double and so it would have been if the Directors had managed the concern intrusted to them with the ability and economy that they ought to have done.

Let us try if we cannot ascertain what under a good system of management should now be the profits of the Bank, and then let us make a due allowance for the management which the affairs of the Bank will receive under the present Directors—

| | | |
|---|---|---|
| Savings—(see Rep.⁵ of Committees) . . . | | £5,000,000 |
| Bank notes in circulation after the necessary reduction—estimated at . . . . . | | 23,000,000 |
| Deposits, Public and Private, estimated at | | 6,000,000 |
| | | 34,000,000 |
| Deduct Treasure to meet demands . . . | | 4,000,000 |
| | | 30,000,000 |
| Suppose these 30 millions to be lent on an average at 4 pc.ᵗ—and if the peace continues that is not too low an estimate they will receive annually . . . . . . | | 1,200,000 |
| Int.ᵗ on capital lent to Govern.ᵗ at 3 pc. . . | | 440,604 |
| For Management of the Debt . . . . | | 280,000 |
| | | 1,920,604 |
| Expences and Stamps . . . | 465,304 | |
| Div.ᵈ 10 pc.ᵗ . . . . . . | 1,455,300 | |
| | | 1,920,604 |
| | | „   „   „ |

If the Bank should have a circulation of 23 millions and manage their affairs well they may continue to pay a dividend of 10 pc. till 1833 when their charter will expire, and a deduction must be made in consequence of the price they must be obliged to pay for a renewal of their priveleges—if they are renewed—and if they are not they may probably divide 130—or 140 for every £100 Stock.—But will they be able to keep 23,000,000 in circulation—certainly not if specie payments are to be restored—that circumstance may probably sink the amount to 15 millions in which case they could not pay more than 8 pc$^t$ div$^d$.[1]

After examining these statements you will be able [to ju]dge whether it would be expedient to [buy] Bank Stock.—I have thought it right to sell [out][2] mine, not much indeed (£2500) being firmly persuaded that it is much too high, and that after a little sober examination the price will fall.[3]

Your brother called on me this morning when I communicated to him my sentiments on this subject.

In great haste I am

My dear Trower

Y$^{rs}$ truly

DAVID RICARDO

## 314. MᶜCULLOCH TO RICARDO [4]
[*Reply to 310.—Answered by 315*]

Edinburgh 30 May 1819

My Dear Sir

Allow me to congratulate you on the signal triumph which the sound principles of political economy have

---

[1] The circulation fell to 17 millions at the end of May 1822, after the resumption of specie payments, and the dividend was reduced from 10 to 8 per cent.
[2] MS torn here and above;

Bonar and Hollander's conjecture is 'some of'.
[3] The price moved only within narrow limits during the next few years.
[4] MS in *R.P.*

obtained in Parliament—I regret the Committees should have countenanced the idea of reverting to specie payments; but I have no doubt that if the Bank gives your plan a fair trial it will be found so advantageous as to gain a general concurrence in the propriety of excluding gold coins from circulation—As far as I have an opportunity of ascertaining the public opinion, your plan is almost universally approved of both here and in Glasgow—It is indeed so well established in your pamphlet, and is so simple in its mechanism, and so obviously beneficial that I am astonished it should have been opposed by persons pretending to any acquaintance with the science—I read the report of your speech[1] in the Times and Morning Chronicle with the greatest satisfaction; not so much because it showed the futility of the objections which had been stated against the measure, and gave a wholesome lesson to the Directors, as because I conceived it to be a proof that you had conquered any little difficulties you might have at first experienced in addressing the House—

In looking over the accounts annexed to the Commons Report, I do not observe any statement of the average annual amount of Bank notes in circulation since the restriction— At page 271 there is an account of the number in circulation on 26 February and 26 August each year; but I presume the mean would not give the true annual average—I think it would be very desirable to have such an account, and if you concur in this opinion, I imagine it could be easily procured— I think it would also be desirable to have an account of the average annual advances to government, and of the average annual discounts—Perhaps some of these accounts may be given in the Lords Report, but this I have not seen; and I have to request as a particular favour that you would be so good as to send me a copy of it—It will I believe come without any expence by the Mail—

[1] Of 24 May; see above, V, 7 ff.

I still am of opinion that with a view to the ultimate success of your plan it would be of importance to obtain an account of the entire expence of the gold and silver currency and of the expence of the Mint establishment from 1695 down to the present period—The accounts relative to the Mint in the Commons Report do not convey this sort of information.

I am getting very slowly and I fear but very indifferently on with my article on Exchange[1]—I think the theoretical part of it may do, but I can make no such supposition relative to that which is practical—If it were not encroaching too much on your valuable time, I would sollicit you to send me a short statement of the manner in which the buying and selling of bills of exchange is actually conducted in London, or that you would have the goodness to say where I could find this information—

I beg leave to return you my best thanks for the honour you have done me in noticing my article on the Corn Laws in so flattering a manner in your second edition,[2] and for the copy of it which you have sent me—I have no object more at heart than to obtain your favourable opinion and to deserve it—

You will regret to learn that our celebrated novellist Scott (for of his being the author of Waverley &c. there is not the shadow of doubt) has been of late very much indisposed—At present however he is, I understand, a good deal better—He has a new novel just about ready for publication[3]—Were works on political science to bring the same price with works on imagination there would be rather more inducement to cultivate it than at present.

---

[1] For the *Supplement to the Encyclopaedia Britannica.*
[2] Above, I, 267 and 318.
[3] '*New Tales of My Landlord, The Third Series,* containing *The Bride of Lammermoor* and *A Legend of Montrose,* in four volumes, will be published on Monday, 21st June.' (Advt. in the *Scotsman,* 12 June 1819.)

Pray have you as yet taken a peep at Sismondis book?[1]— It is the most extraordinary production I ever had in my hand—I think your townsman Dr Purves is the better economist of the two—[2]

Forgive me for troubling you with this letter; and believe to be with the greatest respect

Yours most faithfully

J. R. M<sup>c</sup>CULLOCH

### 315. RICARDO TO M<sup>c</sup>CULLOCH[3]
*[Reply to 314]*

London 22 June 1819

My dear Sir

30 May 1819

22 June 1819    I have too long neglected answering your kind letter, but I have been much engaged; and indeed my energy has been a little impaired by the late hours which the business of the House has compelled me to keep for the last 2 or 3 weeks.

I hope that you have received the Lords Report on Bank Affairs, which I sent you by the Mail. That Report contains an account of the yearly average of Bank notes in circulation for more than 20 years, and is I think precisely the document which you wished to see.[4]

I thank you for your endeavors to inspire me with confidence on occasions of my addressing the House. Their indulgent reception of me has in some degree made the task of speaking more easy to me, but there are yet so many

---

[1] See above, p. 22, n. 2.
[2] 'George Purves, L.L.D.', pseudonym of Simon Gray. Having published under his real name *The Happiness of States...*, London, 1815, 4to (2nd ed., 1819), he then puffed it up in two pseudonymous books, *All Classes Productive* *of National Wealth...*, London, Longman, 1817 and *Gray versus Malthus, The Principles of Population and Production Investigated...*, *ib.* 1818.
[3] MS in British Museum.—*Letters to M<sup>c</sup>Culloch*, VIII.
[4] *Appendix*, B. 2.

formidable obstacles to my success, and some, I fear, of a nature nearly insurmountable that I apprehend it will be wisdom and sound discretion in me to content myself with giving silent votes.

There is a disposition among many of the best informed of the two committees to adopt my plan of currency as a permanent regulation, but they think that it will have more chance of finding supporters, after it has been tried for a few years. I am of the same opinion, and only object to the Bill just passed, because it will impose on the Bank the obligation of buying gold, and preparing for coin payments, in 1821, although such payments may never be necessary.

I fear I cannot obtain the account of the expence of the Mint Establishment for so long a period as you mention. I am sure that Ministers would object to give it, and I am too young a member to move for it without previously knowing that it would be granted.

Bills are bought and sold on the exchange by brokers, who make themselves acquainted with the state of demand and supply. There is a difference in the price of bills, accordingly as they are drawn on persons, and by persons, of undoubted credit. There are also middlemen, who speculate largely on the rise or fall of the exchange and either buy or sell bills, without being entitled to do so from any previous transaction, on the expectation of the future supply and demand of bills. The practice I believe is this. The brokers go round to the different merchants, and ascertain whether they are buyers or sellers of bills. The man of most influence amongst them judging of the relation between the buyers and sellers, suggests a price at which all the transactions of the day are settled, with such deviations as particular bills, on account of their being in very high, or very low credit, may be subject to. In the evidence before the committee you will

22 June 1819 see that merchants in the best credit generally negociate their bills on better terms than the quoted price.—

I hope, Mr., or I believe, Sir W. Scott is recovered from his indisposition. His last novel is just published, but there is so great a demand for the work at present in my house that I have not yet seen it—I shall consent to wave my claim to its perusal till I get in the country. Then also I shall read Sismondi's last work, which I am prepared to find exactly of the description which you give of it—viz a work not less extraordinary than that of Dr. Purves, if there be really any such person in existence.—

You have probably heard that Mr. Mill has got a highly respectable situation in the East India House. Considering the opinions which he has so freely given of the Government of India this appointment reflects great credit on the Directors.[1]

[1] In a letter of 13 Dec. 1819 to Dumont, Mill gives some details of the appointment; after saying that the first ed. of his *History of British India* 'is now wholly sold, and we are actively printing a second', Mill goes on: 'What will more surprise you is, that said book has been the principal cause of placing me in the service of the East India Company. You probably know that what is called the Examiner's Office in the East India House, is the office in which the whole of the correspondence with India, in all the departments of government, except the military, is carried on. I am placed at the head of one of the principal departments in that office. The salary with which I began is £800 a year; but as the Directors proceed in the way of gradual encrease with the salaries of the principal officers in this House I have the prospect of considerable augmentation at no very distant period. The time of attendance is from 10 till 4, six hours; and the business, though laborious enough, is to me highly interesting. It is the very essence of the internal government of 60 millions of people with which I have to deal; and as you know that the government of India is carried on by correspondence; and that I am the only man whose business it is, or who has the time, to make himself master of the facts scattered in a most voluminous correspondence, on which a just decision must rest, you will conceive to what an extent the real decision on matters belonging to my department rests with the man who is in my situation.' (Unpublished, MS in Bibliothèque publique et universitaire de Genève, Ms. Dumont 33. III, p. 41.)

Mr. Malthus with whom I am very intimate speaks confidently of publishing his work on Political economy next
Spring. When we meet we carry on a most active contest but
with the best disposition towards each other possible. Every
opinion of his is subjected to the ordeal of a vigorous discussion between us—I tell him that he has in this respect very
greatly the advantage over me—the truth is he is too timid
and I am too rash.—

I shall probably quit London for Gatcomb Park in the
middle of July. Whether there or in London I shall be always
happy to hear from you.—Believe me to be with great
esteem

Y$^{rs}$ very truly

DAVID RICARDO

### 316. TROWER TO RICARDO [1]
[*Answered by* 317]

Unsted Wood—Godalming—
[*ca.* 4 July 1819] [2]

My Dear Ricardo

As the proceedings of Parliament are drawing to a close,
and as the Dog days are fast approaching, I conclude you are
*beginning to think* of getting out of Town.—No doubt, the
new scenes in which you have been an actor have bound you
still more closely to London; and indeed I should regret to
have your interest devoted to any other object—You must
be highly gratified with the success that has attended your
efforts in the cause of truth and science, and to observe those
doctrines, which used to be treated as dangerous and impracticable theories, now universally admitted, and acted
upon, as undisputed axioms.

---

[1] Addressed: 'To / David Ricardo    Grosvenor Square'.—MS in *R.P.*
Esqr / M.P. / Upper Brook Street /    [2] London postmark 5 July 1819.

No—not *yet undisputed,* as my friend Sam Turner has taken up the cudgells against you, and has the boldness to avow opinions, in opposition to all the professors of the Science! Perhaps he hopes to establish a new School of Political Economy upon the ruins of that which he considers so erroneous! What say you, and what do you hear said of his Pamphlet.[1] No doubt it is popular in the environs of the Bank—and I must do him the justice to say, that his defence of the Directors against *Ministers* is both spirited and successful.—As to the rest, he has not mended the cause of Bank Notes much by representing them in every case as having effects similar to the debasing the Coin!

I observe by the Papers, that Bullion is within 1/- of the Mint price! So, that the remedy is no sooner adopted than the recovery is effected, and without the slightest danger, or even inconvenience, to the terrified patient.

Well! who would have expected to see *you* a Member of a Committee for the furtherance of Mr. Owen's Schemes!! I suppose you have accepted the appointment the more effectually to counteract his impolitic projects! Is it not a very confined, and a very unwise view of the poor, to consider the question of *expence* as the leading point to be attended to in their management? Can it be an improvement to convert the whole Country into a great Manufactory, even admitting it to be well regulated? Surely, with a view to the health, happiness and morality of the poor, the great object is not to *collect* them *into large masses,* (to which, under any system of management, there are innumerable objections,) but to *break them down* into small, unconnected *societies—*

---

[1] *A Letter addressed to the Rt. Hon. Robert Peel, &c. &c. late Chairman of the Committee of Secrecy appointed to consider the state of the Bank of England,* *With Reference to the Expediency of the Resumption of Cash Payments at the Period fixed by Law,* By Samuel Turner, F.R.S. London, for the Author, 1819.

Not to collect them into great Towns, but to scatter them 4 July 1819
over the face of the Country in small villages, and detached
cottages—So to assort them, that every Gentleman resident
in the Country should have an opportunity of creating those
sympathies, and exerting that influence among them, the
feeling and the exercising of which cannot fail to produce the
happiest effects. That the indefatiguable and humane exertions
of a benevolent individual *may* have succeeded in introducing
into a mass of people, who are his *dependents,* that happiness,
morality and good conduct, which are not the *natural growth*
of the congregated multitude, I dont mean to deny; but that
he should *therefore* expect to be able to produce *similar effects*
upon masses of people, *not similarly circumstanced* is I conceive, a conclusion not warranted by experience, nor justified
by common sense. I observed the *qualifications* which you
wisely imposed upon your being nominated on the Committee, and I am therefore prepared to find you deny a
concurrence in Mr. Owens views, but, still, I would rather
his chimeras had not received the sanction of your name even
in appearance—I shall be glad to hear what you have to say
on the subject. What do Geologists say of our friend
Greenough's Book?[1] His style is peculiar, but his pages
evince the extent of the information he has collected on the
subject. Mrs. Trower begs to unite with me in kind remembrances to Mrs. Ricardo, and your family and I remain my
Dear Ricardo

Yrs very sincerely—

HUTCHES TROWER.

What is there new or interesting in the litterary world?

[1] *A Critical Examination of the First Principles of Geology; in a Series of Essays,* by G. B. Greenough, Pres- ident of the Geological Society, London, Longman, 1819.

317. RICARDO TO TROWER [1]
[*Reply to* 316]

London July 8—1819

My dear Trower

You have calculated right—I shall in a few days leave London for Gatcomb, no worse in health for irregular meals, and late hours, during my first Parliamentary campaign. Though not necessary to my health I shall see the green fields, and hills of Gloucestershire, again, with great satisfaction. These objects are always pleasing to me, but will be more so now on account of the contrast which a little leisure will afford me to the busy and bustling life which I have lately been passing. The daily attendance in the House of Commons, and the time necessary to look over the Reports and papers which are so profusely delivered,—to say nothing of Committees which sit in the morning, leave a member no leisure to read even the light publications of the day, so that I am not acquainted with the Legend of Montrose [2] yet, and have not read more than two or three articles in the last Quarterly and Edinburgh Reviews.

The triumph of science and truth in the great councils of the Nation, this Session, gives me great satisfaction, which is not a little increased by observing the present state of the price of bullion and the foreign exchanges. Gold is I believe at £3 18. p.$^r$ oz,—silver at the mint price, and the exchanges very nearly at par. The best friends to the measures lately adopted could not have anticipated less pressure than what has been hitherto experienced, and I think it but reasonable to hope that the permanent price of bullion will settle at the present rate, without adding much to the slight difficulties which we have already suffered. Our opponents, whose

---

[1] MS at University College, London.—*Letters to Trower,* XXVII.     [2] See above, p. 37, n. 3.

prophecies are all proved to be unfounded, now say that we have had great good luck—that the natural course of events has been favorable to us—they will admit any thing but the truth of our principles. Even Lord Lauderdale, whose theory respecting Mint regulations requires that silver should never be under 5/6, that price which he calls the mint price, maintains that the present market price of silver is an unnatural and disturbed price, which cannot have a long duration.[1] I have heard much of Mr. Turner's pamphlet, but I have not seen it—I did not buy it because I have already such a number of publications by me which maintain the same doctrine which he maintains that I did not think it expedient to make the trifling sacrifice which its purchase would cost, to add to the mass. I saw extracts from it in the New Times, which paper has been as loud in his praise as it has been in condemning me.

I am not a member of a Committee to *further* Mr. Owen's plans—the committee was appointed for the purpose of examining, and not of approving those plans. I attended the meeting,[2] and had very successfully resisted all entreaties to let my name be on the committee till attacked by the Duke of Kent and Mr. John Smith. It was in vain that I protested I differed from all the leading principles advanced by Mr. Owen,—that, I was told, was no objection, for I was not bound to approve, only to examine. With very great reluctance I at last consented, and have attended the first

---

[1] Lauderdale argued that according to all the Acts of Parliament, silver, and not gold, was the standard of value. Therefore, the Mint ratio of silver to gold being 14 to 1, while the market ratio was $15\frac{1}{2}$ to 1, now that bank notes were nearly at par with gold they were ten per cent. above their silver parity. (See Lord Lauderdale's speech on 25 June 1819, *Hansard*, XL 1159–63, and cp. his *Three Letters...under the signature of 'An Old Merchant'*, 1819, mentioned above, V, 17, n. 1.)

[2] At the Freemasons' Hall on 26 June; see above, V, 467.

meeting, at which I gave my reasons at some length for dissenting from all Mr. Owens conclusions. The scheme was chiefly examined with a view to a pauper establishment or a well regulated workhouse, but even to that limited plan there are insuperable objections. Owen is himself a benevolent enthusiast, willing to make great sacrifices for a favorite object. The Duke of Kent, his great supporter, is also entitled to the praise of benevolent intentions, but he appears to me to be quite ignorant of all the principles which ought to regulate establishments for the poor—he has heard of Malthus doctrine, and has an antipathy to it, without knowing the reasons on which it is founded or how his difficulty may be obviated. He, Mr. Preston, and Mr. Owen, appear to think nothing necessary to production, and the happiness of a crowded population, but land. We have land; it may be made more productive, and therefore we cannot have an excess of population.—Can any reasonable person believe, with Owen, that a society, such as he projects, will flourish and produce more than has ever yet been produced by an equal number of men, if they are to be stimulated to exertion by a regard to the community, instead of by a regard to their private interest? Is not the experience of ages against him? He can bring nothing to oppose to this experience but one or two ill-authenticated cases of societies which prospered on a principle of a community of goods, but where the people were under the powerful influence of religious fanaticism. I was in hopes that Sir Wm. de Crespigny would have given me an opportunity to state my opinions shortly on this subject in the House of Commons, but he thought fit to withdraw his motion for a Committee, and therefore I was obliged to be silent.[1]

---

[1] On 2 July Ricardo had written to J. H. Wilkinson, from Upper Brook Street: 'I am now going down to the House—I am

Mrs. Ricardo unites with me in kind regards to Mrs. Trower 8 July 1819 and yourself. Believe me ever

My dear Trower very truly Y$^{rs}$

DAVID RICARDO

Torrens tells me he is proceeding with his work on Political Economy.[1] Malthus has been staying a few days with me. He calculates on publishing his book by the end of the year. Mill appears to be well satisfied with his new office at the East India House.—Mr. Bentham's mind and pen are employed at the present moment in elucidating the principles of Government and the safety of extending the representation.

## 318. RICARDO TO MILL[2]
### [*Answered by* 319]

My dear Sir

Ever since I have been here I have been determined not 10 Aug. 1819 to delay writing to you. I was resolved that during this separation I would be the first to commence our correspondence, recollecting as I did with gratitude that you had generally been the one who had written first. I take this opportunity then of renewing my assurances of the undiminished pleasure which I derive from your regard and friendship, and of expressing my hopes that I may continue to enjoy them while you have them to bestow, or I am in a condition to receive them.

meditating a speech on Mr. Owen's plan if I should have an opportunity this evening of saying a few words on the subject. I fear I shall make bad work of it. I had half a mind to speak last night [on Burdett's Motion for a Reform of Parliament] but my courage failed me.' (MS in the possession of the Rev. H. R. Wilkinson.)

[1] Cp. above, p. 22.

[2] Addressed: 'James Mill Esq$^r$ / East India House / London'. Franked 'August eleven'.

MS in Mill-Ricardo papers.

I wish I could have had your company here now. You would enjoy this beautiful weather, and would pronounce our country, now that the fields are green, and vegetation in high perfection, to be more entitled to compete with Bromesberrow, and Pauntley, than when you last visited it. We dine at 3 oClock, on account of the children's holidays, and after dinner we find it cool enough to enjoy very agreeable rides. We have ponies in abundance, and a couple of very quiet horses, so that you would be easily suited with a charger to your mind. Instead of this you are a close prisoner in London, performing with perseverance the new duties which have devolved on you. I by no means however relinquish the hope of seeing you here before we return to London. The Directors must reason as Rob.<sup>t</sup> Owen does—he finds it his interest not to exact too much from those he employs; he finds that he gets more work done by employing them a less number of hours; by so doing, he keeps them in good heart with their energies both of body and mind undiminished. By giving you an opportunity of changing the scene, and of inhaling the balmy air of the country, your strength both of body and mind would be increased, and what the Directors lost in time they would gain in power.—

Mr. Wakefield came here yesterday from Bath, and is gone this morning to Bromesberrow. He is accompanied by Osman, who is more than ever desirous of taking up his residence there, and as one of the houses must be to be let he thinks it may as well be his own at Hyde, as mine at Bromesberrow. I have no objection to his removing, and therefore after a few absolutely necessary repairs at Bromesberrow, he will I believe become its inhabitant. His wife has seen it, and although she is not equally delighted with it as Osman, she is very willing to go there.—We have all been over there lately, on a day when it could not be seen to more advantage, but the ladies of our party did not view the house with much complacency; and even the country about it did not draw from them such warm admiration as we are accustomed to bestow. Mr. Wakefield rode over all my property here—he thought the country very delightful, but not so uniformly beautiful as Bromesberrow and its neighbourhood.—

Mr. and Mrs. Wilkinson[1] have been staying with us—they left us this morning on their way to London. Mr. Wilkinson is enthusiastically fond of fishing, and has scarcely missed a day passing several hours at the side of one of our ponds. His success however has not been equal to his perseverance for he has had but few trophies to boast of.—He is an agreeable companion, being possessed of excellent spirits, and taking a great interest in many books which are universally agreeable. The reading of these of an evening, for the general advantage, made our time pass very agreeably.

I am much interrupted in my studies of a morning, but yet I do not wholly neglect reading. I have got through, with great pleasure, Bayles "Pensées Diverses" and nearly two thirds of Plowden's History of Ireland.[2]—The latter I have not read thoroughly, as I have passed over the account of those periods which are the least interesting to an English reader. The perusal of this book confirms me in the opinion which I have long entertained, that most of the difficulties of Government proceed from an unwillingness to make timely concessions to the people. Reform is the most efficacious preventative of Revolution, and may in my opinion be at all times safely conceded. The argument against reform now is that the people ask for too much, and that Revolution is

[1] J. H. Wilkinson, Ricardo's brother-in-law.
[2] Francis Plowden, *An Historical Review of the State of Ireland from the Invasion of that Country under* *Henry II, to its Union with Great Britain on the 1st of January, 1801,* 2 vols. in 3, London, Egerton, 1803 (2480 pages in 4to).

really meant. Would they be better able to bring about Revolution, if Reform was conceded? I think the disaffected would lose all power after the concession of Reform. Reform may be granted too late, but it can never be given too soon, if the people are sufficiently well informed to know the value of it. If catholic emancipation and a reform in Parliament had been granted to the Irish at the time that Lord Fitzwilliam was Lord Lieutenant would there have been a Rebellion in Ireland? The difficulty would then have been how to direct the councils of two independent countries towards the same objects. One might wish for war, when the other was inclined to peace. One might dethrone its monarch, while the other retained him. In this view the union became desirable, yet it is difficult I think to unite the interests of two countries, and there is great risk that in a legislative body, such as our House of Commons, in which not one sixth of the representatives are chosen by Ireland, the interests of England will prevail in all cases where they may happen to clash with those of Ireland. Is there any remedy against this but independence?—Do you think that a representative Government is more or less disposed to tyrannise over its distant unrepresented possessions than a pure Aristocracy or Monarchy?—

Mrs. Osman Ricardo is reading your history of India—I hope she will persevere.—She is as amiable and as agreeable as when you saw her.—

Believe me

Ever most truly Y$^{rs}$

D RICARDO

Gatcomb Park
10 Aug$^t$ 1819

## 319. MILL TO RICARDO [1]
### [*Reply to* 318]

East India House 14 Augt. 1819

My Dear Sir

I had begun to long for some accounts of you, when 14 Aug. 1819
your acceptable letter arrived. You appear to me to have
been living in high enjoyment; and you draw a picture quite
sufficient to make me wish to be with you. I can easily conceive that Mr. Wilkinson is a very interesting companion
in a place of retirement—his spirits, his enthusiasm, and his
flow of ideas, will communicate a share of the same pleasur-
able qualities to all around him. And then when you talk
of delightful weather, the beauties of your country, quiet
horses, evening rides, evening readings; and last of all, to
tempt me beyond resistance, talk of Mrs. Osman Ricardo "as
amiable and as agreeable as ever", and reading my history of
India,—I know not what to say to you. It is cruelty to
tantalize a man with felicity which he cannot enjoy. And yet
I must glory a little in my own virtue; for though I might
procure leave of absence for the asking, there are so many
despatches to answer, and the happiness and misery of so
many millions are affected by what I write, that I cannot find
in my heart to abstract a day from the labours of this place
till I have got towards an end of my arrears, or at least till
I have replied upon all the more important affairs. If there is
any tolerable weather after that is done, I may after all make
a run down to you of a week.—I cannot help agreeing with
Mr. Osman—if I were in his situation I would live at Bromes-
borrow too, which I would make a paradise of a place. Tell
Mrs. Osman, if she goes there, that positively one of my first
visits shall be to her; I think in consenting to go from the

---

[1] Addressed: 'David Ricardo Esq. / M.P. / Gatcomb Park / Minchinhampton / Glostershire'.—MS in *R.P.*

society of your family, and friends, to a place where she has no acquaintance, and to go without a murmur, is really being "a good girl": although, as she likes you and you like her, it is a sacrifice I regret on the account of both of you— because she was a resource to you, and you would have been of great use to her. By the bye, if she is reading my history, she is bound to send me her criticisms, as she reads; that I may profit by them, just now, when I am preparing for my second edition. As you give me no other family history, than what I have thus adverted to, I conclude that all is going happily with all of you—I have therefore nothing to do but to be happy at the thought of it; and to entreat that Mrs. Ricardo will believe that the future will be like the past, a great deal more good in it than evil. My wife and brats are all well—but we have not yet got back to our house.

I always regret when I hear that you are abridged in your hours of study—because now you ought to consider, that you have it in your power to benefit, by these hours, your fellow creatures, in a degree that few people have—and you are therefore not blameless when you neglect them. It was good that you should make yourself acquainted with the history of Ireland, but there is a monstrous portion of sur-plusage in Plowden, and I half regret the time that it will require to squint him. Your inferences from that history with regard to the importance of concession to the people— contemplating only the narrow interests of the few, and not considering those of the many—are unquestionably just, wherever the few are not sure of being able to crush the many, and compell them to submitt. I never can doubt that it is safe to give the people the benefits of a real representative government unless in very low states of civilization; and even then, they would govern themselves better perhaps in that way, than by any other government that would emanate from themselves. I can have no doubt for example that a real representation of the people would satisfy the population of this country, and secure the interests of the many without violating the rights of the few. I should think a representative government, in regard to foreign dependencies, would act very much like an aristocracy or monarchy—it would, wherever the interests of the foreign country clashed with those of the home, sacrifice those of the foreign—but as it would be more enlightened, and less guided by caprice, the foreign country would suffer only when the incongruity was real; and when the home population would really be benefited by oppressing the foreign. Over taxation, for the relief of the home population would be the grand temptation. But could this go farther than the oligarchy of the East India company goes?—and besides, if the taxation of the home country were as low as I think a good gov$^t$ would make it, the people would have little interest in seeking to relieve themselves, at the cost of their dependents. And a truly representative government will always have the benefit of a truly free press—and that will exercise an efficient controul over the treatment of dependencies, as well as every thing else.

But I must now conclude, and go to talk about Zemindars and ryots, and think of the means of protecting the latter against the former—no easy task.

Most truly Yours

J. MILL

## 320. MILL TO RICARDO [1]

24 Aug. 1819      You recollect that when I rummaged for my copy of
your letter to Perceval on the Economical currency,[2] I was
unsuccessful.—I found it in a snug concealment on replacing
my papers yesterday after the disturbance they had undergone to make way for the workmen. There was however an
envelope to the copy, which had on it a few words, and that
I cannot find.

I cannot enter upon the important topics on which I should
like to converse with you—because I have neither time nor
room. You who have both ought to send me a long letter.

J. M.

East India House 24th [August][3] 1819.


## 321. RICARDO TO MILL [4]
### [*Answered by* 322]

Easton Grey
6 Sept[r] 1819

My dear Sir

6 Sept. 1819      I received your note,[5] with Mr. Napier's letter to you,
only yesterday, and as he must be desirous of having my
answer as soon as possible to the proposal which he has very
much flattered me by making, of contributing the article on
the Sinking Fund to his valuable publication, I lose not a
moment in furnishing you with the means of giving him
one. If I thought I should succeed in such an undertaking
I would most willingly attempt it, but I know myself better
than you, or any other of my friends know me. I know the

[1] Addressed: 'David Ricardo Esq.
/ M.P. / Minchinhampton / Glostershire'.—MS in *R.P.*
[2] Letter 18.
[3] In MS 'July'; London postmark, 24 Aug. 1819. The 'im-

portant topics' no doubt refers to
'Peterloo' (16 August).
[4] Addressed: 'James Mill Esq[r] /
East India House / London'.
MS in Mill-Ricardo papers.
[5] Mill's letter is wanting.

difficulty which I at all times have in stringing a few sentences together, and this difficulty would be incalculably
increased if I felt that I was under an obligation to complete
a task in a given time. When I write I must be free as air;
I must have the privelege of relinquishing my work if I
please, of postponing it if I should think it expedient, and of
committing to the flames whatever may appear to me to
deserve that fate: I am quite sure that I could do nothing,
even if I were placed in the most favourable circumstances,
were I bound by an engagement to accomplish my work in
a definite portion of time. But I am now not placed in the
most favourable circumstances for such an undertaking. In
the first place I very much doubt whether my books at
Gatcomb will furnish me with the facts concerning the
establishment and progress of the sinking fund, and it is
peculiarly important that in an Essay on that subject all the
facts should be minutely and correctly stated. In the second
place I am under a load of engagements, expecting to have
visitors of one description or another in the house with me
for several weeks to come, and although I might if I pleased
entirely withdraw myself from their society of a morning,
and plead my engagement for so doing, yet I know by
experience how difficult this is, and how apt I am to be drawn
away from my work by taking rides and walks about the
country. My best reason however is my inadequacy to the
performance of the work in question, and though I know
that I might rely for great assistance, in the way of correction,
from your friendship, yet I also know I should not get that
which alone could induce me to encounter these and many
more obstacles, I mean literary fame. I am sure that with my
best efforts it would not be deserving of a place in the
company by which it would be surrounded.

Since I last wrote to you I have been at Bath to stay a few

56    *Correspondence*

days with Mr. and Mrs. Clutterbuck. From Bath I went to

Gloster for the Assizes, and served for a few days on the
Grand Jury. On leaving Gloucester Mr. Shepherd accompanied me or rather preceded me to Gatcomb where we
found Lady Mary and you know that in her company there
can be no time for work of any description.[1] While she was
with us the Smiths passed two or 3 days at Gatcomb and we
are now returning their visit. Since thursday we have been
here, and shall probably go back to Gatcomb tomorrow.

I found Mr. Belsham at Easton Grey, he had arrived just
before me from the neighbourhood of Manchester. He is not
much of a reformer, but he speaks with great indignation,
(and says that the same feeling is general in every place in
which he has been staying,) against the conduct of the
Manchester Magistrates. Both here and at Gatcomb we have
had many political discussions, without the least loss of
friendship.—Shepherd, you know, is a tory, and is by inclination and interest devoted to Ministers. Smith is a determined
Whig, and my sentiments are well known to you. When the
expediency of a Reform in Parliament was the subject, the
whig and tory joined against me, but I found myself occasionally powerfully supported by Miss Hobhouse, who is on
a visit to Mrs. Smith, and consequently was of the party at
Gatcomb as well as here. She is very warmly attached to her
brother,[2] and defends the cause of reform with all the energy

[1] Henry John Shepherd, M.P., a barrister, and his wife, Lady Mary, daughter of the Earl of Rosebery. She was the author of several philosophical treatises. 'It has now become high fashion with blue ladies to talk political economy. There is a certain Lady Mary Shepherd who makes a great jabbering on the subject, while others who have more sense, like Mrs. Marcet, hold their tongues and listen.' (Maria Edgeworth to Mrs Ruxton, from London, 9 March 1822. This passage, which is incomplete in *Memoir of Maria Edgeworth*, 1867, has been kindly supplied from the MS by Professor H. E. Butler.)

[2] J. C. Hobhouse.

of a good citizen.—Our party was yesterday increased by 6 Sept. 1819 the accession of Mr. Whishaw, who arrived here at dinner time, accompanied by a young friend of his Mr. Mac Donnel.[1] We had very little politics yesterday. The Manchester and Westminster meetings were of course the subject of discussion but on that subject there does not appear to be much difference of opinion. Sometimes indeed they speak with so much alarm of the numerous and frequent meetings of the people as to impress me strongly with the opinion that they would be willing to forbid them by law altogether.—

Remember that I wish much to see you at Gatcomb, and depend on your availing yourself of any favourable opportunity which may offer to withdraw yourself for a time from your laborious duties.—When you see Mr. Bentham tell him I have him frequently in my remembrance.

Ever truly Y<sup>rs</sup>

DAVID RICARDO

I have been reading Sismondi's work[2]—it is I think a very poor performance. In his attacks upon me he is not candid but misrepresents me in several instances.—He as well as Say attempts to refute the doctrine of rent, because there is no land they say which does not pay rent.

### 322. MILL TO RICARDO [3]
[*Reply to 321.—Answered by 323*]

East India House 7<sup>th</sup> Sept<sup>r</sup> 1819

My Dear Sir

I have just received your letter, and as I am quite 7 Sept. 1819 decided that not one of your reasons is a good one, I shall

---

[1] Alexander McDonnell (1794–1875), Student of Christ Church, Oxford, later Commissioner of National Education in Ireland.

[2] *Nouveaux principes d'économie politique,* Paris, 1819.
[3] MS in *R.P.*

write to Napier that you undertake the article. If you had felt any objection, even founded on feeling, I should have given way—if you had not liked the idea of giving your name to a partnership work—though a work which has the names of Dugald Stewart, Playfair, Walter Scott, Barrow, &.c., can do no discredit to any name—I should have said you were entitled to judge for yourself. But to give only reasons, which, if acted upon, would for ever hinder you from doing any thing, is too bad. As for time, take your own time. I will undertake for you, you shall not be hurried. And then, again, as for your not being able to work for time, it is all a fancy. You are not a puling sentimentalist—a thing that must be *governed by,* not govern, its *fine feelings!* A couple of hours, each day, and a great deal less, would accomplish the thing in a month—and if you want any book, name it, and it shall be sent to you. The last plea, of want of ability, you ought to be ashamed of yourself for stating. So now I hope you are properly scolded, and having kissed the rod, like a good disciple, are taking seriously to your task. You ought to be thankful, if your house is going to be full, of having an excuse, for appropriating a little of each day to yourself. Why, surely, you can manage to get up two hours before breakfast. Mrs. Ricardo is up three.[1]

Whiggery is whiggizing most characteristically on the present occasion. It would like dearly to make a howl about the Manchester massacres for the sake of turning out the ministers; but it is terrified out of its miserable wits to do so, for fear of aiding parliamentary reform, to which it seems to shew pretty distinctly that it would prefer an iron despotism. "Sometimes indeed they speak with so much alarm of the numerous and frequent meetings of the people as to impress me strongly with the opinion that they would be willing to

---

[1] See below, p. 77–8.

forbid them by law altogether." These are your own words,
speaking of the Whigs you have lately had about you. This
is pretty well—is it not? What are you and I to think,
reasonably, about such gentry? About their understandings,
if they are sincere? About something else, if they are not
sincere? If they dread the meetings of the people, because
they worship bad government—they are right—and nothing
will save them, but the degrading despotism they would
prefer. If they dread them, as supposing the people hostile,
or likely to be made hostile to property, it is folly; as the
temperance and self-command of the people on so many
recent occasions might convince them. The displays of talent
and virtue have all changed sides; gone over to the people,
from those inferiors of theirs who call themselves their betters.

I have seen a paragraph in the Times of today about the
health of Brougham, which fills me with alarm—if true, I am
afraid it is his health in a very unhappy sense.

It gives me great pleasure that you had a fellow combatant
and a good one in Miss Hobhouse. I have no doubt, that you
had the victory in every thing except in positiveness of
assertion. I like to hear that she is an admirer of her brother,
in whom I think there is a great deal of stuff of the best sort.
He is a man capable of great things, if he takes pains with
himself, and keeps among right people. You should encourage
him to come about you. It will do him much more good than
tying himself up in the apron-strings of Burdett. If you see
his sister again, you may tell her I said so.—I hardly know
what I have said—for I had but 10 minutes for you—adieu.

J. M. [1]

---

[1] A letter from Mill to Napier, dated 10 Sept. 1819, reads: 'I wrote immediately to Ricardo, telling him you counted upon his half promise as a whole one. I received from him a parcel of excuses—but as there was none of them good for any thing, I wrote to him immediately that I should send you word of his

## 323. RICARDO TO MILL [1]
*[Reply to 322.—Answered by 325]*

Gatcomb Park
9 Sep 1819

My dear Sir

I am to kiss the rod, and take myself seriously to my task! And do you really expect such obedience? I am inclined to shew you a little of my democratic spirit, and tell you plainly that I will not be an author on compulsion, but when I reflect that you have always been a good master and guide to me—that it is to your encouragement that I am indebted for the gratification which my vanity has experienced as an author, I am induced to pause, and not at once rush into open rebellion. If my reasons have not satisfied you, neither have yours removed my objections. I can not agree to enter into any engagement with Mr. Napier to furnish the article required for the Encyclopedia, but I will use my best endeavors to write it. We must both be free as air. He shall himself be convinced, however humiliating to me, that I am not equal to the performance of the task, and he shall be at liberty to reject my work altogether, or to take any ideas from it which may appear to him worth his attention. You must not give him the idea that I can do any thing which he is afterwards to publish, and I confess I should feel

having undertaken the task. I might have heard from him to-day —and as I have not, I conclude he acquiesces. It is unaffected diffidence which is the cause of his unwillingness, for he is as modest as he is able.—At this moment Ricardo's letter is brought up to me. He will put down his thoughts, he says, and send them to you, but that you will have to write the article at last for yourself. But of this there is no fear except his own.... If you have any instructions to send to Ricardo, you may write them either to him or to me.' (MS in British Museum, Add. 36,612, fols. 287–8; incomplete in *Selections from the Correspondence of Macvey Napier,* p. 23, and Bain, *James Mill,* p. 187.)
[1] MS in Mill-Ricardo papers.

more satisfaction if I knew that some other person had undertaken it.

I am not well aware of what I am to do. A history of the Sinking Fund! What has been already done in the work itself on that subject?—I have not my copy here, and cannot send for the particular volume as I do not know under what word the subject is treated. In Rees' Cyclopedia[1] under the head "Funds" there is an account of the first establishment, and progress of the Sinking Fund; may I depend on the accuracy of that account, and shall I state the same facts in my own words? To me it appears of little consequence to enter into minute details of the state of the fund before 1784, when Mr. Pitt first took it in hand. With respect to the facts concerning this fund I believe there is a great deal of information in Hamilton's book[2] which I have here, and I expect to meet with much more in the Parliamentary History and Debates, which I have also got here. It would have been of some advantage to me to have been able to consult the annual accounts of finance laid before the House of Commons, but that I cannot do without going to London. If you should think of any book to which I might refer for instruction pray send it to me, and give me your opinion of the sort of arrangement which you think most desirable. Tell me also how long the article should be. Rees has said all he had to say in 4 pages. Will it be necessary for me to go into the subject much more at length?

I came home on tuesday, but at Smith's earnest request I went over to him again yesterday, and came back at night. We had many discussions on the subject of reform, and I was glad to find that Whishaw conceded so much to me, re-

---

[1] *The Cyclopaedia,* by Abraham Rees, 1819.

[2] Robert Hamilton, *An Inquiry concerning...the National Debt,* 3rd ed., Edinburgh, 1818.

specting the non representation of the people in Parliament, as really to give up the whole question. He of course clung to the favorite position of the Whigs that without nomination in some instances the most distinguished talent would be shut out from the House of Commons, which I did not fail to combat to the best of my ability. I pressed him upon the subject of whig reform which in fact is no reform at all, as it proposes to secure to the aristocracy a majority against the people. Some may wish to extend the suffrage more than others, but the test of sincerity is whether they will allow a majority in Parliament to be bona fide the representatives of the interests of the people. On the whole Whishaw was much more of a reformer than he ever appeared to me to be before, and seemed to lament that the Aristocracy were so determined not to yield any thing to their adversaries, he thought the consequences might be serious of the determined resolution of the *two violent parties* in this contest.

Mr. Mac Donnell, a young Irishman, spoke with admiration of the increased, and increasing knowledge of the people, and he, I am sure is a sincere advocate for at least such a reform as may give to the good sense of the people the choice of their representatives. Previously to our conversation we had been enumerating the different members of the Duke of Beaufort's family who were in Parliament, and all had expressed indignation at the invariable custom which appears to have prevailed in that family for many generations of palming the younger sons of it on the Public. This was not a bad exemplification of the evils of our present system, as it shewed that the public interest was sacrificed to secure votes in Parliament.—

Mr. Smith has an excellent collection of pamphlets published at the time of the sittings of the "Friends of the

People". One caught my attention to which there was no author's name printed, but to which he had put Mackintosh's name as the writer. It is a Letter to Mr. Pitt on his Apostacy from the cause of Reform,[1] and might with great propriety be now addressed to himself. Smith could not recollect his authority for putting Mackintosh's name to it, and Whishaw had no recollection of his having written such a pamphlet. Whishaw read it and is now sure that it was written by Mackintosh. There are two or three very strong and able points in it, in answer to the most popular objections to Reform, and when Smith urged these objections in our argument, I opened the book and read the triumphant answers to them. One was that bad as our parliament was in theory it worked well, and therefore it would be unwise to meddle with it. That argument was urged by Pitt in 1792 when the nation was at Peace and prosperous, and then received its proper answer, which can now not be more justly, but more forcibly applied to it. Did you ever see this pamphlet? An old Lady[2] a relation of Mrs. Smith a clever woman enthusiastically attached to the Whigs listened to our discussion with the greatest interest and attention. She has been accustomed to think that the Whigs are the steady supporters of the liberties, and best interests of the people. She told me she agreed in all the opinions I had given in favor of Reform and always thought those were the opinions of the Whigs. I believe her faith in Whig virtue and pa-triotism is very much shaken by our arguments.

I am exceedingly concerned at what you hint concerning Brougham's health—I hope that your fears are unfounded and that he may not be another added to the list of able men whose services have been denied to their country by the

---

[1] London, 1792.    [2] Mrs Chandler; see below, p. 75.

visitation of one of the most calamitous diseases which afflicts our nature.——

Ever truly Y<sup>rs</sup>

David Ricardo

Do you know where I could get D<sup>r</sup> Price's work on the sinking fund.[1] Hamilton has really done what Mr. Napier wants, why does he not copy his book? If I write I must quote largely from it. Is there any objection to doing so.

### 324. MALTHUS TO RICARDO [2]
[*Answered by* 328]

E I Coll Sep<sup>r</sup> 10<sup>th</sup> 1819.

My dear Ricardo,

I trust you have been spending your time very pleasantly at Gatcomb. After I had the pleasure of seeing you in Town,[3] the Eckersalls changed their abode from Henley to Ray Mill Cottage near Maidenhead Bridge, whither we accompanied them, and continued our excursions upon the water. We finally came to Town the end of July in the *four oar,* having explored above 110 miles of the course of the Thames.

We have been now returned to the College above a month, nearly indeed six weeks, and I have been endeavouring to get on a little with my volume[4]; but I have been delayed and led away as usual by thoughts relating to the subjects of some of our discussions. In pursuing one of the suppositions which I believe I mentioned when I saw you in Town I have been rather struck with the consequences which seem to flow from it.

If we suppose half an ounce of silver on an average to be

---

[1] Richard Price, D.D., *An Appeal to the Public on the Subject of the National Debt,* London, Cadell, 1772.

[2] MS in *R.P.*

[3] See above, p. 47.

[4] *Principles of Political Economy.*

picked up by a days search on the sea shore, money would then always retain most completely the same value. It would always on an average both cost, and command the same quantity of labour. The money price of labour could never permanently either rise or fall; and the accumulation of capital in all cases where capital was used and the same quantity of labour employed, would shew itself in a fall of prices owing to the diminished rate of profits. Corn alone would rise in money price on account of the increased quantity of labour required; but the rise would be inconsiderable, and strictly limited by the diminution of *corn* wages which the labourer could bear.

Under these circumstances I should like to know from you how the profits of stock would be *regulated*. They could not evidently be regulated by the rise in money wages of labour, because labour would not alter in money value.

I am strongly disposed to think that a rise of money wages, supposing money always to retain its value, is by no means absolutely necessary in the progress of cultivation to its extreme limits. It is only necessary that corn should rise to such a point, as with fixed money wages will put a stop to the further increase of population. In general when money wages rise, which is one of the commonest events in the progress of wealth, I am inclined to think, it may be fairly concluded that the value of money has fallen. According to my measure of value indeed I should say at once that money had fallen if it would command less labour; and according to your theory it could only command less labour and yet retain the same value, from the accidental circumstance of capital being employed in the production of it.

I have been saying in my introduction, that my work has been delayed by my respect for your authority, and the fear that I must have overlooked some essential points either in your view of the subject or in my own.[1] But though I have been lately finishing the beginning, I have by no means arrived at the end. I think I have a fourth or a fifth to write yet; and having composed the different parts at different times and not in their natural order, I have still much to put out and put in, before it will be fit to send to the press. I can hardly expect to be out before February or March.

What do you think of this terrible Manchester business.[2] It was a most cruel and unjust proceeding in itself; and I fear it is likely to be attended with the most unfortunate consequences, by giving additional importance and influence to such persons as Hunt.[3]

Mrs. M joins me in kind remembrance to Mrs. Ricardo. All well here. I hope you can make the same report at Gatcomb.

Ever truly Yours

T R Malthus.

325. MILL TO RICARDO[4]
[*Reply to* 323.—*Answered by* 329]

East India House 11th Sept.ʳ 1819

My Dear Sir

A parcel will be sent to you on monday, containing Price on the Sinking fund, Sinclairs Hist. of the Rev.[5] and such other books as may appear to be useful to you.[6]

I have no doubt that the history of the Sinking Fund, up to the date of the Book, and other common-place matter, was given pretty fully in the Encyclop.[7]—Of all this, accordingly, I should in your place give very little, and I have no doubt

---

[1] See above, II, 11–12.
[2] 'Peterloo', 16 August.
[3] Henry Hunt.
[4] MS in *R.P.*
[5] Sir John Sinclair, *The History of the Public Revenue of the British*

*Empire,* 3rd ed., London, Cadell and Davies, 1803–4, 3 vols.
[6] The parcel was being sent by Place, see letter 326.
[7] *Encyclopaedia Britannica,* 4th ed., published between 1801 and 1810.

that for such facts as you need employ, you may trust the article in Rees with safety. Your grand business should be to explain the nature and operation of a sinking fund; and to discuss the questions of policy connected with it. As far as Hamilton, or any other body, has gone before you, in saying what is necessary to be said, you have nothing to do, but to say it after them, telling that you do so; and either taking their words, or your own, as you think best suits the occasion. An article in an Encyclopedia, should be to a certain degree didactic, and also elementary—as being to be consulted by the ignorant as well as the knowing; but the matter that has been often explained, may be passed over very shortly, to leave more space for that which is less commonly known. As for space, you should take much or little, just as the matter requires. Put down every thing which you think it will be instructive to put down—there is no fear of its being too long. When you have made your list of the points which you think the article ought to embrace, it will not require you much time to send them to me. They may suggest some things which you have overlooked. At present I have the subject so little in my head, that I can say nothing hardly about topics. The mode in which a sinking fund, when real, operates to pay debts, is one—the mode in which a sinking fund, when no longer real, may be made to appear real, is another—and a third is (what you have not been anticipated in by any body) the utter absurdity of trusting a government like ours with a sinking fund at all. The last topic is original, and if worked in your best manner will be striking—I know not that you will find any thing to say that is quite new, on any other part of the subject—though to point out as clearly as possible the delusion which was long carried on under the cloak of the sinking fund, will be highly useful, and you will be able to put it into new lights.

I return you many thanks for the reports you have given me of your parliamentary reform discussions. I edify by them very much. Your test of a man who is really, and not pretendedly a reformer, namely, the allowing an effectual majority of *bona fide* representatives to the people, is excellent. I am mightily pleased with your making a convert of the old Whig lady. As for the concessions of Whishaw, they are good for nothing—he is a confirmed party man, and will retract them all tomorrow. I would undertake to make a convert to any thing that would be reform Mr. Canning himself sooner than a confirmed Whig, who politically speaking (I am far from meaning personally) is decidedly the most vicious creature we have amongst us.[1]—I wish you would procure me a sight of that pamphlet of Mackintosh— I have often heard of it, but never been able to see it.

Adieu

J. M.

Remember me kindly to Mr. and Mrs. Smith, and to all of your own family (and that emphatically) who are near you.

---

[1] In the letter to Napier of 10 Sept. quoted above, p. 59–60, n. Mill writes: 'I would undertake to make Mr Canning a convert to the principles of good government sooner than your Lord Grey and your Sir James Mackintosh; and I have now an opportunity of speaking with some knowledge of Canning.'

## 326. RICARDO TO PLACE [1]

Dear Sir

Accept my thanks for the books you have sent me.[2] I have not yet had time to look over them. I fear I shall not be able to accomplish the task I have undertaken. I hope Mr. Napier does not depend on me.

In great haste
Y[rs] very truly
DAVID RICARDO

Gatcomb Park
18 Sep 1819

18 Sept. 1819

## 327. TROWER TO RICARDO [3]
*[Answered by 330]*

Unsted Wood—Godalming—
Sept[r] 19—1819.

My Dear Ricardo

It appears an age since I have had the pleasure of hearing from you, and I am therefore fearful, that I have been a very dilatory correspondent. No doubt, your time has been much occupied of late, as mine has, by company in my house; when it is difficult to steal an hour to oneself. In large families, and great establishments, where visitors are numerous, everyone is left to himself in the morning, to seek his own amusement, but where arrangements are upon a more limited scale, it is not so easy to separate oneself from a companion, to follow one's own pursuits, and to throw him upon his own resources. I am at length alone, and avail

19 Sept. 1819

---

[1] Addressed: 'F. Place Esq[re] / Charing Cross / London'. Place notes on the MS: 'This relates to an article for the Encyclopedia Britannica'.
MS in British Museum (Place Papers), Add. 37,949, fols. 76–7.

[2] See above, p. 66.
[3] Addressed: 'To / David Ricardo Esqr / M.P. / Gatcomb Park— / Minchinhampton'.
MS in *R.P.*

myself of the opportunity, thus afforded, of enquiring after my friends at Gatcomb. I do not find that the manufacturers in Glocestershire have evinced the same restless, troublesome and dissatisfied spirit, that has been so lamentably exhibited in the northern manufacturing districts. Although these disturbances are not of a nature sufficiently serious to create anxiety, they are still very disagreeable; and it is, to say the least of it, unfortunate, that any circumstances should have happened to excite still further the irritated feelings of a distressed population. I am told, and by those, too, who are good authority upon the subject, that the proceedings of the Magistrates, and constituted authorities at Manchester are *perfectly legal*. Of the truth of this, at present, I am by no means satisfied, but shall shortly endeavour to satisfy my mind upon the subject, by examining into the various statutes by which it is governed. But, at all events, I think, even should the legality of the measures be admitted, the result has fully proved their inexpediency. For, so far from having checked the existing mischief, they have greatly aggravated it.—In all the proceedings at Manchester I am surprised not to have seen the name of Mr. Sharpe's friend Mr. Philips, who, I believe, is a resident, of course has great influence, and could not be indifferent on the subject. As a Magistrate I should have expected to have seen him taking *some* part in the proceedings—

I keep my eyes fixed on the prices of Bullion and the Course of the exchanges, and I rejoice to see how steadily they continue at, or near par. Affording conclusive evidence, that they have been brought there, not by accidental and temporary causes, but that the wise measures pursued have brought them back to their proper and *permanent* level.— Are your thoughts still directed to these interesting subjects? The public mind is now in a proper state to receive instruction on these matters; and there is one branch respecting which they are lamentably ignorant. I mean the *principles of taxation.* The question of taxation is never agitated in Parliament without affording abundant proof of this deficiency. All taxes on necessaries are scouted as unwise and unjust, and efforts are constantly making to repeal them.— It is true, that you have already clearly and ably laid down those principles in your Book. But I cannot help thinking that much benefit would arise from having these principles more *fully* explained and insisted upon, and their *application to our particular situation pointed out.* Their importance is enhanced by the peculiar circumstances in which this Country is placed, by the enormous amount of the funded debt, which will render it *absolutely necessary,* in any future war, to depend *almost exclusively* upon supplies raised within the year. It is a question of great interest, and general application, and I know no person so qualified to engage in it, and do it justice as yourself. In short it would be a more enlarged and comprehensive view of a subject you have already treated; *applied to, and illustrated by,* the actual circumstances and situation of the Country. Except the Chapters in your Book I am not aware of any modern work upon the subject.—

Mrs. Trower and the Children are all well, and I hope to have an account equally satisfactory of Mrs. Ricardo and your family. I expect the Autumn will scarcely pass away before Mrs. Trower will have added to our domestic circle! It is a pity your friend Malthus had not been a Physician, instead of a Member of the Church, as probably he might have been more *successful* than Mr. Owen in discovering a check for population![1]

---

[1] The story was that Robert Owen had travelled to France to discover the means which prevented a rapid increase of population and had brought back with him several specimens of the contrivance

I did not know of the nature of Mr. Mills appointment at the India House till I lately saw Mr. Hume. I rejoice at it. He is sure to do it justice, and it affords him a very comfortable addition to his income—

Pray make our kind regards to Mrs. Ricardo and believe me My Dear Ricardo

yours very truly—

HUTCHES TROWER

### 328. RICARDO TO MALTHUS [1]
[*Reply to* 324.—*Answered by* 338]

Gatcomb Park
21 Sep.<sup>r</sup> 1819

My dear Malthus

I must not longer delay answering your kind letter. I have had you often in my mind, and was on the point of writing to you a short time ago, when I received a letter from Mill, inclosing one from Mr. Napier, the editor or manager of the Encyclopedia Britannica, requesting him to apply to me to write an article on the Sinking Fund for his publication. The task appeared too formidable to me to think of undertaking, and I immediately wrote to Mill to that effect, but that only brought me another letter from him,[2] which hardly left me a choice, and at last I have consented to try what I can do, but with no hopes of succeeding. I am very hard at work, because I wish to give Mr. Napier the opportunity of applying to some other person, without delaying

there in use; this was later denied by Owen. (See N. E. Himes, 'The place of J. S. Mill and of Robert Owen in the history of English Neo-Malthusianism', *Quarterly Journal of Economics*, Aug. 1928, pp. 633–40; and cp. below, IX, 62.)

[1] Addressed: 'The Rev<sup>d</sup> T. R. Malthus / East India College / Hertford'.
    MS at Albury.—*Letters to Malthus*, LXIX.
[2] Letter 332.

his publication, as soon as I have convinced Mill and him that I am not sufficiently conversant with matters of this kind. This business has lately engrossed all my time, and will probably continue to do so for at least a week to come.

So you moved from Henley to Maidenhead!—You were determined not to lose sight of the Thames. I shall expect to see your name entered as a candidate for the annual Wherry.

I am glad that you are proceeding merrily with your work. I now have hopes it will be finished. You have been very indolent, and are not half so industrious, nor so anxious as I am, when I have any thing in hand.

I have not been able to give a proper degree of attention to the subject of your letter. The supposition you make of half an ounce of silver being picked up on the sea shore by a day's labour, is you will confess an extravagant one. Under such circumstances silver could not as you say rise or fall, neither could labour, but corn could or rather might. Profits I think would still depend on the proportions of produce allotted to the capitalist and the labourer.—The whole produce would be less, which would cause its price to rise, but of the quantity produced the labourer would get a larger proportion than before. This larger proportion would nevertheless be a less quantity than before, and would be of the same money value. In the case you suppose the rise of money wages does not appear to be necessary in the progress of cultivation to its extreme limits, but the reason is that you have excluded the use of capital entirely in the production of your medium of value. You know I agree with you that money is a more variable commodity than is generally imagined, and therefore I think that many of the variations in the price of commodities may be fairly attributed to an alteration in the value of money. It is difficult to conceive that in a great, and civilized[1]

---

[1] In MS 'civiziled'.

country any commodity of importance could be produced with equal advantage without the employment of capital.

By what you tell me in your letter you have respected my authority much too highly, and I do not consent that you should attribute to that respect the little activity you have displayed in getting your work finished. I wish that Mrs. Malthus and you would come to us here at Christmas. I shall then be quite in the humor to discuss all the difficult questions on which we appear to differ. My family is now in a settled state, and I think I can promise you more comfortable entertainment than I have yet been able to give you here. You must no longer plume yourself on being the principal object of Cobbett's abuse. I have come in for my share of it, and just in the way that I anticipated. Even when he agrees with you he can find shades of difference which calls forth his virulence.[1]—

[1] Cobbett had been advocating for nine years the return to gold; but now that the Bank was to resume payments according to Ricardo's ingot plan, he represented this as a paper-money scheme. In 'Letter X to Henry Hunt, Esq. On the recent Tricks of the Boroughmongers, relative to their Paper-Money' (*Cobbett's Weekly Political Register*, 4 Sept. 1819) he writes from Long Island, 7 July 1819: 'I see, that they have adopted a scheme of one Ricardo (I wonder what countryman he is), who is, I believe, a converted Jew. At any rate, he has been a 'Change-Alley-man for the last fifteen or twenty years. If the Old Lord Chatham were now alive, he would speak with respect of the Muckworm, as he called the 'Change-Alley-people. Faith! they are now become *every thing*. Bar-ing assists at the Congress of Sovereigns, and *Ricardo* regulates things at home. The Muckworm is no longer a creeping thing; it rears its head aloft, and makes the haughty Borough Lords sneak about in holes and corners.' 'This Ricardo says, that the country is happy in the discovery of a paper-money; that it is an *improvement* in political science' (pp. 80, 82).

In 'Letter XI to Henry Hunt, Esq. On the Workings of the Boroughmongers, relative to the Poor-Laws' (*op. cit.,* 11 Sept. 1819) he comments, with much abuse of 'that impudent and illiterate Parson,' Malthus, on Ricardo's speech on Sturges Bourne's Poor-Law bill: 'Mr Ricardo from the 'Change, is *afraid* that this regulation will be an encouragement for the labour-ing people *to go on breeding*, as he

I had the pleasure of passing a few days lately in Mr. 21 Sept. 1819 Whishaw's company at Mr. Smith's at Easton Grey—He was in very good spirits, and very agreeable. We had some political discussion, particularly on Reform, and he was more liberal in his concessions than I have usually found him. I had Miss Hobhouse heartily on my side, and Mrs. Chandler, an enthusiast for the Whigs, declared that mine were the true Whig principles. Mr. Belsham was of the party, but he did not take a decided part.[1] Mr. Macdonnel, who came with Mr. Whishaw, was, I thought, all but an ally. Are you not weary?

Mrs. Ricardo joins with me in kind regards to Mrs. Malthus. Believe me ever

Y$^{rs}$ truly<br>DAVID RICARDO

## 329. RICARDO TO MILL[2]
[*Reply to 325.—Answered by 332 & 337*]

Gatcomb Park
23 Sep.$^r$ 1819

My dear Sir

As I before told you I am anxious that a wrong estima- 23 Sept. 1819 tion of my talents, both by you, and Mr. Napier, may not expose the latter to the inconvenience and delay of not getting the article on the Sinking Fund done in time for the regular period of the publication of his volume, and therefore I have lately been hard at work that you might very soon

says they are *too apt* to do! I wonder whether any plan, bullion or other, has suggested itself to the mind of this great statesman to check the population amongst the loan and script gentry? None of the declaimers against an increase of population ever think of this' (p. 109).

[1] See Belsham's account of this party, in his *Memoirs*, by John Williams, 1833, pp. 701–2.

[2] Addressed: 'James Mill Esq$^r$ / East India House / London'.

MS in Mill-Ricardo papers.

be enabled to decide on the truth of my representation, that I was unequal to the task you required of me. I now send you the fruits of my work, of which I request you to dispose as you think best for my honour and reputation. If you think that with such few alterations and additions as I am capable of giving to it, it may do, return it to me with such suggestions as may offer themselves to you, and with such corrections of language as you may think it requires. If you think, which is my feeling about it, that it contains some hints which may be useful to a better, and more expert writer, send it to Mr. Napier, and let him ask some other person to perform the work, giving him the privelege to avail himself of my hints if he thinks proper. Perhaps after all the best way of disposing of it is to put it in the fire, for it is a thing of shreds and patches, culled from one person's writing, and another persons speech, and is withal in a stile so barbarous that you cannot do better than so to dispose of it.—To complete the article tables are wanted and on this point I am not acquainted with Mr. Napier's wishes. The parliamentary papers would afford me the means of giving copious tables respecting the increase of debt—the growth of the Sinking Fund—the public expenditure—the amount of taxes &c$^a$. &c$^a$. There might be 4 or 5 and as Hamilton has performed this as well as almost every other part of the work, would it be fair to copy his tables?—I send the MS by this days coach to Brook Street, with directions to my servant there, to take it to you to Queen Square, and if you are not residing there, to forward it to you at the India House.

In looking over my work last night, I perceive that what I have said in page 15 is nearly a repetition of what I had before said in the latter end of page 11. Does the repetition tend to clearness, or should one of the passages be left out?—

It was very kind of Mr. Place to send me the books and
Parliamentary papers which he has sent. He selected the
latter with great skill, they are full of information. Say so to
him when you see him. Perhaps he would not object
looking over the MS I send you, and giving me his opinion
of it. I do not think that he and I quite agree in our opinions
about the Sinking Fund.—

With the parcel I send you the letter to Mr. Pitt said to be
written by Sir James, then Mr. Mackintosh. Take care of it
for I have borrowed it of Mr. Smith, and have his permission
to send it to you.—The passage which I read to Whishaw,
and the rest of my adversaries on reform, at Smiths, is that
where he supposes Pitt the minister of Titus,—it came very
apropos for my cause.—

I hope that you and your family are well. We are all well
here still enjoying the fine weather. I expect Grenfell the
latter end of this or beginning of next week.

Ever Y.ʳˢ

DAVID RICARDO

## 330. RICARDO TO TROWER [1]
[*Reply to 327.—Answered by 339*]

Gatcomb Park 25 Sep—1819
My dear Trower

I was well pleased to see your well known handwriting
after the very long interval which had elapsed since I received
your last letter. I was on the point of writing to you, to shew
you that I was not disposed to relinquish my intercourse
with you, imperfect as it is; when your letter arrived, and my
murmuring ceased.

By rising early in the morning I have two hours to myself
for any object I may have in view, without interruption even

---

[1] MS at University College, London.—*Letters to Trower*, XXVIII.

when visitors are in my house, of course when I am alone or when my visitors are those who are nearly related to me there is much more time in the course of the day that I can call my own. It is easier to find time, than to use it profitably. I have been very much drawn away from all serious occupation since I have been in the country by the desire I have felt to enjoy the fineness of the weather. I cannot often refuse the solicitations of my two little girls to accompany them in their morning rides and we are often to be met with in full canter on our respective ponies.

For the last fortnight I have confined myself a good deal to my desk, endeavouring to put my thoughts on paper on the subject of the Sinking Fund. I was requested to do so by Mill, who had been applied to by Mr. Napier to forward such a request to me. Mr. Napier is the Editor of the Supplement to the Encyclopedia Britannica, and he wished for an article on the Sinking fund, from me, to appear in the next half volume of his work. I, at first, refused, but on being strongly urged to do it by Mill, I consented to make the attempt. I have made it, but I have not succeeded, and it is now a very doubtful matter whether I shall persevere in my task. The truth is that Dr. Hamilton's book on the Sinking Fund is so good that very little of original observations can be made on the subject. It would be unjust not to refer to him on all occasions, and if you do so it may be asked whether you have done any thing yourself? The only point of difference between Dr. H and me is this,—he would I believe support the Sinking Fund, I would get rid of it entirely, or leave it at that small amount as to give security that if the revenue suffered any unexpected defalcation there was this surplus to apply to. I am equally impressed with Dr. Hamilton with the importance of diminishing our enormous debt, the question with me is, will the Sinking Fund effect it? I am persuaded that it never will, for it will never be safe from the gripe of ministers. Have you virtue enough to pay a great part of your debt by the sacrifice of a portion of your property? This is the question to be put to the country—if they answer in the negative, then I say the next best thing is to submit to the burden of your debt without aggravating it by new imposts which will certainly be misapplied. But I must remember that I am not now writing my essay, and that I must not forestal the only point on which I think I am entitled to attention.

I have pretty nearly discarded the subject of bullion from my mind. Every thing regarding its price and the foreign exchanges is going on so much to my satisfaction that I have nothing to wish for. I repose in full confidence on the wise checks which have been put on the Bank Directors—if they had been unrestrained they would again have mistaken the object which they ought to have in view; instead of taking measures to equalise the value of paper and gold they would have been thinking of the public good, and under a mistaken idea of promoting that, they would have administered an increased dose of paper.

On the subject of taxation a wide field is open for those, who will patiently think, to give instruction to the Public; but the first step must be to make the first principles of Political Economy known, and that remains yet to be done. Without correct notions of rent, no man can be made to understand that a land tax does not ultimately fall on the landlord, and it would be in vain to talk to him, till he did admit the new doctrine on the subject of rent. We are advancing, and the discussion which Malthus' new work will provoke as well as the other productions which we lately have had, and which we shall have, will tend to the diffusion of right principles. I am very much mistaken indeed if the delay in the publication of Malthus book will not have had the effect of very much improving it. I think I perceive in him a very sensible approach, under different words, to opinions which at first appeared to him most preposterous and extravagant.

This is as it should be. Even Sismondi's errors will be of use to the diffusion of correct opinions. Why do not you give your assistance? It is a path in which much may be done, and in which the stimulus of public opinion and public approbation for success, is not wanting. The truth is you are an idle fellow, and are glad to avail yourself of any excuse, such as a want of time and an abundance of other occupations, rather than undergo the toil of writing.

One word on the Manchester proceedings. I am glad to find that the opinion is general amongst all those whom I meet or converse with that the interference of the Magistrates at the late meeting was unwise and inexpedient. I hope it will appear too that it was illegal, for I hope that no law can be produced to justify the violent interference of magistrates to dissolve a meeting of the people, the avowed object of which was to petition legally for a redress of real or imagined grievances. If the right to petition is only to be exercised at the discretion of magistrates, or of any other body in the state, then it is a farce to call us a free people. These large assemblages of the people may be regretted—they may in their consequences be productive of mischief, but if the security of our freedom depend on our right to assemble and state our wrongs, which in the absence of real representation I believe it does, then we must patiently suffer the lesser evil to avoid the greater.

Accept my sincere wishes that Mrs. Trower may pass through her time of anxiety with safety. My friend Malthus would not have thought your case one which required his

skill, had he been a physician, and possessed of a remedy to    25 Sept. 1819
prevent the too great increase of population. You would be
only legally and beneficially employed in furnishing citizens
to the state, whose exertions might benefit, but whose
reasonable wants could not injure the rest of the community.
Mrs. Ricardo and my family are well they unite with me in
kind regards to Mrs. Trower. I am ever my dear Trower

Truly Yours

DAVID RICARDO

## 331. MᶜCULLOUCH TO RICARDO [1]
### [*Answered by* 333]

Edinburgh 25 Septʳ 1819

My Dear Sir

I have taken the liberty to enclose a proof of the article    25 Sept. 1819
on Exchange written by me for the Supplement to the
Encyclopaedia Brittannica; which I hope you will have the
goodness to read over and return to me with such remarks
as you may think proper, in order that I may have it in my
power, by availing myself of your suggestions, to correct
those errors into which I am sure I must have fallen, before
the article is sent to press—I have bestowed a great deal of
time on this article; but as I was but very indifferently
acquainted with the practical part I cannot flatter myself that
I have succeeded in giving a proper view of the subject.

I was extremely happy to learn that you had agreed to
write the Article Funding System; as well on account of the
great importance of disseminating just views on so very
important a subject, and because it must give additional value
to a work which I consider as reflecting the greatest credit on
the country—

---

[1] MS in *R.P.*

If you have looked into the last Number of the Review, you would perhaps recognise an Essay by one of your friends[1]—The restrictions on the trade between Great Britain and France seem to me to be among the most destructive of all the means which national prejudice ever suggested for cramping and fettering the progress of real opulence and lasting improvement—I trust that ere long the subject will be discussed in Parliament; and in the present situation of the country its agitation in that Assembly would be productive of the best effects—I only express the general opinion of all well informed persons when I say that no one could introduce the subject so properly as yourself—

You will be glad to learn that the University of Saint Andrews, has, with a zeal for the advancement of sound knowledge which reflects the highest honour on that ancient seminary, adopted your great work as their text book on the science of which it treats—

I sent you two Numbers of the Scotsman, which I hope you got safe, containing characters of the late Professor Playfair and Mr Watt[2] written by Mr Jeffrey—I am sure you would be very much gratified with them both. Mr Watts character was most felicitously and beautifully described—

Mr Torrens speech at the meeting at London on the subject of Owens visionary and utopian schemes seemed to me to be extremely good, and indeed one of the best things that I ever recollect to have met with[3]—It is astonishing that a person who could write the Essay on the Corn Trade, and make the

---

[1] *Edinburgh Review,* July 1819, Art. III. 'Commercial Embarrassments—Trade with France', by McCulloch.
[2] *Scotsman,* 21 Aug. and 4 Sept. 1819.
[3] The *Scotsman* of 21 August published 'exclusively' a full report of Torrens' speech on Owen's plan at the London Tavern on 26 July 1819. Torrens reproduced it almost verbatim in his article in the *Edinburgh Review* for Oct. 1819, pp. 464–9 and 475–6 (see below, p. 159, n. 2).

speech in question, should have opposed, and on such un-    25 Sept. 1819
tenable grounds the plan of Bullion payments[1]—I am
My Dear Sir

with the greatest respect

Yours most faithfully

J. R. M^cCULLOCH

332. MILL TO RICARDO [2]

[*Reply to 329*]

E.I. House 28^th Sept^r 1819

My Dear Sir

I ought to have written to you yesterday, and fully    28 Sept. 1819
intended so to do—but I was so often interrupted that I
forgot.

I have read your article, which is excellent. Few observations have occurred to me; and those chiefly in the expression, which I have altered as I went on, in pencil.—Place's
commentary is more voluminous—he has written part of it
in the margin, and part on a separate paper which shall be
sent to you.[3]

I shall possibly not return the M.S. for a few days; as I
shall run it over again; and write more fully what I particularly mark either as excellence or defect. I have a letter from
Napier today who says if he has the article from you any
time in *November,* it will do—So that you see there is no
need for hurry.

---

[1] See R. Torrens, *A Comparative Estimate of the Effects which a Continuance and a Removal of the Restriction upon Cash Payments are respectively calculated to produce: with Strictures on Mr. Ricardo's Proposal for Obtaining a Secure and Economical Currency,* London, Hunter, 1819.

[2] Addressed: 'David Ricardo Esq. / M.P. / Minchinhampton / Glostershire'.

MS in *R.P.*

[3] Place's comments on Ricardo's article 'Funding System' are not extant, but see letters 341–343 which were occasioned by them.

I met your brother Moses at Dr. Lindsays[1] yesterday, along with Mr. Belsham, at a turtle feast. Your brother tells me he is soon to visit you, and tempted me by telling me how much he wished I should go along with his lady and himself.

I shall write to you at length in a day or two—but am anxious you should know as soon as possible that your article will do you all the credit such an article is capable of doing. All old points are well explained; and there are new points which exhaust the subject.

With best compliments to Mrs. Ricardo and the rest of your circle, I am always &.c.

J. MILL

Please to thank Mr. Smith most kindly in my name for lending to you on my account the pamphlet of Mackintosh—it is exactly the pamphlet I had heard of. I beg you will remember me most particularly to himself and to Mrs. Smith. I hope he is not in a great hurry for the volume, as I wish to read Dr. Parrs controversy—and wish for time to make some use of a few things of Mackintosh.

[1] James Lindsay, D.D. (1753–1821), Unitarian minister, political reformer, and an old friend of Mill. (See Bain, *James Mill*, p. 120–1.)

## 333. RICARDO TO McCULLOCH [1]
[*Reply to* 331.—*Answered by* 344]

There is a trifling error in the figures at the top of page 2.[2]  2 Oct. 1819
The second line £100,100 should be £100,000, and in the
third line £89100, should be £89108, for 1 pc.ᵗ on 89108

$$\text{or} \quad \underline{\quad 891\quad}$$
$$\text{make} \quad 89{,}999$$

The same error of considering a premium of 1 pc.ᵗ on one
sum to be equal to the discount of 1 pc.ᵗ; on a similar sum, is
committed in another place. If a commodity worth £100
rise to £200,—it will rise 100 pc.ᵗ; but if it fall again to £100
—it will fall only 50 pc.ᵗ. No commodity can fall 100 pc.ᵗ if
it retain any value whatever. Apply this observation to
beginning of page 8,[3] where you speak of paper being worth
only half its nominal value, "or which is depreciated 100 pc.ᵗ"
should it not be 50 pc.ᵗ?

2 I think the cause of the exchange with the country,
being favorable to London, is owing to rather an excess of
currency in the country.[4] The same cause might produce the
same effect, if nothing but coin were used both in London and
the Country. Diminish the quantity of Country currency, and
the exchange would be in favour of the Country. It never

---

[1] MS (in Ricardo's handwriting) in British Museum.—*Letters to McCulloch,* IX.

This paper contains Ricardo's criticisms on the article 'Exchange' prepared by McCulloch for the *Supplement to the Encyclopaedia Britannica.* The enclosing letter is wanting, but McCulloch's reply (below, p. 125) gives its date as 2 Oct. 1819.

Ricardo's page-references are to the pagination of a proof of McCulloch's article (cp. letter 331); but in the footnotes below they are to the published volume.

[2] *Supplement to the Encyclopaedia Britannica,* vol. IV, p. 205; corrected.

[3] p. 211, not corrected.

[4] McCulloch says, p. 205, that the chief causes of the exchange between London and other parts of the country being invariably in favour of London are 'the demand for bills on London to remit revenue' and 'the superior value of Bank of England currency'.

will be so reduced, because it is the interest of Country Banks to maintain the largest amount possible of Country circulation. I cannot help thinking that in all cases an unfavorable exchange may be traced to a relative redundancy of currency.

Suppose a country to carry on its circulation with coins, its market and mint price of gold to be the same, and its exchanges at par with other countries. Now suppose gold to be in great demand for our manufactures, its price would rise above the mint price, if the coin could not be readily converted into bullion; but it would be converted into bullion, and consequently the coin being reduced in quantity, would rise in exchangeable value with other commodities. A fall in the value of commodities here would encourage the exportation of goods and the importation of gold, and thus by an influx of gold would our currency be again increased in quantity and lowered in value, and till it was so, the exchange would be favorable to England.

But suppose England to carry on its circulation by means of paper only, not exchangeable for gold, and the same demand for gold to arise for our manufactures, gold would rise, estimated in paper, and therefore with the same computed exchange as before it might be advantageous to import gold. But even in this case it may I think be justly said that the exchange was unfavorable to the foreign country because its currency was relatively redundant. Bullion is the commodity in which the value of currencies would be estimated. That of England would be lowered in value for it could command, after the rise in the price of bullion, fewer ounces than before. Those of Foreign Countries (within the limits of the expences of transmission) would be the same as before:— bullion or coin would purchase the same quantity of commodities abroad as before; in England it would purchase more. The same quantity of paper in England would be equivalent to a less quantity of gold—the same quantity of foreign money would be equivalent to the same quantity of gold. The exchange would vary on account of the relatively higher value of the currency of the foreign country[1].

3 You say that the price of Foreign Bills of exchange depends entirely on two circumstances; ["]first, on the value of the currency at the place where they are made payable, compared with the value of the currency at the place where they are drawn; and secondly, on the relation which the supply of bills in the market bears to the demand."[2] From what I have said you will perceive that I see no difference between these two causes—they appear to me to be one and the same. The supply of bills and the demand for them must depend on the previous purchases and sales of goods in the two countries, and these are entirely influenced by relative prices. But relative prices are determined by relative value or quantity of currencies. Increase the quantity of currency in France, goods will rise in France, and will be exported thither from England. Bills on France will fall in England, bills on England will rise in France. The demand and supply will be strictly regulated by the relative value of the currencies of the two countries. Double the quantity of currency in England and commodities will rise to double their former price[3] in England, and twice the quantity of the money of England will be given for the former quantity of the currency of France. This is undoubtedly a mere nominal alteration, the real value both of commodities and bills will be the same as before. In fact the real par is altered, and nothing else. Instead of ascertaining the par by a consideration of what the pound sterling was formerly worth, it should be computed

[1] Actually written 'currency' in MS; the mistake is due to the words 'currency of the' having been ins.

[2] p. 206, unchanged.

[3] 'former price' replaces 'value'.

with reference to its present value, which is to be known by the value of the bullion which a pound can command.

We mean the same thing, but I doubt whether there be any advantage in the distinction which is drawn between real and nominal exchange; by correcting the par, with every altera- tion in the bullion value of money,[1] all would be clear. *See the end of this paper.

[*Note at the end of the paper*] *On further reflection there may I think be real use in the distinction drawn between the nominal and real exchange, but the distinction should be clearly defined. The exchange may be said to be nominally affected to the amount of the difference between the market and mint prices of bullion, and be really affected by any deviation from par exceeding or falling short of this difference. You have I think so defined them.

4 In the article on Foreign Exchange you say "the price of foreign bills depends on the value of the currency at the place where they are made payable, compared with the value of the currency at the place where they are drawn." But soon after it is said "that the comparative value of the currencies of particular countries must depend 1st on the relative value of bullion in those countries and 2dly on the quantity of bullion contained in their coins, or on the quantity of bullion for which their paper money, or other circulating media, will exchange.["][2] Do you not then mean to say that the price of Foreign bills depends on the relative value of bullion in the countries between which they are negociated? Under some circumstances you agree with me that bullion might possess a higher value in Poland, than in England, but a bill on France for 10000 francs would not vary in either of those countries on that account,—the same quantity of bullion must be paid in both for the bill on France, without any

---

[1] The last nine words are ins.
[2] p. 207, unchanged. See M^cCul- loch's reply to the criticism, letter 344.

regard to the quantity of corn or labour that can be commanded by it. It is true that the expences of sending bullion from France to Poland may exceed the expence of sending it to England, but this circumstance will not alter the par, although it will allow of a greater deviation in the exchange from par between the more distant countries, before bullion moves to stop the rise or fall of the exchange. I cannot help thinking that the language of the Bullion Report is correct, and that it would introduce a new and less satisfactory definition if we were to allow of these expences in estimating the par of exchange between different countries.[1] Suppose that the expence of sending silver from Poland to France or from France to Poland, to be 5 pc$^t$ it would in my opinion be correct to say that the exchange was at par when 100 ounces of silver in Poland would purchase a bill for 100 ounces of silver payable in France. According to your explanation I do not know whether you would estimate it to be at par when 105 ounces were given in Poland for a bill of 100 ounces payable in France or when 105 were paid in France for a bill of 100 ounces payable in Poland.

The restraints laid on the exportation of gold may lower its relative value in Spain 3 pc$^t$, and therefore if from that which is usually called the par, there should be a difference in the computed exchange of 3 pc$^t$ against Spain, that deviation may as justly be called a nominal deviation, as if it were occasioned by an abundant paper money not convertible into bullion. The market price of bullion that could be legally exported would in Spain be 3 pc$^t$ above the mint price.[2]

---

[1] M$^c$Culloch, p. 207, quotes and describes as 'obviously incorrect' the definition of the *Bullion Report* (8vo ed., p. 22): 'The Par of Exchange between two Countries is that sum of the currency of either of the two, which, in point of intrinsic value, is precisely equal to a given sum of the currency of the other; that is, contains precisely an equal weight of Gold or Silver of the same fineness.'

[2] This sentence is ins.

5 In this paragraph the word value has an ambiguous meaning. In the first sentence I understand ["]whatever occasions a rise or fall in the relative *value* of the precious metals estimated in commodities must proportionably affect the nominal exchange with other countries["] [1], in which I agree, if you suppose that the precious metals can be forcibly detained in such country;—if they are free to pass, I think it is the real exchange which will be affected, altho' the exportation of the metals will not continue till the exchange is at par—it may remain for a very considerable time unfavorable to the exporting country, within the limits of the expences of transmitting bullion. When you speak afterwards of the "difference between the value of the precious metals in the home and foreign market,["] in what do you estimate that value? If you say in goods, I ask in the goods of which country?

6 This [2] would depend on the abundance of the clipped money. If not in excess the real par would or ought to be estimated, not by what the coin contained of pure metal, but what it would have contained if not clipped. The depreciation of the currency is inferred as a necessary consequence of a clipped coin.

7 On this the same remark may be made as on 6. If the coin notwithstanding the seignorage passes current at a high value, the par of[3] exchange ought to be regulated by such current value. [4]

8 Does not this paragraph[5] confirm the above opinion?

---

[1] p. 208, where the words 'estimated in commodities' are replaced by 'in a particular country'.
[2] *i.e.* M^cCulloch's statement that between two currencies clipped in an unequal degree the real par should be estimated by their relative weights, p. 209. In a footnote Ricardo's qualification respecting the abundance of clipped money is adopted as 'a principle which must be constantly kept in view.'
[3] 'par of' is ins.
[4] p. 210, apparently unchanged.
[5] p. 211, first paragraph.

The real par is justly estimated by the current value of the pound sterling—that current value is depreciated, hence a new real par is, or ought to be, established.

9 Because it rarely happens that the currency of one or other is not redundant. It is redundancy or deficiency which is the cause of balances being paid from one to the other.[1]

10 We should not have imported a single ounce of bullion from Hamburgh, because the real exchange would not be such as to afford a profit on its importation, while there were goods which could be imported to more advantage.[2]

11 Provided money did not alter in value.[3]

12 This is true if the prices of goods do not vary from the same cause that the exchange varies, namely a superabundance of money in one of the two countries.[4]

13 See last observation.

14 I am rather doubtful of this tendency to disappear.[5]

15 I doubt whether an unusual deficiency in the supply of corn ["]must always materially affect the state of debt and credit with foreign countries["][6]. If we import to a greater value, we shall also export to a greater value. If we import an unusual quantity of corn we are less able and willing to purchase the usual quantity of other foreign commodities. The exportation of commodities is supposed here to be caused by the previous effect on the exchange. I believe it to be caused by the unusual importation of foreign goods.

---

[1] Refers probably to p. 218 § 3.
[2] pp. 218–19, M<sup>c</sup>Culloch criticises Bosanquet's argument based on the importation of bullion from Hamburg in 1797–8 (on which see above, III, 170); Ricardo's observation is inserted in the published article.
[3] This phrase was added on p. 219, § 5, second sentence.
[4] The statement that an unfavourable exchange operates as a stimulus to exportation, p. 219, qualified as suggested by Ricardo.
[5] 'Fluctuations in the *real* exchange have a necessary tendency to correct themselves', owing to their effects on exports and imports, p. 219.
[6] p. 220.

16 Here[1] you adopt the usual language and say that the computed exchange with Rio Janeiro would be 5 pc.t in favour of London. As the money of both countries is supposed to be at its mint standard, the computed exchange is the same thing with the real exchange, you agree therefore that the real exchange is favorable to England when it differs from par any part of the expences of transit, and you state the real par to be what the bullion committee defined it, and which definition you quote page 4.[2] The latter part of the paragraph is I think at variance with the first. In the first we are told that when the market and mint prices of bullion agree both in Rio Janeiro and in London and bullion is transmitted from Rio Janeiro to London at an expence of 5 pc.t—the computed, or which in this case is the same thing the real exchange is 5 pc.t unfavourable to Rio Janeiro and 5 pc.t favourable to England; but in the latter part we are told that under the very same circumstances the expence of transit will measure the unfavourable *nominal* exchange. Now by nominal exchange I understand you to mean that percentage of the exchange which is caused by the depreciation of money in either country. But you have not explained what you mean strictly by depreciation of money. I thought you always meant to measure depreciation of money by the agreement of its market with its mint price, but in this place you speak of another depreciation, of relative depreciation. If the exchange be 5 pc.t against Rio Janeiro and money therefore comes to England, I agree with you that it is to that amount relatively depreciated in Rio Janeiro, 105 ounces of silver in one place is really paid to obtain 100 ounces in the other, but the exchange which is the consequence of this relative depreciation should I think be called real and not

[1] p. 223; McCulloch assumes that the expense of conveying bullion from Rio Janeiro to London is 5 per cent.

[2] See above, p. 89, n. 1.

nominal. If you dispute this I do not know what you would call a real favorable exchange. If there were no expences whatever in sending bullion from one country to another the exchange would never deviate from par. It would be as invariable as the price of bullion is in countries where money is freely exchangeable for bullion on demand.—It appears to me essential that a very marked line should be drawn between actual and relative depreciation of money. There can be no unfavorable exchange without relative depreciation—the exchange may be still more unfavourable because of actual depreciation. In this case relative depreciation will be increased. I think we agree in principle, I object to the language.

17 Adopting your language, and making your allowances the exchange can never *be very different from par*. You say "Had the *computed* exchange been less unfavorable, it would have shewn that the real exchange was in favour of London."[1] It could not be either more or less unfavorable and therefore the real exchange could be only at par. Money can be relatively depreciated only from two causes—one the actual depreciation of its value from its bullion standard, the other the expence of sending it from one country to the other, the latter is always the range within which the real exchange varies. You add these together, and then say if there be any thing more than these, in the deviation from par of the computed exchange, then only is the exchange really unfavorable. I ask how can it deviate more, the computed exchange being an accurate exponent of relative depreciation?

18 I agree with the argument here, but I think the word relative in the expression of relative redundancy should be left out,—[2] a real unfavourable exchange, which it is acknowledged facilitates exportation, is always in my opinion accompanied, and may be said to be caused by relative redundancy.

---

[1] p. 223, unchanged.           [2] p. 224, where the word is omitted.

## 334. BROWN TO RICARDO [1]
*[Answered by 336]*

Newcastle upon Tyne
25 Sep. 1819.—

Sir,

When you have done me the honor to peruse this letter, I think you will be able, distinctly to perceive the real motives which have induced me to use such freedom—these motives constitute my apology—I cannot pay you a higher compliment.—A few days ago your treatise on Political Economy and Colquhoun on the Wealth &c of the British Empire were lent, or rather procured for, me by a Friend for a particular purpose—Until then I had never seen either— I was aware of their existence and of the character attached to them chiefly by means of the newspapers—I am no Political Economist in the common acceptation of the phrase —none whatever—I am 50 years of age and for more than half of that period have been connected with the operations of Manufactures, Trade and Agriculture to a considerable extent—like other men I can examine, compare and combine in a certain degree according to the opportunities for doing so that come in my way or attract my attention—for the last ten years I have read very little except the newspapers occasionally,—this has been not altogether from want of inclination—formerly I read not a little according to the leisure I had and the means I possessed.—

I had not then much time for reflexion—Since then I have had more than I could have wished—no man is a competent judge of the value of his own notions or reflexions—I have

---

[1] Addressed: 'To David Ricardo Esq.' Not passed through the post. Received by Ricardo, with the next letter, on 10 October (see his reply).
MS in Mill-Ricardo papers.

A paper, in which Brown expounded his views on the origin and nature of money, was enclosed; although its MS, which covers 4 pages, is extant, it is omitted here.

taken the liberty to inclose a specimen of mine on a subject 25 Sept. 1819 deeply interwoven with what is called Political Economy.—

The powerful intellect, sound judgement and extensive experience so visible throughout your valuable publication will enable you at once to detect the fallacy of my notion if it is not correct or to appreciate the utility of it, if it is.—

I have not as yet read the Book—I have only dipt into it as it suited the purpose I had in view—I could not however refrain from taking an early opportunity of expressing to you my sense of its value, and of my respect for the Author.—

One of the great difficulties attending the solution of the Problem to which you allude in your judicious preface is owing, in my humble apprehension, to the want of defining the words or terms necessary to the elucidation of so very complicated a subject—the true meaning must be sought for and can only be obtained from the invariable or at least general practice of mankind—whether I have succeeded in any tolerable degree with respect to this rule in the instance I have sent you I know not—You will be able to judge, I am certain.

On many other subjects, some of them connected with yours, I have been led to entertain notions or opinions which do not at all correspond with the received doctrines or maxims usually held of such matters and differ in some cases so much from what are considered authority that I have been induced to doubt without being able to know why—

For the present I will avail myself of this doubting faculty, and make my retreat, fearful of being deemed an intruder or guilty of impertinence by one whom I hold in high respect.—

I have the honor to be
Sir,
Your most obedient and very humble servant
James Brown

## 335. BROWN TO RICARDO [1]
*[Answered by 336]*

Newcastle 28 Sep. 1819.—

Sir,

28 Sept. 1819

Before I can possibly know what reception you may give to my first messenger (of 25$^{th}$) I cannot refrain from dispatching another—I have seen a little more of your Book.—

You are in the road to Truth—You merely want a little more scepticism to proceed much farther—perhaps to arrive at the solution of that Problem to which you allude in your preface—In order to this You must lay aside prejudice or reverence for received or admitted doctrines or Maxims— You must suspect them to be false and not only examine them with rigor, but likewise cross-examine them with the utmost severity—Try them by the standard of facts—if they will not bear this—they are false or erroneous—Very few men, Sir, know how to think—In this occult operation of the mind the difficulty is to distinguish cause from effect— the great danger and fruitful source of error is in mistaking one for the other—to avoid these as much as possible first principles must be resorted to and carefully sifted and scrutinised—You are capable of all these—You have done much—if You have not done more it is owing in some degree to your situation in life and to a circumstance I have already noticed—Before proceeding to some observations on some passages in your treatise I deemed it necessary to make these observations, relying on your candour to forgive the freedom with which I have made them.—The passages I allude to begin at P. 560[2] with "M. Malthus appears to me" &c &c—

[1] Addressed: 'To / David Ri-            MS in Mill-Ricardo papers.
cardo Esq. / M.P. / London'.        [2] Above, I, 406.
London postmark, 1 Oct. 1819.

I write on the supposition that you have now the vol. before
You, or the substance clearly in Your mind—

You there contravert the favorite doctrine of Mr. Malthus "that population is only increased by the previous provision of food &c &c"—You are right, Sir, and Mr. Malthus is wrong—His error is in mistaking cause for effect, or not being able to distinguish one from the other—Every fact connected with the history and practice of man is on your side—on his there is nothing but plausible theory and fine writing—When such errors as his are merely theoretical, they are comparatively harmless, but when they are adopted by Statesmen entrusted with the government of a great nation like this, and converted into practical effect, no man can estimate the mischief they are calculated to produce— I suspect Mr. Malthus to be the father of the Corn Law as it now stands—If so, he has produced the most mischievous and illegitimate bantling this country ever saw—It and another delusion are now pressing upon the vitals of this great and powerful nation with a combined force that must be attended with the most ruinous consequences if some adequate remedy is not speedily applied—

This Country is possessed of powerful resources—far beyond those of any other nation—the machinery of action is however so very complicated—its props and joints of so nice and delicate a texture that the prudent management of it can never be understood but from an accurate knowledge not only of the materials of which it is composed but of their relative value in respect to each other—It is so much the fashion to place Agriculture in the front rank that it would be dangerous for any man except yourself to turn her into the rear—I mean as a source of wealth—Yet that is her natural place—

Manufactures, Trade or Commerce and Agriculture—

A very little reflexion will convince you this is their proper order and rank—Agriculture could not exist at all without Manufactures—how could her operations be carried on?—

Without Trade she would be indolent and therefore miserably poor—Where is the *Agricultural Nation* that ever was rich—it will be difficult to find her I believe—Sparta was the only Agricultural nation in the proper sense of the word I ever heard of—Even she was not without Manufactures but she had no Trade—she was therefore poor—Tyre, Carthage and Athens were rich and popolous—Was it their Agriculture that produced their Wealth and population?— Holland, Venice and Genoa have been rich—Look at them— Look at Poland—

The singular advantage of this country is in having the means of carrying on all these sources of wealth together and that we have got the start of other nations to a great degree— if we lose it it will be our own fault and we are now in no little danger—The great cry of the Agriculturists is to export Corn—One year with another it is perfectly evident they cannot supply the home consumption—

Do they mean to sell a part here at 100/p qr. and export the rest at 30/ or 40/.—I really believe they know nothing of the matter or even of their own real and solid interests—

*Do* you proceed a little farther in the road in which You now are and You will soon be able to tell them, and to convince every man of sense, that corn is exported and in the most profitable way for them—namely—in the immense supply of her Manufactures furnished by Great Britain to Foreign Nations called the Export Trade, by means of which she absolutely levies a very heavy tax on every Nation who uses them and without which all this *Unique* piece of mechanism would get into instant confusion, if it did not fall entirely to pieces.—

I am certain You will comprehend me—for the Moment I must stop—assuring you of my respect &c &c.

JAMES BROWN

D. Ricardo Esq.

[The following is written on the back of the cover]

N.C. 29 Sep 1819.—

Sir,

I am rather anxious to save the post.—It is not upon Corn but Butchers Meat that Agricultural prosperity rests— the value of it consumed by the Manufacturing and Trading part of the Community is more I believe than that of all the Corn put together—a very slight research and reflexion will convince you of this—if ever the price of this gives way then the Landed interest as it is called will have reason indeed to cry out—Monday and yesterday all the Keelmen on this river struck work—the Pitmen or Coal hewers will soon follow—their example will be imitated by those on the Wear—30 to 40,000 will be added to the prosolytes or fol- lowers of Hunt &c—Really, Sir, if men like you do not step forward and insist on Parliament being immediately assembled to take into consideration the state of the country, no one can foresee the consequences—What is really the nature of the case? it seems like this—Mr. M. or some one else is the State Physician—he has prescribed—the Corn bill—the Ministry have applied the Physic—the Patient is sick—and runs after a mischievous Quack (Hunt) who tells them of Annual Parliaments, Universal suffrage and Election by ballot being infallible nostrums for all their evils—the people want employment and nothing else.—

They neither understand nor value such impracticable nonsense beyond the pressure of the moment—What

29 Sept. 1819   can Military do? Can they remove Poverty, hunger and want?—

My time will not admit of more than that I have the honor to be most respectfully Sir

Yr mo ob st

JAMES BROWN

### 336. RICARDO TO BROWN [1]
[*Reply to* 334 & 335]

Gatcomb Park, Minchinhampton
Gloucestershire 13 Oct.ʳ 1819

Sir

13 Oct. 1819    Your letters, with their inclosures, were forwarded from my house in London to this place, which is my residence for six months in the year, but as I was absent on a little excursion, I did not receive them till sunday last.[2] Their perusal has given me very great satisfaction. In the first place I am pleased that a mind so capable as your letters prove yours to be, is employed on a subject in which I take a peculiar interest, and which it is generally acknowledged is of great importance to the welfare and prosperity of this and every other country. Political Economy is daily engaging more and more of the public attention, and it is of the first consequence that our errors in legislation on subjects of trade should be made clear and evident to any one who is willing to give to them a moderate degree of attention. In the second place I am pleased that my humble efforts to improve the science of Political Economy have met with your approbation, and have in your opinion been in some degree successful. Your praise is the more valuable from its discrimination, and it would have been more valuable still, if you had

[1] MS in Mill-Ricardo papers. The MS appears to be a fair copy, not a draft; possibly this letter was never sent to Brown.
[2] 10 October.

been more free in your comments on such parts of my book
as in your view require amendment.

On the subject of my difference with Mr. Malthus in the
passage to which you refer me in your letter, I am glad to
find that you are decidedly of my opinion; and here it will
be proper for me to correct a little misapprehension under
which you appear to be respecting Mr. Malthus' concern in
the Corn Law as it now stands. Mr. Malthus is a very
intimate friend of mine, and a more candid or better man
nowhere exists. Although you have not expressed any
doubt, or indeed any opinion of his good qualities, I could
not mention his name without giving this testimony in his
favor. He has I think some erroneous opinions respecting
the expediency of a free trade in corn, but they are honest
conscientious opinions. From the respect which is paid to
every thing that comes from him his views on this subject
may have had great weight in influencing the judgments of
those who were finally to decide on the question in Parliament, but he was never consulted by those who originated
the measure, and his opinions were only collected from his
writings, which did not appear till after the measure was
before Parliament.—

If it were not for the necessity of taxation the business of
Government regarding Agriculture, Commerce and Manufactures would be very easy indeed,—all that would be
required of them would be to avoid all interference, neither
to encourage one source of production nor to depress another,
but the necessity of raising money by taxes renders some
interference necessary. The aim of the legislature should
nevertheless be to press on all equally, so as to interfere as
little as possible with the natural equilibrium which would
have prevailed if no disturbance whatever had been given.
It may I think be a curious matter for speculation, to know

whether Agriculture is more productive of wealth to the country than Manufactures, or manufactures than Agriculture, but however accurate our knowledge might be as to the facts, that would not justify either restraints on one, or encouragements to the other. Every research into this subject convinces me that trade should be left perfectly free, and that taxation should be so managed as to interfere with that freedom as little as possible. Manufactures and trade are alternately the cause and effect of wealth. An agricultural nation without trade and manufactures cannot be rich, because neither an individual or a nation can be said to be rich, if it have only food to eat. An agricultural nation might however have the command of a great quantity of labour besides that employed on the land, which it might expend on war, or in supporting the rude ostentation and magnificence conferred by a great number of retainers. Such a nation would have powerful resources, and would I think be more than a match for a country of the same extent and fertility which was also a manufacturing country. Why have we not heard of any such Agricultural nation? because none ever persevere in the course from which they commence— they prefer manufactures to menial servants—instead of a great man having a thousand persons about him ready to obey his mandates, they are accumulated in workshops manufacturing his lace, his china and his furniture, or they are digging the earth for the purpose of obtaining the precious metals of which he is so greedy. Give a country wealth, or let it acquire wealth, and it ceases to be purely agricultural, not because there is any thing which necessarily obliges it to be any thing else, but because with wealth a desire for manufactures is excited, and this desire becomes a powerful stimulus to the accumulation of capital, in order that the desire may be gratified. Even with this desire for manufactures, a country might continue to be purely agricultural, if by means of trade, she could in exchange for a portion of her agricultural produce obtain a larger quantity of manufactured goods, than, with the capital employed on the production of such portion of agricultural produce as she exported, she could manufacture at home.

It is the accumulation of wealth from Agriculture which first gives the notion and the means of establishing Manufactures. Manufactures in their turn become the cause of new accumulations of capital which tend to produce a fresh demand for labour, an increased population, and a greater consumption of agricultural produce. Thus Agriculture is alternately the cause and effect of manufacturing industry.

Your remark respecting the relative value of the Corn, and the Butcher's meat, annually consumed, is new to me, and does not accord with my preconceived notions. It is important, and deserves particular investigation.—

We all have to lament the present distressed situation of the labouring classes in this country, but the remedy is not very apparent to me. The correcting of our errors in legislation with regard to trade would ultimately be of considerable service to all classes of the community, but it would afford no immediate relief: On the contrary I should expect that it would plunge us into additional difficulties. If all the prohibitions were removed from the importation of corn and many other articles, the sudden fall in the price of corn and those other articles, which could not fail to follow, would ruin most of the farmers, and many of the manufacturers; and although others would be benefited, the derangement which such measures would occasion in the actual employments of capital, and the changes which would become necessary, would rather aggravate than relieve the distress under which we are now labouring.

With most of your definitions and remarks in the paper inclosed in your first letter, I should agree, with the alteration of a few words. In one of your remarks you say that the wisdom of the senate must be estimated according to the nicety or skill with which they restrain and adjust the conflictive interests of those employed in obtaining wealth. You take for granted that some measures of restraint and adjustment on the part of Government are necessary. This should be first proved for it is one of the important points in dispute. In another place you call money a *Pledge* or *Security.* Now according to my ideas of a pledge or security when that is given the transaction is not concluded. A man gives a pledge which he is bound at some future time to redeem—it may be of more or less value than the thing for which it is pledged —but this is not the case with money—money is an equivalent. When I buy a piece of cloth and pay for it in money, I become possessed of the cloth and the seller becomes possessed of the money. I am subject to all the loss which may arise from the fall in the value of cloth, he to all that may take place in the value of money. I have given him value for value—the transaction is for ever closed between us—he has obtained from me an equivalent, and not a pledge.

These Sir are the hasty notions which I have formed on the perusal of your letter and I have as hastily communicated them to you which must be my apology for all the inaccuracies which you may observe in this letter.

I have the honor to be Sir
with great respect
Your obed.<sup>t</sup> and humble Serv.<sup>t</sup>
DAVID RICARDO

James Brown Esq.<sup>re</sup>

## 337. MILL TO RICARDO [1]
### [*Reply to 329*]

East India House Wednesday
[13 October 1819] [2]

My Dear Sir

I have this day sent your M.S. [3] to the coach. I have, 13 Oct. 1819
upon a second and careful perusal seen nothing to suggest,
but a few verbal corrections. They are written in pencil, and
you will distinguish mine from those made by Mr. Place, by
this, that mine are all interlined, and Places are written in the
margin. You will see that I have suggested your putting the
2$^d$ paragraph first, and making the 1$^{st}$ the 2$^d$—If I was to
suggest any thing farther, I think it would be an attempt to
curtail the historical part, by abridging some of the quotations, and giving the substance of them in your own words.
I am ashamed at having kept the papers so long. But for the
last fortnight Sir John Stuart, one of the oldest and best of
my friends, has been in town, not very well, and very lonely,
and I thought it my duty to spend with him almost every
evening [4]—which trenched upon my other operations very
lamentably.

Places criticisms upon you seem to me at bottom to concern only the question of names. He thinks the term Sinking
Fund, in itself, improper. He says there is no fund. A fund
is not an annual income, but the source of an annual income.
What we have to pay debt with is not a fund—it is a portion
of the nation's income—and the only fund or source of this
income is the nations productive powers. To talk of the
Sinking Fund's producing, he says, is nonsense: the sum we

---

[1] Addressed: 'David Ricardo Esq
M.P. Minchinhampton / Glostershire'.
  MS in *R.P.*
[2] Date of London postmark.

[3] 'Funding System.'
[4] See Mill's account of his old
friendship with Sir John Stuart in
a letter to Place, quoted by Wallas,
*Life of Francis Place*, pp. 70–1.

have to pay debt with annually, produces nothing; it is produced.

This is true, at bottom. But to explain the subject in conformity with this language would require the re-casting of the whole piece—and, then, query whether the old language, on such an occasion as this, ought to be altered. Your use of the old language is throughout free from any violation of the true doctrine, except in as far as error is implied in the very existence of false names.

I am reading with a good deal of interest Dr. Parr's pamphlet in Mr. Smiths vol. of Tracts—and unless Mr. Smith is in a hurry for its return, I shall keep it some little time longer.

If all is true which we hear, we shall have you in town before long for parliamentary duties. It appears that the Aristocratical Conspiracy begins to fear that it is found out; and thinks that very serious measures are necessary to prolong its existence. This, with the falling off in the revenue, is astounding the ministry. The section of the aristocratical conspiracy called Whiggery knows not what to do. It cannot set up the cry against the other section without (it fears) increasing the danger which threatens the conspiracy itself.

Truly yours

J. Mill

I began my notes on your M.S. on a bit of paper, before I took to marking with pencil—and as there is one or two things on the paper, I send it.

One thing I had forgot, which is, that you will receive some letters for me. Col. Walker,[1] an old experienced Indian is sending me remarks on my book; and they are so voluminous, that I am ashamed to put my Hon. Masters to so much expense of postage. As I am in no hurry about them, you may forward them only when you have plenty of room.

---

[1] Alexander Walker, an officer in the service of the East India Company.

## 338. MALTHUS TO RICARDO [1]
[*Reply to 328.—Answered by 345*]

E I Coll Oct 14th 1819

My dear Ricardo

I am ashamed to think that I have so long delayed    14 Oct. 1819
thanking you for your letter, and particularly for your very
kind invitation to Gatcomb at Xmas. It would be a most
agreeable visit both to Mrs. Malthus and myself, if we could
accomplish it; but I fear there are insurmountable obstacles
in the way. You forget that Mrs. Malthus is governess to her
own girls, and that I am preceptor to my own boy, when he
is at home, which will be at Xmas. It so happens, further,
that we shall have a nephew with us about that time; and
into the bargain I hope to be very busy correcting the press.
Under these circumstances I fear it is quite an impossible
case, and we must defer our visit till you come to Town.

Whishaw speaks with much pleasure of the two days he
passed at Gatcomb. He is to be at Mackintosh's tomorrow
where we are to meet him at dinner. I am glad to find, from
the account you give of the discussions at Mr. Smith's that
your principles are considered as genuinely whiggish, as
from what has lately happened, and the apparent temper of
the mob, I am certainly not more inclined to Radicalism than
I was, although I am a decided friend to a moderate reform
in Parliament. I can hardly contemplate a more bloody
revolution than I should expect would take place, if Universal
suffrage and annual parliaments were effected by the intimi-
dation of such meetings as have been latterly taking place.
These people have evidently been taught to believe that such
a reform would completely relieve all their distresses; and
when they found themselves, as they most certainly would,

[1] Addressed: 'D. Ricardo Esqr M.P. / Gatcomb Park. / Minchinhampton'.—MS in *R.P.*

entirely disappointed, massacre would in my opinion go on till it was stopt by a military despotism. In the case of a revolution in this country, the distress would be beyond all comparison greater than in France. In France the manufacturing population was comparatively small, and the destruction of it which took place, was not so much felt; but in England the misery from want of work and food would be dreadful. I hope and trust however that these extremities may be avoided.

Your answer to my query was such as I expected, and I agree with you. You observe that my supposition is an extravagant one. It is so. But perhaps it is safer to reject capital and profits entirely, than to apply them in any given way, under the certainty that scarcely any other commodity can reasonably be supposed to have required in its production exactly the same quantity of fixed and circulating capital employed for exactly the same time. On any supposition you can make respecting the capital employed in the production of the precious metals, it is scarcely possible that all your calculations should not be necessarily and fundamentally erroneous.

Pray just tell me whether, when land is thrown out of cultivation from the importation of foreign corn, you consider the new rate of profits as determined by the state of the land, or the stationary prices of manufactured and mercantile products compared with the fall of wages. According to your view of the subject, will not capital be withdrawn from the land, till the last capital yields the profit obtained by the fall of wages in manufactures, on the supposition of the price of such manufactures remaining stationary.

I hope to begin printing the middle or end of next month. I fear I shall have too large a volume when it is finished, although I cannot include taxation and some other subjects

which I wish to discuss. I am making an analysis like  14 Oct. 1819
Sismondi's[1] which will take up a good deal of room.[2]

Mrs. M joins me in kind regards to Mrs. Ricardo.

Ever truly Yours

T R Malthus

## 339. TROWER TO RICARDO[3]

*[Reply to 330.—Answered by 346]*

Unsted Wood—Oct. 26—1819

My Dear Ricardo

Many thanks for your last kind letter, which afforded  26 Oct. 1819
me much pleasure.—I am sensible of the justice of your
*reproaches;* and although I cannot altogether plead guilty to
the charge of *idleness;* yet, I must admit, that my nature is of
so mercurial a composition, that I am rather adicted to the
*active exertions* of life, than to its more sedentary and studious
pursuits. We are very much the creatures of circumstances;
and our lots are greatly influenced by accident.—*I* have taken
up farming, am pursuing it with eagerness, and am endeavouring to improve my little property.—My Magisterial
and other local duties occupy some portion of my time, the
rest is given to my domestic duties, to an attentive observation of the progress of public events, and to the literature of
the day. Thus you see, as a sort of *defence,* you have drawn
from me some account of my proceedings, which, although
they *may* be sufficient to clear me from the charge of *idleness,*
will not, I fear, entitle one to the praise of *exertion.*—

I am rejoiced to find that *you* are following up your *blow*—

---

[1] *Nouveaux principes d'économie politique,* Paris, 1819, 'Table analytique des matières contenues dans cet ouvrage', vol. II, pp. 367–442.

[2] The 'Summary of the Con-tents' in Malthus's *Principles of Political Economy* occupies 70 pp.

[3] Addressed: 'To / David Ricardo Esqr / M.P. / Gatcomb Park / Min-chinhampton'.

MS in *R.P.*

26 Oct. 1819   The amplest success has attended your exertions; you have made the principles of the subject completely your own, and are capable of affording information to the public, on every branch of it. I agree with you, mainly, in your view of the Sinking Fund. And, I should be rather disposed, had we any surplus revenue to spare, to employ it in the annual *actual* discharge of a portion of the debt, than trust to an accumulation, which however promising in prospect, may never realise the benefit expected—But, it appears to me, that there is a *prior,* and a much more important question to determine. How can we *prevent* the *encrease* of that debt? How, in the event of diminished revenue, or of encreased expences, can we raise the funds necessary for our *current expenditure?* This is the point to be labored; this is the question to be spread before the public. It is a subject of interest not only to this Country, but to every Government in Europe.—I am glad, that Parliament is about to meet, because I hope its measures will be calculated to calm the irritated feelings of the public. But, I grieve to see, that Ministers have schemes in contemplation, that I fear will have an opposite effect.[1] Still, I cannot think they will succeed in carrying them; that they will be able to make out a case, which will induce Parliament to adopt them—I should not be surprised if a general, or a partial, change of administration should result from these discussions.—It is impossible, however, not to be alive to the dangers resulting to the peace, and to the *liberties* of the Country, from the frequent meetings of these countless multitudes—And, I am impressed with the necessity of adopting some *regulations,* which whilst they should effectually guard the right of public meetings from the arbitrary will of Government, should, at the same time, secure them from the dangers, not less imminent, of mere physical force.

[1] The 'Six Acts' of November 1819.

Why not limit meetings for political purposes to *parishes,*
and thus diminish the danger by *breaking down the masses?* If
the Votes at elections were to be taken in *Parishes,* there
would be a precedent for the practice; and a fair analogy to
justify its application to public meetings.—The people must
and will meet, but they cannot continue to meet in safety to
the Country, in the immense masses, which now assemble—
If, therefore, these assemblies be not regulated, the liberty
of the people will be endangerd, or the safety of the Country
will be put to hazard. What say you to these matters?

I think the dismissal of Lord Fitzwilliam from the
Lieutenancy very unwise and very unworthy of Ministers.[1]—
It will injure the cause it is intended to benefit; and is an
evidence of bad temper and paltry malice, instead of good
sense and liberal policy. At the same time it cannot be
conceded, that the opposition are unworthily availing themselves of the popular outcry, and are giving countenance to
outrageous conduct, which they cannot but condemn, because
it may afford them an opportunity of pushing Ministers from
their seat!—

After looking very attentively into the *law* upon the
subject, and comparing it with the *facts* of the case, *as they
have appeared in the public papers,* I am rather disposed to
think the Magistrates at Manchester were *not* justified in the
measures they pursued. But, it is really a nice point. Certainly, some of the circumstances attending the Meeting,
were of an unlawful character. The flag with the Motto
"Equal Representation or Death", clearly calls for what the
Constitution *denies,* and is consequently unlawful. The
unusual mode of assembling, marching in regular time, and

---

[1] Earl Fitzwilliam had been dis-
missed from the office of Lord
Lieutenant of the West Riding of
Yorkshire for the part he had
taken in a public meeting at York
to demand an inquiry on the
Manchester massacre. (See *Annual
Register for 1819,* p. 113.)

locked together by each others arms, provided, as many were, with clubs, (accompanied, as it was, by the certain knowledge of multitudes drilling at night,) were circumstances calculated to excite alarm—And, at all events, it seems to be forgotten, that, if the Magistrates *have* erred, they must have done so from *an error of judgment,* (for no man can fairly charge them with an *evil intent,*) and Magistrates, in the conscientious discharge of their duties, are protected by the law from punishment for *errors* in judgment. And, indeed, if it were not so, I wonder what gentleman would take upon himself the troublesome invidious, and anxious duties of the Magistracy!—And yet, the Manchester Magistrates are branded by the name of *Murderers;* and by those, who bawl aloud for *enquiry!* If they really call for *enquiry,* then the Magistrates are *libelled.* If they mean to call for *punishment, then,* are they *condemned without enquiry!*—

These are all very interesting and important questions, and I look with impatience to the meeting of Parliament for their decision—

Pray have you read Peters Letters to his Kinsfolk?[1] They are amusing, and forcibly but coarsely written—If the writer be really *Dr. Morris,* I think he must be one of the most impudent coxcombs that ever existed, and certainly must never mean to shew himself in Scotland again—But I am almost disposed to think, that the D.[r] is an *assumed* character, for the purpose of more effectually concealing the writer. Who is he? What do you hear of him? He seems to set all the rules of decency and decorum at difiance! Is received in Edingburgh with the greatest hospitality, has the run of the Houses of the most distinguished men in it, and makes use of the advantages, which these opportunities afford him, to

---

[1] See above, p. 25, n. 3.

lampoon his friends, and abuse and ridicule their customs   26 Oct. 1819
and their Country!—

But I must stop; for I find I am running this letter to an
immeasureable length; and I must not conclude without
informing you, that Mrs. Trower has added another *Daughter*
to our family, and that she and the infant are both doing
well.—

Pray make our kind remembrances to Mrs. Ricardo, and
family, and believe me

Yrs very sincerely<br>HUTCHES TROWER.

Pray tell me on what *day* the Sheriffs are Sworn in. Is it
on any particular day—and when do they first enter on the
actual discharge of the duties of their Office is there anything
to do before the Assizes?

340. BENTHAM TO RICARDO [1]

Queen Square Place West<br>Oct. 28—1819—

Dear Sir,

Assuming that it would be matter of satisfaction to you   28 Oct. 1819

[1] MS in *R.P.* Written by an amanuensis; only the signature and postscript are in Bentham's hand.
A copy of the first part of this letter (up to 'Babes and Sucklings', p. 116 below) is inserted in a volume of Bentham's tracts, in British Museum, 6025. b. 7 (8); together with it is the following note written by Place to Bentham and endorsed 'F.P. to J.B. Sept. 9. 1822': 'F.P. to J.B. The account of Rosser in the letter to Ricardo is sufficiently correct, without exposing the harsh manner he was treated by his father, while at home with him, but there are several parts of that letter which I think too familiarly written for the public eye, I doubt too the propriety of saying any thing, which is not very general, without its being first shewn to his father who I am sure would be very much hurt at what is said both of his son and himself —like most men of the common cast of mind, he thinks he knows more, and he certainly feels more,

and your friend Mr. Professor Smythe[1] of Cambridge, to give countenance and encouragement to merit in any age, and in particular in early youth, I take the liberty of mentioning, in this view, a young friend of mine, a Pensioner, I think they call it, late of Peter House, now of Trinity College Cambridge. He is, I think, about 20 years of age, son of an opulent perfumer of Skinner Street, London, who, till lately, now that years have suggested the contracting the field of his cares, had another Establishment, I think it was in Bond Street, and a third at Bath—through all which channels put together, he has contrived to extract a considerable sum of money from the pockets of Amateurs, by extracting milk out of Roses with somewhat better success than attended the endeavour of the Laputa Philosopher to extract sunbeams out of Cucumbers. The destination of Henry Rosser was—to serve perfumery behind his Father's counter: happily (I trust) for mankind, however it may be for himself, his destiny has taken a different turn: His education, till t'other day, was adapted to his destination: nor yet, well adapted: being rather beneath it, than upon a level with it. Two or three years ago, some spirit—I either have never known or have forgot what;—perhaps the spirit of

of and for his son now he is dead, than he did while he was living.

'All that it can be necessary to say in addition to the facts contained in your letter to Ricardo is that he pursued his studies successfully, and during the vacation went to Paris to perfect himself in french conversation when bathing with another young man he was drowned.' (I am indebted to Prof. Hayek for this reference.)

Henry Blanch Rosser died in July 1822. He was a close friend of Godwin, on whose side in the Malthusian controversy he is said to have written a pamphlet—presumably *The Question of Population,...being a Detection of the Gross Blunders and Absurdities of the Article on Mr. Godwin's Enquiry concerning Population, which appeared in the...Edinburgh Review* [Anon.], London, Longman, 1821. (See C. Kegan Paul, *W. Godwin: his Friends and Contemporaries*, 1876, vol. II, pp. 261–5, 273–4, 280.)

[1] William Smyth.

contradiction, perhaps the spirit of Tailor Place, through whose means about a year and a half ago, I became acquainted with him, inspired him with the love of liberal learning. He was kept from her embraces (pity that learning is not more decidedly of the feminine gender) with as much anxiety as Pyramus from the embrace of Thisbe. That History became, for his benefit, a prophecy: et vetuere patres quod non potuere vetare. An Index prohibitorius was promulgated for his use: and, with the exception of the Bible, the Account Book, and perhaps a Book on Book-keeping, every Book whatsoever was inserted in it. Never were Books stolen *from,* with more ingenuity, than with more obstinate perseverance he stole *to* them. It has not lain in my way to take any exact measure of the acquirements he has made in the almost nothing of time that he has had for it: he is pursuing his route with seven leagued boots on his legs, towards a possible fellowship in the forcibly conjoined roads of Greek and Mathematics. Politics, Logic, and Etymology are those in which he has travelled longest, and with most pleasure and consequently with most success. I had like to have forgot public speaking: it was that which produced the miraculous conversion of his Father. For about these dozen years there has existed a Society of the lower orders which meets weekly at a room in Great Malborough Street under the name of the Society for Mutual Improvement: it has a common Library, and occupies itself in debate. About 3 or 4 years ago, without the least suspicion on my part, the very existence of any such Society being unknown to me, it had the whimsical fancy to elect me its Patron: and thus to enrol a sworn enemy to sinecurism in the goodly fellowship of Sinecurists.[1] Henry Rosser had been some time a Member.

---

[1] See Bentham's letter agreeing to be patron of the Society, 31 July 1817, in his *Works,* ed. by Bowring, vol. x, pp. 488–9.

He had given out a subject proposing to speak upon it. His father found him out, and nitched himself in a snug corner unobserved to catch him *in flagranti delicto*. He heard a speech of an hour and a half long, and went away in rapture. He declared that his son should be a Gentleman, and for that purpose should be first a University Man, and then a Barrister. You have the original Edition of my Parliamentary Reform Catechism. I know not whether you are acquainted with the Vulgate, vulgarly called Bentham made easy;[1] if you are, it is more than I am, for I have never yet read a line of it. Such as it is, it was made by Henry Rosser. The alterations I understand are not inconsiderable, and from the short accounts I have heard of them, I make no doubt perfectly judicious, and with reference to the class of persons in view, in no small degree instructive and advantageous: omissions some, additions likewise, to explain allusions by historical statements: the structure of the sentences rolled out from the form of a period in which my old age had involved it, into that of a principal clause, and then a qualifying clause, and then a qualifying clause to that—such being the form suitable to the powers and the taste of grown Idlers, as well as of Babes and Sucklings.

Upon politics—upon Logic—no speculations of mine so novel and abstruse, that he does not lay hold of them the Instant a hint is given of them, and make application of them, as if they had been his own. Chrestomathia he has more of in his head than at this time the Author has. T'other day,

---

[1] *Plan of Parliamentary Reform, in the form of a Catechism...* [title uniform with 1st ed.; see above, VII, 261, n. 1], London, 'Reprinted and Republished, with Notes and Alterations, by permission of the Author by T. J. Wooler', 1818; issued 'in Numbers, at a cheap rate, with the style adapted to the popular reader', according to the 'Advertisement' prefixed to it. Cp. Bentham's *Works*, ed. by Bowring, vol. x, pp. 489–90.

from a few hints I gave him he constructed for me a Tabular view, which I believe to be a compleat one, of the whole stock of *Conjugates* (in the Logical sense which is a great extension of the Grammatical one) travelling over and I believe exhausting the whole field of the English Language. The moral part of his character to judge from all I have ever seen or heard, is such as makes a perfect match with the Intellectual. The only department in which I have observed any deficiency is that of the Graces. He stutters and splutters and makes faces and explodes his words to the no small annoyance of a nervous old man, in the bad sense of the word, such as myself: and such is his ardency, that when an honest man has begun a sentence, he will not always let him finish it. As to his stuttering, the curious circumstance is,— that when he has to speak for a length of time without interruption, for example in the aforesaid laudable Society of your humble servant's much respected Patrons, the spell of the bad Enchanter is suspended for the time, and he pours forth his periods as fluantly as Counsellor Anybody. So he has assured me when scolded by me; and on this, as on all other subjects in general, the correctness and frankness of his assertions is, unless I am much deceived in him, not to be exceeded.

T'other day I had to thank you for a Letter dated the 2$^{\text{d}}$ Inst from my—I will venture to say from our—Hibernian friend.[1] You have, I make no doubt, sympathized with him in his exultation. You will have seen in as strong a light as he and I do, the need there is, that for an indefinite length of time, connections so obnoxious should remain unknown: for all the good he can expect to do may depend on it.

Here ends this my Sermon, for time being bitterly scarce and fingers wearied out with scribbling, I have preached it,

---

[1] Not identified.

preached, I mean, not as orthodoxy, but as Methodism and other heterodoxy preaches.

Believe me, with the truest respect,

Dear Sir,

Your faithful Servant,

JEREMY BENTHAM.

David Ricardo Esq.[r]

In a few days we are to have you again. Good: but no thanks to you but to his Majesty's Ministers.[1]

341. RICARDO TO PLACE[2]

Gatcomb Park, Minchinhampton

1 Nov.[r] 1819

Dear Sir

My object, as well as yours, is the discovery of truth, and therefore there is no occasion for apology on either side, for freely commenting on each other's opinions.

You say, that you do make a distinction between a Sink.[g] Fund provided by taxes, and a Sinking Fund borrowed, but that in both cases there is nothing but delusion. "To a S F borrowed," you say, "that there has been no other kind

---

[1] Parliament reassembled on 23 November.

[2] Addressed: 'Mr. Place / Charing Cross / London'. Franked by Ricardo 'November two 1819'.
MS in British Museum (Place Papers), Add. 27,836, fols. 113–16. (A series of reference-marks on the margins of the original MS correspond to sixteen Notes written by Place in reply to this letter, *ib.* fols. 119–20; they are not published.)—*Economic Journal,* June 1893, pp. 289–92; *Letters to Trower,* XXIX.

Place had read the MS of Ricardo's article *Funding System* and made certain criticisms, of which some account is given by Mill in letter 337 above; Ricardo replied to the criticisms in a letter which is wanting; Place wrote a lengthy answer, of which a draft, endorsed 'Sinking fund observations on Mr. Ricardo's letter sent to Gatcomb. Oct. 30. 1819', is in British Museum, Add. MSS 27,836, fols. 111–12 (unpublished; quotations from it will be found in the present letter, which is a reply to Place's observations).

since 1793." Now I cannot agree[1] to this; I wish to ask whether during a portion of the time from 1793 to the present day, there was not, in consequence of that which you deem an unfounded and delusive name, less debt contracted than there would have been if no such name had existed. Twenty millions for example were required for the extraordinary expences of 1796. Besides a million a year for interest, 200000 p.$^r$ Ann.$^m$ were also provided, by taxes, for what was improperly called Sinking Fund. Suppose this to go on for several years, say ten years is it not true that we shall, at the end of those years, be less in debt, than if we had continued our expenditure of twenty millions, and had provided only one million per ann.$^m$ for interest? It is demonstrable that the difference of our debt would be precisely equal to the sum which £200000 p.$^r$ Ann.$^m$ for ten years, another 200000 for nine years, another for eight years, and so on, would amount to, at compound interest, in ten years, and therefore in comparing these two modes of providing for expenditure together, it conveys no erroneous idea, to say, that we shall owe less in one case than the other, by all the amount of the sinking fund, and its accumulations. Strictly speaking there is no fund, for there can be no fund, and no accumulation, while we are in debt. All that is received[2] is applied to the payment of debt, or to prevent the contracting of it, but still it is correct to say that the difference between A and B is equal to all the accumulations which a fund of any named amount would yield in a given time. Now suppose the S. F. to be borrowed every year, then indeed you may justly say that the whole is a delusion, for it may be demonstrated that with a given expenditure you will be just as much in debt at the end of 10, or any other number of years, without, as

---

[1] Replaces 'Now supposing that I agree'.

[2] 'All that is received' replaces 'The fund'.

with a sinking fund. Is there not a very marked difference between the effects of one or other of these sinking funds, yet your language would lead us to suppose there was none, for you say "that neither in the one case nor in the other is there any thing but delusion." Suppose Mr. Pitt's plan to have always been fairly acted upon, and I should ask any of its supporters what benefit we had derived from it in diminishing or in preventing the accumulation of debt, would he not be correct if he shewed me the amount of stock standing in the names of the commissioners, and told me that but for the operation of the Sinking Fund the nation would really have owed that amount in addition to the unredeemed debt. How then can you call the whole a delusion? I say that the delusion is in ministers not having performed what they promised—they did not provide what they have always called a sinking fund from the taxes, but have *for the last few years* not only borrowed the sinking fund on the loans which they have created, but have not even provided the interest for them, and therefore it has become necessary to take the interest from the sinking fund.—I hope now I have made myself understood; I concede to you that there is no real fund, nor can there be, while we are in debt, but that no delusion will arise from considering the Sinking fund as a real fund, if we wish merely to make a comparison between the actual state of our debt, with a certain provision to check its accumulation, and its state if no such provision were made.

You deny that Mr. Vansittart took any thing from the S F when he made his arrangements in 1813, you say "there was nothing to take." We will suppose a country to owe 20 mill$^s$ p$^r$ Ann$^m$, and to consent to pay 25 millions p$^r$ Ann$^m$. It pays the 5 millions with the intention of arriving at a term when it shall not be called upon to pay any thing, or in other words it prefers paying 25 millions p$^r$ Ann$^m$ for a limited number of years to paying 20 millions p.$^{r}$ Ann.$^{m}$ for ever. With the 5 millions p.$^{r}$ Ann.$^{m}$ payments of capital are to be made, but without affording any relief to the country which is always to pay 25 millions, till the whole debt is paid. The first year 20 millions are paid to the public, and 5 millions to the Commissioners;—the second year 19,750,000 to the public, and 5,250,000 to the Commissioners; and so from year to year the payments to the public diminish, while those to the Commiss.$^{rs}$ increase. Suppose that at the end of a certain number of years, 7 millions only are annually paid to the public, 18 millions to the Commissioners; and suppose at this time the minister requires a loan of 20 millions. If he provides 1 million from the taxes, for the interest of this loan, he will pay annually for interest and sinking fund on debt 26 instead of 25 millions, and though the debt will increase, the sinking fund will not diminish, but suppose he does not so provide the million for interest, he will only pay 25 millions p.$^{r}$ Ann.$^{m}$: instead however of paying as before 7 millions for interest, and 18 millions to the commissioners, he must now pay 8 millions for interest, and 17 millions to the commissioners; and if foreseeing that he shall want loans of an equal amount for several years to come he should obtain an act of Parliament allowing him to reduce the payment to the commissioners to 11 millions, and increase that to the public, by the creation of new debt, to 14 millions, will he not have made a substantial inroad on the plan for the payment of debt? This is what Mr. Vansittart has done, and yet you say, "Nothing was in fact taken, nothing could be taken, because there was nothing to take."

If you say so because strictly speaking there is no fund, I will not dispute the matter, for it is in fact a dispute about words. But you observe that it is not a dispute about words, what then do we differ about? If we have not the means of paying off our debt so quickly as we otherwise should do, or if we cannot check its increase so effectually in consequence of the new arrangement proposed by Mr. Vansittart, then I say he has taken something, and not nothing. Call it S F, or call it what you please, he has diminished the necessity for laying on new taxes, but he has done so, by accelerating the increase of debt.

"A S F from taxes can only exist when the taxes produce more money than the[1] current expenses of the Government consumes, and this has never been the case in any one instance since 1793, so there has been no sinking fund from taxes." This is in other words saying "I call nothing a sinking fund which does not actually diminish debt." My idea of a sinking fund is not so strict as yours,—it is a fund which holds out a fair prospect of one day being effective to the diminution and the annihilation of debt. If we had a surplus of permanent revenue above permanent expenditure of 20 millions, and for one year only expended more than our permanent income you would say that we had no sinking fund that particular year—I should on the contrary contend that inasmuch as we had 20/m p.$^r$ Ann.$^m$ *for ever* to set against one single years expenditure of 21/m we had a very substantial and a very efficient fund. "If we had lent out a sum at compound interest, notwithstanding our continual borrowing, we should have a real sinking fund and might in time pay off our debts, but this we have never done, and never can do." That we have not lately done it I agree, but why the thing is impossible, except from the bad faith of ministers or parliament I can not see.

What reason do you give why we can not do it? "because we can not create stock with the produce of the taxes" but the commissioners can appropriate the interest on stock

---

[1] 'amount' is del. here.

already created with the produce of the taxes, and this will  1 Nov. 1819
be attended with precisely the same effects as if they had lent
the money at compound interest. If you admit which you
unequivocally do that if we lent out a sum at compound
interest notwithstanding our continual borrowing, we should
have a real sinking fund and might in time pay off our debts,
you must admit that an equal fund given to the commissioners
to purchase stock in the market with the power of appropriating the dividends on the stock purchased to the making
of new purchases, would be equally efficacious. You must
withdraw your first admission or you must be prepared to
yield the second—it is impossible consistently to maintain one
of these propositions and to refuse one's assent to the other.

I am Dear Sir<br>Truly Yours<br>DAVID RICARDO

Be so good as to shew this letter to Mr. Mill that he may
judge between us.

342. PLACE TO RICARDO [1]<br>[Answered by 343]

London Monday Nov. 1. 1819.

Dear Sir

Looking at Dr. Hamiltons book last night for another  1 Nov. 1819
purpose I met with a passage in which the Dr. shows that
there cannot [be][2] a S. F. from taxes,[3] I had some desire to
send it to you but I was restrained from apprehension of
being too officious—so I mentioned it this morning to
Mr. Mill and at his desire it is now sent.

[1] MS in British Museum (Place Papers), Add. 27,836, fol. 112. This is a draft in Place's handwriting.
[2] Omitted in MS.
[3] *An Inquiry concerning the Rise and Progress...of the National Debt*, 3rd ed., Edinburgh, 1818, probably pp. 46–50.

## 343. RICARDO TO PLACE [1]
### [*Reply to* 342]

Gatcomb Park
3 Nov.[r] 1819

Dear Sir

3 Nov. 1819     I have looked carefully at the passage which you quote from Dr. Hamilton, but do not see that the Dr. shews that there cannot be a sinking fund from taxes.

The case he supposes of borrowing money at simple interest and lending it at compound interest, I do not clearly understand. If the nation borrows a loan of a million, for which it taxes itself 50000£ p[r] Ann[m], to pay the interest, and then employs the million at compound interest in the discharge of debt, it will the first year discharge the debt of the million, and will from that time employ £50000 pr ann. at compound interest in the discharge of old debt. In fact it taxes itself £50000 p[r] Ann[m] for a Sinking Fund. When a nation or an individual borrows money at simple interest, and lends it at compound interest, it has the interest to pay every year, but never receives any thing in return while it continues[2] the original loan, or which is the same thing, the annual interest of it, at compound interest. So far from this case proving your proposition, it appears to me to establish mine. A nation taxes itself £50000 p[r] Ann[m] without increasing its expenditure. If the revenue and expenditure were before equal this surplus of £50000 p[r] Ann[m] being devoted to the payment of debt, will produce the same effects, as if it were lent to A or B at compound interest, and when arrived at a certain sum were employed for the payment of debt. Do you mean to say (I am sure Dr. Hamilton does not) that if

---

[1] Addressed: 'F. Place Esq[r] / Charing Cross / London'.
   MS in British Museum, Add. 27,836, fols. 117–18.—*Economic*

*Journal,* June 1893, pp. 292–3;
*Letters to Trower,* XXX.
[2] 'to lend' is del. here.

our income exceeds our expenditure £50000 p.$^r$ Ann.$^m$, and 3 Nov. 1819
is devoted to the payment of debt, that it will not diminish
our debt at a compound rate of interest? Shall we not be less
in debt by £50000 the first year, £52500, the second,
£55125 the third and so on. Call this a S F or what you
please, for I will not dispute about a name, will not this be
the result? If you say it will what is our difference? On this
subject I agree entirely with Dr. Hamilton—pray look at
Page 53, and following pages of the last edition of his book.—

I am

Sincerely Y$^{rs}$

DAVID RICARDO

I am very much obliged to you for sending me the account of the proceedings at the Westminster election—I
have read it with a great deal of interest[1].

## 344. M$^c$CULLOCH TO RICARDO [2]
[*Reply to 333.*—*Answered by* 349]

Edinburgh 2$^{nd}$ Nov 1819

My Dear Sir

I trust to your goodness to excuse me for not sooner 2 Nov. 1819
acknowledging receipt of your most friendly and valuable
communications of the 2$^{nd}$ October—But having been in the
country for a few days at the time when your letters reached
this, I got so much in arrear, that this is the first moment
I have been able to devote to the agreeable task of answering
the communications of those on whose friendship I set the
highest value—

By means of your suggestions, I have, I think, considerably

---

[1] *An Authentic Narrative of the Events of the Westminster Election,* London, Stodart, 1819, a volume of pp. vii, 412, compiled by John Cam Hobhouse and Francis Place.
[2] MS in *R.P.—Letters of M$^c$Culloch to Ricardo,* II.

improved my Article on Exchange, and I have also added an explanation of the cause of its rise in 1815 and 1816[1]—I cannot, however, agree, notwithstanding the extreme distrust I feel of the correctness of any opinion on such a subject different from yours, to reject the consideration of the expence of the transit of bullion in estimating the *real par* of exchange[2]—It appears to me that whatever affects the relative worth of the circulating media of different countries, whether it consists in a diminution of the quantity of bullion contained in their coins, or in the quantity for which their paper money will exchange, or in a diminution of the comparative value of the bullion itself, must be held to affect the nominal and not the real exchange—You have stated in your answer to Mr Bosanquet that Spain can never have an unfavourable exchange with her colonies;[3] and by this statement I always understood you to mean that any given amount of the precious metals in Spain, was worth more than the same amount in South America, and that therefore the nominal exchange must be proportionably in favour of the former—You would admit that if gold and silver were accumulated by means of restrictive regulations in a particular country, that its nominal exchange would be rendered proportionably unfavourable—Now, why should the case be different when the same effect is produced by natural causes, such as the possession of productive mines, &c? I cannot help thinking the example I gave of the case of sugar decisive—It could not surely be maintained that the exchange was at true par, if a bill which cost 200 hogsheads of sugar in London only brought 100 in Jamaica—

I think you err in stating that if there were no expences

---

[1] *Supplement to the Encyclopaedia Britannica,* vol. IV, p. 220–1.

[2] See Ricardo's fourth remark, above, p. 88–9.

[3] Above, III, 171.

whatever in sending bullion from one country to another
the exchange would never deviate from par—This principle
would hold good if *no time* as well as no expence were required in the transportation of bullion, but not otherwise—
Although bullion could be brought free of expence from
South America to restore any derangement in the equilibrium
of the value of money in Europe, yet it is clear this derangement could not be adjusted for many weeks—

I was very sorry to learn that you did not mean to write
an Article on the Funding System for the Supp to the E.B.
but only on the Sinking Fund—I hope you will yet be prevailed on to proceed with the former—The subject is one of
the greatest possible interest, and it is one which has never
been properly or, I may say, at all discussed—You would
have an opportunity not only of tracing the comparative advantages and defects attending the providing for extraordinary
expences by means of loans, as contrasted with the advantages
and defects attending the providing for them by means of
a sudden increase of taxation; but would also be enabled to
point out the ruinous effects attending the accumulation of a
large debt—Neither would the discussion be at all difficult—
It would only be giving a practical application to the grand
principles which you have already established—Nothing will
give me greater pleasure than to hear that you are going on
with the Funding System, and I am sure that a Dissertation
by you on that subject would be of infinite importance—

I am particularly gratified with what you state respecting
my Article in the Review on the Trade with France;[1] and
I hope that you will endeavour to afford a practical proof of
the efficacy of the principles on the freedom of trade—However much I am disposed to concur in your opinion on other
subjects I beg to dissent entirely from what you say as to the

---

[1] See above, p. 82, n. 1.

2 Nov. 1819 person who should agitate that question in the House of Commons—If the public opinion is to have the least influence in such matters, I am certain it would be decidedly in favour of *your* agitating it; and in your hands I have no doubt whatever that a recognition of the great principles on that subject would soon be obtained—

I had a letter from Mr Torrens yesterday—He says he is to send me some of these days a copy of a reply he has written to your theory of value[1]—I regret that so excellent a political economist as the Major should be so wedded to his preconceived opinions—I shall send you a copy of the Article on Exchange addressed to your House in London—And hoping to be honoured with a letter from you at your convenience I remain with every sentiment of respect and esteem

My Dear Sir
Yours most faithfully
J. R. M^cCULLOCH

## 345. RICARDO TO MALTHUS[2]
[*Reply to* 338]

Gatcomb Park
9 Nov! 1819

My dear Malthus

9 Nov. 1819 I am sorry to find by your letter that there are so many difficulties in the way of your and Mrs. Malthus' paying us a visit at Gatcomb during your next vacation. According to your account of them they appear to be insuperable, and I must content myself with hoping that circumstances may be more propitious on some future occasion.—I shall go to London, alone, on the 22^d, and of course I shall continue there until Parliament adjourns for the holidays:—perhaps

[1] See below, p. 138.

[2] MS at Albury.—*Letters to Malthus,* LXX.

you may have occasion to visit town during that time, if so, I shall have a bed at your service, and such fare as can be furnished by my factotum in Brook Street.—

I am glad that Mr. Whishaw has expressed satisfaction with his very short visit here. I was very much pleased with his company—no one could be more agreeable, nor more disposed to be satisfied with every thing about him. We had many conversations on the subject of Parliamentary Reform, and I was glad to find that our sentiments accorded much more than I had previously imagined—I should be quite contented with such a reform as Mr. Whishaw was willing to grant us. I am certainly not more inclined than I was before, to Radicalism, after witnessing the proceedings of Hunt, Watson and C°,[1] if by Radicalism is meant Universal Suffrage. I fear however that I should not think the moderate reform which you are willing to accede to, a sufficient security for good government. Your scheme of reform, if I recollect right, is as much too moderate, as the universal suffrage plan is too violent,—something between these would give me satisfaction. Do you think that any great number of the people can really be deluded with the idea that any change in the representation would completely relieve them from their distresses? There may be a few[2] wicked persons who would be glad of a revolution, with no other view but to appropriate to themselves the property of others, but this object must be confined to a very limited number, and I cannot think so meanly of the understandings of those who are well disposed, as to suppose that they sincerely believe a reform in Parliament would give them work, or relieve the country from the payment of the load of taxes

[1] Henry Hunt and James Watson, the leaders of the people at Spa Fields in 1816 and (the former) at St Peter's Fields, Manchester, in 1819.
[2] Replaces 'many'.

with which we are now burthened,—neither do I observe in the speeches which are addressed to the mob any such extravagant expectations held out to them. If there were I am sure they know better than to believe the speakers who make such delusive promises. I expect that we shall have a very stormy session of parliament.—

With respect to my calculations, I have only this to say in defence of them, that I never brought them forward for any practical use, but merely to elucidate a principle. It is no answer to my theory to say that "it is scarcely possible that all my calculations should not be necessarily and fundamentally erroneous," for that I do not deny, but still it is true that the proportion of produce in agriculture or manufactures, retained by the capitalist who sets the labourers to work, will depend on the quantity of labour necessary to provide for the maintenance and support of the labourers.

You ask me "whether when land is thrown out of cultivation from the importation of foreign corn, I consider the new rate of profits as determined by the state of the land, or the stationary prices of manufactured and mercantile products compared with the fall of wages." You have correctly anticipated my answer: "Capital will" I think "be withdrawn from the land, till the last capital yields the profit obtained (by the fall of wages) in manufactures, on the supposition of the price of such manufactures remaining stationary.["]—

I am glad to hear that your book will be so soon in the press, but I regret that the most important part of the conclusions from the principles which you endeavour to elucidate, will not be included in it, I mean taxation. In a letter which I have lately received from Trower,[1] he is full of regret

---

[1] Letter 327.

that the important subject of taxation receives so little attention from Political Economists:—at this time he thinks it peculiarly important, and I cannot but agree with him.—As soon as you have launched your present work, I hope you will immediately prepare to give us your thoughts on a subject in which are all practically interested.—

I have received a letter also very lately from M'Cullock[1]— he has been writing an article on Exchanges for the Ency. Brit. which is very well done, I think; altho' I cannot agree with one or two of his definitions.

I finished in my hasty way the article I had undertaken to do on the Sinking Fund, and then became so disgusted with it, that I was glad to get rid of it.—I have given so many injunctions not to regard my supposed feelings in deciding whether it shall or shall not be published, that I much doubt whether it will ever see the light.

Mrs. Ricardo joins me in kind regards to Mrs. Malthus

Ever Y<sup>rs</sup>

D. RICARDO

## 346. RICARDO TO TROWER[2]
[*Reply to* 339]

Gatcomb Park—12 Nov! 1819

My dear Trower

Think not I pray you that I meant to make a charge of idleness against you—I knew full well that if you were not employed in sedentary occupations, that you were nevertheless usefully employed. Nothing can be more useful to the public than that enlightened men, with no motives for the misapplication of the powers entrusted to them, should take

[1] Letter 344.

[2] MS at University College, London.—*Letters to Trower,* XXXI.

upon themselves the duties of magistrates. I am convinced
that you are performing very essential services to the community about you by settling the disputes,—preserving the
peace, and affording securities for the protection of property
within the circle of your influence. Nor do I undervalue
your farming pursuits; I am well satisfied that great benefits
arise from men of education and liberal views engaging in
such speculations. They contribute much to introduce improvements in agriculture, and to break down those obstinate
prejudices against innovation, which are perhaps more conspicuous in farming concerns than in any other. My regret
was perhaps selfish. Wishing ardently[1] for the diffusion of
correct principles in Political Economy, I wanted the assistance of one to effect that object who appeared to me to have
imbibed correct opinions himself, and to be qualified to aid
in the further improvement of the science. The subject you
mention is very important to be well analysed, and explained
—namely, the best means of raising the funds which may be
necessary for future expenditure; it is highly interesting and
merits the most patient investigation. The difficulty which
encompasses it is almost sufficient to deter one from entering
upon it. For my own satisfaction however, and not with any
hope to throw much light on so very intricate a question,
I would employ my time upon it, if I had any time at my
command, which at present I have not: on some future day
I will bend my whole mind to the consideration of this
subject.

I am sorry to find that Malthus, whose work I believe is
now actually in the press, has left off, without treating on the
subject of taxation.[2] Political Economy, when the simple principles of it are once understood, is only useful, as it directs

---

[1] First written 'ardendly', then      [2] See above, p. 108–9.
imperfectly corrected 'ardendtly'.

Governments to right measures in taxation. We very soon arrive at the knowledge that Agriculture, Commerc[e], and Manufactures flourish best when left without interference on the part of Government, but the necessity which the state has for money to defray the expences of its functions, imposes on it the obligation to raise taxes, and thus interference becomes absolutely necessary. It is here then that the most perfect knowledge of the science is required, and I cannot but regret that Malthus has not given us his thoughts on this part of the subject. I hope he will immediately after publishing his volume seriously set about it.—

I am pleased to find that you are friendly to the preservation of the right to the people to meet, and to state their real or supposed grievances. This right may occasionally be attended with grave inconveniences, but I do not think that you can provide against these, in the way you mention, without making the privilege itself a mere nullity. A Government is free in proportion to the facility with which the people can overthrow it. What security for freedom should we have if no meeting, larger than a parish meeting, was legal. Such meetings might indeed talk of their grievances, but their talking would be no motive to their rulers to alter their measures, but might indeed be an inducement with them to get rid of such meetings altogether. The fear of insurrection, and of the people combining to make a general effort are the great checks on all governments—these we might have thro the means of a reformed House of Commons—now we have them by the privilege which the people have of meeting— I can not consent to weaken the latter check without having some security for the obtaining of the former, and even if we did obtain it, I am doubtful how far it might be safely accepted as a substitute for the privilege which we now enjoy.

I agree with you in thinking that the ministers have shewn very little wisdom, and as little liberality, in their dismissal of Lord Fitzwilliam;—as for the conduct of the opposition, in taking advantage of the present circumstances, or any other which may occur, to oust ministers from their places, it is quite in the regular course of ministerial and opposition tactics,—they appear to me to have no more chance of succeeding now than on many former occasions.

Before I go any further let me congratulate you and Mrs. Trower, which I most sincerely do, on the birth of your daughter. I am glad to hear that mother and infant are doing well.

I have not read Peter's letters to his Kinsfolk, they are in our book society but have not yet reached me.

I was sworn in as sheriff at my own house, by, I believe, the Clerk of circuit, or Arraigns, in London, and in the month of Feb.ʸ or march—perhaps April. I was not called upon to do any act in discharge of the duties of the office, till I went to meet the Judges at the Assizes.

I hear with great concern that an application will be made to Parliament to defer the payment of bullion for paper, at the rate of £4. 1–pr oz. in gold, from feb.ʳʸ next the time fixed by law, to a later period. I am told that ministers have not discharged any part of the Gov.ᵗ debt to the Bank, and are disposed to accede to the wishes of the Directors and of their friends to the undefined issues of paper, on condition of more time being granted to them for the payment of the money.[1] Surely Lord Liverpool will disgrace himself by

[1] On 30 Nov. 1819, Grenfell asked the Chancellor of the Exchequer what progress had been made by the Government in re-paying five millions to the Bank of England as they were pledged to do by April, 1820, under the plan for the resumption of gold payments. The Chancellor replied that although 'a very considerable sum' had been paid it was unlikely that any further payment

listening to any such compromise—nor can it be possible that after the solemn and grave consideration this subject has undergone Parliam$^t$ will consent to further procrastination. What will you say of the House of Commons if it consents?

Have you heard any thing of an intention to propose an income tax of 5 pc$^t$? I do not see the necessity for it. If the revenue is very deficient, it can hardly be so much so, as to leave us without any surplus at all for a sinking fund. If we are to be taxed only for the purpose of creating a sinking fund, I for one dissent from it. Besides is it fair to infer that because the revenue is from peculiar causes deficient this year, it should therefore be deficient also for years to come. Ministers told us last session that they were then arranging a system which was to be the permanent system of the country and that they did not see any probability of their requiring any further assistance excepting only a loan for five millions.—Why do they not raise the interest on ex-chequer bills? What reason have they to persevere in their endeavors to borrow money at 3 pc. when the market rate is 5 pc$^t$? Before you come to this place you will be heartily tired with this letter—I hasten now to relieve you. With the united wishes of Mrs. Ricardo and myself for your and Mrs. Trower's happiness

I am ever yours

DAVID RICARDO

could be made to the Bank in the near future 'unless that body chose to afford the usual accommodation with respect to the loan'. The Bank, however, had declined that accommodation (*Hansard,* XLI, 514). The position of the Bank Directors was that in view of the impending resumption of gold payments they were compelled to limit their issues of paper; and unless the resumption were deferred they could not make the usual advances to the subscribers for the instalments of the loan.

## 347. SAY TO RICARDO [1]
*[Answered by* 352]

10 Oct. 1819     Permettez-moi, Monsieur, de vous offrir un exemp$^{re}$ de la 4$^e$ edition de mon Traité d'Economie politique qui vient de paraître.[2] Vous verrez par les corrections que j'ai faites, notamment dans les premiers chapitres du Livre 2$^e$ sur la Distribution des richesses, combien vos critiques m'ont été utiles, puisqu'elles m'ont obligé à remettre sur le métier les parties les plus délicates de ma doctrine. Je m'estimerai bien heureux si ces corrections et quelques autres parviennent à vous ramener sur les points peu nombreux où j'ai eu le malheur de ne pas me rencontrer avec vous. J'espere que dans les occasions rares où je me suis permis de vous combattre, vous ne trouverez pas que je me sois ecarté des égards que l'on doit à vos excellentes intentions et à vos vastes lumieres.

J'avais ecrit quelques notes sur vos *Eléments*,[3] uniquement pour mon usage, et par conséquent j'avais dû laisser sans remarquer, les endroits de votre ouvrage où mes raisonnemens ne pouvaient etre qu'une répétition des vôtres, à moins de ne pas les valoir. Un libraire qui fesait traduire l'ouvrage, a eu connaissance de ces notes et m'a persecuté jusqu'à ce qu'il les ait obtenues de moi. Lorsqu'elles ont été imprimées, j'ai voulu vous en adresser un exemplaire que j'ai porté à la *Diligence* où l'on m'a dit, qu'à cause des douanes, on ne se chargeait pas des paquets directs pour Londres, et qu'il fallait adresser le mien à un correspondant

---

[1] MS in the possession of Professor J. H. Hollander, to whom I am indebted for a photostat. (See Maggs Bros., Cat. 360, 1917.)

This letter was received by Ricardo on his coming to London on 22 November; see below, p. 149 and cp. above, p. 128.

[2] *Traité d'Économie politique,... Quatrième édition, corrigée et augmentée...*, 2 vols., Paris, Deterville, 1819.

[3] Ricardo's *Principles;* on the French translation, annotated by Say, see above, VII, 361, n. 1.

à Douvres, où malheureusement je n'en avais point. Le 10 Oct. 1819
paquet est donc resté sur mon bureau jusqu'à ce que je
pusses trouver une occasion d'ami: ce qui a tardé si longtems que je n'ai plus osé vous l'envoyer, trouvant fort
ridicule de vous envoyer un livre que vous auriez vu depuis
longtems. Telle est l'histoire naïve de cette négligence dont
vous me voyez très confus. Je me flatte que ce paquet-ci
sera plus heureux.

Agréez, Monsieur, l'assurance de ma haute considération
et de mon très sincère dévouement

J. B. SAY

Paris 10 october 1819
M. David Ricardo à Londres

### 348. MᶜCULLOCH TO RICARDO [1]
*[Answered by 349]*

Edinburgh 5 Decʳ 1819.

My Dear Sir

By permission of my friend Mr Napier I have had the 5 Dec. 1819
pleasure of reading your Article on the Sinking Fund—
I think it excellent—It is not only sound in its principles but
it gives the clearest and most satisfactory account of the
effects of the various schemes for discharging the national
debt which has hitherto been published—In writing this
article you have done an essential service to the public; and
have added another to the many obligations you have already
conferred on your country—I trust you will not suppose that
I am now merely indulging in the language of compliment;
and to convince you that this is not the fact, I will take the
liberty to state that I think that with a very little additional
you might still add considerably to its value—You have in
fact written an article on the Funding System in general, and

---

[1] MS in *R.P.*—*Letters of MᶜCulloch to Ricardo*, III.

5 Dec. 1819   not on the Sinking fund; and all that is necessary to give it this shape is to transpose a few of the pages—to begin with the general discussion respecting the best methods of raising the supplies; and then to proceed to state the progress of our National Debt, and the history of the various devices which have been adopted for extinguishing it. This I think would increase the value of the article (not merely by the additional *quantum of labour*) by rending it more perfect and complete;— there is abundance of time to make the alterations provided you should think it advisable to adopt this suggestion.

Colonel Torrens lately sent me a paper of which he mentioned he had also sent a copy to you[1]—It occurs to me that our gallant friend has misunderstood your theory—His statement of the grounds of difference between his theory and yours is altogether inaccurate—He considers that when a capital of 50 days accumulated labour is applied in paying the wages of 50 workmen that 200 days labour are expended in the production of the commodity resulting from this labour— This I conceive to be a radical mistake—for it is supposing that the capital is applied *twice* to produce a given effect whereas it is only applied *once* by the agency of human hands —The other cases all proceed on the mistaken hypothesis that it is required in your theory that labour should be applied by the instrumentality of workmen; while it is altogether immaterial, provided the quantities be the same, whether it is by human hands, by machines for making beef, or by the action of natural juices in the process of fermentation—

I see Mr. Malthus has his book in the press—I presume (judging from its title)[2] that it will be a defence of his tenets respecting the Corn laws, and if so I think that justice will

---

[1] This paper has not been traced. See above, p. 128 and below, p. 142.
[2] 'Mr Malthus will soon publish, in octavo, *Principles of Political Economy, considered with a view to their practical application.*' (*Monthly Literary Advertiser,* 10 Nov. 1819.)

not be shown either to the science or the country, if it be not handled pretty roughly—You will forgive me for saying that I consider Mr. Malthus reputation as an Economist to be very much overrated; and were it not that he is a particular friend of Jeffreys,[1] who would most likely oppose his veto, I should attempt to reduce him to his just magnitude—

Though very far from being an alarmist I think it must be admitted by all that the situation of the country is now critical in the extreme—With ignorant and despotic ministers, a million of paupers, a taxation three times as oppressive as in any other country in the world, and corn laws forcing the cultivation of the poorest soils and proportionably reducing the rate of profit, it is quite impossible to suppose, provided the science of political economy be any thing better than a mere ignis fatuus that this country can bear up under the difficulties with which she is surrounded without a total change of system—It is worse than ridiculous to talk of the present distresses being temporary—They will at least continue as long as the causes by which they are produced—

I enclose you a Copy of the Article on Exchange—If it has any merit it is chiefly if not entirely owing to my having studied your invaluable works with considerable attention—

I shall be particularly happy to be honoured with a letter from you when your other more important avocations will permit; and with the greatest respect and esteem

I am

My Dear Sir

Yours ever faithfully

J. R. M<sup>c</sup>CULLOCH

I wish you would allow me to send you a copy of the Scotsman. Perhaps it might occasionally afford you some amusement.

---

[1] Francis Jeffrey, editor of the *Edinburgh Review.*

## 349. RICARDO TO M<sup>c</sup>CULLOCH [1]
### [*Reply to* 344 & 348]

London 18<sup>th</sup> Dec<sup>r</sup> 1819

My dear Sir

18 Dec. 1819    I have two of your letters now before me, the first dated the 2<sup>d</sup> Nov<sup>r</sup>, the second the 5<sup>th</sup> of Dec<sup>r</sup>, and the only excuse which I have to offer for not writing before is that my occupations have been such as to have left me little time for any thing else. With your last I received your article on Exchanges, which I have not been able yet to read throughout: from what I have seen of it, I conclude that there will be no other difference between us, but that which forms a part of the subject of your first letter.[2] With respect to that difference too, I think that we cannot clearly understand each others terms, for I contend for nothing more than is conceded in page 208 of your article, beginning with the words "In estimating the comparative quantity" &c<sup>a</sup>,[3] you appear there to admit the definition of the par of exchange given by the Bullion Committee,[4] but which, in page 207, you contend to be incorrect. If sugar were the circulating medium of the world I should think it right to say that the exchange was at par when a bill "which cost 100 hogsheads of sugar in London only brought 100 in Jamaica." You appear to think that this opinion is not quite consistent with that (to which you refer in your letter) in my answer to Mr. Bosanquet. You say you understood me to mean that any given quantity of the

---

[1] MS in British Museum.—*Letters to M<sup>c</sup>Culloch*, X.
[2] Above, p. 126.
[3] 'In estimating the comparative quantity of bullion contained in the currencies of different countries, a particular coin of one country, such as the British pound Sterling, is selected as an *integer* or standard of comparison, and the proportion between it and the coins of other countries of their *mint standard weight and fineness* is ascertained by experiment. A *par* of exchange is thus established.'
[4] See above, p. 89, n. 1.

precious metals in Spain being worth more than the same amount in South America that therefore the nominal exchange must be proportionally in favor of the former. If you substitute the words "real exchange" for "nominal exchange" you have exactly expressed my meaning, which I think agrees with the view I now entertain on this subject. Your remark that if no expences whatever attended the transmission of the metals from one country to another the exchange might nevertheless deviate from par on account of the time necessary to transmit them is quite correct, I consider the loss of interest for the time occupied in transmitting them as a part of the expence.

I cannot express how much pleased I am with what you say respecting the article I have written for the Supplement to the E B. on the Sinking Fund. I was so dissatisfied with it that I requested Mr. Mill, who transmitted it to Mr. Napier, to tell him that I hoped he would use no ceremony in rejecting it, if he thought it unworthy of a place in his work,— what you say of it is most gratifying, and if the public think only half as well of my efforts, I shall be amply recompensed for my fears and anxiety. You have spoken too favorably of the article to make it prudent in me to attempt the alteration you propose. It is highly probable that I should make it worse rather than better, by further meddling with it. You judge of me by yourself, a standard by which I should be glad if justice would permit me to be tried. You can transpose passages, and new model the productions of your pen with great facility—I with the greatest difficulty. To compose is to you an easy task, with me it is a laborious effort—I must not then risk spoiling an article which is distinguished by your approbation. Other engagements and pursuits too would probably interfere to prevent me from paying that attention to it which would be required.

You will see by the papers that I attempted in the House to express in a short speech[1] some of the opinions which I hold on the questions which circumstances have rendered particularly interesting at this time. My difficulty in speaking is as great as in writing, and therefore I cannot judge how far I succeeded in making my audience understand what I offered. I touched slightly on the subject of free trade, which you have treated of in so able a manner. To institute the necessary improvements in our system requires firmness and perseverance qualifications which we shall not find in our present ministers: they appear to be satisfied when they have removed an immediate difficulty by deferring its pressure for one or two years.

Col. Torrens shewed me the paper which is a copy of the one he sent to you. I am more convinced than ever that the great regulator of value is the quantity of labour required to produce the commodity valued. There are many modifications which must be admitted into this doctrine, from the circumstance of the unequal times that commodities require to be brought to market, but this does not invalidate the doctrine itself. I am not satisfied with the explanation which I have given of the principles which regulate value. I wish a more able pen would undertake it—the fault is not in the inadequacy of the doctrine to account for all difficulties, but in the inadequacy of him who has attempted to explain it.

After I shall have read Mr. Malthus' next work, that, I mean, now in the press, I shall be able to make up my mind whether his abilities as a political Economist have not been overrated. I confess that his dangerous heresy on the corn laws affords a strong presumption in favor of the conclusion to which you have arrived.—I will be obliged to you to send me the Scotsman and to inform me at the same time to whom

---

[1] On 16 December, see above, V, 30 ff.

I am to pay the subscription for it here. I want to know this
not only on my own account but on account of my brother
Ralph who is uneasy at the arrears of his debt. Before I
received your letter I asked Col! Torrens to put me in the
way of becoming a subscriber to that newspaper.—I remain
with great esteem, My dear Sir

Very truly Y<sup>rs</sup>

DAVID RICARDO

## 350. RICARDO TO HEATHFIELD [1]

Upper Brook Street,<br>19th December, 1819.

Sir,

    I ought, long before this time, to have thanked you for
the present of your excellent pamphlet,[2] on the means of
paying off the national debt, and to have expressed to you
the pleasure which I derived from its perusal; but I have
been so much engaged of late, that, till now, I have not had
leisure to make the few remarks which I was desirous of
submitting to you on some parts of your clear and perspicuous statement.

[1] Printed in a pamphlet entitled
*Speech on the State of the Nation,
delivered in the House of Commons,
on the Third Reading of the Reform Bill, on Tuesday, March 20,
1832, by General Palmer. To
which are prefixed, a Letter from
the late Mr. Ricardo to Mr.
Richard Heathfield, on the Liquidation of the Public Debt, and some
Observations thereon*, London,
Longman, 1832. Gen. Charles
Palmer in this speech recommended the adoption of Heathfield's plan for paying off the
national debt by means of a tax
of 15 per cent. on all property.
The 'Observations' are signed by
Heathfield and dated '8 Regent
Street, London, 12th April, 1832';
they contain a reply to Ricardo's
objections.—*Letters to Trower,*
XXXII.
    Richard Heathfield (ca. 1775–
1859) was an accountant.
[2] *Elements of a Plan for the
Liquidation of the Public Debt of
the United Kingdom; being the
draught of a Declaration, submitted to the attention of the
Landed, Funded, and every other
Description of Proprietor of the
United Kingdom. With an Intro-
ductory Address*, London, Longman, 1819.

I entirely concur with you in your general view of the desirableness of extinguishing our debt, and declared my opinion to that effect in a publication of mine, given to the public about two or three years ago.[1] During the autumn which is just passed, I have been employed in giving my thoughts rather more in detail, on the same subject, in an article written for the Encyclopaedia Britannica Supplement, and which was to have been published last month. Mr. Napier, the editor of this work, had my article in October last, but has deferred the publication of it till the next period of publication, because he found that he could not reach the Letter to which it was to be appended, without making the volume just published too bulky. As our opinions coincide remarkably on this question, I thought it right to make you acquainted with these facts, that you might not suppose that I had, without acknowledgment, borrowed your arguments. The chief difference between your opinions and mine are the following. You would pay the stockholder at 100. I think he will receive a full measure of justice, if he is paid at the present market-price, or about 70, for his three per cents. As we are now proceeding in the payment, or rather, non-payment of debt, he can never reasonably expect to receive 100, but may more justly expect to be eventually a

---

[1] *Principles;* see above, I, 247–8, and cp. the speech on 16 Dec. 1819, above, V, 34–5. Ricardo's and Heathfield's 'fanciful plans' were jointly attacked by an anonymous radical writer in *A Letter to the King; shewing, by incontestible facts, the Fundamental Causes of our Unexampled National Distress; and containing a Proposition whereby we may hope to obtain Substantial and Permanent Relief compatibly with the* Preservation of the Established Order of Society: in contradistinction to the Puerile Schemes and Fallacious Theories of Messrs. Baring, Ricardo, Heathfield, and the whole Fraternity of Paper Money Men without Real Capital, By A Commoner, London, W. Benbow, 1820. See also Cobbett's 'Letter to Lord Liverpool on Heathfield's Plan for Paying Off the National Debt', in *Weekly Political Register,* 22 April 1820.

loser of the whole of his capital. Your reasoning on this point, page 25, is not satisfactory, for you there assume that the stockholder would re-invest his capital at an interest of three per cent; such a fall in the rate of interest being, in your judgment, the natural effect of the payment of the debt: but why interest should fall from five to three per cent, without any increase of capital, or diminution of population, I cannot conjecture, and I do not perceive that you have said anything in favour of such a conclusion.

We differ, too, on the effect which the reduction of the debt would have on the agriculture of the country. It would not, in my opinion, enable us to compete with foreign growers of corn, in a degree the least more favourably than we now can do, and, consequently, I think that if a corn law be now necessary to favour our landed interest, it will be as necessary when the national debt is paid. You say (page 10) "that under the supposed relief from impost, the people would be cheaply fed, and that great and powerful impulse to the agriculture of the United Kingdom would be experienced." You think, too, (page 11) "that the remission of duties and taxes would greatly augment the demand for manufactures:"—I cannot help thinking that we should not experience any such advantages.

I am sure you will forgive me for the remarks which I have taken the liberty of making on your ingenious pamphlet. If you are desirous of knowing the reasons on which these remarks are founded, I shall be glad to state them to you on any morning that you will favour me with a visit. I will make a point of being at home, any hour that may be most convenient to you.

I am, Sir,

Your obedient Servant,

DAVID RICARDO.

Richard Heathfield, Esq.

## 351. RICARDO TO TROWER [1]

London 28 Dec! 1819

My dear Trower

At length we have obtained a little breathing time, and I am enabled to sit down and have a chat with you. All the important business in the house has been dispatched, and we are now to look forward to a long holiday: indeed I think we deserve one for our labours have been incessant during the last month, and it is matter of surprise to me how ministers undergo the fatigue of midnight watchings, added to their other duties. Mr. Tierney is evidently much the worse for it, although his attention to the business, even of the House, is by no means unremitting he declares himself that he can no longer undergo the harassing duty of a close attendance at the debates of the House of Commons. You, I have no doubt, approve of all the measures which have been adopted to suppress the public discontent[2]—I consider them as serious infringements on our liberties, and deprecate them because I expect that they will not allay the causes of discontent, but increase them. The people complain that they have not a due share in the formation of their government, and they are deprived of a portion of that which they really had. To me it appears that[3] the radical reformers are very unfairly treated —they are all lumped together—without proof or even examination they are declared to be revolutionists in disguise, and on this assumption they are condemned without being permitted to say one word in their defence. That there was cause for apprehension from the large meetings of the people, and from the publication of atrocious libels, no one can deny, but the efficiency of the laws already in force was

---

[1] MS at University College, London.—*Letters to Trower,* XXXIII.

[2] The 'Six Acts'.

[3] 'even' is del. here.

never fairly tried, and ministers were not justified in adopting new measures of rigour until the old measures had failed of remedying the evil complained of.

Our finance does not seem so very bad as had been represented—the deficiency this year must be serious, but not so great as to absorb the whole of the Sinking Fund, and unless the whole is absorbed I do not see either the policy or necessity of imposing new taxes. I suppose we shall now go on without any important measure in finance till a new war breaks out, and then it appears to me impossible, if faith is to be kept with the public creditor, to raise the annual supplies for the expences of such war, but by taxes equal to such expenditure.

There must I think be an end of loans; we cannot go on adding to a debt of 800 millions. A great deal more has been said than I intended there should be of an incidental observation of mine respecting the payment of the debt,[1] as it usually happens I am attacked by the most opposite parties. By some stockholders I am accused of not doing justice to them, by suggesting that they are not fairly entitled, in ready money, to £100, for £100–3 pc$^{ts}$, but to the market price of £100 stock, or £70. By another party—the landholders, I am accused of wishing to give the lands of the country to the stockholders, and it is more than hinted that I have an interested view in making the proposal. I may be ignorant or prejudiced, but I am not conscious of being influenced by any motives of interest, and it would really be very difficult

---

[1] 'Ricardo's notion of repaying the National Debt by a tax on real property seems at best a wild sort of notion; and it was not very discreet to let it out in an *accidental* manner, in a speech upon the employment of the poor. It is after all something of a radical notion, and is not unlikely to be taken up by the Reformers as a happy scheme to get rid of taxation.' (J. L. Mallet's MS Diary, entry of 19 Dec. 1819.) See Ricardo's speech of 16 Dec. 1819, above, V, 34–5.

for me to determine how my particular interest would be affected by the adoption of the measure.

The most serious obstacle which I see against the adoption of the plan is the state of the representation of the House of Commons, which is such as to afford us no security that if we got rid of the present debt, we should not be plunged into another.

The debates have been very interesting—those of the last week[1] afforded an opportunity for the display of great eloquence and great talent, both on the part of Sir J Mackintosh and Mr. Canning. This display was admirable, and I am told by those who have long had seats in parliament, has not of late years been surpassed. Plunkett and Brougham also have shewn very great abilities.—

I hope Mrs. Trower and your children are well, and are enjoying without alloy the festivities of this season, usually devoted to mirth and chearfulness. Pray give Mrs. Ricardo's and my kind regards to them.

I suppose you will be selected for the Sheriff for the ensuing year, in your County. I hope you will find the office an agreeable one, and that it will not be attended with any unusual portion of responsibility from the unsettled state of the times. Adieu my dear Trower,—Believe me ever

Most truly Y$^{rs}$

DAVID RICARDO

---

[1] On the Blasphemous Libels and Newspaper Stamp Duties Bills.

## 352. RICARDO TO SAY [1]
[*Reply to 347.—Answered by 356*]

London 11 January 1820

Dear Sir,

I received with very great pleasure on my coming to London, your present with the letter which accompanied it. I remember you remarked when I had the satisfaction of seeing you in Paris, that we should in every edition of our respective works approach more nearly to each others opinions, and I am persuaded the truth of this remark will be verified. We have already advanced some steps, and in proportion as we become better acquainted with the points of difference between us, we shall discover that many of them are merely verbal. Your chapter on value is, I think, greatly improved; but I cannot yet subscribe to all your doctrines on that most difficult part of the science of Political Economy.

In that Chapter you appear to have misapprehended a position of mine. I do not say that it is the value of labour which regulates the value of commodities, for that is an opinion I do all in my power to overthrow; but I say that it is the comparative quantity of labour necessary to the production of commodities, which regulates their relative value.

You appear to me to have mistaken also an opinion of mine on which you comment in a note of the translation of my book. My argument respecting rent, profit and taxes, is founded on a supposition that there is land in every country which pays no rent, or that there is capital employed on land before in cultivation for which no rent is paid. You answer

11 Jan. 1820

[1] MS (a copy in Say's handwriting) in the possession of M. Raoul-Duval; the original MS is missing. —*Mélanges*, pp. 103–5; *Œuvres diverses*, pp. 414–15 (in French translation).

11 Jan. 1820 the first position, but you take no notice of the second. The admission of either will answer my purpose.[1]

I beg your acceptance of the second edition of my book. It contains nothing new; I did not like to charge myself with the trouble of recasting it.

Political economy is making progress in this country. Every day correct principles advance, and your work continues, as it ought, to be regarded as of the first authority. The proceedings in parliament last sessions gave great satisfaction to the friends of the science. The true principles of currency were at length solemnly recognized; and I should hope that we never again can go astray.

Jeremy Bentham and M. Mill are both well. I saw them both not long ago. I hope your family are all enjoying good health. I beg you to give my respectful compliments to them.

I remain, my dear sir, very truly yours

DAVID RICARDO.

### 353. LORD GRENVILLE TO RICARDO[2]

Dropmore Jan^y 11
1820

My dear Sir

11 Jan. 1820     I am unaffectedly gratified by knowing that the general view which I take of the causes of the present distress is sanctioned by your high authority.

---

[1] Cp. above, I, 412–13, n.
[2] MS in *R.P.*

Apparently the reply to a missing letter from Ricardo which discussed Lord Grenville's speech on the State of the Country, in the House of Lords, 30 Nov. 1819. The propositions alluded to occur in the opening part of the speech,

where Lord Grenville ascribes the distress prevailing in the manufacturing districts to 'the operation of one general and leading principle of political economy', viz.: 'In peace, and under the happy influence of domestic tranquillity, the capital of every civilised community, especially

The proposition to which you refer is certainly stated more broadly than the argument required. But I still cannot help thinking that it is true, limited as it is to the *natural tendency* of relative increase, and excluding therefore the operation of *extraneous* causes.

The greater productive *power* of population, in the case you mention, I should not dispute. But you must consider that this power has its *natural* check in the difficulties of increased subsistence.

As far as I can judge, my notion seems confirmed by all modern history. Of antient history, with respect to these points, we know too little to reason with much confidence, and besides, all our inferences are disturbed by the existence and extent of domestic slavery among them. Yet I think the state of the European provinces of the Roman Empire, before and after the irruption of the barbarous nations, might afford no unapt illustration of both parts of my pro-position—Of the effect of peace on the one hand, and of war on the other.

Excuse my defending myself against my master in this science, and believe me Ever My Dear Sir

Most truly and faithfully Yrs

GRENVILLE

if permitted to find for itself its most profitable employment, tends naturally to increase in a more rapid proportion than the population; and the effect of this its augmented and growing pre-ponderance, is felt in the corre-spondent increase of all which constitutes national prosperity. But it operates most immedi-ately, and visibly, to the benefit of the lower classes of society.... The tendency of war is, in all re-spects, opposite to this....It is therefore, to a long continuance of this great calamity, that we must ascribe our present distress' (*Hansard*, XLI, 452–3). The publication of the speech as a pamphlet by Murray early in 1820 was probably the occasion for Ricardo's remarks.

## 354. RICARDO TO TROWER [1]

London 28 Jan.ʸ 1820

My dear Trower

I very much regretted not seeing you at dinner on the day I met you in the Strand, we had a very agreeable day, and some discussions in which you would have liked to participate. [2]

[1] MS at University College, London.—*Letters to Trower,* XXXIV.

[2] Perhaps the dinner at Ricardo's on 12 January, of which the following account is given in J. L. Mallet's MS diary (anecdotes about Campbell, Rogers, Windham and Horne Tooke are here omitted):

'14 Jan. 1820. Dined the day before yesterday at Mr Ricardo's where I met Whishaw, Mr Grenfell, Sharpe, Macdonnell, Mr Tooke and Mr Boddington. I had never seen Pascoe Grenfell, of financial celebrity. He is a particular friend of Ricardo's: a clearheaded sensible, moderate man, without pretensions. Mr Tooke is a Russia Merchant, also a man of sense and information, who was examined by the Bullion Committee [of 1819]. Sharpe and Whishaw led the band. *Ivanhoe* was rather severely criticised: the 3rd volume not liked. Speaking of Literary property, it was observed that an author ought never to part with his copy right if he can avoid it…. Mr Ricardo never made anything. He gives his works to Murray but then they consist of pamphlets, and of his *political oeconomy,* which has not been read by 200 persons in the country, altho' the Edinburgh Review got off the first edition.…

'It is impossible to be in company with Ricardo and not to admire his placid temper, the candour of his disposition, his patience and attention, and the clearness of his mind; but he is as the French would express it "*herissé de principes*" he meets you upon every subject that he has studied *with a mind made up,* and opinions in the nature of mathematical truths. He spoke of Parliamentary reform and vote by Ballot as a man who would bring such things about, and destroy the existing system tomorrow, if it were in his power, and without the slightest doubt as to the result. And yet there was not one person at Table, several of them Individuals whose opinion he highly valued, who would have agreed with him. It is this very quality of the man's mind; his entire disregard of experience and practice, which makes me doubtful of his opinions on political oeconomy. His speech on paying off the national debt has very much damaged him in the House of Commons, which cannot but be regretted. He and Mr Tooke, and Grenfell, and Sharpe appeared to me to regard the state of the Country in much too favorable a point of view: the

I am glad to hear that you are again looking at the subject of Political Economy, and that you still see no reason to doubt the truth of the principles which I have endeavored to establish. I have looked to the passages in my book to which you refer.[1] I quite agree with you that in most cases of taxes on income, or on profits, no effect would be produced on prices, and the burthen, which in every case would be equal, would fall on the producer, or the man enjoying the income. But I have supposed a case of our having the mines which supplied our standard, in this country, and that the profits of the miner were not taxed, then commodities would rise in price to the amount of the tax, or the miners business would be more profitable than any other, and consequently would draw capital to that concern. If then all commodities rose in price what would they rise? not in proportion to their value, but in proportion to the capitals employed in their production, and therefore as commodities selling for £4000 may be the result of the employment of the same amount of capital as commodities which sell for £10000, these commodities would not rise in proportion to their prices but if one rose £200—the other would also rise £200. Now in this

only circumstances upon which they laid any stress was the transfer of capital abroad: but as to losses of capital at home, deterioration of fixed capital, wages without adequate returns, lessening of consumption, agricultural sufferings, they made light of these things; it was enough that they were provided for and classed under their proper heads, with the natural remedies, in Books of Political oeconomy. Among other things, they maintained that the Paper Money System had given no facilities to the Government for carrying on the late War; and that we might have done all that we did by the Bank paying in specie.—I doubt it; but the arguments would be too long.

'Ricardo knows Owen intimately. He says that he is a thorough necessitarian; but being at the same time a Deist, he believes that all works for the best. It were to be wished, upon this principle, that he would be less pertinacious in his efforts to alter the state of society.'

[1] Presumably above, I, 205–210.

situation of things suppose money to rise in value and the goods which sell for £10200 to fall to £10,000 the other goods which sell for £4200 will fall to £4000, but if money should continue to rise in value and consequently the goods which sold for £10000 should fall to £5000, then those which sold for £4000 would fall to £2000. Up to certain point then they fall in proportion to the capitals employed in their production, but subsequently in proportion to the value of the goods themselves. This is the opinion which I wished to express, whether it be a correct one is another question. On the hasty consideration which I can now give it I see no reason to doubt it.

A tax imposed on goods, exactly equal[1] to the tax on profits which each man would have to pay, will have precisely the same effects.

I never contemplate as a good and practical measure, a tax on profits, without also taxing all other sources of income. Profits can never be known without a minute scrutiny into the affairs of those concerned in trade, other sources of income are well known and may be easily come at. The landlord cannot well conceal the amount of his rent, nor the stockholder the amount of his dividend, and therefore it might become a question whether you should not tax the profits of trade indirectly, by taxing wages, or necessaries; and other incomes directly, as rent, dividends, annuities &c.ᵃ &c.ᵃ

As a political economist I say that there is no tax which has not a tendency to diminish production, in the same way as a deterioration of soil or the loss of a good machine, but I mean nothing more than that it is an obstacle opposed to production. You say it is such obstacles as these which stimulate to exertion, and experience proves they are always

---

[1] 'equal' replaces 'in proportion'.

overcome. I have no doubt that there is a degree of difficulty in production which acts in the way you mention; if too strong however it will oppose a physical difficulty which can not be overcome. I think the difficulties in our case are not precisely in the proper degree to ensure[1] the greatest production. Still it is correct to record the obstacle and acknowledge it to be one. You compare the expences of the rich proprietors and the expenditure by Government of money received in taxes. With respect to future production it is indifferent whether this portion of the general revenue be expended by one or the other, excepting in this that in the expenditure of government a tax will be required for the future increased production as well as for that which is usually produced and this may prevent[2] the production of the increased quantity altogether. A tithe on land which cannot afford a rent will prevent that land from being cultivated until the price of corn rises. If there were no tithe the same land might be cultivated for the proprietors benefit. If all I am to get is to be expended by the state I will not produce, if it is to be expended by me, I will. After it is produced it is not of much importance whether the state or I expend it, to the public at large, but it is of immense importance in determining me to be active or idle. Taxes for the benefit of trade itself such as for Docks, canals, Roads, &c. &c. are on a different footing from all other taxes, and produce very different effects, they may and generally do promote production instead of discouraging it.—I am glad you have not persuaded yourself that taxes are very delightful things. I am very sorry to be obliged to agree with you that there are a very few who are perfect masters of the science of Polit. Econ.

I have been much entertained by reading Ivanhoe though

---

[1] 'ensure' replaces 'stimulate to'.    [2] 'prevent' replaces 'deter'.

not in an equal degree as by reading some of the other novels written by the same author.

Mrs. Ricardo joins with me in kind remembrances to Mrs. Trower.

Ever Y<sup>rs</sup>

D RICARDO

## 355. RICARDO TO M<sup>c</sup>CULLOCH [1]
### [*Answered by* 358]

London 28 Feb.<sup>y</sup> [1820] [2]

My dear Sir

It is a long time since I have written to you, and now I fear I have little to say worthy of engaging your attention. The death of the King has suspended all public business, and the great object of interest with all those by whom I am surrounded is the approaching election. [3] To some it is an object of hope, and to others of fear, but as far as regards the strength of the two parties opposed to each other, I am told by the learned in those matters, that the ensuing parliament will not materially differ from the present one. My seat I believe is very secure, I shall represent the same place for which I am now returned. There has not been the least foundation for the report that I was to be a candidate for the County of Gloucester; I have not been invited to become such, nor if I had been, should I have consented to embark on so perilous an undertaking as a contest with the family of Beaufort. [4] Col! Torrens will I fear have little chance of

---

[1] Addressed: 'J. R. MCulloch Esq<sup>r</sup> / College Street / Edinburgh'.
MS in British Museum.—*Letters to M<sup>c</sup>Culloch*, XI.
[2] In MS '1821'; but Ricardo's frank on the cover and the post-mark are dated 1820.

[3] George III died on 29 Jan., and Parliament was dissolved on 28 Feb. 1820.
[4] The Duke of Beaufort, whose son Lord R. E. H. Somerset was again returned for the County with Sir B. W. Guise. Mallet, in

success at Rochester, and the probability, I think, is, that he 28 Feb. 1820
will decline going to a Poll.[1]

I read with great pleasure the able articles which I see
every week in the Scotsman. They continue to advocate the
good cause without being betrayed into violence and intemperance of language. For the support which you have
given to my hint in the House of Commons about the
payment of the National Debt I am grateful.[2] It always gives
me satisfaction to find my opinion confirmed by yours, and
I am glad to know that you think it desirable that we should
submit to the necessary sacrifices, to get rid of the over-
whelming incumbrance which palsies all our efforts. The
Stockholders are a very unreasonable class, and in all their
remarks on my proposal, complain bitterly of my thinking
they should not receive more than 70 for their 3 pc$^{ts}$. I do
not know what they would say to you, who propose to pay

a Diary entry of 1823, after mentioning 'the respect entertained
for Mr Ricardo by his country
neighbours and the gentlemen
of the County' which he had
observed during his visit to Gloucestershire in 1817, adds: 'but
I am sorry to say, that an il-
liberal political feeling was gen-
erated by his exertions in the
House, in favour of financial and
political reform, and more particularly against all criminal proceedings for matters of opinion
and works of religious controversy. This feeling grew so
strong that notwithstanding his
station in the County, his large
landed property, his endeavours
to promote industry and true
charity in his neighbourhood, and
the general esteem in which he
was held, the Duke of Beaufort
declined three years ago placing

him in the Commission of the
Peace for the County.' (*Political
Economy Club, Centenary Volume,*
1921, p. 213.)
[1] Torrens was induced, apparently
after some resistance, to withdraw
in favour of the other opposition
candidate, Ralph Bernal, thus
securing the latter's unopposed
return together with a Government candidate. He announced
his decision in a somewhat em-
bittered speech to the Rochester
Electors on 6 March (reported in
the *Scotsman*, 18 March 1820).
[2] 'Expediency and Practicability
of Mr. Ricardo's Plan for paying
off the National Debt', leading
article in the *Scotsman*, 8 Jan. 1820.
In this article M$^c$Culloch proposes paying off the 3 per cents.
at 60, minus a further 15 or
20 per cent. because of the rise in
the bullion value of money.

them only at 40. A Reformed House of Commons, if ever we should possess so great a good, and if we should not the debt I believe may as well remain as it is, should on this question of price, do strict justice between the payers and receivers of taxes, and not heed the clamour which the selfish on either side should raise. From what I observe I am confident that this will not be the mode in which we shall get rid of the debt. Our burthens may, and will probably, continue to weigh us down for many years to come, but finally they will be forcibly thrown from our shoulders, and the stockholders instead of complaining, with injustice, as I think, that they were not to be paid at 100 for their 3 pc$^{ts}$, will have justly to complain of losing both their principal and interest.

The landholders and those concerned in Agriculture are loud in their complaints of the present corn laws, and will I expect make a forcible appeal to Parliament for their improvement, as they will call it. If we are to have laws to protect the landed interest I agree with the complainers that they should not be in the form in which they now exist, for they are calculated to produce the most mischievous variations in the price of corn which can neither be desirable to the grower nor to the consumer. A permanent tax on importation, to the amount only of the peculiar taxes to which the growth of corn[1] is subject, would be I think the wisest policy, but it is probable that such a limited tax would be far from satisfying the landed interest. We should then have to chuse between a higher permanent tax, or a tax varying with the price. If the object be to sustain the price of corn at 80/p$^r$ quarter it might be allowed to enter duty free when at that price—to pay a duty of 1$s$. p$^r$ q$^r$ when it fell to 79—2 when it fell to 78, and so on. A serious objection against this latter mode is that 80/- would become in some measure the maxi-

---

[1] 'the growth of corn' replaces 'land'.

mum of price, whilst no means could be adopted to fix a 28 Feb. 1820 minimum. The corn grower would not have much chance of selling his corn under any circumstances above 80/, but there is no limit to the low price, at which, on other occasions, he might be forced to sell. This is a disadvantage to which no other trade is exposed—if a manufacturer be subject to a glut of his commodity, and consequently to low prices, he is also benefited at times by an unusual demand and high prices. It is true the farmer might make allowances for this peculiar disadvantage, and might therefore insist on a greater general average of profits on that account. If he did so, this would of itself be in its operation a tax on corn, for it would necessarily fall on the consumer, and not on the landlord. Before any discussion takes place in the House of Commons I mean to refresh my memory with the substance of your excellent article on the Corn Laws.[1] I do not at present recollect whether you have made any observation on that part of the subject on which I have now been writing.

I was very much pleased with Col. Torrens essay in the last Edinb<sup>h</sup> Review.[2] I do not think there is more than one proposition in it which I should be disposed to dispute.[3] Mr. Malthus, who passed 2 or 3 hours with me last week, was fully persuaded, till I undeceived him, that the article was written by you; he could hardly believe that Col. Torrens agreed so completely with the doctrines which both you and I have advocated.[4] Mr. Malthus continues stoutly to deny that demand is only limited by production—he thinks that capital might be very mischievously augmented in a country,

---

[1] In the *Supplement to the Encyclopaedia Britannica*.
[2] *Edinburgh Review*, Oct. 1819 (this was then 'the last' number; that for Jan. 1820 was not published till March, see below,
p. 164), Art. XI, 'Mr. Owen's Plans for relieving the National Distress'. Cp. above, p. 82, n. 3.
[3] See below, p. 227.
[4] Cp. below, p. 376.

and he intends in his new publication to make some remarks on this which he conceives to be an erroneous doctrine on the part of the Reviewer.[1] His book has been in the press a very long time, and must now be nearly ready for publication. In our conversation the other evening he maintained stoutly the opinions which he has long held, and which I cannot but think very far from being the correct ones. On the whole however he appears to me to have made some approximation to us, and I suspect that in his book the differences between us will not appear so great as they do in our conversations.

I hope your other engagements will not prevent you from bestowing a portion of your time on Political Economy. The science is already greatly indebted to you, but the public mind is not yet so informed as not to stand in need of all the aid which your pen can give it—I hope to see an article of yours in the next number of the Review.

I have lately seen Mr. Leonard Horner.[2] On enquiring of him after you I was glad to find he was acquainted with you, and had so good an account to give of your health. Mr. F. Horner was a great loss to the House of Commons, he was a powerful supporter of all the good principles of Political Economy.

I am with the greatest esteem
Yours very faithfully
DAVID RICARDO

---

[1] See Malthus's *Principles of Political Economy*, above, II, 313 ff.
[2] The brother and biographer of Francis Horner; he was one of the early members of the Geological Society.

## 356. SAY TO RICARDO [1]
[*Reply to* 352]

Paris, 2 mars 1820

Mon cher Monsieur,

Sans aucun doute, nous finirons par nous entendre. La vérité est en un point; quand on la cherche de bonne foi, on finit par se rencontrer, à moins que notre vie ne se termine avant nos recherches. Peu s'en est fallu qu'il n'en arrivât ainsi de moi; une espèce d'attaque d'apoplexie m'a averti du peu de fond que nous devons faire sur notre existence.

Je vous avoue que je ne comprends pas trop la différence que vous établissez entre *la valeur du travail qui ne détermine pas la valeur des produits,* et la *quantité de travail nécessaire à leur production qui détermine la valeur des produits.* Il me semble que vous ne pouvez déterminer la quantité et la qualité du travail que par le prix que l'on paie pour l'obtenir. C'est du moins ce que j'ai toujours entendu par la quantité de ce service productif que j'ai appelé *service industriel.* Son prix fait partie des frais de production, et vous même établissez très-justement que l'ensemble des frais de production règle la valeur du produit.

Vous blâmez une des notes que j'ai mises à la traduction française que Constancio a donnée de votre ouvrage (je crois que c'est celle de la page 249, tome I du français). J'avoue que je ne vois pas trop comment la seconde partie de la proposition fait passer la première. N'importe: si la critique est juste pour cette première partie, je conviendrai volontiers que vous avez raison pour la seconde. En effet, quand un fermage ne sert absolument qu'à payer l'intérêt du capital qu'un propriétaire a répandu sur sa terre, et qu'un impôt survient, le propriétaire n'abandonnera pas sa terre, et par conséquent le profit que rend son capital, pour ne pas payer

---

[1] *Mélanges,* pp. 106–7; *Œuvres diverses,* pp. 415–16.

2 March 1820 l'impôt. Dès-lors l'impôt ne porte pas sur le propriétaire en tant que propriétaire, et il augmente les frais de production, et par conséquent le prix des produits bruts. C'est un cas qui montre, en dépit des physiocrates, que tout impôt ne retombe pas sur les terres.

Agréez de nouveau, etc.

J.-B. SAY.

## 357. RICARDO TO TROWER [1]

London 13 M[ch] 1820

My dear Trower

13 March 1820 Mr. Mill is so constantly occupied at the India House that I seldom see him, except on sundays, and therefore I delayed answering your letter till after I had met him yesterday. He, as well as I, are much obliged by your invitation, and we have agreed to accept it, if it will suit you to receive us on saturday the 1st, or, the following saturday, the 8th of april. Mr. Mill is obliged to stipulate for Saturday, as that is the only day on which he can leave the India House. Our visit will necessarily be a short one, but if the weather should be as fine as it now is, we shall have an opportunity of seeing the beauty of the country immediately about you.

My late constituents at Portarlington appear to be a very good tempered set of gentlemen, and will I am assured elect me without hesitation to the next Parliament. The report of my being a candidate for the county of Gloucester never had the least foundation, and was put forth I imagine with no other view than to provoke a contest. I do not soar so high, and am the most unfit of all men to engage in an undertaking

---

[1] Addressed: 'Hutches Trower Esq[r] / Unsted Wood / Godalming' —not passed through the Post.      MS at University College, London.—*Letters to Trower*, XXXV.

so difficult and so expensive as that of contesting a county 13 March 1820
with an old and powerful family.[1]

The plot in Cato Street[2] must no doubt be favorable to
ministers in the general election, and yet at Brookes' they
confidently anticipate rather an accession than a diminution
to the ranks of opposition. On this point I am very little
anxious, as whether the ministers have a majority of 200, 100,
or 50, will not, I think, in any degree affect the important
questions about which the country should be most particularly solicitous.—I should be glad to have some enlightened
commercial men added to the small number usually in the
House, and therefore I regret that Sharp has been defeated
at Maidstone—I hope however that Haldimand will succeed
at Ipswich. He is brother to Mrs. Marcet and appears to be
a clever man. He is rich, and has much influence amongst
his brother merchants.[3] Sir Wm. Curtis's commercial knowledge will not add much to the general stock.[4]

My thoughts have not been engaged upon any particular
branch of Political Economy exclusively, but have wandered
over the whole field. At one time I have to defend and
explain one principle against an adversary, at another time
another, and I have the satisfaction of observing that the
opinions which I deem the correct ones are daily gaining
ground. Col. Torrens is becoming one of the most efficient
advocates for the right principles, as may be seen both in his

[1] The Duke of Beaufort; see above, p. 156, n. 4.
[2] The plot of Thistlewood and four others to kill the Ministers on 23 February. The conspirators, who met in Cato Street, were betrayed by a spy and hanged.
[3] William Haldimand, an ex-director of the Bank of England who had been strongly in favour of the resumption of cash pay-

ments. M.P. for Ipswich 1820–26.
[4] Sir W. Curtis, a banker, had lost his seat for the City of London in 1818, and regained it in 1820. 'He was a man of great importance as head of the Tory party in the City, though he was a pitiably bad speaker, very badly educated, and the constant butt of all the whig wits' (*Dictionary of National Biography*).

review of Owen in the Edinburgh,[1] and in the last edition of his work on the impolicy of restraints on the importation of corn.[2] Lord King too, with whom I have lately conversed, is also marshalled on our side. M'Culloch has I am told an article in the Edinburgh just printed, in favor of free trade, and I dare say it is a good one.[3] That we are improving is manifest from this that a petition is preparing in the city to Parliament in favor of free trade, in which the merchants (the petitioners) with great ability urge the advantages which would result from unrestrained commerce. It is very respectably signed and will be presented to the H of Commons by Mr. Baring. That the merchants should condemn and expose the mercantile system is no unimportant evidence of the progress of liberal opinions.[4]

I am glad that you are not to be plagued with a contested election in Surry. As Sheriff it would have involved you in a degree of anxiety and responsibility from which you must be glad to escape.

Mrs. Ricardo unites with me in kind wishes to Mrs. Trower.

Believe me Ever

Truly Y[rs]

DAVID RICARDO

[1] See above, p. 159, n. 2.
[2] *An Essay on the External Corn Trade,* 2nd ed., Edinburgh, Constable, 1820.
[3] Jan. 1820; see below, p. 165, n. 2.

[4] The Merchants' Petition for Free Trade was presented by Baring to the House of Commons on 8 May 1820; see above, V, 42.

## 358. M<sup>c</sup>CULLOCH TO RICARDO [1]
[*Reply to 355.—Answered by 359*]

Edinburgh 19 March 1820

My Dear Sir

Permit me to return my best thanks to you for your kind letter of the 28<sup>th</sup> ulto—I am always most happy to hear from you; nor is there in point of fact any thing of which I am so proud as of the honour of your correspondence—

I presume that ere now you have seen the 65<sup>th</sup> Number of the Review—You will have little difficulty in ascertaining who wrote the article on Taxation and the Corn laws[2]—I thought it was the best way in order to render the article *frappant,* and that you know either is or ought to be the great object of a Reviewer, to endeavour to shew the effect of the Corn laws as a tax—I do not think I have at all exaggerated the burden they impose on the country, and an arithmetical statement of the kind in question, if it is nearly correct, will make a more powerful impression than the best conducted argument— I should like to know what you think of the soundness of my opinion relative to the comparative rapidity of the increase of taxation[3]—If I am well founded in the statement I have made would it not afford a pretty strong argument against the sudden increase of taxation that would be required to enable a country to raise the supplies for carrying on a war

[1] Addressed: 'David Ricardo Esq M.P. / Upper Brook Street / London'.

MS in *R.P.—Letters of M<sup>c</sup>Culloch to Ricardo*, IV.

[2] *Edinburgh Review,* Jan. 1820, Art. IX. This article, which is by M<sup>c</sup>Culloch, was ascribed to Ricardo in the *Gentleman's Magazine* of May 1820 (p. 425).

[3] *ib.* pp. 163–4; 'a slow and gradual increase of taxation, by adding to the efficacy of the principle of moral restraint, has a tendency to raise the rate of wages'. But a sudden increase of taxation, precluding as it does the possibility of previously modifying habits, 'is unaccompanied by any alleviating circumstance. The mischiefs which it occasions are pure and unmixed.'

within the year? I regret I did not get your scheme for paying off the debt spoken of in the manner I should have liked to have done,[1] as Mr. Jeffrey thought it would be better to postpone any examination of it to a subsequent period—However I am under no apprehensions but I shall still have it in my power to do it justice, and to defend it against the cavils of those by whom it has been ignorantly attacked—

I agree with you in thinking that if there were no other alternative a permanent tax on the importation of corn, or even a tax varying with the price, might on the whole be preferable to the present system—But I trust you will, in the first instance, oppose all such taxes and all restrictions whatever on the trade in corn—Your concurrence in any scheme, however modified, for restricting the freedom of this trade, would be the most fatal event that could possibly happen to blast the hopes of those who are confidently looking forward to the ultimate and complete triumph of those principles you have done so much to establish—Excuse the freedom which I take, and forgive me for saying that on this fundamental point you must make no compromise—It is for the interest of all—even of the landlords—that the present vicious system should be abandoned—Any attempt to improve or amend what is in itself bottomed on radically unsound principles, however advantageous in the meantime, must in the end aggravate the disease and render a return to a healthy state more difficult—When the question of the Corn laws comes to be agitated in Parliament, every person who has emancipated himself from the shackles of the vilest prejudices, or who would wish to see his country again in a flourishing condition, will look up to you as their representative; and

---

[1] *Edinburgh Review,* Jan. 1820, Art. IX, p. 180: the scheme is described as a 'bold and decisive measure', but 'at all events to be considered as a *dernier resort*'.

will expect you to recommend not palliatives or soporifics, 19 March 1820 but such a mode of treatment as will effectually extirpate the disease which is now preying on our vitals—

I am anxious to see Mr. Malthus work. He deserves to be very roughly handled—The assistance which he has given to the supporters of our factitious and exclusive system, renders the task of exposing his errors, however ungracious, indispensibly necessary—

I am much gratified with what you say of the Scotsman; and I hope it will continue to deserve your approbation—It is no light matter I assure you to put your hand to any paper in this City in which the government is not to be the subject of eulogy—I believe a political writer would have an equal chance of justice in Madrid and Edinburgh[1]—Juries are here no protection for they are invariably packed, and the Bench is filled with mere servile partisans who must have starved had they continued at the Bar—Whatever intelligence or public spirit may exist in Scotland, exists in despite of the public institutions of the country, which are infinitely worse than you could have any idea of—I shall hope to hear from you when you have leisure. And I remain with the greatest regard and esteem

Yours most faithfully<br>J. R. M^cCULLOCH

[1] 'The first number of *The Scotsman* newspaper was published in January 1817. The incalculable importance of this event can only be understood by those who recollect that shortly before this the newspaper press of Edinburgh, though not as much fettered as in St. Petersburgh (as it has been said to have been), was at least in as fettered a condition as any press that is legally free could be.' (H. Cockburn, *Memorials of his Time,* Edinburgh, 1856, p. 308.)

## 359. RICARDO TO M^cCULLOCH [1]
[*Reply to 358.—Answered by* 360]

London 29 March 1820

My dear Sir

I received with great pleasure your kind letter of the 19^th inst., and I take advantage of this period of inaction to enter into a little discussion with you on some of the points contained in your article on taxation, in the last number of the Edinb^gh Review,[2] knowing, as I do, that we have both the same object in view, namely the establishment of truth; and therefore I feel no more hesitation in making you acquainted with my sentiments when they differ from your own, than when we are fully agreed. In the article in question, you have, with your usual force and ability, advocated the great truths of the science of Political Economy, which you have yourself before so satisfactorily and so clearly explained; but there are some minor points on which you touch that I request you to reconsider, and if you detect any error in the reasoning by which I support an opinion contrary to yours, have the goodness to communicate it to me, that I may examine it with that care and attention to which I am sure it will be entitled.

The labouring classes in all countries have the very greatest interest in keeping the supply of labour rather under the demand, but they are then most happy when the funds for the support of labour, and consequently the demand for it increase with the greatest rapidity, and their means for supporting their families and contracting of marriages is at the highest level to which it can be raised. It is only because taxation interferes with the accumulation of capital, and diminishes the demand for labour, that it is injurious to the

---

[1] MS in British Museum.—*Letters to M^cCulloch*, XII.
[2] January 1820.

working classes. Sometimes it only retards the rate of accumulation, at other times it arrests it altogether, and on some occasions the taxes by being supplied at the expence of capital itself actually diminish the means of the country to employ the same quantity of labour as before. Wages may be regulated, and may continue for a series of years, on a scale which shall allow the population regularly to increase from year to year in such a proportion as shall double it in 25 years. Under other circumstances this power of doubling may not be possible in less than 50, 100, or 200 years—or population may be so little stimulated by ample wages as to increase at the slowest rate—or it may even go in a retrograde direction. Wages being regulated according to some one of these states may or may not be affected most injuriously to the working classes by taxation.

Suppose them to be in that state of abundance as to encourage the doubling of population in 25 years, and suppose a tax to be laid directly on wages, or on the necessaries on which wages are expended, of 20 pc^t, what effect will such a tax have on the real comforts of the labourers?[1] None whatever, I answer, unless it diminishes the demand for labour, because it will be immediately transferred to the employers of labour, and will consequently diminish the profits of stock. Suppose wages not to be increased after the tax, every body could employ the same quantity of labour as before, and to that demand would be added the additional demand of government for labour, who cannot expend these

---

[1] M^cCulloch's answer (*Edinburgh Review*, Jan. 1820, pp. 160–1) is that the labourer 'is unable to raise his wages in proportion to the increased price of the commodities he consumes; and for this obvious reason, that, while the competition for employment, or the number of labourers continues undiminished, the demand for their services, however much it may be lessened, cannot be increased by the imposition of the tax.'

taxes without employing soldiers, sailors and many other labourers. This of itself would soon raise the price of labour, and transfer the burden to the employer of labour. If I before employed 10 gardeners, after wages have thus risen, I may not be able with the same funds as before to employ more than 8, and thus the tax of 20 pc.$^r$ falls on me—no more men are employed, but two men are dismissed from my service, and are taken into the service of Government. The rate of accumulation goes on as before, and no other effect is produced than what would have been produced if a tax of an equal amount had been directly laid on me. Whatever may previously have been the rate of wages, the tax obviously never deteriorates the situation of the labourer unless it diminishes the demand for labour, by affecting the rate of accumulation. Taxes will generally affect the rate of accumulation, and therefore they are generally injurious to the labourer, but when we are carrying on an expensive war and it is necessary to raise large funds within the year, either by loan, or by taxes equal in amount to such loan, the former will I think be most injurious to the labourer, because it will more materially affect the accumulation of capital.[1] If an individual is called upon to pay an annual tax of £100 p.$^r$ Ann$^m$ instead of a sum of £2000 for once only, he will not make so great an effort to save, because he is seldom sensible that a tax of 100 p.$^r$ Ann$^m$ is equivalent in value to £2000,—and therefore a system of loans is more destructive to the national capital than a system of heavy taxation to an equal amount.

I must quickly dispatch my remaining observations. Page 157 The distress of the poor is considered as synonymous with diminished resources. Suppose a nation to increase its capital annually at the rate of 2 pc.$^t$ but that at the same time its population increases at the rate of $2\frac{1}{2}$ pc.$^t$ is it

----

[1] Cp. the same argument above, I, 220–2.

not clear that there will be annually new demands on its
charitable funds? Its annual net revenue, and with it the
means of expenditure and enjoyment to the higher classes of
society would increase but would be accompanied with a
diminution of happiness, if not positive misery to the great
mass of the people.

The employment of machinery I think never diminishes
the demand for labour—it is never a cause of a fall in the
price of labour, but the effect of its rise. If one man erected
a steam engine because it was just cheaper to employ the
engine than human labour, and if this were followed by a fall
in the price of labour it would be no other man's interest to
prefer also the use of the machine. Loans, then, if made from
capital, will be supplied from circulating and not fixed capital
particularly if the expenditure of government, even with a
slight diminution of capital, should as it generally does
increase the demand for people. Fixed capital such as
buildings, machinery &c^a cannot furnish the means of
loans—they, after they are once erected must be employed
as capital or thrown by as useless.[1]

You lead the reader to infer that the great discoveries and
improvements made by us in machinery and manufactures

---

[1] M^cCulloch argues that 'the factitious and unnatural prosperity' during the war was partly due to the loans, because 'the capital lent to the State would, if it had remained in the hands of the subscribers, have...been chiefly devoted to the increase of fixed capital, or machinery. But, although it would have thus contributed to the lasting benefit of the country, it would not have occasioned the same immediate demand for labour.' He adds: 'The fixed capital invested in a machine, must always displace a considerably greater quantity of circulating capital,—for otherwise there could be no motive to its erection; and hence its first effect is to sink, rather than increase, the rate of wages.' *Edinburgh Review,* Jan. 1820, pp. 170-1. This latter principle is taken from Barton (*Observations on the Condition of the Labouring Classes,* 1817, p. 16, but cp. pp. 55-6) of whose pamphlet the article is nominally a review.

have been particularly favorable to this country.[1] Excepting for an inconsiderable portion of time are they not equally advantageous to every other country, even if they are retained in this country only?

You say that the corn laws have the same effect as if a tax of 24 millions and a half were levied from the consumers of corn for the public expenditure.[2] I should add, provided the 24 millions and a half received by the landholders be all expended as revenue, and no part be added to capital.

Perhaps you may think me fastidiously minute in my observations—I think so myself, but my object is to ascertain exactly whether our opinions coincide or differ. The general reader would perhaps prefer that his attention should not be distracted by the consideration of such niceties and it may not be material that it should. It is however important to my theory of providing for a heavy expenditure when it arises, by taxes within the year in preference to loans,[3] that I should shew that it is more favorable to the accumulation of capital, to the demand for labour, and to the general happiness.— The single man amongst the labouring class may bear and often does bear his portion of taxation, but the married labourers has the means of repaying himself by commanding increased wages, unless the amount of the tax is so heavy, however laid, that it disturbs the rate of accumulation.

You must not have the least fear of my compromising my opinion on the Corn laws, I have already spoken out, on that subject, and shall again, if I can muster up courage to speak at all. You know however that I have always maintained that the growers of corn in this country should be protected from any peculiar burdens to which they may be subject, but then they should shew that they are so burthened—the fact I

---

[1] *Edinburgh Review,* Jan. 1820, pp. 168–9.  [2] *ib.* p. 180.  [3] See above, IV, 185 ff.

believe is that every other trade is taxed in a proportion greater than the growth of corn. My principle is that we may impose restrictions to restore things to their natural relation, but never to destroy it.

I have lately been at Mr. Malthus for a couple of days—he shewed me a chapter of his new work, perhaps that in which his difference with me is most particularly noticed.[1] I am an interested judge and my decision must be received accordingly. To me it appeared to offer no objections which might not be easily disposed of.

After reading this long letter I am strongly tempted to commit it to the flames—yet I am so doubtful whether a new attempt to convey my opinions to you will be more successful that I think it most prudent to let it go with all its imperfections. In you I know I have a partial judge ever inclined to view my errors and omissions with indulgence. I remain with great esteem

Faithfully Yours

DAVID RICARDO[2]

---

[1] Probably Chapter III, 'Of the Rent of Land', of Malthus's *Principles of Political Economy.*

[2] In *Letters to McCulloch*, pp. 60–61, there is printed a memorandum, described as being in Ricardo's handwriting, which was found in a copy of the 1st ed. of Ricardo's *Principles* in the library at Gatcombe. This memorandum touches upon some of the points discussed in this letter. The handwriting of the MS, however, though similar in general appearance to that of Ricardo's, differs in essential details and is unlikely to be his.

## 360. MᶜCULLOCH TO RICARDO [1]
[*Reply to* 359.—*Answered by* 361]

Edinburgh 2 April [1820] [2]

2 April 1820

My Dear Sir

I have to return you my best thanks for your kind letter of the 29 Ulto; and for the remarks which you have been so good as to make on my article in the last No of the Review —If I could suppose that whatever sums are paid into the Exchequer as taxes would in the hands of Government give employment to the same number of labourers as if they had been allowed to remain in the possession of the contributors, I should have no hesitation about subscribing to your opinion that such taxes would, immediately after their imposition, or at least in a very limited period, fall on the capitalist, and that wages would be proportionably augmented—But I am convinced that a little reflection will satisfy you that any such supposition is altogether out of the question—Suppose that in order to pay a subsidy to the Russians a duty of 6$^{\text{d}}$ is laid on every quartern loaf, by what means will the labouring class be able proportionably to raise their wages? Yet such subsidies form a constant and important part of the expenditure of every war—But, admitting that the taxes are totally expended on the maintenance of home soldiers, it is plain, from the incomparably greater waste that must take place in providing for troops, and from the expenditure in the shape of *munitions de guerre,* that instead of the sums raised by Government setting the same quantity of labour in motion as they would have done had they not been thrown into the Exchequer, we shall be a great deal too liberal if we suppose

---

[1] Addressed: 'David Ricardo Esquire / M.P. / Upper Brook Street / London'.

MS in *R.P.*—*Letters of MᶜCulloch to Ricardo,* V.
[2] In MS '1819'. Ricardo notes 'Qu? 1820'; post-mark, 1820.

them to have *half* that effect—In various years of the late
contest the expences on account of the war alone exceeded
70 millions, and on the supposition that the wages of labour
amounted to £30 that would have afforded the means of
subsistence to above 2 millions of individuals—at least
100 per cent more than have at any period been directly or
indirectly employed by government—Although, therefore,
in estimating the effects of taxation the additional employment which it enables the government to afford ought not
to be lost sight of, yet this is but a very poor and inadequate
compensation for the diminished employment afforded by
the contributors—Hence when a country, in which the increase of capital and of population had been nearly equal has
the misfortune to be involved in hostilities, I can have no
doubt that if a sudden check be not given to the principle of
population, the condition of its inhabitants must be degraded
—This, as it appears to me, is the great evil of excessive and
especially of suddenly increasing taxation—Increased exertion might make some amends for the destruction of capital;
but when the sentiments of the people are once depressed—
when they submit to be sunk in the scale of existence—
when, in short, the extortion of government has reduced
them to the situation, for example, of the Irish, their capacity
of improvement is at an end, and their condition becomes
altogether hopeless and desperate—

I perfectly agree in your opinion that if population increases
faster than the means of subsistence, a country even though
not taxed at all, must ultimately sink into the extreme of
misery—But, I think I have stated enough to shew that the
increase of population has not been by any means the main
cause of the poverty with which the lower classes in the
country are now assailed—

For want of throwing in an additional sentence an erroneous impression may be made by what I stated on the subject of the Corn laws—I did not mean to say that the $24\frac{1}{2}$ millions went into the pockets of the landlords—This sum goes partly into their pockets, but by far the largest share, perhaps two thirds must be expended *en pure perte* on the increased cost of production—

I should consider it as a very great obligation to the many other I am already under to you, if when Mr. Malthus work is published you would have the goodness to favour me (and you may be assured I shall not communicate them to any other individual) with notes of your opinion of his objections to the fundamental principles involved in your theory of political economy—I beg to hear from you at your convenience—And with the greatest respect and esteem

I am

My Dear Sir

Yours most faithfully

J. R. M<sup>c</sup>Culloch

### 361. RICARDO TO M<sup>c</sup>CULLOCH [1]
[*Reply to 360—Answered by 366*]

London 8 April 1820

My dear Sir

I write immediately after the receipt of your letter, because the subject is now fresh in my mind, and I am desirous that we should clearly understand what our difference really is. You appear to me to misapprehend it. I do not deny that war is attended with waste and extravagance, and that its evils, even as far as regards taxation, are by no means limited to the mere transferring of disposable labour from the em-

---

[1] MS in British Museum.—*Letters to M<sup>c</sup>Culloch*, XIII (where it is misdated 6 April).

ployment of individuals to that of the state; on the contrary I fully agree that its usual effects are to destroy or to prevent the accumulation of capital. But I contend that the poor suffer from this dissipation of capital, not on account of the peculiar taxes which are imposed upon them, but on account of the disturbance which it gives to the usual demand for labour. It matters not, I say, whether the taxes be laid on wine, silks and velvets, the luxuries of the rich, or on the corn and clothing consumed by the laboring class, the specific evil is in both cases, not the tax, but the annihilation of capital to which the tax gives rise. Destroy that capital by a loan of 30 millions in the year, with only taxes to pay its interest; or raise the thirty millions within the year by taxes on luxuries, or on the necessaries of the poor, and the effect will be the same—the poor will suffer because 30 millions of capital is withdrawn from active employment.

I understood you to advance a very different doctrine in the passage of the article in the Review in page 160 beginning "The labourer is, in this respect, placed in a much more disadvantageous &c^a, &c^a."[1]—I acknowledge that the labourer may be made wretched under adverse circumstances of taxation &c^a, but it is only because capital is reduced and the demand for labour lessened. If a loan was raised for a subsidy to Russia, or if the amount of the subsidy were supplied by a tax of 6d. on every quartern loaf, or a tax of 100£ on every pipe of wine; provided, in every case, the sum raised was equal in amount, it would be a matter of comparative indifference to the labouring class by which means it should be raised; the great evil is in the amount of the sum raised, and not in the mode of raising it.—

When I have read Mr. Malthus book I will make known to you my opinion on the passages which will be found in it

---

[1] See the quotation given above, p. 169, n. 1.

8 April 1820    in opposition to our theory. I am flattered by the request. I shall as freely comment on those passages to Mr. Malthus himself. Since we have known each other, we have always freely discussed each other's opinions, and it is a subject of wonder to our friends that after the innumerable contests we have had together, there should still be such serious difference between us.

The merchants of London have prepared a petition to the House of Commons on the subject of free trade, which you will be pleased to see. I send you a copy of it but I must request you to say nothing of it in print till after it is presented. When its presentation has taken place, I know it would be agreeable to the leading parties in it, if you expressed your approbation of their petition, should it, as I think it will, appear to you to be entitled to it.[1]

Believe me

Truly Yours

DAVID RICARDO

## 362. RICARDO TO McCULLOCH [2]
### [*Answered by* 366]

London 2 May 1820

My dear Sir

2 May 1820    In the Scotsman of Saturday last, which has just reached me, I perceive with much satisfaction that you have with your usual ability met Mr. Malthus, on what I consider his strongest ground.[3] I assure you that I am highly gratified in

---

[1] The Petition (on which see above, p. 164, n. 4) was supported by an editorial paragraph in the *Scotsman* for 13 May 1820.
[2] Addressed: 'J. R. M'Culloch Esq.r / College Street / Edinburgh'. Franked by Ricardo 'May three 1820'.

MS in British Museum.—*Letters to McCulloch*, XIV.
[3] The *Scotsman* of 29 April 1820 in a long review of Malthus's *Principles of Political Economy* defends Ricardo's theory of value.

2 May 1820

having succeeded so well in my imperfect statements, as to engage you in their defence, for I should have no chance of procuring their admission into other people's mind, without your powerful assistance. From the very complicated nature of the subject of value, Mr. Malthus has, I think, more chance of discovering some flaw in my argument in the chapter which treats of it, than in any other part of the book, and this chance is increased by my supposition of a medium which shall itself be invariable. This medium may be supposed to be produced under a variety of circumstances. It may either be the result of the employment of labour only, as supposed by Mr. Malthus,[1] when he supposes it to be picked up on the sea shore, in which the advance of only one days sustenance is required; or it may be produced under all the variety of different portions of fixed capital, and employed for different portions of time. If produced by labour only—if half an ounce of silver could be picked up on the sea shore by a day's labour, the natural price of labour would be always half an ounce of silver, it could neither rise nor fall. Corn might however be produced with more difficulty, and by the rise of its price, the wages of the labourer would be less adequate to procure him comforts and conveniences. In this case I should say wages would rise, because I always measure the rise of every thing by the quantity of labour necessary to produce it, and the wages though less in quantity would require more labour to produce them.—But if much fixed capital was employed in the mines, or if a considerable time must elapse before the circulating capital is returned by the sale of the silver, labour might be exceedingly variable in such a medium. Every commodity measured in such a medium would rise when labour rose, if it were the produce of labour only, or of a less portion of fixed capital than was employed

[1] Above, II, 81.

in the production of money, and on the contrary from the same cause those commodities which were produced by larger proportions of fixed capital, or required more time to finish, would fall in price. This is all implied in my book, but I have not been sufficiently explicit, for I ought to have said that if the medium is produced under certain circumstances, there are many commodities which may rise in consequence of a rise in labour, altho' there are many others which would fall, while a numerous portion would vary very little.[1]

You, I know, understand me, but I fear that I have not been particular enough in shewing the various bearings of this question. After the best consideration that I can give to the subject, I think that there are two causes which occasion variations in the relative value of commodities—1 the relative quantity of labour required to produce them 2$^{dly}$ the relative times that must elapse before the result of such labour can be brought to market. All the questions of fixed capital come under the second rule, which I will endeavor to explain if you should wish it.—

I thought of noticing the particular points on which Mr. M and I differ, and to have offered some defence for my opinions, but I should have little else to do but to restate the arguments in my book, for I do not think he has touched them. Mr. M adopts a measure of value very different from mine, but he no where adheres to it. Sometimes when he speaks of the rise of commodities he means their rise in money, at other times their rise in labour. His very standard is spoken of as rising and falling. In what medium does it rise and fall? in commodities whose value is estimated by the quantity of the very standard which he is thus measuring. Cloth has risen, he would say, because 100 yards of it will command more labour. Well then the variation is in the

---

[1] See above, I, 63 and cp. 43.

cloth, and labour is the standard by which it is measured;
but labour is abundant, the population is excessive, wages
are low, and the proof is that more labour is given than
before for 100 yards of cloth, and for many other commodities.—

The most objectionable chapter in Mr. Malthus' book is
that perhaps on the bad effects from too great accumulation
of capital, and the consequent want of demand for the goods
produced.[1] This doctrine naturally leads to the conclusion
which Mr. Malthus draws from it. I could not have believed
it possible, if I had not read it, that so enlightened a man as
Mr. Malthus should recommend taxation as a remedy to our
present distresses.[2] He is not aware that the produce of a
country is always consumed, and that saving means only that
a larger portion shall be consumed by those who reproduce
a value superior to their consumption. From the insufficient
numbers of labourers, they may be enabled to command such
a quantity of the produce as to leave little for profits, and
thereby to deter capitalists from employing any additional
capital in reproduction; but these low profits, if society be
not at the end of its resources, arise only from the insufficient
number of labourers to do the work required. It can never
happen that capital and labour can be at the same time redundant, except as I said before you have arrived at the end
of your resources, but Mr. Malthus talks of low profits from
a want of demand, and thinks it quite possible that you may
have more capital than you can employ, with a redundancy
of people.

According to him you produce too much and consume too
little, and as you are so obstinate that you will not consume
yourself he recommends that taxes should be imposed, and
that government should expend for you.

[1] Ch. VII, Sec. 3.      [2] Above, II, 432–3.

Mr. Malthus does not appear to have understood me respecting improvements on the land. I have not denied that
eventually they will be very beneficial to landlords, but their
immediate effect is to lower rent. When the same land is again
cultivated in consequence of increased population the landlords corn rent will be higher, but his money rent will be the
same as before[1], for the price of corn will be lower. As however inferior lands can be cultivated with a lower price of
corn, the improvement cannot fail to become, at no distant
period, very beneficial to the landlord. All this I think I have
allowed—if I have not, I ought to have allowed it. He has
not acted quite fairly by me in his remarks on that passage in
my book which says that the interest of the landlord is
opposed to that of the rest of the community. I meant no
invidious reflection on landlords—their rent is the effect of
circumstances over which they have no control, excepting
indeed as they are the lawmakers, and lay restrictions on the
importation of corn.[2]—

I am surprised that rent should be still spoken of as a
surplus produce, differing in that respect from the produce
of manufactures. Is it any thing but a value transferred?
Could it exist in the same degree as it does if the lands were
all more fertile or varied less in relative fertility? Might we
not have more produce with less rent?

These are all the observations which I intend making on
Mr. Malthus' work. If you should write any remarks upon
it I should very much like to see them, and should without
scruple say to you whatever might occur to me on perusing
them. At present I feel a real difficulty, for I confess I do not
very clearly perceive what Mr. Malthus system is. He and
I differ in our opinions on the benefits resulting from foreign

[1] 'the same as before' replaces    [2] Cp. above, II, 117.
'lower'.

trade, but what his opinion is I do not well know. I have 2 May 1820 read his book rather in haste, and after different intervals of time, so that I have not strictly done it justice—I mean to go over it carefully again.

I am expecting the Merchants petition to be presented in a few days.[1] I am glad to see that the doctrines of the advantages to be expected from a free trade are daily gaining converts. I am sure that the public are much indebted to you for enlightening them on that important subject.—

I remain with great esteem<br>Very faithfully Y<sup>rs</sup><br>DAVID RICARDO

363. RICARDO TO MALTHUS [2]

London 4 May 1820

My dear Malthus

You, and Mrs. Malthus, will hear with pleasure that 4 May 1820 Mrs. Ricardo is quite well, and bears her late loss[3] with much more tranquility and composure than could have been expected. Osman and his wife, with Mr. Clutterbuck, and my daughter Henrietta, have been with us for some time,— their presence has been very acceptable on this sad event.

I have read your book[4] with great attention. I need not say that there are many parts of it in which I quite agree with you. I am particularly pleased with your observations on the state of the poor—it cannot be too often stated to them that the most effectual remedy for the inadequacy of their

---

[1] It was presented to the House of Commons by Alexander Baring on 8 May 1820.
[2] Addressed: 'Rev<sup>d</sup> T. R. Malthus / East India College / Hertford'.

MS at Albury.—*Letters to Malthus,* LXXI.
[3] The death on 17 April of Ricardo's daughter Fanny (wife of Edward Austin).
[4] *Principles of Political Economy.*

wages is in their own hands.[1] I wish you could succeed in ridding us of all the obstacles to the better system which might be established.—

After the frequent debates between us, you will not be surprised at my saying that I am not convinced by your arguments on those subjects on which we have long differed. Our differences may in some respects, I think, be ascribed to your considering my book as more practical than I intended it to be. My object was to elucidate principles, and to do this I imagined strong cases that I might shew the operation of those principles. I never thought for example that practically any improvements took place on the land which would at once double its produce, but to shew what the effect of improvements would be undisturbed by any other operating cause, I supposed an improvement to that extent to be adopted, and I think I have reasoned correctly from such premises. I am sure I do not undervalue the importance of improvements in Agriculture to Landlords, though it is possible that I may not have stated it so strongly as I ought to have done.[2] You appear to me to overvalue them, the landlords would get no more rent while the same capital was employed as before on the land, and no new land was taken into cultivation, but as with a lower price of corn new land could be cultivated, and additional capital employed on the old land, the advantage to landlords would be manifest. Because the landlord's corn rent would increase without these conditions, you appear to think he would be benefited; but his additional quantity of corn would exchange for no more money, nor for any additional quantity of other goods. If labour were cheaper he would be benefited in as far as he would save on the employment of his gardeners, and perhaps some other menial servants, but this advantage would be

[1] See above, II, 262.          [2] Cp. above, II, 116 ff.

common to all who had the same money revenue, from whatever source it might be derived. The compliment you pay
me in one of your notes[1] is most flattering. I am pleased at
knowing that you entertain a favorable opinion of me, but
I fear that the world will think, as I think, that your kind
partiality has blinded you in this instance.

I differ as much as I ever have done with you in your
chapter on the effects of the accumulation of capital.[2] Till a
country has arrived to the end of its resources from the
diminished powers of the land to afford a further increase,
[I hold][3] it to be impossible that there should [be, at the]
same time, a redundancy of capital, and of [population. I]
agree that profits may be for a time very l[ow] because
capital is abundant compared with [labour but] they cannot
both I think be abundant at one [and the same time.]

Admitting that you are correct on this [point, I doubt if
the] inference you draw is the correct one, and i[t does not
seem to me] wise to encourage unproductive consumption.
If individuals would not do their duty in this respect, Government might be justified in raising taxes for the mere purpose
of expenditure.—

M Culloch has a short review of your book in the last
Scotsman—it is chiefly on the subject of value—he differs
from you but does so with the greatest civility and good
humor.

Torrens has an interest in, (I believe he is Editor of)
the Traveller evening paper—He also has some remarks on
your book written in the right spirit, and as his arguments
are on my side I of course think his criticism just.[4]

[1] Above, II, 222–3.
[2] Chapter VII, Section III.
[3] MS torn here and below: similar
statements occur below, p. 278
and above, II, 426.

[4] 'The *Traveller* is not a new,
but a newly-conducted evening
paper; which, if it has not much
wit or brilliancy, is distinguished
by sound judgment, careful in-

4 May 1820

Pray give our kind regards to Mrs. Malthus and believe me ever

Truly Y$^{rs}$

DAVID RICARDO

## 364. RICARDO TO SINCLAIR[1]

11th May 1820.

Sir,

11 May 1820

I agree with you on the benefits resulting from a paper, instead of a coin circulation, *and I never wish to see any other established in this country;* but we differ on the means of regulating its value and amount. That I think is to be done best, by making it exchangeable for bullion, at a fixed rate. I do not deny that the public has suffered much pressure from the limitation of circulation, but Parliament is not responsible for more than about 5 or 6 *per cent.* of that pressure, the limitation having taken place, and the currency having risen in value, to within 5 or 6 *per cent.* of the mint value, before the Bank Committee was appointed. An increase of currency now, would undoubtedly lower its value, raise all prices, and very much lighten taxation; but no measure could, I think, be more impolitic.

It would be unjust to all creditors, and proportionally advantageous to debtors. If the payment of the interest of the national debt is a greater burden than we can bear, which I

formation, and constitutional principles' (*Edinburgh Review*, May 1823, p. 368). Torrens was the new proprietor and Walter Coulson, who had been an amanuensis of Bentham, was (or became shortly afterwards) the editor: 'Colonel Torrens himself wrote much of the political economy of his paper'

(J. S. Mill, *Autobiography*, p. 86). Two articles, unsigned, on 'Mr Malthus's New Work' appeared on 26 April (on profits and on free trade) and 1 May 1820 (on rent); a sequel was promised, but did not appear.

[1] *Correspondence of Sir John Sinclair*, vol. 1, pp. 372–3; *Letters to Trower*, XXXVI.

think it is not, and cannot well be, the fair way would be, to compound with the public creditor, and not make him only a pretended payment.

Respecting the paying off the national debt, we do not materially differ. I would pay it off entirely, and never allow any new debt, on any pretence whatever, to be contracted. You would only pay off a part, and would not object to contract a fresh debt, on any pressing emergence. You would not exempt foreigners from the necessary contribution. I would. You calculate that we consume as much corn, and other things, when prices rise from a scarcity, as when they are cheap from abundance. This I think impossible. If there were an equal consumption, there could be no scarcity, and consequently no rise of price. You would give the home grower of corn the monopoly of the home market, while the operation of paying the debt is going on. I would, when it was completed, take off all restrictions on importation. I would leave the law as it is during the paying off, and would gradually take off all restrictions afterwards. To induce capital, by a monopoly, to go into agriculture, and then remove it afterwards, would be attended with ruin to the agriculturists. The restrictions, I think, should not be increased with a view, finally, to get rid of them.

I fear that no plan for paying off the debt will receive any countenance from Parliament. Men do not like to make an immediate sacrifice for a future good; and they please themselves with imaginary riches, from which they really derive no advantage. Are not those imaginary riches, from the possession of which we only derive a revenue, which we are immediately obliged to pay to the tax-gatherer? I remain, Sir, your faithful servant,

DAVID RICARDO.

Sir John Sinclair, Bart.

## 365. RICARDO TO NAPIER [1]

London 15 May 1820

Sir

15 May 1820　　I return the *Proof* of the article on the Sinking Fund which you sent me; I wish it was more worthy of insertion in your valuable publication.

The table at the end has little to do with the subject—it contains some information and may be omitted or inserted as you think best. [2]

I will be obliged to you for 2 or 3 separate copies of the article.

I am Sir with great esteem
Faithfully Yours
DAVID RICARDO

## 366. MᶜCULLOCH TO RICARDO [3]
[*Reply to 361 & 362.—Answered by 368*]

Edinburgh, 15 May 1820

My Dear Sir

15 May 1820　　I was exceedingly gratified by your letter of the 2nd— Although I think I understand your theory pretty well, still if you could spare as much time from your other and more important engagements, as would enable you to send me a brief abstract of your opinions respecting the effect that the relative times which must elapse before commodities can be brought to market must have on their comparative value, it

[1] Addressed: 'To Macvey Napier Esqʳ'—not passed through the post.
MS in British Museum (Correspondence of Macvey Napier) Add. 34,612, fol. 358.—*Letters to Trower*, XXXVII.

Macvey Napier (1776–1847), editor of the *Supplement to the Encyclopaedia Britannica*, 1814–1824, succeeded Jeffrey as editor of the *Edinburgh Review* in 1829.
[2] It was omitted.
[3] MS in *R.P.*—*Letters of MᶜCulloch to Ricardo*, VI.

will be of particular service to me; and will enable me the
better to support the sound principles of the science against
the attacks of those who will avail themselves of the authority
of Mr. Malthus to revive all those errors which Dr. Smith
would have been the first to have abandoned—I do not
exactly know whether Mr. Jeffrey will allow me to review
Malthus—I rather think he will not[1]—However no commendations will be bestowed on his work and I will occasionally
shew the hollowness of particular parts of it—Perhaps I am
wrong, but it appears to me that there is much more of art
than of ingenuousness in Mr. Malthus work—There is no
clearness in his statements and no force in his reasoning. The
former is loaded with modifications and limitations, and the
latter is weakened by an affectation of candour, a quality of
which the book is in reality but too destitute—Should I write
a Review of it I shall certainly send you the proof sheets for
your revisal—I have desired Mr. Napier to allow me to write
the article Value in the Supplement;[2] so that I will then have
an opportunity of discussing the new doctrines at length, and
of doing all in my power to assist in their dissemination—

I cannot help differing with you on the subject of taxation.
Exclusive of the destruction of capital I think there is a very
great difference in the effects produced by taxes on luxuries
and taxes on necessaries—Suppose Ireland is obliged to remit
a subsidy of 10 millions to Russia and that there are two
methods of raising it—a duty on potatoes and a duty on
claret and coaches—If the first method be adopted it is plain
wages will not rise in proportion to the duty; for as the
subsidy is to be remitted to a foreign country it cannot enable

---

[1] The first ed. of Malthus's *Political Economy* was not reviewed
in the *Edinburgh Review*.
[2] 'Value' is not a separate article
in the *Supplement to the Encyclo-*
*paedia Britannica;* it is dealt with
in Part III, Sec. IV of the article
'Political Economy', by M<sup>c</sup>Cul-
loch.

the Government to employ more labour, and as the number of labourers will remain the same, and the demand for their labour is not increased, they must continue to suffer the extreme of misery untill the pressure of famine or the slackened operation of the principle of population shall have equalised the supply and demand—But an increased duty on claret and coaches would be productive of these effects only in a very slight degree—The love of accumulation must on the average be always stronger than the passion of expence—The increased duty on luxuries would be met by a proportionable saving on those and other articles of expence; and few or no labourers would be thrown out of employment, inasmuch as this would in fact lessen the means of paying the duties—

But although I am of opinion that it is better to impose taxes on luxuries than on necessaries, I should object to any scheme for repealing the taxes on commodities and substituting a property or income tax in their stead—Such a measure would most certainly add to the public distresses—It might no doubt give a momentary relief; but it would widen the basis of taxation, and enable ministers to divert a much greater portion of the wealth of the country into the coffers of the Treasury—

I have sent Colonel Torrens a copy of an article I have written for the Review on the subject of our restrictions on foreign commerce[1]—Though it is entirely practical and hardly worth your attention, I desired him to put it into your hands—I hope the present session will not be permitted to elapse without some specific motion on the subject of the trade with France being brought forward—Nothing I am sure would give greater pleasure to the country at large than to see this subject in your hands.

I was exceedingly sorry to learn from Col. Torrens the

[1] *Edinburgh Review,* May 1820, Art. III.

misfortune which has occurred in your family¹—I will expect    15 May 1820
to have the pleasure of hearing from you at your convenience
—And I am with every sentiment of respect and esteem

Yours most faithfully

J. R. M<sup>c</sup>CULLOCH

367. RICARDO TO BENTHAM ²

Dear Sir

     I am obliged to be in the City to-morrow which will    18 May 1820
prevent me from meeting you in the morning. I shall take
my chance of finding you in the Green Park on Saturday at
the usual hour.

Y<sup>rs</sup> very faithfully

DAVID RICARDO

Upper Brook Street
18 May [1820]

368. RICARDO TO M<sup>c</sup>CULLOCH ³

[*Reply to 366.—Answered by 372*]

London 13 June 1820

My dear Sir

     A number of engagements, to which I have been obliged    13 June 1820
to give my time and attention, has prevented me from answering your letter before. I fear I shall have some difficulty

---

¹ See above, p. 183, n. 3.
² Addressed: 'Jeremy Bentham Esq<sup>r</sup>'. Docketed by Bentham— '1820 May 18 Ricardo Upp Brook Str to JB. Q.S.P. Appointment to walk.'—Not passed through the post.
     MS at University College, London, Bentham Papers, Case No.

165, 'Correspondence respecting Chrestomathic School'.
     From other letters (*ib.,* unpublished) it appears that they were to discuss the lease of the site in Bentham's garden in Queen Square Place on which the school was to be built.
³ MS in British Museum.—*Letters to M<sup>c</sup>Culloch,* XV.

in explaining myself on the effects which the relative times before commodities can be brought to market, have on their prices, or rather on their relative value. All commodities which have value are produced by labour. The labour employed in making a steam engine, may be the same in quantity, and exerted for the same length of time, as the labour employed in making a valuable piece of furniture, consequently the steam engine and the furniture, would be of the same value. The upholsterer sells his furniture at the end of a year for a thousand pounds—the steam engine is also worth a thousand pounds, but it is not sold, it is to be employed the following year as capital. If profits be 10 pc$^t$, independently of the quantity of labour and circulating capital which the owner of the steam engine must employ, and in which he is on a par with the upholsterer, he must have his steam engine replaced in its original state of efficiency at the end of the year, and must charge upon his goods £100—for the profit of the £1000 capital employed as fixed capital. If it be two years before he can receive the return from the work done by the steam engine, he must have £100 for the first years profit, and £110 for the second, and this is totally independent of the quantity of labour actually accumulated in the commodity brought to market. Now if I employ valuable machinery from which I have no return for two years, at the end of the two years, my machinery and my goods together, must be of the value of all the labour employed in producing them, besides the accumulated profit on the capital which yielded me no return for that time. But the same result would take place if I employed circulating capital only and could not bring my commodity to market for two years[1]—at the end of the two years, the commodity will not be worth only all the labour bestowed on it, but also all the accumu-

---

[1] Last eleven words are ins.

lated profits for the time that my capital was so employed. Strictly speaking then the relative quantities of labour bestowed on commodities regulates their relative value, when nothing but labour is bestowed upon them, and that for equal times. When the times are unequal, the relative quantity of labour bestowed on them is still the main ingredient which regulates their relative value, but it is not the only ingredient, for besides compensating for the labour, the price of the commodity, must also compensate for the length of time that must elapse before it can be brought to market. All the exceptions to the general rule come under this one of time, and as there are such a variety of cases in which the time of completing a commodity may differ, it is difficult to fix on any one commodity which may properly be chosen as a general measure of value, even if we could get over the difficulty of not having one which always requires the same quantity of labour to produce it. The two extremes appear to be these: one, where the commodity is produced without delay, and by labour only, without the intervention of capital; the other where it is result of a great quantity of fixed capital, contains very little labour, and is not produced without considerable delay. The medium between these two is perhaps the best adapted to the general mass of commodities; those commodities on one side of this medium, would rise in comparative value with it, with a rise in the price of labour, and a fall in the rate of profits; and those on the other side might fall from the same cause. Mr. Malthus has taken advantage of this defect in my measure of value, from which his own is not free, and has not failed, as he justly might do, to make the most of it. Mr. Malthus in fact keeps to no one measure of value—sometimes he speaks of a rise or fall of goods, and means a fall or rise in their money price— sometimes he estimates their fall and rise by their power of commanding labour, and sometimes by their exchangeable value in corn. His real measure of value is itself variable, and in a degree not inferior to the variableness of most other things, and he speaks of this variableness without appearing to be aware that he thereby shews how unfit his measure of value is for any useful purpose.

It must be confessed that this subject of value is encompassed with difficulties—I shall be very glad if you succeed in unravelling them, and establish for us a measure of value which shall not be liable to the objections which have been brought against all those hitherto proposed. I sometimes think that if I were to write the chapter on value again which is in my book, I should acknowledge that the relative value of commodities was regulated by two causes instead of by one, namely, by the relative quantity of labour necessary to produce the commodities in question, and by the rate of profit for the time that the capital remained dormant, and until the commodities were brought to market. Perhaps I should find the difficulties nearly as great in this view of the subject as in that which I have adopted. After all[,] the great questions of Rent, Wages, and Profits must be explained by the proportions in which the whole produce is divided between landlords, capitalists, and labourers, and which are not essentially connected with the doctrine of value. By getting rid of rent, which we may do on the corn produced with the capital last employed, and on all commodities produced by labour in manufactures, the distribution between capitalist and labourer becomes a much more simple consideration. The greater the portion of the result of labour that is given to the labourer, the smaller must be the rate of profits, and vice versa. Now this portion must essentially depend on the facility of producing the necessaries of the labourer—if the facility be great, a small proportion of any commodity, the result of capital and labour, will be sufficient to furnish the labourer with necessaries, and consequently profits will be high. The truth of this doctrine I deem to be absolutely demonstrable, yet I think that Mr. Malthus does not fully admit it.—

The case you put to support your opinion that it is of great importance to the labourers whether taxes be imposed on the luxuries of the rich or on their own necessaries, is well chosen. You suppose a subsidy to be (*annually,* I believe) remitted from Ireland to Russia, and you ask whether it will be of no consequence whether the taxes to raise that subsidy be imposed on potatoes, or on claret and coaches? As no more labourers will be employed by Government, and consequently there can be no increased competition for them, you conclude that notwithstanding the taxes on the necessaries of the poor, their wages will not be raised till after they are reduced to the extreme of misery, and famine, or the slackened operation of the principle of population have equalized the supply to the demand. According to your own view of the case, when the demand has to operate on the diminished supply, wages will rise very high, not only so high as to compensate the labourer for the tax imposed on him, but much higher, for on no other conditions can he replace the void which misery had made in the number of labourers. Before the tax, his wages were only sufficient to keep up the supply equal to the demand. If you add the tax to his wages, he can do no more; and therefore if famine and misery have occasioned depopulation, there must be an extraordinary stimulus to place things on their former footing. I should say then that according to your admission the labourer would on an average have his wages increased equal to[1] the amount of the tax, but he would first suffer from

---

[1] Replaces 'have wages increased by'.

their being extraordinarily low, and then benefit from their rising extraordinarily high. In truth, however, I think that they will neither be very low nor very high, but that they will undergo such a moderate increase as will compensate the labourer for the tax laid on his necessaries. It is the interest of all parties that they should so rise. I consider that the quantity of necessaries which the wages of a labourer will enable him to purchase, is really the efficient regulator of the population. The circumstances of the country require that the population should continue to increase at the same rate after the subsidy is granted to Russia as before, for there is no diminished demand for labour, and the question between us comes to this. Will the population be in the first instance very much depressed, and then afterwards violently stimu-lated, or will it continue in that course which the circumstances of the capital and the demand for labour originally required it to be? The value of things I believe to be influenced, not by immediate supply and demand only, but also by con-tingent supply and demand. You must not suppose that I am arguing in favor of taxes on necessaries, in preference to taxes on luxuries, for that is not the question—but I am endeavoring to ascertain in what these taxes really differ. I quite agree with you, and for the reasons you give, that an income tax is by no means a desirable tax, situated as we are, instead of the taxes now levied.—

What I said on the Agricultural question in the House of Commons[1] has been in many respects imperfectly reported. I assure you that I maintained stoutly those principles which you know I think the correct ones. Mr. Brougham very much misrepresented what I said and he himself advanced principles which were wholly untenable, but the House was much too partial to one view of the subject, to allow me to

[1] On 30 May; see above, V, 49 ff.

enter into a refutation of them. I shall probably have some other opportunity of doing so.[1]

Your article in the Edin. Review is exceedingly good, and I am sure will be of great use in forwarding the good cause.[2] Your article on Corn in this days Scotsman is also calculated to convince the honest sceptics.[3]

You are mistaken in thinking that I could be of use in Parliament by bringing forward the question of free trade with France. In the first place I have not talents for such an undertaking, and in the second I am treated as an ultra reformer and a visionary on commercial subjects by both Agriculturists and Manufacturers. Do you not observe that even Mr. Baring, the professed but I think lukewarm friend of free trade, did not nominate me on his committee.[4]

Y^rs ever

D Ricardo

## 369. BENTHAM TO RICARDO[5]

Q.S.P. 17 June 1820

Dear Sir

I question whether I have ever observed to you, that a main cause, and by far the most material one, of my reluctance to see the School quit that place[6] is this—that in doing so it would lose the benefit of the inspection of Mr Mill, who, my garden being his, may as it were in no time perform that office, as often as need shall be: which is what, especially considering his engagements at the India House,

---

[1] No opportunity seems to have arisen during the Session.
[2] See above, p. 190, n. 1.
[3] 'The Proposed Alterations in the Corn Laws', leading article in the *Scotsman,* 10 June 1820.
[4] The Select Committee on Foreign Trade appointed by the House of Commons on the motion of Alexander Baring, 5 June 1820.
[5] MS in *R.P.*
[6] Bentham's garden; see above, p. 191, n. 2.

he could not do any where else. His assistance in that way is of capital importance: not only in itself but in respect of the confidence it will inspire, by the proofs afforded by the progress of his son John, as exhibited in a letter, which I believe you saw, and which, though I have never told him so, I intend to trumpet forth in print, by means which I have over and above the very inconsiderable ones that would be afforded by any publication under my own name.

The letter in question is one written by John Mill in answer to one from my Brother to me, concerning the progress made by him in his studies.[1]

This is a topic which Mr. Mill could not do justice to himself, and it is therefore necessary that I should endeavour to bring it under your view. He knows not of my writing this, nor can he have any the least suspicion of it.

Yours truly

J. B.

Had it not been for the assurance of his assistance, as above together with Mr. Place's, I never should have written the Book that I wrote,[2] nor taken any other part in the business.

## 370. RICARDO TO MILL[3]

Upper Brook Street<br>3 July 1820

My dear Sir

    I should be exceedingly sorry if Mr. Bentham should be disappointed in his wish of having the school in his garden.

---

[1] This letter, written by J. S. Mill to Sir Samuel Bentham on 30 July 1819, was published (apparently for the first time) by A. Bain in his *J. S. Mill, A Criticism*, London, 1882, pp. 6–9.

[2] *Chrestomathia;* above, VI, 112.

[3] MS at University College, London, Bentham Papers, Case No. 165, 'Correspondence respecting Chrestomatic School'.

The MS of the revised agreement for building the School in Bentham's garden in Queen Square

I think the difficulties may now easily be got over.[1] I have, I know very imperfectly, endeavored to sketch the alterations which I think necessary in his draught of the Agreement. Be so good as to look at my paper, and supply what may be deficient in it. After doing this give it to Mr. Bentham and let him suggest such corrections as he may think requisite. He and I are to meet on wednesday morning when we may talk over the business together. Mr. Bentham will of course understand that I am expressing only my own opinion.

At your leisure read my paper on the importation of corn.[2] If you could return it on saturday or sunday I shall be glad.

Truly Y<sup>rs</sup>

D Ricardo

J. Mill Esq<sup>r</sup>

## 371. TROWER TO RICARDO [3]
### [*Answered by* 373]

Unsted Wood—Godalming.<br>July 5—1820.

My Dear Ricardo

London has become more than ever the centre of attraction! The proceedings going on in Parliament are most important, and their consequences most fearful.[4] What

*3 July 1820*

*5 July 1820*

---

Place (to which this letter refers), written by Ricardo and annotated by Bentham, is in the British Museum Newspaper Library, Place Collection of Newspaper Cuttings, vol. 60, No. 25.
[1] 'Bentham imposed harder and harder conditions, and in 1820, after an enormous correspondence, his offer of a site was finally declined, and the project given up.' (Wallas, *Life of Place*, p. 112.)

[2] This paper has not been found.
[3] MS in *R.P.*
[4] On 4 July a Committee of the Lords, having examined the papers on the conduct of Queen Caroline, which had been laid before the House in two sealed bags, reported that the documents contained allegations 'charging her majesty with an adulterous connection with a foreigner...and attributing to her majesty a con-

is to become of this Pandora's Box? Are its contents to be spread abroad and scatter mischief among us? Is the investigation to be pursued? Is it possible after all, that the Q. is really innocent? Or, is she presuming upon the difficulty of proving her guilt? If so, hitherto, her bullying has been most successful, since she has succeeded in exciting a feeling in her favor, which will not dispose the public to be very impartial judges in her cause. It will require some better evidence than what *foreign* accusers can afford, to satisfy the biassed mind of John Bull. Her advisers must indeed feel confidence in her case to allow her thus to put everything to hazard, and to rise in her demands as the hour of trial approaches. If she should be successful, I consider a change of Ministers *certain;* it is impossible they can continue to hold their places after having exposed the K. or rather perhaps after having allowed him to expose himself, by such useless, such mischievous, such senseless proceedings. Under such circumstances a change of Ministers might be beneficial, it would be calculated to tranquilise the public mind, and we should have a right to expect, that those who have so long, and so loudly *preached* about economy, would, as soon as the opportunity was afforded them, set about *practising* it.—

I am glad to see you lose no opportunity of standing up in your place in Parliament to assert the true principles of political economy. It is only by reiterated representations of sound doctrines on this subject that we can hope to see

tinued series of conduct highly unbecoming her majesty's rank and station, and of the most licentious character.' Thereupon Lord Liverpool announced that the next day he would bring in a Bill of Pains and Penalties against the Queen. (*Hansard,* N.S., II, 167 ff.) The proceedings on the Bill in the House of Lords, usually referred to as the Queen's Trial, occupied the attention of the whole nation for the next four months, till the Bill was withdrawn on 10 November.

them reduced to practise.—What do the Economists say of ⟨5 July 1820⟩
Malthus's Book[1]? Has he obtained any converts? Has it
excited any interest? Have you begun your proposed
epistolary controversy with him? I have made but little
progress in his Book yet; but, hitherto, I cannot think he has
succeeded in overturning any of your positions. He labors
hard to prove, that the prices of commodities are not regulated by the *cost of productions,* and, yet, I think, he admits
the point, even by his mode of reasoning the subject; for, he
allows, that the costs of production have a most powerful
effect upon prices. "But," he adds, "the true way of considering these costs is as the *necessary condition* of the supply
of the objects wanted."[2] Now, if the *supply* of the objects
wanted *depends* upon the *price,* covering the *costs of production; and that price* depends upon the relation between the
*supply* and demand, *then,* must that *price* be governed by
these costs of production, because if that *price* be not adequate,
the relation between *supply* and demand is altered, and the
*price* is necessarily affected. After all, I confess, it appears to
me little more than a dispute about terms, a different mode
of stating the same question; and I am at a loss to know why
he considers these points, "as two systems, having an essentially different origin, and requiring to be carefully distinguished."[3]—No doubt, Mr. Malthus's high reputation,
his long devotion to these subjects, entitle his opinions to
very mature consideration; but, if he be correct in this view,
I do not think he has succeeded in making his reader
acquainted with the foundation of his arguments, at least he
has not succeeded in satisfying or convincing me.—Nobody
disputes that the prices are affected *immediately* by the relations between supply and demand, and he has not shewn,

[1] *Principles of Political Economy.*  [3] Above, II, 44.
[2] Above, II, 49.

that they do not *ultimately* depend upon the cost of production. Adam Smith himself says "that the natural price is, as it were, the *central* price to which the prices of all commodities are continually gravitating."[1]

When is Parliament likely to rise—I suppose you are a fixture in London till that event takes place. Has any account been yet laid before the House of the amount of the Savings Banks Funds? I want to know what has been the encrease. Notwithstanding the difficulties of the times our accumulation goes on here; and I am happy to say, that our poor rates are diminishing.

I am amused to observe the incessant activity of our friend Hume in Parliament. No subject whatever escapes his notice. He is a compleat Ferret; and must be abominated by those Rats who are fond of "Cheese Parings and Candles ends!". It is a pitty, however, that he does not apply the principles of *Economy,* which he advocates so strenuously to his own exertions! He would raise considerably the value of these exertions, if he would diminish their supply. But, I fear they must continue in abundance, as the *production* seems to *cost* him nothing!—

Mrs. Trower begs to join with me in kind remembrances to Mrs. Ricardo and your family and believe me My Dear Ricardo

Yrs very truly—<br>HUTCHES TROWER

---

[1] *Wealth of Nations,* Bk. 1, ch. vii; Cannan's ed., vol. 1, p. 60.

## 372. M^cCULLOCH TO RICARDO [1]
[*Reply to 368.—Answered by 375*]

Edinburgh 16 July 1820

My Dear Sir

I trust to your goodness to excuse me for having so
long delayed acknowledging the receipt of your most
valuable and excellent letter of the 13th ulto—It will be of
great use to me in framing the article Value for the Supplement[2]—I am not so presumptuous as to imagine that I shall
be able to fix on a measure of value which will not be liable
to any of those objections which have been urged against
those hitherto employed; but I think that all that is necessary
to set your theory of value in a sufficiently clear point of
view, is to compare commodities produced under different
circumstances with standards also produced under different
circumstances—Such a comparison might be instituted without occasioning any great intricacy of statement, and if it
were properly conducted would exhaust the subject as far as
actually existing standards are concerned, and explain many
of the seemingly anomalous appearances which occur in the
relation of commodities to each other—This is nearly all
I ever intended attempting, and with your assistance I may
perhaps hope to succeed.

I have been thinking of trying my hand on an article on
the subject of Tithes for the Review.[3] Tithes as you have
shewn (for it is to you that I acknowledge myself indebted
for almost all that I know of political economy) are merely
a tax on corn—But they are tax levied in the most revolting
manner, and it will also be necessary to give the reasoning

16 July 1820

---

[1] Addressed: 'David Ricardo Esq
M.P. / Upper Brook Street, / Lon-
don'. Re-directed: '13 Artillery
Place / Brighton'.

MS in *R.P.*
[2] See above, p. 189, n. 2.
[3] See below, p. 222, n. 2.

by which your conclusion has been established a greater degree of extension, and if possible a more popular shape— It would be most gratifying to me to receive any suggestion from you relative to this subject—

I perceive you have been moving for some papers connected with the trade in French wines—This is a subject of which I should like to be master—Do your motions embrace the quantities of French wines imported and consumed for a long period back? and do they distinguish the different rates of duty? Permit me to say that this is what I think they ought to embrace, and not to be restricted to a few years or to the port of London[1]—Mr. Brougham, in his celebrated speech on the state of the Nation in March 1817 refers to a petition presented by Mr. Sharpe as containing an accurate history of the wine trade[2]—I have never been able to obtain a copy of this petition; and if I might use so much freedom I would beg you would have the goodness to send me, if it can be easily procured, a copy of it, along with the papers you have moved for, and whatever brief remarks may be necessary to make me understand them—

The discussions about the Queen, and still more the discussions about the Professorship of Moral Philosophy have for the last five or six weeks made a complete breach in my studies—However one of these interruptions will speedily be removed, and as I presume by the election of Wilson— He is as thorough a knave as is to be found in the country, but he is connected with the son in law of Sir Walter Scott who has got Lord Melville to interfere in his behalf, and that I suppose will be enough—Almost all the respectable part of

---

[1] See below, p. 214, n. 1.
[2] The petition of the importers of wine, mentioned by Brougham on 13 March 1817, had been presented to the House of Commons by Richard Sharp on 25 February the same year; see *Hansard*, XXXV, 639 ff. and 1034, and *Journals of the House of Commons*, vol. LXXXII, p. 107.

the Tory party have protested against this most disgusting of all disgusting jokes—Wilson, I know for certain, once dined at Mr. Jeffreys country house, and he very soon after published a most false and offensive account of what took place at the table of his accomplished host, and even ridiculed Mrs. Jeffrey!—Yet this is the most venial of a thousand other offences of which this protegé of ministers has been guilty— I have to apologise for obtruding this on your attention; but I am sure you cannot but be indignant at this vile attempt to degrade the most efficient Seminary in the kingdom[1]—I am with the greatest affection and esteem

16 July 1820

Yours most faithfully<br>J. R. M<sup>c</sup>CULLOCH

Have the goodness in future to address me at
*No 10 Buccleūgh Place*

---

[1] In the end, John Wilson was elected. M<sup>c</sup>Culloch, who had a personal feud with Wilson (see below, IX, 205), conducted a vigorous campaign against him in the *Scotsman;* and after the election J. G. Lockhart, the son-in-law of Scott, celebrated the success of his friend with a poem ('The Testimonium', in *Blackwood's Magazine,* July 1820) in which he lavished abuse on 'The Galovegian Stot (I mean Macculloch)'. The Professorship combined the subjects of Moral Philosophy and Political Economy, and when in 1825 M<sup>c</sup>Culloch's friends proposed to establish for him a Chair of Political Economy at Edinburgh, Wilson succeeded in defeating the project by appealing to Government for protection of his vested interest. On that occasion Wilson, under the pseudonym of 'Mordecai Mullion, Private Secretary to Christopher North', issued *Some Illustrations of Mr. M<sup>c</sup>Culloch's Principles of Political Economy,* Edinburgh, Blackwood, 1826, in which he exposed M<sup>c</sup>Culloch's practice of reprinting over and over again the same articles, representing them as fresh ones, in the *Scotsman,* in the *Edinburgh Review,* in the *Supplement to the Encyclopaedia Britannica* and in his books. However, as Prof. Ferrier writes, 'in after life Professor Wilson and Mr M<sup>c</sup>Culloch were thoroughly reconciled.' (See A. Lang, *Life of Lockhart,* 1897, vol. 1, pp. 239–43; Mrs Gordon, 'Christopher North', *A Memoir of John Wilson,* 1879, p. 297 ff.; J. Wilson, *Works,* ed. Ferrier, 1855, vol. 1, p. 140, n.)

## 373. RICARDO TO TROWER [1]
*[Reply to 371.—Answered by 376]*

Brighton 21 July 1820

My dear Trower

I have been here above a week, and ought, before this time, to have acknowledged the receipt of your kind letter of the 5ᵗʰ inst! All business of consequence had been dispatched in the House of Commons before I quitted London, and as my family had left me alone, in my large house, I was anxious to join them in this place, which they had chosen for their residence for a few weeks, previous to our journey into Gloucestershire. They are much more partial to Brighton than I am, and are much more persuaded also of the beneficial effects of sea air to all persons, and to all constitutions, than I ever shall be—I should have preferred going straight to Gatcomb as soon as I could quit London. It does not appear likely that public business will allow me to stay long in Gloucestershire this year. The enquiry into the charge against the Queen, will, no doubt, make a very early meeting of the House of Commons necessary, and when we meet we shall not I think be very soon discharged from our attendance. I am sorry that this unfortunate business was not settled without an appeal to Parliament. Under all the circumstances of the case I do not think that ministers were justified in making it an affair of state. It can have no other effect but to bring royalty itself into disgrace, and to weaken the attachment of the people to monarchical government. If these proceedings should lead to a change of ministers I am very far from expecting that the proceedings of the whigs when in administration will be essentially different from those of

---

[1] Addressed: 'Hutches Trower Esqʳ Unsted Wood Godalming'. MS at University College, London.—*Letters to Trower,* XXXVIII.

the men they will displace—something they must do to preserve an appearance of consistency, but it will be very little indeed—they are in their hearts as little friendly to any real reform as the tories.

You say more than I deserve in my praise for asserting the true principles of Political Economy in my place in Parliament. I feel that I am quite unequal to do what a better speaker might do, and I am more than usually daunted by observing that on every point where an abuse is to be got rid of there are such powerful interests to oppose, who never fail of making the worse appear the better reason.

I have not met with many persons who have yet read Malthus' book. I am pleased however with the observations you make on what he has said respecting my doctrine, of price, being ultimately regulated by cost of production. By the very definition of natural price, it is wholly dependent on cost of production, and has nothing to do with demand and supply. The terms on which a commodity can be produced, so as to remunerate the producer, will remain the same altho' the demand should be for 5 times the quantity produced. We all acknowledge the effect of such a demand on market price.

Mr. Malthus pays me a very unmerited compliment at the end of his chapter on the rent of land,[1] but he is very unjust to me in his comments on my doctrine of rent and profit, in that same chapter. He represents me as holding the landlords up to reproach, because I have said that their interests are opposed to those of the rest of the community, and that the rise of their rents are at the expence of the gains of the other classes. The whole tenor of my book shews how I mean to apply those observations. I have said that the community would not benefit if the landlords gave up all their rent—

---

[1] Above, II, 222–3.

such a sacrifice would not make corn cheaper, but would only benefit the farmers.—Does not this shew that I do not consider landlords as enemies to the public good? They are in possession of machines of various productive powers, and it is their interest that the least productive machine should be called into action—such is not the interest of the public—*they* must desire to employ the foreign greater productive machine rather than the English less productive one. Mr. M. charges me too with denying the benefits of improvements in Agriculture to Landlords. I do not acknowledge the justice of this charge, I have more than once said, what is obvious, that they must ultimately benefit by the land becoming more productive. Perhaps I have not expressed myself so strongly on this point as I ought to have done, but it was evident that I acknowledged the principle. I refer you to the last Chap. of my book, and particularly to the paragraph beginning "Another cause of the rise of rent, according to Mr. Malthus &c. &c.,"[1] for the truth of my assertion.

Pray look at Page 237 of Mr. M's book[2] and you will see an instance of a great (unintentional I am sure) misrepresentation of an adversary's argument. I contend for free trade in corn on the ground that while trade is free, and corn cheap, profits will not fall however great be the accumulation of capital. If you confine yourself to the resources of your own soil, I say, rent will in time absorb the greatest part of that produce which remains after paying wages, and consequently profits will be low. Not only individual profits but the aggregate amount of profits will be diminished, notwithstanding an increase of capital. The whole net produce will be increased, but less will be enjoyed by capitalists (see Chap. on Profits, Pages 128–129 2$^{\text{d}}$ edition[3]). Now how does Mr. M

---

[1] Above, I, 412.
[2] Above, II, 221–2.
[3] Above, I, 122–4.

apply my argument? Do not let cheap corn be imported, says he, because if you do you will lose a part of that portion of your surplus produce which now appears in the form of rent. I agree that this would be the consequence, but then it is known that I contend this would be more than compensated by increased profits, but Mr. M was my authority for the very opposite conclusion: you will have no compensation in increased profits, he says, and I appeal to Mr. Ricardo for the correctness of this opinion, who has admitted that not only each individual capital in the progress of society will yield a continually diminishing revenue, but the whole amount of the revenue derived from profits will be diminished. I admit it! yes I do, but in the case of high rents and a high price of corn,—not in the opposite case to which he applies it of low rents, and a low price of corn.

Pray look to Section 6—Page 192 and you will observe that all the points on which my theory is raised are admitted. There are only 2 causes for a high[1] price of corn. A fall in the value of money. An increase in the quantity of labour and capital necessary to produce corn. After this admission is it not wonderful that any thing should be said in *favor* of a rise in what Mr. M calls real rent when it is[2] caused by an increase in the quantity of labour and capital necessary to produce corn? and yet this I consider to be Mr. M's argument, for according to him high rent is in itself a good, independently of its being a sign of wealth and power. Is it not a good to obtain all your productions by the least sacrifice of labour and capital? I could fill sheet after sheet with what appears to me to be false reasoning and inconsistencies in this book, but I will spare you.

You have no doubt observed that Hume has undergone

---

[1] 'relative' is del. here.

[2] 'when it is' replaces 'which can only be'.

the ordeal of an election committee with success.[1] The ministers have not a more formidable opponent. He never speaks without a formidable array of figures to back his assertions, and he pores over documents with persevering zeal and attention, which most other men fly from with disgust and terror. His manner of speaking is I think improved—he is however generally too diffuse—speaks too often—and sometimes wastes his own strength, and his hearers patience, on matters too trifling for notice.—He justifies this indeed by saying that he contends for sound principles, which are as much outraged by an unjust expenditure of a few hundred pounds, as of a million. He is I think a most useful member of parliament,—always at his post and governed I believe by an ardent desire to be useful to his country.

I hope Mrs. Trower and your girls are well. Mrs. Ricardo joins me in kind remembrances to them.—

Believe me ever My dear Trower

Very truly Y<sup>rs</sup>

DAVID RICARDO

I have seen no account of the Savings Bank Fund on the table of the House, but I believe one is ordered to be presented

## 374. RICARDO TO MILL[2]

Brighton 27 July 1820

My dear Sir

I hope that Mrs. Mill is, before this, relieved from her anxiety and apprehension, and is safe in bed with a healthy

---

[1] A petition against the return of Joseph Hume for the Aberdeen District of Burghs had failed. (*The Times*, 13 July 1820.)

[2] Addressed: 'James Mill Esq<sup>re</sup> / Examiner's Office / East India House / London'.
MS in Mill-Ricardo papers.

and thriving infant.[1] The week or two previous to final relief, on these occasions, are generally the most unpleasant, both to the lady and her husband, particularly if the time be protracted beyond the period looked for. We shall be very glad to see you on friday se'nnight—there are coaches go from London at all hours, and if you cannot get away at 10 oClock in the morning, you will find a very expeditious coach leaving the Spread Eagle at 3 oClock.

I have read with great pleasure the article on Government which you have written for the next volume of the Encyclopedia—I think it excellent, and well calculated to serve the good cause. It is written in the true philosophic temper— the best reasons are given for the propositions advanced, and they are made clear, and convincing. There is no attack in it on other people for their opinions, no calling of names, but a correct, a consistent and clear development of your own views. I like it very much indeed. I dare say you had good reasons for not explaining the influence of public opinion on government, but as it is one of the checks, and a most powerful one in such a government as ours, I should have expected that you would have noticed it. I think you did right in not entering into the consideration of the securities for a good election, even after the right of suffrage is given to the people generally: it would have given the article too much the appearance of an essay on Reform of Parliament which it was perhaps desirable to avoid. That is a part of the subject so important however that I hope you will take some opportunity of writing upon it, and of advancing all the powerful arguments by which it may be supported. I have not sent you the article back—I wish to read it again, and can give it you when we meet here. If you want it before, send me a line, and it shall be returned immediately.—

---

[1] Henry, the Mills' seventh child, was born this year.

I have had no books here but Malthus's and my own.
I am reading the former with great attention, and noting the
passages which I think deserving of comment. They are
more numerous than I expected. If I were to answer every
paragraph, containing what, I think, an erroneous view of
the subject on which the book treats, I should write a thicker
volume than his own. The attack on Say's and your doctrine
of accumulation, is supported by the weakest arguments,
inconsistent with many of his own declared opinions, and
so palpably fallacious that one's wonder is he could have
deliberately written it.—

I have by no means given up my intention of going into
Gloucestershire—I hope to be there very soon after your
visit to Brighton, and shall expect you to follow me within
a very moderate time. My first destination will be to
Gloucester, where the Assizes will be held on the 9$^{th}$. I hope
you will be able to come to us on the 16$^{th}$. I have so far
altered my plan that I shall not return to London, but shall
go direct from this place. Be so good as to let Mr. Bentham
and Mr. Place know of this. If the agreement[1] is ready for my
signature you will perhaps bring it with you—my presence
in town for any purpose connected with this agreement
cannot be necessary. Mrs. Ricardo and the family will all go
back to London, and will from thence proceed to Gatcomb.

Altho' the house of Commons will meet on the 21 Aug$^{t}$
I think it very improbable that they will proceed to business
before October or November. It is impossible that the
Lords should have passed the bill before that time. If you
have any reason to think otherwise, or have heard any good
opinion on that subject, pray let me know it, as in that case
I should stop the preparations which are now in course for
our removal to Gatcomb.

[1] See above, p. 198, n. 3.

My family have benefited by the air of this place, particularly Mrs. Clutterbuck, who was much of an invalid when
she first [came][1] here. They all desire to be most kindly
remembered to you. Mrs. Osman is the bravest sailor of the
party, she never loses her good looks in the most boisterous
weather, while all about her think their last hour arrived.
The men suffer much more than the ladies.—

Ever truly Y<sup>rs</sup>

DAVID RICARDO

Lord Folkestone is here—I lent him your paper to read
as I know him to be a good reformer. On returning it he
spoke very much in its praise—said it was impossible not to
agree with the conclusion—but he lamented that the argument was not more dilated. The commencement and the end
he thought a little too abrupt.

## 375. RICARDO TO M<sup>c</sup>CULLOCH [2]
### [*Reply to 372.—Answered by 377*]

Brighton 2 Aug 1820

My dear Sir

I have been for sometime in this place enjoying the sea
breezes. My own inclination would have led me into the
more retired situation of my own house in Gloucestershire,
but my family were very desirous of a few weeks residence
here, and I was induced to comply with their wishes. I shall
be at Gloucester on Wednesday, and at Gatcomb Park in a
very short time after. This is the proper place for me to
request you to give directions to have the Scotsman sent
to me at Minchinhampton, and it is also the place to ask
you to direct the agent of the paper, in London, to receive

---

[1] Covered by seal.

[2] MS in British Museum.—*Letters
to M<sup>c</sup>Culloch*, XVI.

from my brother, and me, our respective subscriptions, which I understand from him they now will not do without instructions.

It will be some time before your article on value can appear in the Supp.$^t$ of the Encyclop. Brit. I shall be very eager to see it, for I am sure you will divest the subject of value of some of the clouds in which it is at present enveloped. I am glad too that the subject of Tithes has engaged your attention. You will not fail to make the nature of this tax, on which much error and misapprehension prevail, well understood. Nothing occurs to me to say upon it at present, which can have the least claim to your attention.

The papers which I moved for respecting the duties on French and other wines I have directed to be sent to you. There is another set not yet printed which will continue the information till July last, they shall be sent to you also.[1] I moved for them at the request of a committee of the trade, who expected that they would convey information on which they might found a petition which they would have requested me to present, but I understand that the facts which these papers disclose are not exactly such as they expected, and therefore they have abandoned their intention of presenting a petition. I believe that they contain the information you wish to have. I hope you will find them useful. When I wrote to the vote office to request Mr. Mitchell to send the papers to you I mentioned the petition to which you refer presented by Mr. Sharp and begged if they had it to forward it to you. I fear it is of too old a date to be in the Vote Office.

---

[1] 'Accounts of the Number of Gallons of Foreign Wines, distinguishing French from other Wines', ordered to be printed 29 June 1820, in *Parliamentary Papers,* 1820, vol. XII, pp. 201–3; the sequel, ordered to be printed 5 July 1820, *ib.* pp. 208–10. The quantity, the amount of duty paid and the amount drawn back on exportation are given for each year from 1787.

I was sorry to see that Mr. Wilson was elected to the Professorship of Moral Philosophy, after all the meritorious exertions you had made to shew how improper a person he was for so dignified a situation. The world is getting better than it was but, I fear we are yet at a great distance from that time when merit will be considered as the best claim to such important offices.

Since I have been here I have been giving a second reading to Mr. Malthus' book. I am even less pleased with it than I was at first. There is hardly a page which does not contain some fallacy. He dwells incessantly on the importance of giving increased value to commodities, which he thinks of much more consequence than securing an abundant supply of them. He is always for sacrificing the interest of the consumer to the interest of the merchant. His increased profits are of the greatest moment, altho' they may be partial, and really derived from a partial monopoly. To be consistent he ought to be friendly to all kinds of monopolies, for there can be no doubt that these would benefit merchants and dealers at the expence of consumers, and would give a high value to commodities. If you increase the quantity of commodities by means of facility of production (he says) you do an injury to society, unless they give as much or a greater employment to labour.[1] This is clearly not true, for if with less labour you can obtain the same quantity of commodities, one of two things must happen, either you will give employment to the same or a greater number of people, and still further increase your means of enjoyment, or you will by the payment of the same or even less wages in money enable the employed to command more commodities, and if they prefer indolence to the rewards of labour they may with less labour command the same quantity of enjoyments. How an abundance of

---

[1] Above, II, 350 ff.

productions can lead to a less demand for labour I cannot make out. Mr. M appears to me to confound two things which ought ever to be kept very distinct. A man may produce commodities the return for which may not repay the value of the labour that has been bestowed on them. Such commodities would be cheap, and we should say they were abundant, but their cheapness would be attended with this effect—the national capital would be diminished by their production. But when commodities are produced in abundance, and at a cheap price, from facility of production, and really more than replace the capital employed on them, it is an unmixed benefit, and is essentially different from the other case. That the first sometimes happens cannot be denied, but it is always the effect of miscalculation. It may take place with respect to one, or to a thousand commodities, but cannot at once happen to all.

Mr. Malthus speaks of an indisposition to consume being very common—I say it never exists any where, not even in South America to which he has so triumphantly alluded.[1] In South America there is no indisposition to consume, the indisposition is to produce. To entitle a man to consume there as well as elsewhere he must produce, but he prefers indolence to the gratification which the commodity he would demand would give him, and this Mr. Malthus calls an indisposition to consume, and makes him deny the proposition that effective demand depends upon production. If one man were industrious, and all others idle, it is possible that he might produce commodities which no other person might have the means of buying, but what was his object in producing them—he can have but two, either to consume them himself, or to exchange them with others for the objects which he wishes to consume. If he does the last, when there

[1] Above, II, 337.

are no others to give him the objects he wants, he is guilty of miscalculation—he should have produced directly the objects he wants. How then can the accumulation of capital be mischievous? It may be under certain circumstances without benefit to the capitalist, and then it will be proportionally more beneficial to the labourer. Unless it be beneficial to the capitalist it will cease; on that point we are all agreed, but how can it be said to be prejudicial to the whole community, and to be as injurious to the labourers as it is to their employers? This appears to me as great an absurdity as to say that twice 2 do not make four.

Believe me to be with great regard

Very truly Y$^{rs}$

DAVID RICARDO

## 376. TROWER TO RICARDO [1]
### [*Reply to 373—Answered by 380*]

Unsted Wood—Godalming
Aug. 13. 1820—

My Dear Ricardo

Many thanks for your last kind letter. Perhaps you are not aware, that I still am, and have been for more than 5 weeks, a prisoner on the Sopha. I, unfortunately, violently dislocated my knee, in getting over a gate, and although I dont suffer from *pain,* I fear I shall, for some time, have to suffer from confinement. I cannot blame myself for any boyish trick, not suited to my *staid* time of life, as I was jumping down very quietly from the top of a field gate, on which I had been sitting. Thus circumstanced, I look to my *Library* for my principal resource, and the Volumes of Ricardo and Malthus occupy no small portion of my time,

---

[1] Addressed: 'To / David Ricardo Esqr. / M.P. / Upper Brook Street— / Grosvenor Square'.—MS in *R.P.*

and my thoughts. No doubt, Malthus' Book is a very elaborate performance, and must have occasioned him much labor. As far as I have *hitherto* advanced in his work I perfectly agree with you in thinking, that he has left all your main and substantial points untouched. His objections appear to me as applying to the *qualification* of your principles, and not to the *principles themselves.* On the question of Rent I conceive, that even, *by his own shewing,* he has surrendered the point in dispute. He admits there may be some land which pays only wages and profit, and that the price of corn must be limited by the cost on the worst land.—That *peculiar quality* in the land, about which he says so much, and which he considers the source of *Rent;* is nothing more than that *surplus produce,* which both in *raw produce* and *manufactures* is the *source of profit.* No doubt, if there were no surplus there would be no *rent,* but it does not, on that account follow, that this *positive* surplus will *produce rent.*

I agree with you in thinking, that much false reasoning, and many inconsistencies, are to be found in his pages. Have the goodness to turn to page 125. where he says, that "when labor commands the smallest quantity of food it commands the greatest quantity of other commodities," &. &. and to page 128. where he says—"at a period when a given quantity of *corn* will command the *greatest quantity* of *necessaries* and a given quantity of *labor* will always command the *smallest quantity of such objects*" &. Surely these cant both be true? Labor commands the smallest quantity of food and the greatest quantity of necessaries in *an advanced state of society,* where Corn is of high value and necessaries of low value; therefore, I take the position in page 125 to be *true.* But, when *Corn* can command the *greatest* quantity of *necessaries,* its exchangeable value in relation to *necessaries* must be high.

And when the value of Corn is *high* in comparison with necessaries, although the wages of labor may be such as to enable the laborer to obtain a small supply of *Corn*, with that portion of his wages, which he allots to *food*, yet they will enable him to obtain an *ample* supply of *necessaries* with *that portion* which he allots to that purpose.

In page 145. The inferences he draws from the supposed diminution of $\frac{1}{2}$ of the fertility of the land appear to me incorrect. His object seems to be to shew, that the largest portion of the lands would be thrown out of cultivation, *not in consequence of the diminished demand by the destruction of the consumers,* but because the quantity of produce being only half of what was before obtained by the same labor and capital it could not pay the costs of production. But surely in such a deplorable case wretched as must be the condition of the survivors the price of produce required for the people would be sufficient to cover the costs of production—it *must be carried up to that pitch,* be it what might. It might be such as to leave no surplus for profit, and then none but cultivators could exist, and the quantity of land cultivated, in *proportion* to the number of the people would be double what it was before.

I have not yet made much progress in Malthus' Book, but I shall continue my enquiries in which I feel much interest.

In page 566. of the first Edition of your Book[1] you say, "In the natural course of things the *Demand* for all Commodities *precedes their Supply,*" and on page 560[2] you say "It is not the abundance of necessaries which raises up Demanders but the *abundance of demanders* which raises up necessaries" —

Is this true? I doubt it. Is not population limited by Capital? and do not *necessaries* constitute a *part of Capital?*

[1] Above, I, 409.    [2] Above, I, 405, n. 2.

Must not some time elapse before the fruits of labor are gathered? And during that *interval* must there not be a *preexisting supply* to satisfy the laborers wants? Does not an *encrease of capital occasion* a *demand* for labor? And is not a *demand* for labor, the same thing as a *supply* of necessaries? Are not *capital* and *labor* equivalent to *supply* and *demand*? How could labor be demanded, if the demander had not, in his possession, or within his command, a supply of necessaries to satisfy the immediate and indispensable wants of the laborers? Again, what are the *profits* of Capital but a surplus of commodities, over and above the wants of the community? But, a surplus of commodities, is the same thing as an *abundance,* and in proportion to the amount of that *abundance* is the rate of profit? No doubt there is an action, and a reaction of capital and labor maintained constantly in every progressive Country; but how could these operations have *commenced* if there had not been a *previous supply of necessaries?* What would have become of our illustrious *first parent* if *he* had not been sent into a World *provided* with necessaries suited to his condition; or in other words, if *supply had not preceded demand!*

I venture to throw out these observations for your consideration. They have had considerable influence upon my opinion on the point in question, and I should be glad to know what you have to say to them.

When do you come up to the *horrible* investigation? I am not without hopes it may yet be avoided. No doubt, the circumstances of the case are such as to *warrant enquiry;* but, the object is not of such importance as to render it expedient to hazard the *peace* of the Country in prosecuting it. And, the opinion of so large a portion of the public has been so strongly expressed, that it is *doubtful* what effect might be produced by altogether disregarding it. The address of Lord

J. Russell will of course have *no effect.* The arguments it contains have long been before the public; but I should have expected from a Noble Lord, from a Senator, and above all, from an *author,* that the materials would have [been] better arranged, and more happily concocted. But the letter and address are both written in a very careless and slovenly manner, and are not at all suited to the important occasion which called them forth[1]—

There is a very good reply to them in the Chronicle signed an Old Whig. Which however affords proof that the New Whigs think they spy a vista view of Downing Street through the Columns of Addressers who are constantly marching to the Queens House!—

Adieu My Dear Ricardo pray make our united kind Compliments to Mrs. Ricardo and your family and believe me

Yrs very sincerely

HUTCHES TROWER.

I have referred to the passages of Malthus quoted in your letter and agree with you in what you say upon them.

Pray tell me, have you made any alterations in the 2 edition of your Book, is it necessary to enable me to pursue my examination of the points in dispute between you and Malthus.

[1] Lord John Russell's open letter to Wilberforce, and his proposed petition to the King against the prosecution of the Queen had appeared in the newspapers. (*Scotsman,* 12 Aug. 1820.)

### 377. MᶜCULLOCH TO RICARDO [1]
[*Reply to 375.—Answered by* 381]

Edinburgh, 10 Buccleugh Place
24 August 1820

My Dear Sir

24 Aug. 1820
      I return you my best thanks for your excellent letter of
the 2nd inst—The different communications with which you
have favoured me relative to Mr. Malthus late work are not
only extremely valuable as criticisms on that publication, but
as developing principles and opening up views of the greatest
importance—They will be of very great use to me in my
future inquiries—

      I send you herewith the sheets of my article on Tithes[2]—
You will I hope excuse me for having done so—I know it
contains nothing of which you were not previously aware;
but I am anxious that you should see all my labours, however unimportant, and I thought you would not be displeased
to see a farther practical application of those principles which
you have so successfully and admirably developed—In
treating this subject I was a good deal fettered—I should like
to have handled the clergy a little more roughly; but the
circulation of the Review in England and their very great
influence rendered a considerable degree of *menagement* quite
indispensable—However if the public attention could be
excited to a proper consideration of the subject of Tithes,
a great deal of good would be effected; and an improvement
in one branch of the Church establishment might pave the
way for it in another—

      I have some intention of preparing an article either for the
Supplement to the E.B. or the Review on the National

---

[1] MS in *R.P.*                    [2] *Edinburgh Review,* Aug. 1820,
                                     Art. III.

Debt[1]—In this article I should endeavour to give an outline and a criticism of the different plans which have been proposed for ridding the country of this enormous load. Of course I would have to review that which you have patronised—I think I am pretty well acquainted with the advantages which might be expected to result from its adoption, and also with the difficulties which would undoubtedly attend any attempt to carry it into effect— However if you could command as much leisure, I should be much gratified by your favouring me with your remarks on some of the most popular and strongest objections which have been made to it—

I hope you receive the Scotsman regularly at Minchinhampton—I shall order receipts for your subscription and that of Mr. Ralph, to be sent to you when you return to London—I have not heard from Mr. Ralph for a very long time—I hope he has not forgot me altogether, and I shall feel much obliged if you will present him with my compts, and assure him that I shall not be long in replying to his next letter to me—

The public here are very much interested in the case of the Queen—It is a revolting and a disgusting business; whether she be innocent or guilty is a matter of very inferior consideration—The evil consists in the abominable and infamous nature of the inquiry—

I shall expect to hear from you at your convenience and with every sentiment of esteem and regard I remain

My Dear Sir

Yours most faithfully

J. R. M^cCULLOCH

[1] The article did not appear in the *Supplement to the Encyclopaedia Britannica;* see *Edinburgh Review,* Oct. 1823, Art. I, 'Funding System—British Finances' and cp. below, p. 238, n. 1.

## 378. MALTHUS TO RICARDO [1]

*[Answered by 379]*

E I Coll August 28th 1820.

My dear Ricardo,

I dont know whether this will find you at Brighton, but I write at a venture. Our vacation was rather longer than usual, but we have been returned now some little time, and I have been constantly intending to write.

We staid about five weeks at Paris, and passed our time very agreeably. I saw most of the principal people whom I wished to see, and got some insight into the state of France, which is curious, but the subject is too large to enter upon now.

I found some persons who had read your work, but they did not appear to me to understand it, and were not on the whole favourable. [2] From this general remark however I should except the Duc de Broglie who seemed inclined to adopt your views. He is one of the *Doctrinaires* who are considered as very theoretical both in Politics and Political Economy. Monsr. Garnier the Translator of Adam Smith [3] attacked you violently, though it appeared to me that he agreed with you in many essential points, perhaps without

---

[1] Addressed: 'D. Ricardo Esqr MP. / West Cliff. / Brighton'. Received by Ricardo at Gatcomb; see opening of next letter.
MS in *R.P.*

[2] One of these was the widow of Dupont de Nemours, the Physiocrat, who in a letter to Sismondi, 6 Nov. 1820, acknowledging the latter's article against the Ricardo school (see below, p. 376, n. 2) wrote: 'Je vous scais bien bon gré mon bien cher ami d'avoir si bien répondu a ce *Ricardo* je vous admire de l'avoir fait avec tant de

modération car les déraisonnemens de cet auteur sont faits pour impatienter. Je suis bien charmée que vous ayez rendu justice a notre bon Malthus. Je dis *notre* parceque pendant son séjour a Paris il m'a donné a lire son dernier ouvrage en anglais dans lequel il bat aussi Ricardo.' (MS in Biblioteca Comunale, Pescia, Tuscany.)

[3] Germain Garnier (1754–1821); his translation of Adam Smith, in 5 vols., was published in 1805.

knowing it. He thinks of publishing a new edition of Adam 28 Aug. 1820 Smith with a volume of notes to refute all the modern writers who have differed from him.

I took a copy of my book for Mr. Say; but he had already got it, and answered that part of it which refers to him. He had sent his manuscript[1] to the printer, but it had not come out before we came away. He had sent me his last edition,[2] but it never reached me; and he said it was owing to my not having seen it that I made the remarks which he has answerd; but upon looking at the edition I found there was little or no difference in the Chapter Des Debouchés.

Generally speaking the French read but little political economy. There is such a prejudice against it in the Government that Mr. Say was induced actually to change the denomination of the lectures he is about to give, and substitute the term *industrielle* for *Politique*.[3] He says however that the younger part of the society is making a considerable progress. The bookseller who undertook the translation of your work[4] told me that he had sold 900 copies, which under all the circumstances is I think a favourable report. My book was translating.[5] I saw a few sheets, and fear it will not be very well done. Few, of course, had read it. Those who had, agreed with me about value, and in the main; but doubted a little about my doctrine respecting accumulation. It is indeed not likely to apply much to France, on account of the great division of landed property. The check to production in France under its actual system will be chiefly want of power, not want of demand. But the more I see, and the more I

---

[1] *Lettres à M. Malthus;* see below, p. 227, n. 1.
[2] *Traité d'Economie politique,* 4th ed., 1819.
[3] Cp. below, p. 291, n. 2.
[4] J.-P. Aillaud; see above, VII, 361, n. 1.

[5] *Principes d'Economie politique, considérés sous le rapport de leur application pratique,* 'par M. T. R. Malthus,...traduits de l'anglais par M. F. S. Constancio', Paris, J.-P. Aillaud, 1820, 2 vols.

28 Aug. 1820 think on the subject, the more I feel convinced, that the doctrine I have laid down on the immediate causes of the progress of wealth is essentially just, and that the actual phenomena in society cannot be accounted for without it. I have seen nothing since my return. Pray tell me if you know of anything that has been written against me? Has Torrens gone on in the Traveller?[1] What says Maculloch on the subjects of value?

What do you think of this strange trial? and how are we to get out of the difficulty.

Mrs. Malthus joins with me in kind regards to Mrs. Ricardo who we hope is well with all your family. I am going into Lincolnshire this evening but shall be back in less than a week.

Ever truly Yours

T R MALTHUS.

## 379. RICARDO TO MALTHUS[2]
[*Reply to 378.—Answered by 388*]

Gatcomb Park
Sept.r 4—1820

My dear Malthus.

4 Sept. 1820 I was very desirous of hearing from you and was on the point of telling you so when your letter reached me from Brighton. Mr. Hump.y Austin a neighbour of mine told me he saw you at Paris, and I had heard of your safe arrival in England. I am quite pleased to hear that your journey has been agreeable to you; it could not fail to be so when it gave you the opportunity of seeing and conversing with the principal literary men of France, and of hearing their opinions on

[1] Cp. above, p. 185
[2] Addressed: 'Rev.d T. R. Malthus / East India College / Hertford'.

MS at Albury.—*Letters to Malthus*, LXXII.

4 Sept. 1820

the present state of that important country. I hope in that quarter there will be no interruption of the present order of things for sometime to come, but if they do make a move-ment I trust it will be for the purpose of securing more effectually the liberty of the people, by perfecting as far as human means can perfect the representative system. There is nothing on which the happiness of the great body of the people so much depends.

I did not expect that I had so many readers in France as the number of copies of the French translation which you tell me have been sold would seem to imply. I am not sur-prised that you found few who understood my theory cor-rectly, and still fewer who were disposed to agree with me. I have not yet succeeded in making many converts in my own country, but I do not despair of seeing the number in-crease—the few I have are of the proper description, and do not want zeal for the propagation of the true faith.

I have seen Say's letters to you[1]; it appears to me that he has said a great deal for the right cause, but not all that could be said. In one point I think he falls into the same error as Torrens in his article in the Edin. Rev.[2] They both appear to think that stagnation in commerce arises from a counter set of commodities not being produced with which the commodities on sale are to be purchased, and they seem to infer that the evil will not be removed till such other com-modities are in the market. But surely the true remedy is in regulating future production,—if there is a glut of one com-modity produce less of that and more of another but do not

---

[1] *Lettres à M. Malthus, sur différens sujets d'économie politique, notamment sur les causes de la stagnation générale du commerce,* par Jean-Baptiste Say, Paris, Bossange, 1820.

[2] Oct. 1819 (see above, p. 159, n. 2). In Torrens's article the 'error' occurs on p. 471 ff. In Say's *Lettres*, p. 5, *et passim.*

let the glut continue till the purchaser chuses to produce the commodity which is more wanted. I am not convinced by any thing Say says of me—he does not understand me, and is frequently at variance with himself when value is the subject he treats of. In his fourth edition[1] 2 Vol Page 36 he says every thing falls in value, as the quantity is increased, by facility of production. Now suppose that you have to pay for what he calls "services productifs" in these commodities which have so fallen in value, will you give the same value if you give for them the same quantity of commodities as before? certainly not, according to his own admission, and yet he maintains page 33 that productive services have not varied if they receive the same quantity of a commodity, notwithstanding the cost of production of that commodity may have fallen from 40 to 30 francs p.$^r$ ell. He has two opposite notions about value, and I am sure to be wrong if I differ with either of them.[2]

I am sorry that the Government of France is prejudiced against Political Economy. Whatever differences of opinion may exist amongst writers on that science, they are nevertheless agreed upon many important principles, which are proved to demonstration. By an adherence to these, Governments cannot fail to promote the welfare of the people who are submitted to their sway. What more clear than the advantages which flow from freedom of trade, or than the evils resulting from holding out any peculiar encouragement to population?—

I have been reading your book a second time with great attention but my difference with you remains as firmly rooted as ever. Some of the objections you make to me are merely verbal, no principle is involved in them—the great and lead-

[1] *Traité d'Économie politique*, 1819.  [2] Cp. the same criticism above, I, 280 ff.

ing point in which I think you fundamentally wrong is that which Say has attacked in his letters.[1] On this I feel no sort of doubt. With respect to the word value you have defined it one way, I another. We do not appear to mean the same thing and we should first agree what a standard ought to be, and then examine which approaches nearest to an invariable standard the one you propose, or that which I propose.

I have not heard of any thing further having been written against you either by M Culloch or Torrens, nor do I know that they have any thing in contemplation. M'Culloch has written me two letters since I saw you last, he does not say any thing about value and it will probably be a year or two before he can publish any thing on that subject in the Supplement to the Encyclopedia. In the next Review there will be an article of his on Tithes which I have seen—his principles are right but I do not like his remedy for the existing evil.[2]

Mill has been with me here for a fortnight and will stay sometime longer. He has it in contemplation to write a popular work on Political Economy, in which he will explain the principles which he thinks correct in the most familiar way for the use of learners. It is not his intention to notice any person's opinions, or to enter into a controversy on the disputed points.—

I have been looking over my first chapter, with a view to make a few alterations in it before the work goes to another edition. I find my task very difficult, but I hope I shall make my opinions more clear and intelligible. I did intend to defend myself against some of your attacks, but on reflection I think that to do myself justice I must say so much that I should very inconveniently enlarge the size of my book, be-

[1] The point in question was the causes of the general stagnation of trade.

[2] See below, p. 237.

4 Sept. 1820    sides which I should be constantly drawing my readers attention from the [ma]in[1] subject. If I defend myself at all, I
must do it in [some] separate publication.

Respecting the trial of the Queen I am more than ever
convinced of the impolicy and inexpediency of the proceedings which have led to it, and am quite sure that the plea set
up that it is a state question is a false one—it is entered into
merely to gratify the resentment and hostility of one individual who has himself behaved so ill that whatever he may
have to complain of he so fully merits, that no one is bound
to enter into his quarrels or wish for punishment to follow
offences to which his own conduct has been so instrumental.

Mrs. Ricardo unites with me in kind regards to Mrs. Malthus. Gatcomb is very delightful, I wish you and Mrs. Malthus could give us your company here before we go to
London.

Mr. Mill desires to be kindly remembered

Ever Y[r]

DAVID RICARDO

### 380. RICARDO TO TROWER[2]
[*Reply to 376.—Answered by 384*]

I have been here since the 9th of Aug[t]

Gatcomb Park
15 Sep[t]—1820.

My dear Trower

15 Sept. 1820    I learnt with great concern that you had had the misfortune to dislocate your knee. Besides the pain which you
must have endured, it was a cruel grievance to one so fond
of moving about as you are to be confined for so great a
length of time, as you already had been when you wrote, on

---

[1] Covered by seal.

[2] MS at University College, London.—*Letters to Trower*, XXXIX.

the sopha. I hope you were able to resume your accustomed active pursuits before that interesting day to most country gentlemen, the 1ˢᵗ of Septʳ, and that the next account I receive from you will be that you are quite recovered, and looking after your plantations and improvements with the same interest and enjoyment as hertofore.

I have suffered too long a time to elapse without writing to you, but Mr. Mill is partly to blame. He has been staying with me for more than three weeks, and as he is fond of exercise we have taken advantage of the fineness of the weather, and have been pretty constantly on the move. Our last excursion was down the Wye from Ross to Chepstow— From Chepstow we went to Malvern and passed a few days with my son[1] who is settled in that neighbourhood. Mill speaks well of my house and grounds at Gatcomb, but he greatly prefers those of my son. The soil about us is poor, the trees are chiefly beech which grow very luxuriantly, but we have few oaks. In the country where my son lives the soil is good and oaks flourish better than any other tree; the ground too is beautifully diversified. I wish you would come to see me, and let me shew you the various beautiful spot[s] within a moderate circuit of us. We were greatly delighted with the scenery on the Banks of the Wye. Report has not exaggerated its beauty—my expectations were at any rate surpassed. We travelled in a low phaeton which I have lately bought, and to save a few miles in our journey, and also to see some country which we had not before visited, we resolved to cross the Severn in a boat, instead of going over the bridge at Gloucester. When we arrived at the Ferry, opposite Newnham, it was low water, and by the direction of the boatman I drove first over the dry sand, and then into the water alongside the boat which was ready to receive us.

---

[1] Osman, who was now living at Bromesberrow Place.

I proceeded with perfect safety till I got within 3 or 4 feet of the boat, when the carriage began to sink in the sand, and the horses to plunge violently in their efforts to extricate themselves from the place where they also were sinking. The men became greatly alarmed at our awkward situation, in a moment half a dozen of them, besides my servant, were in the water, and if they had not united their strength to support us on the side which was sinking fastest, Mr. Mill, two young ladies[1] who were behind, and myself, would have been all overturned into the water. The first object was to disengage the horses from the carriage, the next to carry us into the boat. The poor horses were so exhausted with their struggles that they lay on the ground with their heads just above water without making any further effort to get out and for a short time I thought I should lose them both. At length however they got on their legs, and reached firmer ground, but it was nearly an hour before the carriage was lifted up from the sand in which it had sunk. By the aid of levers and the united strength of the men this was at last effected. With the utmost difficulty the horses were made to get into the boat. The carriage was put in after them, and we all at length landed in safety at Newnham, with the very slightest damage to the harness, and the horses quite uninjured. Our two young ladies behaved like heroines.

I am glad that you have been employing your leisure time in reading Malthus, and examining the grounds of his difference with me. I have turned to Page 125 of his work as you requested and I think it must be admitted that when corn rises from difficulty of producing it, manufactures will generally fall from facility of producing them, which will make a rise of wages on account of a rise in the price of corn often unnecessary. I quite agree with you that the passage

[1] Ricardo's younger daughters, Mary and Birtha.

in 128 is inconsistent with this doctrine for in one place he says when corn is high, labour will command a great quantity of other things besides corn, and in the other he says that under the same circumstances it will command only a small quantity of them. The passage in 128 is very faulty, and proceeds on the supposition that "when *corn* compared with *labour* is *dear, labour* compared with *corn* must necessarily be *cheap.*" But to say that *corn rises* and will therefore command *more labour,* is a very different thing from saying that *labour falls* and therefore will command *less corn;* for when we talk of a thing rising or falling we always mean in reference to something which we suppose does not move. Because labour falls in reference to *corn* it does not necessarily undergo any variation in reference to *other things,* and therefore in fact *labour does not fall*—it is improper to say it does, the truth being that labour is of the same value, but one of the commodities on which wages are expended has risen in value, not only in reference to labour, but in reference to every thing else. Now if we suppose that the same circumstances which are favorable to a rise of corn are also favorable to a fall of manufactures, which was Mr. Malthus doctrine Page 125— not only will labour not fall in reference to manufactured commodities, when it falls in reference to corn, but it will do exactly the contrary, it will rise in reference to those commodities while it falls relatively to corn. This however would not be the correct way of explaining what was taking place— I should say that[1] labour continued *uniformly* of the *same value,* but that corn one of the objects on which wages were expended rose in value, while manufactured goods the other objects on which wages were expended fell in value.

Mr. Malthus argument for using a mean between corn and labour as a standard and measure of value is full of fallacy

---

[1] 'wages' is del. here.

when patiently examined. Corn rises because it is more difficult to produce it. In consequence of the rise of this prime necessary, labour rises also, but not in the same degree in which corn rises. Now here are two things which rise in value, and Mr. Malthus, chuses a mean between the two as a good measure of value. Altho' they both rise in value yet comparing them with each other and making each the measure of the other, one will appear to fall. Here then says Mr. M I have two commodities which vary in opposite directions, and therefore a mean between them is an admirable measure of value. Suppose corn to rise from 80 to 100 p.$^r$ quarter, and labour from 10 to 11/- p.$^r$ week, nobody would deny that they both rose. Now compare corn and labour, a quarter of corn at 80/ would command 8 weeks labour, at 100/- it will command more than 9 weeks labour. Corn has risen as compared to labour and is therefore dear, but if corn is dear[1] compared with labour, labour must be cheap as compared with corn. 8 weeks labour would command a quarter of corn, 9 weeks labour must now be given for it, who can doubt that labour is cheap? Do you not observe that the whole argument from beginning to end is completely fallacious? and that a commodity really become dear is stated to be cheap?

I do not think that Mr. Malthus is wrong in Page 145. I think he means to say that if you diminish the fertility of the land so much that the whole produce must go to the cultivators there can neither be surplus produce to afford profit or rent. If it should be even enough to afford a trifling profit there could be no rent because no worse land could be taken into cultivation. Now says Mr. Malthus if you diminish the fertility of the land one half you will place us in this condition. This is a question of fact and degree, not of principle, and it is one of my complaints against him that he

[1] 'says' is del. here.

does not answer your principle but wishes to shew that you have taken your case so wide, that it could under no circumstances exist; but however limited might be your case, the same principle is involved, and it is that which should be answered.

No commodity is raised unless there is a demand for it. If it were raised without a demand, it would sink in value, and not afford the price necessary to remunerate the labour bestowed upon it, and to afford the usual profits of stock. If this be true, in what respect is corn different from silk, wine, or sugar? Those who manufacture, or grow, these commodities, will be losers if they produce more than is equal to the demand at a certain price, but is not the producer of corn in the same condition? he will not raise corn if there be no demand for it at the remunerating price. If any man wishes to increase his capital he produces that which he has good reason to think he can sell at a remunerating price. It is with money he is to pay labour, and it is money which he seeks to obtain. He may indeed anticipate that the commodity which will be immediately demanded in greater quantity than before will be corn, but then he will produce that as a means to an end, in the same way as he would produce any other commodity. Corn is produced because it is immediately demanded, or an additional demand for it is reasonably anticipated, but we should not on that account be justified in saying that corn raises up its own demanders, or that its plenty bribes people to come into existence, because that always supposes a price of corn below the natural or remunerating price, and it is no man's interest to produce it on such terms. An increased demand for labour is not immediately supplied by an additional number of people—higher wages induce the same number of people to do more work. An increase of capital, then, and a demand for labour, does not necessarily produce an increased demand for food, but an increased demand for other things agreeable to the labourer. It is those things which will be produced in the first instance, and corn will not be demanded, in any unusual quantity, till the number of children are increased: then the commodities demanded in the first instance will be relinquished, and an increased demand will take place for corn. I hope you will think this a justification of the opinion which I have given that corn does not raise up demanders, any more than coats raise up wearers, or wine, wine drinkers. A producer has a right to demand either his own commodity or some other. If he intends to add to his capital he naturally seeks to possess himself of that commodity which will be in demand by those whose labour he wishes to dispose of: it may be corn, but there is no more necessity for its being corn than cloth, shoes, stockings, tea, sugar, iron or any other thing. I do not think then with you, that a demand for labour is the same thing as a supply of necessaries. Labour and necessaries may come in additional quantity into the market at the same time in which case neither of them will fall; they will both be supplied and demanded in greater abundance. Suppose the necessaries only to come into the market in additional quantity, that will not occasion any greater demand for labour than if an additional quantity of iron was brought to market, for no one wishes to consume it. The way most effectually to increase capital is to produce a commodity that you know will be demanded and consequently will not fall in value, not one that will not be demanded and will fall in value. Pray understand that I am answering Mr. Malthus who contends that there is something peculiar about corn which gives it a character of being able to raise up demanders different from all other things—I contend on the contrary, that there is no difference between them that nothing is pro-

duced until it is wanted unless from mistake and miscalculation.

You must be tired of reading this long letter. One word only about the Queen. Whatever her conduct may have been can ministers shew that the real interests of the country required a bill of pains and penalties under the circumstances of the cruel usage she has received? Every one must answer this question in the negative.

Mrs. Ricardo unites with me in kind comp.$^{ts}$ to Mrs. Trower.

Very truly Yours<br>DAVID RICARDO

There is nothing new in the second edition of my book.

381. RICARDO TO M<sup>c</sup>CULLOCH [1]

[*Reply to 377*]

Gatcomb Park<br>Minchinhampton<br>15 Sept.<sup>r</sup> 1820

My dear Sir

I have read your article on Tithes with great satisfaction.
You have made that clear which to many minds was before obscure, and I hope have laid the foundation for some beneficial change in this most oppressive and irritating tax. I do not quite agree with you in the justice of subjecting those to the tax whose lands have hitherto been exempted from it. Many tithe free farms are yearly brought to market, and an additional price is paid for them in consequence of the peculiar advantage they enjoy. It would surely be very unjust to subject such a proprietor to a tax after his paying a valuable consideration to be exempted from it. I think that it would be almost equally unjust to impose this tax on those who have retained the property in their own hands for the three

[1] MS in British Museum.—*Letters to M<sup>c</sup>Culloch*, XVII.

hundred and fifty years of which you speak. I also differ with you on the expediency of substituting for the tithes, a poundage on rents; this would be to tax exclusively a particular class of the community. I speak without any consideration of my interest as a landholder, and I assure you that I am not possessed of any tithe free land.

I am glad that you are about preparing an article on the National Debt, and on the different plans suggested for paying it off.[1] I am not well acquainted with the objections which are made to the discharging ourselves from this heavy burden. The principal one that I have heard, is the large quantity of land which a proprietor would be obliged to part with in order to redeem himself from the payment of his annual taxes. It is difficult to make these men understand that the payment of £1000 p$^r$ ann$^m$, is a heavier burden than the payment of £20000 once for all. I suspect too that they imagine their consequence would be lessened by so great a diminution of their landed property as the payment of the debt would require, and perhaps they might be in some measure right in this opinion if the payment did not affect them all and did not leave them when made precisely in the same relative situation to each other as that in which they now stand. Another objection which I have heard, and which I think is the most plausible, is that it would relieve from taxation all those who are in professions, and whose incomes are derived from wages or salaries. This I have endeavored to answer in my article,[2] but it requires your talents to give it weight. There is some difficulty with respect

[1] McᶜCulloch made extensive use of the arguments in this letter in an article on 'Taxation—Retrenchment—Reduction of the Public Debt', *Edinburgh Review*, Oct. 1827 (Art. V), p. 409 ff.; the arguments on the issue of exchequer bills and on the title of land are there reproduced almost verbatim, p. 412.
[2] 'Funding System'; above, IV, 188–9.

to the time required for such an immense operation, and the means of effecting it. I have sometimes thought that it would be desirable to issue a particular paper money to facilitate the payment. Suppose Government were to commence the business by issuing exchequer bills to the holders of 50 millions of stock, which bills should be receivable in payment of the contributions of capitalists, and if not used for that purpose, then payable in money on a day to be fixed; fifty millions might by these means be paid off without any considerable demand of the circulating medium of the country, and by immediately reissuing the bills, and renewing the operation from time to time, the whole payment might be effected in a moderate time. Some precautions would be necessary to prevent people from concealing their property, or sending it abroad, to withdraw it from a share of the burden. Mr. Brougham made an objection in the house[1] to the plan, that it would throw the landed property of the country into the hands of low and designing attornies, but his objection is I think easily answered. By act of Parliament the title of all land sold for the purpose of raising money necessary for the landholders contribution should be held to be a perfect title, whatever might be its insufficiency for any other sale. Suppose A paid it, and that hereafter it should appear to be the property of B—B would suffer no injury or injustice, for had he been before possessed of it, he must have equally with A, have contributed the portion to which the act has given a good title. No landed property in the country would have a better title, and it would therefore be preferred above all other by a purchaser—it could never require the interference or advice of low attornies. Nothing further offers itself to me on this subject at the present moment.

I receive the Scotsman regularly here. When Parliament

---

[1] On 24 Dec. 1819; see above, V, 40–1.

meets *for business* I will thank you to send it to me again in London. I have not seen my brother Ralph since I received your letter. As he is become a father as well as a husband, we do not see each other out of the neighborhood of London so often as heretofore.

I agree in every thing you say about the Queen. The question of her innocence or guilt is not the important one, — she has been abominably treated, and no grounds have been, or can be stated, to prove this disgusting enquiry either just, or necessary for the public good.—

I am with great esteem<br>
Very faithfully Yours<br>
DAVID RICARDO

382. MILL TO RICARDO [1]<br>
[*Answered by* 383]

Queen Square West! 16ᵗʰ Sept! 1820

My Dear Sir

16 Sept. 1820    The enclosed, along with the vol. of the Supp.,[2] I found on my arrival here. The best thing to do was, I thought, to send you the letter, and beg you to hint to me what I should say. As I think it very likely if I were with you, that you would ask me for my opinion, I will take the liberty, to mention it unasked. I think you should accept payment, and say that it is a money which you have pride in receiving; but that you will not accept any thing beyond their common rate of remuneration, whatever it may be. It is I think 10 gˢ per sheet. At least, I have received according to that scale, except for the article Govt, for which he has sent me more.

[1] MS in *R.P.*
[2] *Supplement to the Encyclopaedia Britannica,* vol. IV, part II, containing the articles 'Funding System', by Ricardo, and 'Government', by Mill. The enclosure (a letter from Napier) is wanting.

I need not waste your time in giving my reasons for this
opinion, because you will easily conceive them. If they are
not satisfactory to you, it only remains that you tell me your
opinion as frankly as I have mentioned mine.

I beg to be most kindly remembered to all *mes cheres
amies*. I make use of a French scrap, for the sake of the
feminine gender, because the ladies were principally in my
recollection, from whom I have received during the last
month so many marks of partiality, and from whose society
I have derived so great a degree of pleasure. In using, however, this feminine gender I am far from forgetting Mr.
David, of whom I would be bound to make a great deal of
all that is good; and to whom I would send my best comp.ts
if I did not know that he will be absent.

Here I found all in good health, and every thing as it
should be.

I hear that the procession of the sailors, when they went
to address the queen, wore a very imposing aspect—that
such a number of that particular kind of men, taking a part,
which they never did before, in political matters—men never
afraid of the most desperate sort of fighting, and ready to
begin a struggle at any time—has excited unusual fears.
Lord Wellesley who passed through them going to his
bankers, said, if this happens often, the game is at an end.

A letter which came here on thursday from Mc Culloch[1]
(I suppose about his dinner) Mrs. M. who thought it might
be of importance, has I understand troubled you by enclosing.

A meeting is in preparation for framing an address to the
queen, upon the present state of her prosecution, to be
presented by the inhabitants of the Metropolis generally, by

[1] No doubt William McCulloch (see below, p. 251, n. 1). On
Thursday, 14 September, Mill was still at Gatcomb.

16 Sept. 1820 a procession of coaches. It is expected that every coach in London will be in requisition. The Marybone procession they say was such as to warrant such an expectation.

Mr. Bentham, whom I have not yet seen, is well.

Most truly yours

J. MILL

383. RICARDO TO MILL [1]

[*Reply to* 382]

Gatcomb 18 Sep.^ 1820

My dear Sir

18 Sept. 1820 We were glad to hear that on your arrival in London you found all your family well.

Your *cheres amies* received your remembrances with great satisfaction; they have all grieved for the loss of your society, and speak of the time you passed with them with the greatest animation and pleasure. Mrs. Ricardo and myself were gratified with the few words you said of David—I believe he is a well disposed young man.

You were quite right in anticipating that on the subject of Mr. Napier's letter to you, I should wish particularly to hear your opinion—I am glad you have given it, and I determine to be guided by it, if on further reflection you see no reason to alter it. It is impossible that I should be offended by any offer of a fee which Mr. Napier might make to me,—nor does my pride stand in the way of my accepting of it, if it is usual for persons who are amateurs, and not worthy to be called authors, to be paid for their articles.—You must know what the practice is in the case of the Edin. Review.

My scruples are of two kinds, first, I have a miserable opinion of the article itself and the most trifling compensa-

---

[1] MS in Mill-Ricardo papers.

tion in a mere commercial view would be an overpayment. Secondly I am afraid that I may be thought mean in accepting a fee when it must be known that it formed no part of the motive which induced me to write the article. After saying thus much, I leave the matter wholly to your better judgement.[1]

The meetings and processions in London must I think have some effect on the higher powers. I wish however that the Queen may be able to prove her innocence. Mr. E. Clutterbuck[2] yesterday told me that the people in Cheltenham hearing that Denman was on his road to that place, wanted the bells rung to welcome him.[3] The clergyman refused to give the keys, in consequence of which above a thousand persons went out to meet him, to the great terror of Mrs. D. who was with him. They drew the carriage in triumph thro' the town, after which Denman made them a

[1] Mill wrote to Napier, in a letter dated 20 Sept. 1820: 'I had been spending a month with Ricardo in Glostershire, and I and your letter to me arrived at home on the same day. As I felt no difficulty in talking to Ricardo himself about the point which you have referred to me, I transcribed what you had said. I have his answer in which he says, he would have no pride in refusing, but rather a pride in receiving such remuneration, if it is customary for amateurs in such circumstances to do so. On that point he refers to me, and as I am ignorant, I must transfer the reference to you. Ricardo adds, that his scruples about receiving are of two kinds—first on account of the article, which he says is not worth payment—secondly, because payment having formed no part of the motive which induced him to write the article, he reckons himself not entitled to payment. He then prays me to decide for him—but says he will on no account receive more than at the rate of your most ordinary allowance. As I think this decision is remarkably proper, you will know how to proceed.' (MS in British Museum, Add. 34,612, fol. 383; printed inaccurately, and misdated 20 November, in Bain, *James Mill*, pp. 190–1.)

[2] Edmund Clutterbuck and James Clutterbuck, J.P., mentioned below, were uncles of Ricardo's son-in-law.

[3] Thomas Denman, M.P. (afterwards Lord Denman), was Solicitor-General to Queen Caroline.

18 Sept. 1820 speech in which he said that his royal mistress was innocent, or he should be able to prove her innocence, and her honour would shine with as much brilliancy as the stars which he was then looking at. He recommended them to disperse, and go to their homes. This they did not do till they had broken every window of the parsons house. Mr. James Clutterbuck who was the only magistrate in the town could do nothing with them, and was obliged at last to call on Denman for his assistance. Denman readily gave it, again addressed the mob when they immediately dispersed.

The Wilkinsons have left us for London this morning. It is raining slowly but without cessation. Mrs. Ricardo Mary and Birtha desire to be kindly remembered.

Y<sup>rs</sup> truly

D RICARDO

384. TROWER TO RICARDO [1]<br>[*Reply to* 380.—*Answered by* 387]

Unsted Wood—Sept. 20. 1820

My Dear Ricardo—

20 Sept. 1820     You will be surprised at my returning so early an answer to your last kind letter. The fact is, I am desirous of making some observations on a question to which I called your attention in my last letter. The point is important, and as I confess your reasoning has not satisfied my mind, I am anxious, if I am in error to request your assistance to set me right. But, I must, first of all, congratulate you upon your escape from the very alarming predicament, in which you, and your friends, appear to have been placed, in crossing the river you mention. It would not have been a very glorious

---

[1] Addressed: 'To / David Ricardo Esqr / M.P. / Gatcomb Park— / Minchinhampton'.—MS in *R.P.*

termination to your career, to have been swamped! and you are one of the last men I should have suspected, *on any occasion,* of getting out of your *depth!*

You say "you do not think with me, that a *demand* for labor is the same thing as a supply of Necessaries." And "that an additional quantity of necessaries will not occasion any greater demand for labor than if an additional quantity of iron was brought to market."

The foundation of all Wealth is the power, which man possesses, by means of his labor, in conjunction with the powers of nature, to produce *more* of any commodity than is necessary for his own use—Hence arises the *surplus produce* of Commodities, which is the fund of profit, and revenue, and from which proceeds the growth of capital—

In a Country, in any degree advanced in civilization, its productive capital and labor will naturally divide themselves into *two parts.* that employed in land, and that in manufactures. These, for the purpose of my argument I shall class under the two general heads of *Necessaries,* and of *Conveniences*—By *Necessaries* meaning food and those other commodities, which, under any given state of society, constitute the support of the laborers, and lower classes of the people—And by *Conveniences* meaning all those commodities, of whatever description, which administer to our comfort and enjoyments; and which are consumed, in different degrees, by all classes *above* that of laborers. There will, then, be an annual *surplus* produce of *Necessaries,* and of Conveniences. And these will be exchanged for each other.

But, the surplus produce of *Necessaries* must, in the *first instance* have *preceded* the surplus produce of *Conveniences;* for, if there had not been *any such surplus,* Conveniences could not have been produced. The producers of *Necessaries,* creating more commodities than are requisite for their own support, employ that *surplus* in setting to work laborers (not required for the production of Necessaries) upon the production of Conveniences. And the producers of Conveniences also create more of their Commodities than they require for their own use. But, they cannot employ their surplus in the employment of *laborers,* because, it does not consist of *articles required* by the *laborer.* If their object is to encrease the amount of the Commodities they produce, they must exchange their Conveniences for *Necessaries,* or, if their object is to encrease their *comfort* they will exchange their Conveniences for other Conveniences.

You say, "no Commodity is raised without there is a demand for it." It is perfectly true, that no Commodity will *continue* to be raised unless there is a demand for it. But, it is in the nature of all Commodities to *create* their own demand. The amount of the *surplus* produce of *Necessaries limits* the whole amount of labor, which can be employed upon the production of *Conveniences.* But, *within that limit,* these conveniences may be multiplied and varied, according to the taste and desire of the Consumers.

But, here there is an action and reaction; for, in proportion as conveniences are multiplied, the desire to possess them is encreased. This desire is felt, in common, by the producers of *necessaries,* they encrease their produce, in order to possess these Conveniences, and, by this encreased produce of *Necessaries,* enable the producers of *Conveniences* to employ more labor for *their* further production.

What is the *surplus produce* but an *excess* of the Commodity produced over the expence of producing it? When that excess consists of *Necessaries,* it may be disposed of, either in the employment of *more* labor in the production of the *same Commodities;* or in the employment of more labor in

the production of *Conveniences;* or in the employment of more
nonproductive labor. If productively employed, then, *Non-productive* consumers may be converted into *productive* ones:
But, in whatever way it is employed, it occasions an increased
demand for *some sort of labor.* If that encreased *demand* is not
met by an encreased *supply, then,* the *whole* of *this surplus
produce,* which consists of Necessaries, is distributed among
the *existing laborers;* and their condition is improved accordingly; and from *this improvement* it is, that the increase
of population proceeds. It is true, that this increase does not
*necessarily* take place, nor for some time, but, this *surplus*
is the *fund,* and the *only fund,* which can occasion it.

Now, let us suppose this surplus to consist of an excess of
*Conveniences.* How can it be disposed of? Not in the employment of *labor,* because it does not consist of *Necessaries.*
It may be exchanged for *Necessaries*—and *then,* those Necessaries may be productively employed; or it may be exchanged
for other Conveniences, but its power of employing *labor*
must depend upon its power of *first obtaining necessaries.*
How, then, can Necessaries and *Iron* have similar effects.
There is a natural division, which takes place in the distribution of labor and capital, in every Country; and upon the
*actual* division corresponding with this *natural* division,
it appears to me, principally depends the prosperity of
States—

Suppose, that natural division to require, that *one fourth*
part of the population and a proportionate amount of capital,
should be employed in producing *Necessaries,* for the whole
population—Suppose *another fourth,* with its due proportion
of Capital, to be employed in the production of *Conveniences;*
and the other *two fourths* to be nonproductive consumers—
If this were the *natural state,* any considerable deviation from
it, must be attended with sensible inconvenience; and

especially, if any material reduction should take place in the portion allotted to the production of *Necessaries;* either, by too large a proportion being engaged in producing *conveniences;* or, becoming *non productive consumers.* It is true, that no great deviation from this natural point could *long continue;* Capital and labor would again find their proper station; but, it is *during these intervals* that those inconveniences and sufferings take place, by which the prosperity of states is affected.—

You say you do not think with me "that a demand for labor is the same thing as a supply of Necessaries."

You admit (561)[1] "that the general progress of population is affected by the increase of Capital," and you define Capital (93)[2] ["]that part of the Wealth of a Country which is employed in production, and which *consists of food, clothing* &&." It follows, therefore, that the general progress of population is affected by the increase of food and clothing. But, food and clothing are *necessaries,* therefore the growth of population is affected by the increase of *necessaries.* And, what is an *increase* of necessaries, but an *additional supply* of necessaries, by which the progress of population is affected? And how can the progress of population be affected by this additional supply, unless *preceeded by it;* and, if preceeded by it, then, "the abundance of necessaries raises up demanders." You also admit (561) "that an increase of Capital occasions a *demand* for labor, and a rise of wages." And, is not a *demand* for labor the same thing as a supply of necessaries? How could labor be *demanded;* if the demander had not a *supply of necessaries,* ready provided for the labor he demanded; or, what amounts to the same thing, did he not possess the means of providing those laborers with the supply of food

[1] Above, I, 406. The references    [2] Above, I, 95.
are to ed. 1.

and clothing they would require? No amount of capital could enable him to make that demand for *labor,* unless it consisted of that portion of the productive capital, which *is composed of necessaries,* or unless it had the *power of commanding them.* Here I will stop, for this is enough for one dose, and I am afraid *you* will think *too much.* And, indeed, in reading over my letter, I think I might have condenced the matter into smaller compass. But, I am anxious that you should understand my argument, and if I am wrong, that you should point out the *source* of the error for it is an important question.

Have you seen Mr. Say's letter to Mr. Malthus in the New Monthly Magazine for Sep:[1]—And what think you of it?

The argument he urges against Mr. Malthus is in some degree connected with the question I have been here considering. He contends there can be *no excess of commodities,* and that it is production, which opens the market to produce.

But, I confess, I think, this proposition must be *limited,* as I have endeavoured to limit it above, by the *due distribution* of the capital of the Country. For, to me it appears obvious that if too small a proportion of the capital of the Country should be employed in producing *necessaries,* owing either to the low profits on land, or the High profits on Manufactures, that such commodities might (during that state of things) continue in excess.

Mr. Say's notion of *immaterial services* &. appears to me fanciful and useless, and his notion, that any man, who writes upon political Economy should banish from his thoughts the distinction between *durable and perishable* commodities, altogether erroneous—But, really I must have done, or you

---

[1] A translation of the first of Say's *Lettres à M. Malthus;* the other letters were published in subsequent numbers.

will not have patience to read my letter with that attention which I wish you to do.

I am happy to say, that my knee is a great deal better, but I move cautiously, and, as the *pleasure* of exercise is gone, at least for a time, I take only that quantity which I consider necessary to health.

I wish I could see my way through this horrible affair of the Queen. Serjeant Onslows proposition[1] is *Monstrous*— You Gentlemen of the Commons are tyrants enough at present; and what you *might* become when possessed of the power of examining on Oath, I, for one, am not desirous of ascertaining! It would be sacrificing *principle* for the sake of present convenience; and would be the means of establishing a most dangerous precedent, pretences for acting upon which there would hereafter be no difficulty in finding.

Mrs. Trower begs to join with me in kind remembrances to Mrs. Ricardo, and believe me My Dear Ricardo

Yrs very sincerely

HUTCHES TROWER

### 385. MILL TO RICARDO[2]
*[Answered by 386]*

East India House 23ᵈ Septʳ 1820

My Dear Sir

I am now going to write to you about a subject of very great importance; and I am very strongly persuaded that you can have no good objection to the proposition which I am going to make to you. I have mentioned to you before now with something of the air of a jest, but with not a little of the reality of earnest, my wish that you were an East India

---

[1] For a bill to enable the House of Commons to examine witnesses on oath. (*Hansard*, N.S., III, 51.)  [2] MS in *R.P.*

Director. In conversation just now with Mr. M<sup>c</sup>Culloch,[1] 23 Sept. 1820 when he was lamenting to me the prospect created by the present race of aspirants, and telling me what some even of the leading directors themselves thought of it, I seized the opportunity which I have been on the watch for, and said, I wish that Ricardo could be prevailed upon to offer himself. He started up, even from his chair, and said, "Oh God, if Ricardo could be prevailed upon, he might come in next April! The Court of Directors would jump at him. He would have all their support. If he would undergo the canvas, I would lay my life that he comes in."

This you will observe is said by a man who knows more about the field than any other man living; and who is one of the men of the soundest judgement that I have ever known. I consider then the fact that you would come in with ease, if you chose it, as out of dispute—and that being the case I am quite sure that you ought not to hesitate. It would put you in a situation in which your means of doing good to your fellow creatures would be prodigious; it would increase your dignity and importance in a very high degree; and the occupation which it would afford would add to your happiness—for to your mind, which has so long been intensely employed, one of the principal inconveniences of your present situation is, that it affords not objects of immediate interest to employ it—and hence your occasional feelings that life is but a stale possession, and that at 60 years it would be sufficiently long. On your own account, therefore, on account of the millions of your fellow creatures over whose happiness and misery you would be invested with so much power, on account of your family to whose dignity and

[1] William M<sup>c</sup>Culloch, the Examiner of India Correspondence at the East India House; on his retirement in 1830 Mill succeeded him as head of the department. (See Bain, *James Mill*, pp. 194, 355–6.)

23 Sept. 1820 advantage it would redound in so many ways, and on my account, whose welfare I am sure is a matter of no small importance to you, I hope you will give the subject not only a most serious but a favourable consideration.

I write in a great hurry, and shall content myself with barely opening the proposition. If you write to me with any encouragement, MᶜCulloch will instantly proceed to sound, and to give you the necessary information. And he is a man in whom you may implicitly confide. He is as discerning and judicious as he is honourable; and I know no man who surpasses him in either. This is written with his concurrence and by his advice.

Most truly Yours<br>J. MILL

## 386. RICARDO TO MILL [1]
*[Reply to 385.—Answered by 389]*

Gatcomb Park<br>25 Sepᵗ 1820

My dear Sir

25 Sept. 1820 The proposition which you have made to me has been incessantly present to my mind since I received your letter.— I have considered it in every way—have not been insensible to the reasons which you urge in favour of it, but after all I cannot bring myself to agree to it. In the first place I cannot believe that I should have the support of the Directors— I am little known to any of them personally, and I cannot think that the sentiments which I have expressed publicly on various occasions, would recommend me much to their favour. I have always understood that support from the Directors was generally bestowed from personal favour and

---

[1] Addressed: 'James Mill Esqʳ / East India House / London'.
MS in Mill-Ricardo papers.

25 Sept. 1820

attachment. Secondly,—without any affected modesty, I have not the requisite talents to fill the situation of a Director of the East India Company. My want of information on many points might be removed by study and application, but I have no pretensions to entitle me to take upon myself so important and so responsible an office. You say, or may say, that the present aspirants are more ignorant than I am, that may be true, and yet it would not justify me for thrusting myself into an office for which I am unfit. 3$^{dly}$ This scheme would not contribute to my happiness. You are mistaken in supposing that because I consider life on the whole as not a very desirable thing to retain after 60, that therefore I am discontented with my situation, or have not objects of immediate interest to employ me. The contrary is the case— I am very comfortable, and am never in want of objects of interest and amusement. I am led to set a light value on life when I consider the many accidents and privations to which we are liable.—In my own case, I have already lost the use of one ear, completely—and am daily losing my teeth, that I have scarcely one that is useful to me. No one bears these serious deprivations with a better temper than myself, yet I cannot help anticipating from certain notices which I some- times think I have, that many more await me. I have not I assure you seriously quarrelled with life,—I am on very good terms with it, and mean while I have it to make the best of it, but my observation on the loss of esteem and interest which old people generally sustain from their young rela- tions, often indeed from their own imperfections and mis- behaviour, but sometimes from the want of indulgence and consideration on the part of the young, convinces me that general happiness would be best promoted if death visited us on an average at an earlier period than he now does. If I were an East India Director I should be kept from my family more than I now am—I should not be able to absent myself from London for six months together as I now do; In addition to the business of the House of Commons I should be almost daily obliged to go into the city to attend the duties of my office. Notwithstanding then that I am aware of the increase of dignity which the situation would give me (though by the by I am no seeker after increased dignities)— of the many advantages which my family or friends might derive from the power which it would give me, and notwithstanding my regard for your welfare, which is, and ever will be, an object of great interest to me, it would be unwise in me to hazard the step which you recommend.

Mr. M'Culloch may be a good judge of the probability of success in such cases as these, and I am very much flattered by the favorable opinion he expressed of my success, if I would undergo the canvas; yet I cannot help thinking that his opinion was formed on a very imperfect knowledge of my qualifications, and of the degree of influence I enjoy in the city, and among East India Proprietors. As to my qualifications he may have derived his information from your too partial report, and of my influence he may judge by my reputed wealth, very unsafe criterions by which to arrive at a correct judgement. I believe that no man with half my real wealth, or with one fourth my reputed wealth, ever had so little influence as I possess. I have never taken the least trouble to obtain it. Under these circumstances my dear friend I must decline moving in this business.

Truly Y$^{rs}$

DAVID RICARDO

## 387. RICARDO TO TROWER [1]
[*Reply to 384.—Answered by* 390]

Gatcomb Park
26 Sept.[r] 1820

My Dear Trower

You see that I follow your good example, and while the
subject is fresh in my memory offer the best reasons I have
in vindication of the view which I take of it. The point in
dispute is this, Does the supply of corn precede the demand
for it, or does it follow such demand? You are of the former
—I of the latter opinion. You have not answered one important objection I made to you, namely, that if the supply
of corn preceded the demand it must be at a lower price than
the grower could afford to produce it—this is the inevitable
consequence of supply exceeding demand—who under such
circumstances would be induced to grow the surplus quantity
of corn? Your mistake appears to me to proceed from considering the case too generally. It is undoubtedly true that
if production were wholly under the control of one individual,
whose object it was to increase population, he could not
better effect his object than by growing more corn in the
country than the existing community could consume—it
would in that case be at a low price, and the greatest stimulus
would be given to population. We might indeed then justly
say that it was the abundance of corn which raised up consumers, and that in this respect corn differed from iron, silk
or any other commodity, but this is not the question under
consideration, what we want to know is, whether, in the
present distribution of property, and under the influence of
the motives which invite to production, corn is produced for
any other reason than that iron, silk, wine &c. &c. are
produced—whether they are not all produced on account of

---

[1] MS at University College, London.—*Letters to Trower,* XL.

an actual or expected demand for them, and whether this
demand is not always indicated by the relation of the market
price to the natural price? If the supply existed one moment
previously to the demand, the market price must sink below
the natural price, and the manufacturer of the commodity or
the grower of the corn, whichever it might be, would not get
the usual and general rate of profits, and would therefore be
unwilling to produce such a commodity.

What all producers look steadily at is market price, and
its relation to natural price. Suppose you to be disposed to
add from your revenue to capital this year, it would not
induce you to change the nature of your production, for
whether you spent your revenue, or employed it as capital,
the next year, your immediate object would be to realize it
in money. But with your increased capital what would you
produce next year? Corn undoubtedly, if the price indicated
that the supply did not equal the demand, or if you had good
reason to expect that but for your production the supply
would not equal the demand. Now what I ask is would not
the same motives induce you to employ your additional
capital in the manufacture of cloth, iron, silk, &c., if you
answer it would not, then I request you to give me your
reasons why you, or any other producer, would so obviously
neglect your best interest. If you answer that the motives for
the production of either of these commodities are the same,
then there is an end of the dispute, for this is all that I am
contending for. Suppose a man intent on saving were to
employ his savings in producing corn—he would do unwisely if he did not expect the price of corn to be at least as
high as its natural price,—in this you must agree—he will
not then produce corn. But corn is as high as its natural
price, then there is an end of the argument, for it can not be
so if the supply preceded the demand. You will not say that

he may as well produce corn as any other commodity, because it is possible that corn and all other commodities may be under their natural price, for that would be to adopt the great and fundamental error of Mr. Malthus, who contends that there may be at one and the same time a glut of all commodities, and that it may arise from a want of demand for all—he indeed argues that this is the specific evil under which we are at present suffering. This is I think the only defence you can make for your opinion, and if you do make it, I shall know how to deal with you in a subsequent letter— at present I shall content myself with saying that I have no conception of any man knowingly and wilfully producing a commodity which will sell under its natural price. I do not deny that it is often done, but then I say it is from error and miscalculation, and cannot continue for more than one or two years.

You say that "the surplus produce of necessaries must in the first instance have preceded the surplus produce of conveniences," but did the surplus produce of necessaries precede the demand for them?—this is the question—I say they did not, for the men who had their labour to offer in exchange for them were the effective demanders of this surplus produce, and the conveniences are the result of this demand.

A man first produces necessaries because he himself has a want or demand for them—he produces more of these necessaries because he wants conveniences, and he can obtain them by other men's labour, which his necessaries will command. Hitherto he has produced nothing for which there is not a demand. But he wants to increase his possessions, and it can be done only by having the power to employ more people; must not his first step be to provide necessaries for such additional number of people? Not absolutely, because he may have the power of employing more people, and others may have the means of employing fewer—his capital will increase whilst that of another man diminishes. But no other mans capital diminishes! The aggregate capitals will be increased! If labour cannot be procured[1] no more work will be done with the additional capital, but wages will rise, and the distribution of the produce will be favorable to the workmen. In this case no more food will be produced if the workmen were well fed before, their demand will be for conveniences, and luxuries. But the number of labourers are increased, or the children of labourers! Then indeed the demand for food will increase, and *food will be produced in consequence of such demand.* It would be wrong to infer always that an increase of capital will procure an increased quantity of work to be done, it will be followed by no such effect if the labourers happen to be in a position to enable them to command the whole addition to the fund for the maintenance of labour, without doing any more work.*

I thought of leaving off half an hour ago but my pen runs on. I cannot even now conclude without expressing my satisfaction at the improvement in your knee—I hope all traces of your late accident will soon be lost.

Ever Y.$^{rs}$

DAVID RICARDO

There is a part of your letter I have not noticed, I mean that part which refers to M. Say's doctrine of demand being only limited by production. His doctrine appears to me to be correct. You say it must be limited by the due distribution of capital. Undoubtedly you are right, but M. Say would answer that private interest would always lead to such a due

* It is on this ground that I dispute your position that a demand for labour is the same thing as a supply of necessaries.

[1] 'at the usual price' is del. here.

distribution. He would not deny that errors might be made, and more of one, two, three, or of 50 commodities be produced than what there was any effective demand for, but he would not agree with you that for any length of time there could be high profits on manufactures and low profits on land. High profits are the consequence of high price—high price of increased demand—increased demand of an imperfect distribution of capital, it is the remedy and not the grievance.

26 Sept. 1820

## 388. MALTHUS TO RICARDO [1]
[*Reply to 379.—Answered by 392*]

E I Coll Sep^r 25^th [1820]

My dear Ricardo,

I am glad to hear that you are enjoying yourself at Gatcomb. I have no doubt it looks very delightful now, and it would give me great pleasure to pay you and Mrs. Ricardo a visit there, if we were not so completely tied by the leg in the intervals between the vacations. You will leave it I have no doubt with regret in October to attend on this terrible business of the Queen. I am inclined to think perhaps that there is rather more in the *State part* of the question than you do; but whatever evils might have arisen from her having all the rights and privileges of a Queen, they would have been less than the evils attending the present unfortunate discussion. One can hardly see any tolerably good termination to it.

When I received your letter I had not seen Say's publication.[2] He promised to send it to me and I had been expecting it, but at last I got tired of waiting, and sent to my bookseller for it. I do not think it is a very able performance. There are

25 Sept. 1820

[1] Addressed: 'D. Ricardo Esqr MP. / Gatcomb Park / Minchinhampton / Gloucestershire'.

Postmark, 1820.
MS in *R.P.*
[2] *Lettres à M. Malthus.*

more contradictions in it than those which relate to value, and there are some doctrines, besides those which directly concern me that appear to me to obscure, rather than to throw light on the general subject. I cannot agree with him in making no distinction between services and products, in his strange and useless application of the term utility, in his opinions respecting the immateriality of revenues, and in his mode of reasoning by exclamations which enable him to stop short when he comes to the stress of the argument. After all, in a note referring to you p. 101 he fully concedes all that I contend for. He says "qu'il y a beaucoup d'epargnes qui ne se placent pas lorsque les emplois sont difficiles, ou qui etant placées se dissipent dans une production mal calculé"—and this he illustrates by the present state of France. The present state of things indeed in England America Holland and Hamburgh still more than in France does appear in the most marked manner to contradict both his, and your theory. The fall in the interest of money and the difficulty of finding employment for capital are universally acknowledged, and this fact, none of your friends have ever accounted for in any tolerably satisfactory manner; but what confidence can be placed in a theory, as the foundation of future measures which is absolutely inconsistent with the past and the present state of things.

I quite agree with you in regard to the error committed by Say and Torrens about the necessity of counter commodities in all cases. The commodity in which there is a glut should as you say be produced in less quantity; and the true question is, whether the capital and labour so withdrawn can with certainty find employment without any other fall of profits than that which arises necessarily from the state of the land, or temporarily from the improved condition of the labouring classes. You say that no other fall can take place. I say, not that such other fall *must necessarily* take place, but that it *may* take place according to the justest theory of demand and supply, and may occasion a positive diminution in the will and power of capitalists to command labour, which will of course throw labourers out of employment and deteriorate their condition. On these two different statements I conceive issue is joined between us. I am very sorry that a second attentive reading of my book has made no sort of impression upon you: but greatly as I respect your authority, yet if yours, as you say, is the true faith, I much fear that in spite of my orthodox tendencies, I must continue a heretic. I do not acknowledge however that I am heretical in reference to my former doctrines as stated by Say. I never affirm that necessaries if distributed to the labourer in abundance will not increase population rapidly; But I affirm that if the farmer has no adequate market for his produce, he will soon cease to distribute more necessaries to his labourers, an event which is continually occurring all over the world. This important distinction however Say does not make for me, but runs off into an 'Eh! Monsieur!'

It is quite true as you observe that we do not mean the same thing in speaking of value, and I am willing that the question should be tried by the relative *utility* of the two definitions in an inquiry into the nature and causes of the wealth. It is not however merely a question of arbitrary definitions. You assert that with few exceptions the quantity of labour employed on commodities determines the rate at which they will exchange for each other. This is a *proposition;* and one that is not well founded, so that I should doubt whether you will be able to alter your first chapter satisfactorily to yourself. I shall like however much to see it, and am very glad to hear that you are preparing another edition. I am surprised that Torrens has not continued his remarks

25 Sept. 1820 in the Traveller. I shall like to see Mccullochs article on tithes. I doubt whether I agree with him quite in the principle. Pray when you see or write to Mill remember me kindly to him. I shall expect his work on political economy with great pleasure though I think that an elementary treatise on this subject should be delayed for a few years.

I have not yet seen the last volume of the Encyclopaedia, where your funding paper is, but I expect it soon.

Mrs. Malthus sends her kind regards to Mrs. Ricardo. We hope all the family are well at Gatcomb.

Ever truly Yours

T R MALTHUS.

## 389. MILL TO RICARDO [1]
### [*Reply to 386.—Answered by 394*]

My Dear Sir

26 Sept. 1820      I do not mean to pester you on this subject—because I think it as well, in the present state of things, that the deliberation should stand over till you come to town. But I think it necessary to tell you without loss of time that your reasons are by no means satisfactory. I however anticipated them all, and told M<sup>c</sup>Culloch [2] what sort of an answer we should receive. In truth there is not one of the inconveniences you alledge which is not either unreal, or much less than you conceive—except that alone of your not being able to live six months in the year at so great a distance from London. That, however, I think there is more than enough to compensate. You would be needed at the India House seldom more than once a week.

[1] MS in *R.P.*—Cp. below, p. 293,      [2] William M<sup>c</sup>Culloch.
n. 2.

But I shall say no more at present. I hope you all remain well. Mr. Osman has now got his rain. I send my regards to my faithful servant, my Attorney General, whose talents and exertions in my service are no doubt improving. She will in time be entitled to the highest rewards.[1]

26 Sept. 1820

Truly yours

J. MILL

E. I. House
  Tuesday [26 Sept. 1820]

The above was written and intended to be sent yesterday. But Ravenshaw the Director[2] came into my room, and staying till after four oclock I forgot to send it to the post office. McCulloch was with me at the same time, and Ravenshaw lamenting the prospect of supply for the Court of Directors, McCulloch said to him, I want, Ravenshaw, to ask you a question point blank and without preparation. Do you think that the Directors, that is, a decided majority of the Directors, would support Ricardo, if he was to offer for the Direction. Ravenshaw replied instantly, There is not a doubt about it. If he were to call this hour upon the Chairman and state any such intention, the Chairman would hail it as a God-send; and so, he added, would all of us, who have the respectability of the Direction in the smallest degree at heart. We then stated to him a little of what had previously passed between McCulloch and myself, and I mentioned some of your objections—and we had a good deal of talk. You must therefore by no means look upon the chance of success, if you can be, as you ought to be, prevailed upon, as in any degree doubtful.

27 Sept. 1820

Wednesday [27 Sept. 1820].

[1] Mrs. Osman Ricardo.
[2] J. G. Ravenshaw, Director of the East India Company from 1819, Chairman in 1832.

### 390. TROWER TO RICARDO [1]
*[Reply to 387.—Answered by 391]*

My Dear Ricardo

29 Sept. 1820　　I am rejoiced to receive so early a reply to my letter; because, I am desirous of satisfying my mind upon the point in question between us, which, appears to me, to involve some very important consequences. I shall, therefore proceed to reply to your objections; sensible, however, that I am rashly engaging in a very unequal contest. "Haud aequo marte feroci"!

I admit most fully, that Commodities will not *continue* to be produced if they do not pay the *costs of production.* I admit there is a sort of *rough level* of profit on productive capital; that *this* directs capital to its most advantageous employment, and, that the *price,* that satisfies these costs, is the *natural price* of Commodities. I admit also, that there is a constant action and reaction, going on, between capital and labor and supply and demand; but what I contend for *is,* that, *in the very nature of things, supply must precede demand.*—

You say, "I have not answered one important objection vz.ᵗ, that if the *supply* of Corn preceded the *demand* it must be at a *lower price* than the grower could afford to produce it; that this is the inevitable consequence of supply exceeding demand." Let us put *price* out of the question. You will allow, that, although the circumstance of fixing upon one commodity, as a general medium of exchange, has altered the *appearance* of things, it has not altered *their real nature.* But the exchangeable value of Commodities is still regulated by their *relative supplies*—These supplies being governed by the costs of production. That, although the introduction of *money*

---

[1] MS in *R.P.*

has occasioned the man, who carries *money* to market to be called a *Buyer* (or a *Demander*) and the man, who carries *commodities* to market, a *Seller* (or a *Supplyer*) yet that, in fact, they are *both sellers and both buyers;* and that the exchangeable value of their Commodities depends upon their *relative supplies.*—The foundation of all Capital, and all profit, is the power, which the labor of man possesses, in conjunction with the powers of the earth, to produce more *food* than is necessary for his own consumption. The *whole,* which he produces is called the *Gross produce;* the expences attending production, the providing for the laborers employed, and replacing the capital consumed, are called the *costs of production;* and that produce, which *remains* after deducting these charges, is called the *surplus produce.* And this *surplus* constitutes the *profit of capital;* it is the fund from which Revenue is derived, from which *alone* capital can be augmented—And is not this *surplus,* from the very terms in which it is expressed, a produce *over and above* the absolute wants of the producers? As the process of production necessarily occupies *some time,* how could the laborers employed in production, *subsist,* unless there was a *previous* supply of necessaries, for their support; to be *replaced,* out of the new fund arising from their labor? In consequence of the cessation of Barter, and of the use of *money,* as a medium of exchange, it became necessary to add the *profits of capital* to the *costs of production* and to include them *both* in the prices of Commodities. But, in the *nature of things Profit* is quite *distinct* from these Costs, and is what *remains after these Costs are satisfied.* Suppose a man possesses a capital of 1000. Quarters of Corn, and that he employs it in setting to work 100. men, who, during the process of production, consume 1000 Quarters; and that they produce 1200. Quarters. It is obvious, that the Gross produce is *1200* Quarters the costs 1000 Quarters, and the *surplus*

29 Sept. 1820 *produce 200.* Quarters. Now, *this* is the *profit;* which is equal
to 20 pC.ᵗ. There can be *no profit* if there is *no surplus*—And
the whole of this profit, *for a time,* is an addition to the
*capital* of the Country. But, it is of such a nature, that it
must speedily be consumed. It may be consumed in the
support of unproductive labor, or in the production of
necessaries, or in the production of conveniences. If this
fresh creation of capital should not be accompanied by any
*increase* of population, it will go to improve the condition
of the existing laborers, and eventually to produce an *increase.*
This surplus produce diminishes (for a time) the exchangeable
value of the Commodity produced; but, as it is the *inevitable
condition* upon which *all profit exists,* it is going on, in the
same manner, in *every* employment of productive capital;
so, that the *general level* of exchangeable value is preserved.
And this furnishes me with an answer to your objection,
that Corn produced, *without a demand,* would sell under
its natural price. No doubt, if Corn were the *only* article so
produced it *would*—But, as the circumstances attending the
production of *all Commodities is the same;* vz.ᵗ that there is
*no profit, without a surplus;* it follows, that, *for a time* the
natural prices of *all* Commodities *alters,* so that the *level* is
still preserved. This effect, it is true, is *temporary,* because
population follows, after capital, with such rapid strides; but,
*still,* the *operation* of the principle is the same, and it is for the
*truth of the principle* I am contending.

In reference to a state of *Barter,* I should say, that no
Commodity will be produced, that does not afford a *surplus*—
That *that* Commodity will be produced, in *preference,* which
affords the *largest surplus*—And that as long as *any* surplus
is afforded, there is *no limit* can be fixed to such surplus, *under*
which Commodities will not be produced—Provided that
surplus possesses an exchangeable value. And, that the

exchangeable value of Commodities is in proportion to their
*relative surplus.*—

In reference to a state of *Money* I should say, that no
Commodity will be produced, that does not pay the costs
of production—That those which afford the largest profits,
will be produced in preference. And that as long as *any*
profit is afforded, there is no limit can be fixed to *such* profit,
under which Commodities will not be produced—Provided
no better opportunity for the employment of capital exists.
And, that the exchangeable value of Commodities is regulated by their costs of production.—

You say, "what we want to know is, whether, in the
present distribution of property, and under the influence of
the motives which invite to production, *Corn* is produced for
any other reason than *iron,* silk, wine & are produced;
whether they are not produced on account of an actual, or
*expected,* demand for them, and whether this demand is not
always indicated by *the relation* of the market price, to the
natural price"—I answer, that the motive for the production
of *all* commodities is *alike,* and that demand is always
indicated by this relation—And, this answer is perfectly
consistent with the view I have been taking. There is not,
*nor can there be,* any difference between us, as to what regulates the supply of one commodity in *preference* to *another.*
*Profit* is the mighty hinge, upon which all productive capital
turns. What I contend for is, that *all Profit* is *Surplus Produce,*
and that all surplus produce is, for a time, an addition to
Capital. That this addition to capital is constantly going on
(although much of it may be rapidly consumed) with regard
to all capital productively employed, that it is the only source
of Wealth. That if that profit is supposed to be at a general
average rate (as *is* supposed) it does not alter the exchangeable
value of Commodities *one with another*—But, if this growing

profit is not accompanied by a proportionate growth of *population,* it alters the relative proportion of *capital* and *labor,* and the exchangeable value of Commodities, in reference to *labor.* The Costs of Production on all Commodities are then encreased, the surplus produce is diminished, and the rate of all Profits reduced.

When you say "that *Corn* cannot be at its *natural price* if the *supply* preceded the *demand."* You do not seem to recollect, that the case of *Corn* is the case of *every other Commodity;* and that consequently its *natural price has altered* together with the natural price of all other Commodities.— Shew me in what *other way* the profits of productive capital can be realised, *than* in the *surplus produce* of Commodities— If it cannot; *then* must there be an annual addition made to the capital of the Country; and this addition must have the effect (for a time) of *lowering the rate of profit;* if not accompanied by a proportionate encrease in the amount of productive labor. The exchangeable value of Commodities is in proportion to their relative *supplies.* Now, Commodities must be divided under *two* distinct heads; because they produce different effects upon the state of a Country— 1. Necessaries. 2 Conveniences. An increase of *Necessaries* in relation to Labor, has the effect of lowering the exchangeable value of Necessaries in regard to labor; of encreasing the costs of production, improving the laborers condition, and *ultimately* of adding to its number; for, the supply of *labor* depends upon *its costs of production* being paid, as well as any other Commodity.—Now, an increased supply of Conveniences produces a *different* effect. In the ordinary state of things there is no *direct* exchangeable value between Conveniences and Labor, for the laborer is not a *consumer* of Conveniences. An increased supply of Conveniences in relation to *Necessaries,* diminishes the exchangeable value of

Conveniences, (for a time) and increases the Costs of their production. Because, a larger portion of Conveniences must be given in exchange for those Necessaries, required to supply the labor, employed in production of Conveniences—The Consumers of Conveniences obtain them upon easier terms and the comfort and accommodation of the Society is increased. But they have no immediate effect in adding to the population of the Country—It is only by stimulating the producers of Necessaries to encreased production, by offering to them, in exchange for Necessaries, objects of desire that *they* contribute to the growth of population—An increased supply of Necessaries affords *immediate means* for an increase of population; although *that* effect may not always result. But, an increased supply of Conveniences affords *no* such immediate means. It adds to the comforts of society, but cannot contribute to the increase of the people, except in forcing the growth of Necessaries. This may be accomplished either by converting nonproductive consumers into pro-ducers of Necessaries, or producers of Conveniences into producers of Necessaries. What I contend for *is*, that there are two great principles constantly at work, upon the opera-tions of which depends national prosperity. 1. That principle, which regulates the proportion between the relative supplies of Necessaries and Labor. 2. That principle, which regulates the proportion between the relative supplies of Necessaries and Conveniences. *You* will say *Profit* is that principle. I admit it; but then I ask what regulates *Profit*. You will say the *Costs of production*. I admit it; but then I again ask, what regulates the *Costs of Production?* And here, I think, the only satisfactory solution is to be found in the proportionate distribution of the capital and labor of a Country, to which I have been adverting; and in that distribution it appears to me, that the capital and labor employed in the production

of Necessaries occasion effects very different from those
arising from the Capital and labor employed in the production
of Conveniences.—

You say and justly, "that it would be wrong to infer
always, that an increase of capital will procure an increased
quantity of work to be done"; but I dont see what ground
*that* affords "for disputing my position, that a demand for
labor is the same thing as a supply of Necessaries." If an
increase of capital will *not* procure an increased quantity of
work to be done, it only proves, that the *demand for labor has
not been satisfied.* I do not say, that a supply of capital
*generally,* but that ["]a supply of that portion of capital which
consists of *Necessaries* is the same thing as a demand for
labor." There could be no demand for labor made, if that
supply of Necessaries did not exist.

In answer to what you observe with respect to Mr. Say,
I agree, that a great inequality in the profits afforded by
productive capital will not *long exist.* But, they may exist long
enough to produce much individual suffering and national
mischief; and it is important to remember, that the interests
of States and of individuals are most seriously affected by
*deviations* from the natural course; and not by the ordinary
operations of affairs. The Science of Political Economy owes
its interest, and its importance, to its teaching us to trace to
their true causes the *disorders,* which are constantly occurring
in the course of human affairs, and thus enabling us to avoid
the evils they occasion, by ascertaining the symptoms by
which they are to be distinguished.—

Pray make our united kind remembrances to Mrs. Ricardo
and your family and believe me

Yrs ever truly—

HUTCHES TROWER

## 391. RICARDO TO TROWER [1]
*[Reply to 390.—Answered by 397]*

Gatcomb Park
3 Oct.[r] 1820.—

My Dear Trower

We are agreed upon so many points, connected with the subject under discussion, that I do not think we can long differ upon that on which there is now a contrariety of opinion. You are perfectly right in estimating profits in the way you do. If the expenditure of 1000 q[rs] of corn would procure 1200 q[rs], 1200 q[rs] would be the gross income, and 200 the net income, or profit. If the expenditure of 1000 lbs. of iron would ensure a return of 1200 lbs, 200 lbs would also be the net profit; but your mistake, I think, is this, you suppose that because when 1200 q[rs] of corn are produced, and by the same expenditure 500 cwt of iron and 100 pieces of cloth, and consequently, they are all of the same value, therefore when the quantity of each of these commodities is doubled they will still be of the same value:—it may affect the division of the gross produce you think between the capitalist and the[2] labourer, but as this will affect all commodities alike, their relative values will remain the same. If one is below, for a time, its natural price, all will be so. Now on the truth of this doctrine depends the whole question. I contend that in all ordinary cases some commodities will under the circumstances supposed be very much below their natural price, that is to say below the relation which they should bear to other commodities. If 1200 q[rs] of corn be of the same value as 500 cwt of iron, and 100 pieces of cloth, as before supposed, those are the relations which should be preserved between them to keep them all at their natural

3 Oct. 1820

[1] Addressed: 'Hutches Trower, Esq[r] / Unsted Wood / Godalming / Surry'; franked 'October four'.

MS at University College, London.—*Letters to Trower*, XLI.
[2] 'producer' is del. here.

value, and to afford equal profits to the producer of each, however their quantity may be multiplied. But the market price of every commodity depends on the relation between demand and supply, and it is the interest of all the suppliers of commodities to cease producing them when they fall below their natural value. The demand for corn, with a given population, is limited; no man can have a desire to consume more than a certain quantity of bread, if therefore more than that quantity is produced, it will fall in relative value to those commodities which are produced only in such quantity as is required. But the demand for commodities such as luxuries; or for services, such as are performed by gardeners, menial servants, builders &c. &c. is unlimited, or rather it is only limited by the means of the demanders. Under these circumstances it is not necessary to produce any thing for which there is not a demand, and therefore it is not necessary that any thing should be under its natural price. If the demand for corn were for 1000 $q^{rs}$ it would be absurd to employ 1000 $q^{rs}$ when we knew that the result would be 1200 $q^{rs}$ for 200 $q^{rs}$ would be unnecessary, and it would be much better policy to employ 833 $q^{rs}$ to obtain 1000, and the remaining 166 to obtain some convenience or luxury the demand for which could be positively anticipated. The same remark applies to iron, cloth &c. &c. If we were under any obligation to produce them, or to produce nothing, there might be an universal glut, and the glutted market of one commodity might continue in its former relations to the glutted market of another commodity, but there would be no glut of any commodity, because the capital of the country could be always employed in producing commodities for which there would be a demand. If in the division of the gross produce, the labourers commanded a great proportion, the demand would be for one set of commodities—if the masters had more than a usual share, the demand would be for another set. Suppose the labourers were so well off, they would not demand more corn than they wanted for themselves, but yet none of their revenue would remain unexpended, an unusual quantity of the luxuries and conveniences of the labourer would be demanded. When would the demand for an additional quantity of corn commence? then only when an unusual number of children were born, and this would eventually take place for it never fails to follow the easy and happy situation of the labourer. Before this there would be no demand, and before this there would be no supply. It follows I think irresistibly from your own doctrine. "Profit is the mighty hinge, upon which all productive capital turns." In every state of society there will be a demand for some commodities, and it is these which it will be the interest of capitalists to produce. If they produced corn before there was a population to consume it, they would produce more of that commodity than could be consumed, and consequently it would fall in relative value to those things which would be demanded. If I satisfy you on this point the argument must be at an end. The capitalist says, "if I produce corn, I shall lose, for it will fall in relative value." "If I produce iron in greater quantity, that may perhaps not be wanted, but if I produce those luxuries required by the labourer I am sure I shall find a market for them, and their price will afford me a better profit than if I produced more corn or more iron.["] If all commodities were on a par, and whichever I produced would glut the market, then I should agree with you, but being perfectly sure that there would be a demand for commodities of some description,—on the part of the capitalists if profits were high—on the part of the labourers if wages were high—I feel confident that the production of no commodity, except from miscalculation, precedes the demand or anticipated demand for it. Our difference then is [that][1] you say that if corn and all other commodities be increased in [the] same proportion, they will continue at the same relative value to [each ot]her. To which I answer If the population do not immediately increase, there will [be no] additional demand for corn, but there will be an additional [dem]and for other things, consequently corn cannot be produced without affording less profits than can be obtained by the production of those other things. It is most true that "if this growing produce is not accompanied by a proportionate growth of population it alters the relative proportion of capital and labor, and the exchangeable value of commodities, in reference to labor" but the labourers will chuse what commodities they shall buy with their additional wages, we are quite sure that corn will not be one of them, and as sure that some convenience or luxury will be chosen. I recollect that if the production of corn costs more, on account of the rise of labour, so will also the production of other things, and therefore if they bore the same relation to each other, there could be no motive for producing one rather than the other; they might all then be in great abundance. But I say they will not continue in the same relation to each other, one will be demanded the other will not. It is not a question of cost of production, but of the relation of market price when produced, to cost of production. Look into your own household and tell me what would be the effect of doubling your income. You would spend it all, but would you double your demand for every commodity you now consume in your family? Should you purchase twice the number of loaves, twice the quantity [of][1] meat, poultry, horses, carriages &c. &c.? No; you would con[sume] more bread—you would probably have a little more m[eat] and fish because you would

[1] MS torn here and below.

keep more company, but you [would] spend much more than double what you now do on pictures and many other [things] to please yourself, and Mrs. Trower. No mistake can be greater than to suppose that the demand for every thing increases in the same proportion. You say the labourer is not a consumer of conveniences. Is this true? If he is not, must we not impute it to his poverty? Give him the means, and do you think he wants the inclination? Will he not improve his house and furniture, his clothing, and that of his wife and children—will he not purchase more fuel, and indulge himself in the enjoyment of better beer, tea, tobacco and snuff?

I forget what I said about M. Say's doctrine, but whatever it was I agree with you that a great inequality in the profits afforded by productive capital may produce much individual suffering, by the inducement which it offers to the change of employments. This evil however generally follows from bad legislation. If free trade were now established, how many individuals would suffer! Political Economy would teach us to guard ourselves from every other revulsion, but that which arises from the rise and fall of states—from the progress of improvement in other countries [than] our own, and from the caprices of fashion:—against these [we can]not guard, but we are not permanently to deprive our country [of many] and important benefits because the adopting of a good instead of [a bad syst]em, will be attended with loss to individuals—I would make [the]ir fall easy, but I would not to support them, perpetuate abuse, and countenance bad laws. It is a safe rule to legislate for the public benefit only, and not to attend to the interests of any particular class. In these sentiments I have no doubt I shall have your concurrence.

I have answered your letter without delay, because I expect a few friends to-morrow, and my time will for some time be fully engaged.—

3 Oct. 1820      Mrs. Ricardo unites with me in kind remembrances [to]
Mrs. Trower.

Y.$^{rs}$ very truly,

DAVID RICARDO

## 392. RICARDO TO MALTHUS [1]
[*Reply to 388.—Answered by* 395]

Gatcomb Park
[9][2] Oct.$^{r}$ 1820

My Dear Malthus

9 Oct. 1820      The Queen's defence appears to be going on well—a
few more such evidence as Sir W.$^{m}$ Gell and I think the Lords
cannot pass the bill: in that case I shall not be called to town,
and if you are in this part of the world at Christmas perhaps
we shall see you at Gatcomb.

Warburton is staying at Easton Grey, and has paid us a
visit of two or three days with the Smiths—he was very agreeable. He does not speak quite positively, but I think he is
one of my disciples, and agrees with me on some of those
points which you most strongly dispute.

I quite agree with you in thinking that M Say's letters
to you are not very well done. He does not even defend his
own doctrine with peculiar ability, and on some other of the
intricate questions, on which he touches, he appears to me to
be very unsatisfactory. He certainly has not a correct notion
of what is meant by value, when he contends that a commodity is valuable in proportion to its utility. This would be
true if buyers only regulated the value of commodities; then
indeed we might expect that all men would be willing to give

[1] Addressed: 'The Rev.$^{d}$ T. R.
Malthus / East India College / Hertford'.
    MS at Albury.—*Letters to Mal-
thus,* LXXIII (dated 10 October).

[2] In MS '10'; but the cover is
franked by Ricardo 'October
Nine' (replacing 'Ten').

a price for things in proportion to the estimation in which they held them, but the fact appears to me to be that the buyers have the least in the world to do in regulating price—it is all done by the competition of the sellers, and however the buyers might be really willing to give more for iron, than for gold, they could not, because the supply would be regulated by the cost of production, and therefore gold would inevitably be in the proportion which it now is to iron, altho' it probably is by all mankind considered as the less useful metal.

I think more may be said in defence of his doctrine of services—they are I think the regulators of value, and if he would give up rent, he and I should not differ very materially on that subject. In what he says of services he is quite inconsistent with his other doctrine about utility. He appears to me to talk very ignorantly of the taxation of England. In the note, Page 101, he concedes too much. The difficulty of finding employment for Capital in the countries you mention proceeds from the prejudices and obstinacy with which men persevere in their old employments,—they expect daily a change for the better, and therefore continue to produce commodities for which there is no adequate demand. With abundance of capital and a low price of labour there cannot fail to be some employments which would yield good profits, and if a superior genius had the arrangement of the capital of the country under his controul, he might, in a very little time, make trade as active as ever. Men err in their productions, there is no deficiency of demand. If I wanted cloth, and you cotton goods, it would be great folly in us both with a view to an exchange between us, for one of us to produce velvets and the other wine,—we are guilty of some such folly now, and I can scarcely account for the length of time that this delusion continues. After all, the mischief may not be so great as it appears. You have fairly represented the point at issue between us—I cannot conceive it possible, without the grossest miscalculation, that there should be a redundancy of capital, and of labour, at the same time.

When I say mine is the true faith I mean to express only my strong conviction that I am right, I hope you do not attach any thing like arrogance to the expression. I am in the habit of asserting my opinion strongly to you, and I am sure you would not wish me to do otherwise. I am satisfied that you should do the same by yours, and I dare say you will agree with me that you are not more inclined to yield to mere authority without being convinced than I am. I affirm with you that "if the farmer has no adequate market for his produce, he will soon cease to distribute more necessaries to his labourers" with a view to the production of more necessaries, but will he therefore leave that part of his capital inactive, will not he, or somebody else, employ it in producing something which will meet an adequate market. You speak of the relative *utility* of our two definitions of value. I confess that your definition does not convey to my mind any thing approximating to the idea I have ever formed of value. To say that real value as applied to wages implies the quantity of necessaries given to the labourer, at the same time that you agree that these necessaries are as variable as any thing else, appears to me a contradiction. Political Economy you think is an enquiry into the nature and causes of wealth—I think it should rather be called an enquiry into the laws which determine the division of the produce of industry amongst the classes who concur in its formation. No law can be laid down respecting quantity, but a tolerably correct one can be laid down respecting proportions. Every day I am more satisfied that the former enquiry is vain and delusive, and the latter only the true objects of the science. You say that my proposition "that with few exceptions the quantity of labour employed on commodities determines the rate at which they will exchange for each other, is not well founded" I acknowledge that it is not rigidly true, but I say that it is the nearest approximation to truth, as a rule for measuring relative value, of any I have ever heard. You say demand and supply regulates value—this, I think, is saying nothing, and for the reasons I have given in the beginning of this letter—it is supply which regulates value—and supply is itself controlled by comparative cost of production. Cost of production, in money, means the value of labour, as well as profits. Now if my commodity be of equal value with yours its cost of production must be the same. But cost of production is with some deviations in proportion to labour employed. My commodity and your commodity are both worth £1000—they will therefore probably have the same quantity of labour realized in each. But the doctrine is less liable to objections when employed not to measure the whole absolute value of the commodities compared, but the variations which from time to time take place in relative value. To what causes,—I mean permanent causes, can these variations be attributed? to two, and to two only; one insignificant in its effects—a rise or fall of wages or what I think the same thing a fall or rise of profits—the other, of immense importance, the greater or less quantity of labour that may be required to produce the commodities. From the first cause no great effects can follow, because profits themselves constitute but a small portion of price, and no great addition, or deduction can be made on their account. To the other cause no very confined limit can be assigned, for the quantity of labour required to produce commodities may vary to double or treble.

9 Oct. 1820    The subject is difficult, and I am but a poor master of language, and therefore I shall fail to express what I mean. My first chapter will not be materially altered—in principle I think it will not be altered at all.

We are all well here and all unite in kind regards to Mrs. Malthus.

Ever truly Yours

DAVID RICARDO

### 393. SAY TO RICARDO [1]
### [*Answered by* 430]

10 Aug. 1820    Je vous envoie, Monsieur, un exemplaire de mes *Lettres à M. Malthus*,[2] petit ouvrage où je me suis glorifié de votre appui dans les endroits où vous avez été pour moi, et où j'ai pris la liberté de combattre vos opinions dans les cas où elles m'etaient contraires.

Je desire vivement que les explications que je donne ici de ma doctrine des valeurs, vous satisfasse mieux que celles qui se trouvent dans mes précédens ecrits. Cette doctrine me semble maintenant digne d'etre adoptée et étendue par vous; et j'attendrai avec impatience les premiers ecrits que vous publierez pour savoir ce que vous en pensez; car je crois avoir montré qu'elle n'est autre que la vôtre en d'autres termes, puisque'elle admet que la valeur d'une chose n'est que la faculté qu'a cette chose d'obtenir en échange (to command) une *quantité quelconque d'utilité:* et que cette *valeur* est proportionnée à la *quantité d'utilité* qu'elle peut obtenir. *Valeur* et *quantité d'utilité* sont donc les termes egaux d'une même

[1] Received by Ricardo on 14 Oct. 1820 (see below, p. 284). MS in the Baker Library of Harvard University. I am indebted to Prof. Arthur H. Cole for communicating letters 393 and 489.
[2] See above, p. 227, n. 1.

équation; et nous ne différons pas vous et moi, lorsque nous ⟨10 Aug. 1820⟩ fesons entrer, vous, l'un de ces termes, moi, l'autre, dans la définition des richesses.

J'espere que votre santé aura toujours été bonne, et je vous prie, Monsieur, d'agréer l'assurance de ma haute estime et de mon profond dévouement.

J. B. SAY

Monsieur David Ricardo a Londres
Paris 10 aout 1820

P.S. Voulez-vous avoir la bonté de faire tenir à M. Malthus, l'exemplaire que je lui presente dans le paquet ci-joint. J'espère qu'il lui parviendra avant qu'il y en ait en vente, quoique j'aie découvert que mon libraire en a envoyé en feuilles à Londres avant que l'ouvrage fût broché à Paris, et par conséquent avant que j'aie pu en avoir.

## 394. RICARDO TO MILL [1]
[*Reply to 389.—Answered by 398*]

Gatcomb Park
14th Oct! 1820

My Dear Sir

I am writing to you in the evening, at that time of the ⟨14 Oct. 1820⟩ day when I am generally attacked with a sleepy fit, so that if you perceive any thing more than ordinarily stupid in this letter, you will know to what cause to ascribe it. I have within these few days received two letters of application for my vote on the next vacancy for the Direction. This is as it should be, I am glad that the candidates are so early in the field, and are so active in their operations, as it will satisfy

---

[1] Addressed: 'J. Mill Esq! / Examiner's Office / East India House / London'. Franked by Ricardo 'October Fifteen'.
MS in Mill-Ricardo papers.

your prudence, if your judgment is not already satisfied, that it would be inexpedient for me to aspire to the honor of sitting at the Honb.<sup>le</sup> Board, which in name, if not in reality governs so many millions of men. The more I reflect on the proposal you were induced to make, the more I am convinced that I should be wrong to be tempted by it. There is no commoner mistake for men to make than to place themselves in situations for which their habits and talents render them unfit;—this they often discover too late, when to retreat is a matter of difficulty, and they are left exposed to all the mortifications which a responsible situation under such circumstances cannot fail to bring with it. I shall act very unwisely if I deviate from the quiet sober path in which I am now moving—it is not one in which I can do *much* good, but still it affords me opportunities of doing *all* the good which I am capable of performing.

Since you left us, we have had a visit from the Smiths, the Miss Bayleys, and Mr. Warburton, and on monday next we are engaged to go to pass a few days with them at Easton Grey. Mr. Knyvett[1] accepted the invitation we gave him, and Mr. Smith no further kept his engagement of meeting him, than by staying one night at Gatcomb.—I had to entertain Mr. K by myself, and as I have often before experienced, the task was not so difficult as I apprehended. He is a good natured man—has seen a good deal of the world, and is very well disposed to be agreeable and satisfied—he went away, I hope, quite contented with his visit.

The walk is finished from the house up the hill, and down it on the further extremity, till it joins the field. On monday we begin the walk in the field, where we projected the shrubbery, to hide the wall which is now so conspicuous from the house. The other walks are all in contemplation.

[1] A musician.

I have disposed of the Coppice to Mr. Playne[1] for £1600, and the right of throwing a net in the lake is relinquished by him. Under his superintendance, and by his advice, I am building a wall across the lake to prevent the fish from going up the Brook, where he says they are mostly destroyed. This wall will be rather ornamental, as it will give me a waterfall—and it will be useful too as forming the side of a small pond which will answer as a preserve for fish. Since selling the Coppice I have bought a field of Mr. Playne, which rather impertinently intruded itself amongst mine. So much money was asked for it, that I confess I was not disposed to purchase it, but by the advice of friends, but still more for the sake of peace and quietness, as Mr. Warburton observed, I have sacrificed my money. It appears to be doubtful whether the road from Nailsworth will be undertaken,—the projectors are disposed to be very civil to me, and to do nothing without my consent.—

I take advantage of every leisure hour to work on my reply to Malthus—I consider it as an agreeable amusement, and say every thing that offers. It will not probably be desirable to publish it—if I do send it forth it will want a great deal of lopping. I hope you are proceeding with your work.—In a letter I received from Malthus, a short time ago,[2] he begs to be kindly remembered to you. In speaking of your projected work, he observes that it should not be done till the disputed points are settled. If you waited till we had his assent to these points, your work would I fear never appear.

I have done what I at present think necessary to my first chapter, and have laid it by for fresh inspection after I have

---

[1] Probably William Playne, a mill-owner at Minchinhampton and a neighbour of Ricardo. (See A. T. Playne, *History of the* *Parishes of Minchinhampton and Avening,* Gloucester, 1915, pp. 41 and 140.)
[2] Letter 388.

forgotten it a little. I am too familiar with it at present to be able to form a tolerable judgment of the repetitions &c.ª &c.ª.

I received from London, to day, M Say's letters to Malthus, sent by himself, and a very kind letter accompanying it[1]— he says "Je desire vivement que les explications que je donne ici de ma doctrine des valeurs, vous satisfasse mieux que celles qui se trouvent dans mes précédens ecrits. Cette doctrine me semble maintenant digne d'etre adoptée et etendu par vous &c.ª &c.ª"—In this I cannot agree with him —it will be necessary I think to take some notice of his late publications in the next edition of my book, for he says ["]J'attendrai avec impatience les premiers ecrits que vous publierez pour savoir ce que vous en pensez; car je crois avoir montré qu'elle n'est autre que la vôtre en d'autres termes."

Mrs. Osman Ricardo's father Mr. Mallory is dead—he has suffered very much for this last twelvemonths, and his best friends must rejoice that his afflictions are at an end.

Well, what do you think of the Queen's defence? It is not exactly what I wish, but still much more satisfactory than I ventured to expect. What a storm has been raised! How glad ministers would be to go back to their position at the King's death! What will be the end of it? Surely the House of Lords cannot now pass the bill. The Queen preaches pure radicalism. Church and state are treated by her with very little ceremony.

Mrs. Ricardo, Mary and Birtha desire to be most kindly remembered to you—they are the only parts of my family now at home. David is gone to Cambridge, and my sister Rachel who came to us a fortnight ago, to Bath—she will return in a few days.

Ever most truly Y.ʳˢ

DAVID RICARDO

[1] Letter 393.

## 395. MALTHUS TO RICARDO [1]
*[Reply to 392.—Answered by 402]*

E I Coll Oct 26th [1820]

My dear Ricardo,

As it [is][2] possible that the note of M. Say, if such note there be, may contain something which requires an answer; I shall be obliged to you to open the packet, and if you find anything of the kind inclose it to me. Of course I am in no hurry for the work itself.[3]

I shall be very happy to renew our old discussions on the interesting topics which have been so often the subject of our conversations. I also fancy that I am fortified with new arguments to prove demonstratively that a neat revenue is *absolutely impossible* under the determination to employ the whole produce in the production of necessaries, and consequently that if there is not an adequate taste for luxuries and conveniences, or unproductive labour, there must necessarily be a general glut. But I want more particularly to talk to you about these parts of the subject where you think I have misconceived and mistaken you. You know I would not do it intentionally; but I think there may be some parts where the words will fairly bear out my construction, and yet you may not have intended to be so understood, in which case I may not be so much to blame. I am preparing a new edition[4] and shall be glad of any corrections and suggestions which you will give me, both in reference to those parts which relate to you, and any others.

26 Oct. 1820

---

[1] Addressed: 'D. Ricardo Esqr MP. / Gatcomb Park / Minchinhampton / Gloucestershire'. Postmark, 1820.
MS in *R.P.*
[2] Omitted in MS.

[3] See letter 393, postscript. A letter from Ricardo is evidently wanting.
[4] The second edition of Malthus's *Principles of Political Economy* was published posthumously in 1836.

With regard to your new definition of the objects of Political Economy, I own it appears to me very confined; and if it be just, I should say that political economy would be at once converted from a science which I have always considered as the most practically useful in the whole circle, into one which would merely serve to gratify curiosity. In the same manner when you reject the consideration of demand and supply in the price of commodities and refer only to the means of supply, you appear to me to look only at the half of your subject. No wealth can exist unless the demand, or the estimation in which the commodity is held exceeds the cost of production: and with regard to a vast mass of commodities does not the demand actually determine the cost? How is the price of corn, and the quality of the last land taken into cultivation determined but by the state of the population and the demand. How is the price of metals determined? And why are the prices of wood poultry hogs &c according to Adam Smith so much higher than formerly.[1]

Do fifty oak trees valued at 20£ each contain as much labour as a stone wall in Gloucestershire which has cost 1000£. But the Post waits

In great haste.

Ever Yours

T R Malthus

---

[1] *Wealth of Nations*, Bk. 1, ch. xi, pts. ii and iii; vol. 1, pp. 166–7 and 224–5.

## 396. GRENFELL TO RICARDO [1]

Brookes's Friday
[10 Nov. 1820]

My dear Ricardo

The Bill[2] is *lost* in the Lords—So you may either come    10 Nov. 1820
up or not I presume as you best like on the 23d

108—for

99—against

Majority only  9—

Upon which Lord Liverpool came forward and abandoned
the measure. The Town is to be illuminated. This is [the][3]
best answer I can give to your Letter that I have just
received from Taplow.

Yours very truly
PASCOE GRENFELL

## 397. TROWER TO RICARDO [4]
*[Reply to 391.—Answered by 403]*

Unsted Wood—Nov. 12. 1820

My Dear Ricardo

I perceive by the date of your last kind letter, that I have    12 Nov. 1820
suffered too long a time to elapse without answering it. But,
I have been absent from home, and the hour glass has run out
much faster than I was aware of.—It has been an eventful
period, and one, which will never be forgotten in the history
of this Country! Thank God the Bill is abandoned by
Ministers. If the investigation had been taken up in your
House, when would it have ended; how would it have been

---

[1] MS in *R.P.*—The date is inferred from the contents.
[2] The Bill of Pains and Penalties against the Queen.
[3] Omitted in MS.

[4] Addressed: 'To / David Ricardo Esqr / M.P. / Gatcomb Park— / Minchinhampton'.
MS in *R.P.*

conducted! However, I confess, I am not one of those, who consider the Queens innocence established. To my mind there was abundance of evidence to establish her guilt. But, under all the circumstances of the case, the unconstitutional nature of the measure, the rank of the party, the bad character of many of the witnesses, the incompetency of the tribunal before which she was tried, (as far as judicial proceedings are concerned) and the extreme unpopularity of the measure, with the whole mass of the people out of doors, all these considerations rendered it altogether inexpedient to legislate upon the subject. But, what now is to be done? I should be glad to see proposed, on the part of some of the most independent Members of the House, a resolution declaratory of the sense of the House with respect to the impropriety of the Queens conduct; something of the nature hinted at by Lord Elenborough, which, whilst it expressed in strong terms how shamfully she has disgraced the rank and dignity of her station, should, at the same time, assert, that the charges were not without foundation. If *you* consider her innocent, of course you would not approve of such a measure; but, if you deem her *guilty,* though not to the extent charged, you must think, that that guilt should not be passed by unnoticed. Perhaps, it may be said, that the carrying of the Bill to the third reading affords a sufficient evidence of the opinions entertained by a majority of the House. And if it had been so carried by a large and decisive majority, that evidence would have been sufficient; but there are many, who voted against the Bill, as unconstitutional and inexpedient, who are, nevertheless, persuaded of the Queens guilt, and there are still others, who, though not persuaded of the *legal* proof of her guilt, have no *moral* doubt upon the subject. A resolution, therefore, to the effect I have mentioned, might command the support of a large majority of the House, and

would, I think have a wholesome effect out of doors. Surely
this woman must not remain here; mischievously disposed,
as she has shewn herself, in her scandalous answers to the
addresses, as a rallying point for the disaffected, and as a
fruitful subject of excitement to the people.

I am in daily expectation of hearing, that Ministers have
resigned; for, I think they can scarcely keep their places after
the loss of character and confidence, which must attend the
defeat they have sustained. But the cry is, who is to succeed
them? No doubt, that is a difficult question; and I agree in
an opinion expressed by Brougham, not long ago, that the
Country will not be satisfied with an Administration taken
exclusively from either side of the House. I confess I am
anxious to see a Ministry, who will sweep away many of our
Commercial restraints; who will purge and purify our
criminal law; who will remove all disabilities from the
Roman Catholicks; who will retrench our expences; and who
will place our finances on a firm footing. These are the
cardinal points to be attended to in the system of our domestic
policy, and, if our statesmen do not avail themselves of the
breathing time, which peace affords, to accomplish those
great objects; in the name of common sense, in what condition will this Country find itself, when forced again to draw
its sword from the scabbard. I have suffered this subject of
*politicks* to occupy so large a portion of my letter, that I have
not space left to reply to your remarks on my last politico
economical arguments. I shall take another opportunity of
touching upon them; only observing, for the present, that
I am happy to find that, in point of fact, there is little or no
difference between us: and that a fuller explanation of my
view of the subject will, I hope, satisfy you, that I am not an
advocate for the doctrine, which contends in favor of a
general glut of commodities. My mind has been drawn off

from these subjects for some time, and I find it requires no little consideration to bring it back to that familiarity with it, which is necessary to enter into its discussion, so I forbear for the present.

Have you seen Godwins Answer to Malthus Essay on Population?[1] Is it worth reading?—Dont forget to let me have the article with which you are to furnish one of the Cyclopedias. Do you hear whether anybody proposes answering Malthus' Principle of P. E.

Pray tell me whether you have reduced the wages of labor in *your* neighbourhood. In *this* they have been reduced from 12/ to 10/ a week in consequence of the fall in Corn and Provisions.

Mrs. Trower begs to join with me in kind remembrances to Mrs. Ricardo and your family, and believe me

My Dear Ricardo
Yrs very truly
HUTCHES TROWER

## 398. MILL TO RICARDO [2]
### [*Reply to 394.—Answered by* 400]

East India House 13th Nov! 1820

My Dear Sir

I have been hindered from answering your last letter, because I have been busy writing my article Jurisprudence, for the Encyclop. Suppt., and have been obstructed both in that and my other occupations by a touch of the gout in my right hand. I have not however had any thing of importance to say. There has been but one public event;[3] and about that we could pretty well anticipate one another's sentiments. You are happy, I doubt not, at the mode of its termination, because it saves you an early removal to town, and all the

---

[1] See below, p. 291, n. 3.                [3] The end of the Queen's trial.
[2] MS in *R.P.*

drudgery of the investigation. For my part, I am not sure whether I ought to be pleased or not. There is but one fundamental good to this country at this time; and that is, the showing what an aristocracy essentially is. The present inquiry has done much toward that greatest of ends; but a good deal still remains to be done. You must think, and better think, how the work is to be forwarded. I have attempted to lay the foundation, at least to explain and make known the principles, in the article Government.[1] By the bye, I have just had a letter from Say, complimenting me upon it. He says it is "serré de raisonnemens, et gros de consequences". He says also he shall often have occasion to quote me in a course of lectures which he is just about to commence. I know not what is to be the subject of a course of lectures in which he will often have occasion to make mention of me.[2] I am in hopes I have done still more to the subject of Law, in my article Jurisprudence, than to that of Government in the other. I am myself at least better pleased with it. In short I have been able to go much farther than I expected in making every thing clear, and establishing it on the ground of evidence; in shewing what is necessary to be done for accomplishing completely the ends in view, and in shewing that it may be done easily. I am a little anxious to know whether it will appear to others as completely clear, as it does to myself —If so, it is a great job done.

Have you seen Godwin against Malthus?[3] To me it

---

[1] In *Supplement to the Encyclopaedia Britannica.*

[2] J.-B. Say had been appointed Professor of Industrial Economy at the Conservatoire des Arts et Métiers; see his 'Discours d'ouverture du cours d'économie industrielle, prononcé le 2 décembre 1820', in *Œuvres diverses,*

p. 133 ff. Cp. below, IX, 192, n. 1.

[3] *Of Population. An Enquiry concerning the Power of Increase in the Numbers of Mankind, being an Answer to Mr. Malthus's Essay on that Subject,* by William Godwin, London, Longman for the Author, 1820.

appears below contempt. He seems not to know the point in dispute; and like so many others, is incapable of distinguishing an argument from a petitio principii, _or begging of the question; the established and approved mode of proving all orthodox opinions, in religion, and in politics.

I am not at all moved by any thing *you say about the Direction.* The only points that weigh with me as any thing to counterbalance the strong reasons for—are the time and toil necessary for canvass, and the length of time a director is employed in the subordinate details, and has little means of employing himself to the best advantage. But as I said before we shall talk about all these things when we meet. That, I am sorry to say, will not be now till after a considerable interval. The interval I hope will by you be vigorously employed in making yourself more and more fit for all manner of high exertions. You want nothing but to believe that you are what you are. Backwardness would not then hinder you from doing the very considerable things which you are capable of doing, and which the conjunctures of the time call upon you to do. It is not enough for a man, who is good for something, to let himself be merely carried along the stream. It is not what he owes to the family of his fellow creatures. It is not what he owes to his own happiness.

I have not been very well. My stomach has been very liable to disorder; and I have found it hardly possible to keep the digesting process in proper train. I hope I am a little better—and now having done with Jurisprudence, I intend to go on vigorously with political economy. I shall be glad, when you have finished your notes on Malthus and Say, and have formed any conclusion about the mode of producing them, if you will transmit them to me, and give me an opportunity of advising with you; because, the time about

which you will most probably come to town, will be the time
best for publication.

I hope Gatcomb, and all its outlying members, are well.
I long to hear how Mr. David has made his commencement
at Cambridge. I was much edified with the account of your
walks, formed and about to be formed. For pedestrians, like
me, you will add exceedingly to the attractions of the place.
I am glad you have disposed of the coppice—but not so
glad that you have given more than its worth for Plaine's
land. I wish all manner of good things to Mrs. Ricardo, and
send my best affections to the dear girls, whom I heartily
thank for remembering me. John is at Montpellier and now
attending classes in the university, with other sorts of lessons
which have not yet been all reported to me.[1]

Most truly yours

J. MILL

## 399. MILL TO RICARDO [2]
### [*Answered by* 400]

Bentham has imposed upon me the task of begging you
to try to recollect, what those papers consisted of which he
lent to you on the subject of his annuitty notes.[3] He has

[1] See J. S. Mill, *Autobiography*,
pp. 57–8. John's letters to his
father from France are in British
Museum, Add. MSS 31,909.
[2] MS (in Mill's handwriting) in
*R.P.* It was found, with letter
389, in a bundle entirely made
up of letters of Sept.–Dec. 1820.
[3] Bentham's plan of 'Circulating
Annuities', first published as
'A Plan for saving all the Trouble
and Expense in the Transfer of
Stock, and for enabling the Proprietors to receive their Dividends
without Powers of Attorney,
or Attendance at the Bank of
England, by the Conversion of
Stock into Note Annuities' in
*Works,* ed. by Bowring, Edinburgh, 1843, vol. III, pp. 105–53.
Bowring notes: 'The papers from
which the following work is
edited, were written by Bentham
in 1800,—and the principal part
of the first four Chapters then
printed: the Editor has been

14 Nov. 1820 mislaid them. He wishes to know in particular whether the printed papers consisted of two Tables, or of three Tables—the third being the note, in the form intended to be issued—and besides the table, whether there were not two printed sheets, and the half of a third.

Please to answer me these questions as nearly and as expeditiously as you can. He is for making a present of his scheme to the Spanish Cortez, from whom he is in expectation of an invitation to make a code.[1]

I forget what were your objections to his notes, as a currency.

I wrote to you yesterday and have nothing to add.

Perry[2] is working hard to get in the Whigs—but I am told the King is highly pleased with his ministers—and has thanked Lord Liverpool for his exertions.

Tuesday [14 Nov. 1820]

## 400. RICARDO TO MILL[3]
[*Reply to* 398 *&* 399]

Gatcomb Park
16 Nov.r 1820

My Dear Sir

16 Nov. 1820 Your last note must be answered first, and I am sorry that it cannot be answered satisfactorily to Mr. Bentham, for to most of his questions I must answer "Non mi ricordo".[4]

able to discover only a single copy of those Chapters.' A copy (F. Place's) is in British Museum, 6025. d. 7 (1); it is headed simply *Circulating Annuities, &c.*, and consists of 48 pp. and two folding tables, the second being the 'Form of a proposed Annuity Note'.

[1] 'The Cortes of Spain in this year [1820], came, in fact, to a unanimous resolution to avail themselves of Bentham's services in the preparation of codes of law for that country' (Bowring, in *Works of Bentham* vol. x, p. 514).

[2] James Perry (1756–1821), editor of the *Morning Chronicle.*

[3] Addressed: 'James Mill Esq.r / East India House / London'.

MS in Mill-Ricardo papers.

[4] 'I do not remember'; this was the Italian witnesses' usual reply to embarrassing questions at the Queen's trial.

The only recollection I have on the subject of the annuity notes is something of the plan itself, but nothing of the papers, or of their form, which gave me the knowledge I have. I am sorry that I can be of so little service to him, but mine is the worst head for recollection in the world.

My objections to Mr. Bentham's scheme was, I believe, that it did not appear to me the best mode of establishing a paper money. It is clear that the whole advantage that can be obtained by the use of paper money is from the substitution of a commodity of little or no value, as an instrument of trade, instead of a very valuable one. This advantage may be enjoyed by the State, or by one or more individuals. I think it should be enjoyed by the State, and that you cannot go too directly to the object. Mr. Bentham seemed to me to aim at this advantage by a circuitous and intricate course, and this I believe formed the principal ground of my objection.

The whigs I think have little chance of coming in. I wish they were tried once more. Good would I think result from it. Either they would do something for the people and then the result would be good, or they would follow the course of all other aristocratical administrations. In the latter case we should at least derive this good from the trial, that the eyes of the public would be opened, and they would know that the means for good government must be sought in another direction and could be only obtained by their own strenuous exertions. It would more thoroughly convince us of the justness of your conclusion, provided it be a just conclusion, that an aristocratical engine will never give us those improvements in our institutions which are so much required.

I am glad that there is at length a termination to the persecution of the Queen. The joy that is felt in this neighbourhood cannot be described. At Wotton, Tetbury, Stroud, and

Hampton there has [been][1] an incessant ringing of bells—
in some of those places they have roasted oxen whole, illuminated every house and cottage, and not a poor person is
seen without a label, a cockade, or a sprig of laurel in his hat. If
Parliament is not prorogued before tuesday I think I shall go
to town. I have written to Hume to ask for information from
him of the intentions of the leaders on both sides the house.[2]

My notes on Malthus (such as they are) are finished.
I cannot think of imposing on you the task of reading them,
particularly as it would be necessary for you to read also the
passages in Malthus on which I comment. I sometimes think
of writing to M'Culloch and offering to send them to him.
He is so warm in the subject that he might perhaps not
dislike going over the points in dispute between Malthus and
me. You do not give me any great wish to read Godwin.
How strange it is that the real question respecting population
should not be known to all who make the subject the object
of their attention and consideration.

I am glad you have finished the article Jurisprudence for
the Supplement to the Encyclopedia,—I long to see it, and
augur well from what you say concerning it.—

With respect to myself I shall say nothing except this that
I am not destined by my talents or knowledge to fill the place
in society to which your partial judgment would raise me.
The least I can do in return for your good opinion is to
employ myself in endeavoring to get useful information,—
this I will not neglect doing.

I am sorry that you have complaints to make of the state
of your stomach, and digestive organs. I hope a perseverance
in an abstemious regimen will soon set all to right.

---

[1] Omitted in MS.
[2] Hume's reply, dated London, 16
Nov. 1820, says that various reports are in circulation but
nothing is known for certain.
(MS in *R.P.*)

You will now be going on with your Political Economy
and will be able to ascertain whether you can explain all the
principles of the science without defining value.[1] I hope you
may succeed in making the difficult points clear.

I am glad you have good accounts of John. I hope Mrs.
Mill and your family are well, pray remember me kindly to
them.—

Mrs. Ricardo has been very unwell—she is now re-
covering. A faulty digestion has been the cause of her
suffering, but she is now relieved from the immediate inconvenience. She and my girls are obliged to you for your
kind remembrances and beg me to assure you of their good
wishes.

David is pleased with his residence at College,[2] and assures
me in his letters that he is studying with assiduity and
diligence.

Ever truly Yours

DAVID RICARDO

## 401. RICARDO TO MᶜCULLOCH[3]
[*Answered by* 406]

Gatcomb Park, Minchinhampton
23 Nov! 1820

My Dear Sir

I have been employed for some little time in writing
notes on Mr. Malthus' last work, which as yet I have shewn
to no one. Indeed I fear that none but the initiated would
understand them, and even they would think it a heavy task
to get through them; for I have, wherever I met with a
passage on which I wished to animadvert, quoted the page,
and the first few words of the passage, and then have written

---

[1] Cp. below, p. 337.
[2] Trinity College, Cambridge.
[3] MS in British Museum.—*Letters to MᶜCulloch,* XVIII.

my short comment. If the criticism were just, and the principles I advocate correct, still it would not I think be desirable to publish it—first, because Mr. Malthus book, I am told, has not excited much interest, and these dry, and perhaps not very clearly expressed comments upon it, will excite still less. You once asked me[1] to send you any remarks that I might have to make on Mr. Malthus' work, and if you would look at the first few pages of these notes, without thinking that I made an unreasonable demand I would now do so. There is I fear too much of repetition. From this fault I could not escape, for it is the great error of the work upon which I have been commenting. I doubt whether you will be able to read it, for I have not taken a fair copy of it, and it is full of interlineations.

I suppose you have seen M Say's letters. Amidst a great deal of truth there appear to me to be some very grave errors —I have noticed some of them in a few pages set apart for that purpose, but there are some with which I have not meddled.[2]

I hear very contradictory accounts of the sale of Mr. Malthus' book. From himself I have lately heard that he is preparing a second edition,[3] but by others I am told that it has a very dull sale.[4]

M Say sent me a very kind letter[5] with a copy of his letters to Malthus. In his letter he speaks confidently of having obviated all just objections to his doctrine of value, in his 4th edition,[6] and in the letters to Malthus, and calls upon me to embrace it. He wishes to see some early publication of

---

[1] Above, p. 176.
[2] On Ricardo's Notes on Say's *Lettres à M. Malthus*, see below, p. 301.
[3] Letter 395.
[4] This had been reported to Ricardo by his brother Samson,

who had heard it from Murray at the end of August. (Letter of Samson Ricardo, 15 Nov. 1820, MS in *R.P.*)
[5] Letter 393.
[6] *Traité d'Économie politique,* 4th ed., 1819.

mine that he may know my sentiments on it. I do not know whether you are well acquainted with his work on Political Economy;—I have looked over carefully all the new matter in his fourth edition without discovering any thing to induce me to alter the opinion which I have given of the confusion of his ideas respecting value. Utility, riches, value, according to him are all the same thing. A commodity is more valuable because it is more useful. A man is rich in proportion as he is possessed of value—of utility[1], and it makes no difference whether commodities are of a low value or of a high value. Erroneous as I think these views are he has not the merit of uniformly adhering to them, for he often acknowledges that commodities will fall in value if their cost of production be diminished, altho' they preserve the same utility. The book I think is altogether an able one, but I am quite convinced that M Say does not see quite through the subject.

Let me hear from you whether you have any wish to look over my speculations.—You may probably be very much engaged at this time, and I cannot promise you any novelty; it is but the old story repeated. I calculate that all I have written would not fill more than 150 pages.

Are you not surprised at the conduct of ministers towards the Queen? They had their option to proceed with the bill or to drop it:—they chose to do the latter, and on every principle of fair dealing, of common liberality, they should I think cease persecuting her. That however does not appear to be their intention, if we may judge from their refusal to grant her a palace, and a suitable establishment.

Believe me ever with great esteem

very truly Yours<br>DAVID RICARDO

J. R. MCulloch Esq<sup>r</sup>

---

[1] 'of utility' is ins.

## 402. RICARDO TO MALTHUS [1]
*[Reply to 395.—Answered by 404]*

Gatcomb Park Minchinhampton
24 Nov! 1820

My Dear Malthus

I have been living in a state of great uncertainty whether I should be obliged to go to London or not. It seems to be settled that Parliament will be prorogued, and therefore I do not think it necessary to take a journey to town for the sole purpose of hearing the usher of the black rods give his three taps at the door of the House of Commons with his rod of office, and which we are assured by Hobhouse would be laid about his back, if he presumed so to disturb a reformed House of Commons. The political horizon does not appear to be clearing up.—It is always unwise for a Government to set itself against the declared opinion of a very large class of the people, and it is more particularly so when the point in dispute is one trifling in itself, and of no real importance to the state. Should the public be kept in this agitated state on a question whether the Queen should be allowed a palace, or whether her name should be inserted in the Liturgy? Nothing can be more unjustifiable than to risk the public safety on such questions as these, for after raising the discussion there is no safety either in yielding or resisting.

You say in your last letter "that you are fortified with new arguments to prove demonstratively that a neat revenue is absolutely impossible under the determination to employ the whole produce in the production of necessaries, and consequently that if there is not an adequate taste for luxuries and conveniences, or unproductive labour, there must necessarily be a general glut." I shall not trouble you to

---

[1] Addressed: 'The Rev⁴ T. R. Malthus / East India College / Hertford'.     MS at Albury.—*Letters to Malthus,* LXXIV.

bring forward these arguments, for with a very slight alteration I should entirely concur in your proposition. If I recollect right, it is the very exception which I made, and
which you mention in your book.[1] You must collect your
stock of arguments, to defend more difficult points than this.

I am quite sure that you are the last man who would
mistate an adversary, knowingly, yet I find in your book
some allusions to opinions which you represent as mine and
which I do not really hold. In one or two cases you I think
furnish the proof that you have misapprehended me, for you
represent my doctrine one way in one place, and another
way in another. After all the difference between us does not
depend on these points and they are very secondary considerations.

I have made notes on every passage in your book which
I dispute, and have supposed myself about publishing a new
edition of your work, and at liberty to mark the passage with
a reference to a note at the bottom of the page. I have in fact
quoted 3 or 4 words of a sentence, noting the page, and then
added my comment. The part of your book to which I most
object is the last. I can see no soundness in the reasons you
give for the usefulness of demand, on the part of unproductive
consumers. How their consuming, without reproducing,
can be beneficial to a country, in any possible state of it, I
confess I cannot discover.

I have also written some notes on M. Say's letters to you,[2]
with which I am by no means pleased. He is very unjust to
me, and evidently does not understand my doctrine; and for
the opinions which we hold in common, he does not give
such satisfactory reasons as might I think be advanced. In

[1] See above, II, 312.
[2] Ricardo's Notes on Say have
not been found. It appears (cp.
below, pp. 341 and 344–5) that
they covered much the same
ground as the passages on Say
added in ed. 3 of Ricardo's *Principles,* above, I, 279–87.

fact he yields points to you, which may almost be considered as giving up the question, and affording you a triumph. In Say's works, generally, there is a great mixture of profound thinking, and of egregious blundering. What can induce him to persevere in representing utility and value as the same thing? Can he really believe that our taxation operates as he describes, and can he think that we should be relieved, in the way he represents, by the payment of our National Debt?

I shall not dispute another proposition in your letter "No wealth["] you say "can exist unless the demand, or the estimation in which the commodity is held exceeds the cost of production." I have never disputed this. I do not dispute either the influence of demand on the price of corn and on the price of all other things, but supply follows close at its heels, and soon takes the power of regulating price in his own hands, and in regulating it he is determined by cost of production. I acknowledge the intervals on which you so exclusively dwell, but still they are only intervals. "Fifty oak trees valued at £20 each do not contain as much labour as a stone wall in Gloucestershire which costs £1000." I have answered your question let me ask you one. Did you ever believe that I thought fifty oak trees would cost as much labour as the stone wall? I really do not want such propositions to be granted in order to support my system.

I think it is now certain that we shall stay here till Jan.$^y$ Perhaps you may be in this part of the world—if so we shall expect to see Mrs. Malthus and you at Gatcomb—your visit would give great pleasure both to Mrs. Ricardo and to me. We unite in kind regards to Mrs. Malthus.—

I am

Ever truly Y$^{rs}$

DAVID RICARDO

## 403. RICARDO TO TROWER [1]
*[Reply to 397.—Answered by 410]*

Gatcomb 26 Nov.ʳ 1820

My Dear Trower

Hardly a day passes, without some new and extraordinary circumstance occurring, to keep up the agitation in
the public mind, respecting the Queen. What could induce
ministers to prorogue parliament without finally concluding
their proceedings against this persecuted woman? If they
thought the bill expedient, why did they not send it to the
commons? If they thought a vote of censure necessary, as
appears to be your opinion, why not now propose it to
parliament. What good can be expected from putting off this
question, which so engrosses the public attention, for two
months longer, and put it off too in such a manner, by
proroguing the parliament without a speech from the throne?
Can the Queen do otherwise than court the mob? Has she
any hopes of safety from the malignancy of her enemies but
in the support of the people. To that she has hitherto been
indebted for protection;—without it she would have been
crushed by her enemies; and while these proceedings are
hanging over her head she will be greatly to blame if she
suffers the spirit which has been raised in her favor to subside.

I am glad that you are pleased with the proceedings in the
House of Lords stopping where they did. For my part I think
they should never have commenced, and never can I consent
to hold up my hand to censure or degrade the Queen, with
the knowledge I have of the means which have been used
to ruin her. If she has had an adulterous connection with

---

[1] Addressed: 'Hutches Trower Esqʳ / Unsted Wood / Godalming', and franked by Ricardo 'November Twenty seven'.

MS at University College, London.—*Letters to Trower,* XLII.

Bergami, which I think is by no means proved, never had woman so many reasons of justification to urge in extenuation of her fault. Considering all the circumstances, a veil of oblivion should have been thrown over her conduct, instead of employing the basest means for detecting and proving her guilt. I most heartily join in feelings of indignation against all the Queen's persecutors, and of compassion for her. Though it is to be lamented that she is the rallying point of the discontented and disaffected—she is absolutely driven to such an alliance, and the only way of detaching her from her present connections is to cease to persecute her.

I very much fear that we shall have no change of ministers, and I am not sanguine, if we have, in my hopes of their adopting the wise measures which you think so essential to our safety, and future prosperity. What ministers, with the present constitution of the House of Commons, can succeed in sweeping away many of our commercial restraints, particularly the greatest, the restraints on the importation of corn? What ministers will dare to encounter our financial difficulties, in the only way in which they should be met, or will seriously commence the work of retrenchment in our expences? We may probably find men who will remove the disabilities from the Roman catholics, and make some amendments in our criminal laws, but this will be all, we must not expect much more improvement, and when we are involved in another war, then will come the time for those efforts which, if we were wise, we ought to make now.

I am glad to find that you do not think our difference great on the question which we have lately been discussing.— I fully expected that we should approximate in our opinions when we came fully to understand each other. I have been lately employed in writing notes on Mr. Malthus work, with a view to defend my opinions, when fairly attacked—to place

them in a true light, when unintentionally mistated—and to
detect the fallacies which appeared to me to lurk under the
author's arguments. My task is now ended, but with what
success must be left to the judgment of others. The whole
might occupy about 150 pages if printed. It is not however
probable that I shall publish them, because they are not in an
inviting form, and would consequently have few readers.
Wherever I have met a passage against which I have an
objection to make I have quoted the few first words of it, and
then written my comments,—in this way for example
Page 103[1] "If we were determined &c. &c." ["]If equal
capitals yielded commodities of nearly equal value, there
might be some grounds for this argument; but, as from a
capital employed in valuable machinery, such as steam engines &c. a commodity of a very different value is obtained,
than from a capital of the same value, employed chiefly in the
support of labour, it is at once obvious that the one term
thought to be the more correct by Mr. Malthus, would be
the most incorrect that could be imagined." This being a
short comment I have copied it as a specimen, and you will
from it be able to judge how little interest general readers
would take in such a performance. I have also added a few
comments on M. Say's letter to Malthus, which I think is
written with more self satisfaction than its merit deserves.[2]
I remember a remark of yours on a passage in Page 128 of
Malthus work, and as I fully agree with you in your comments, and you will only have the trouble of reading what
I write, I am tempted though it is long to copy what I have
said as another specimen of my labours. Page 128. "Though
neither of these two objects, &c. &c."[3] "A complete fallacy
seems to me to be involved in the whole of this argument.

[1] Above, II, 74.     [3] Above, II, 96.
[2] See above, p. 301, n. 2.

Corn is a variable commodity says Mr. Malthus, and so is labour variable, but they always vary in different directions: if therefore I take a mean between the two, I shall probably obtain a measure of value approaching to the character of invariability. Now is it true? do corn and labour vary in different directions? When corn rises in relative value to labour, labour falls in relative value to corn, and this is called varying in different directions. When cloth rises in price, it rises as compared with gold, and gold falls as compared with cloth; but this does not prove that they vary in different directions, for at the same time gold may have risen as compared with iron, hats, leather and every other commodity except cloth. What then would be the fact? that they had varied in the same direction;—gold may have risen 10 pc. in value compared with all things but cloth, and cloth may have risen 25 pc. compared with all things, excepting with gold, relatively to which it would have risen only 15 pc. We should think it strange in these circumstances to say that we should in chusing a measure of value take a mean between cloth and gold because they varied different ways, when it is absolutely demonstrable that they have varied the same way. This is however what Mr. Malthus has done in respect to corn and labour. A country finds increasing difficulties in supplying the corn necessary for a continually increasing population, and in consequence corn rises as compared with all other commodities. As corn rises, which forms so material an article of consumption to the labourer, though not the only one, labour also rises, but not so much as corn;—if corn rises 20 pc. labour may probably rise 10 pc. In these circumstances, estimated in corn, labour appears to have fallen—estimated in labour corn appears to have risen, but it is evident that they have both risen though in different degrees for they will both be more valuable estimated in all other commodities. A mean then is taken between two commodities which are confessedly variable, and it is taken on the principle that the variation of one, corrects the effects of the variation in the other; as however I have proved that they vary in the same direction, I hope Mr. Malthus will see the expediency of relinquishing so imperfect, and so variable a standard. From Mr. Malthus' argument in this place, one would suppose that labour fell when corn rose, and consequently that with a given quantity of iron, leather, cloth &c. &c., more labour would be obtained; the contrary is the fact; labour as well as corn rises as compared with these commodities. Mr. Malthus says so himself in Page 125 'In the progress of improvement and civilization it generally happens, that when labour commands the smallest quantity of food, it commands the greatest quantity of other commodities,' what is this but saying that when a great quantity of other commodities is given for food, a great quantity of other things˙ is also given for labour; or in other words that when food rises, labour rises?" I would not have troubled you with this if it imposed any heavier task on yo[u than][1] reading it.

I have not seen Godwin's answer to Malthus. Mill writes to me that it is a most contemptible performance.[2]

I send you my article on the Sinking Fund. Tell me freely your opinion of it.

I believe they have lowered the price of labour here, but I, as a gentleman I suppose always pay the same. Mrs. Ricardo unites with me in kind regards to Mrs. Trower. Believe me

Ever my d.ʳ Trower

Yʳˢ truly

DAVID RICARDO

My man filled my lamp too full of oil I have let 3 drops fall on the first sheet pray take it with all its imperfections.

[1] MS torn.          [2] Above, p. 291–2.

### 404. MALTHUS TO RICARDO [1]
[*Reply to 402.—Answered by* 405]

E I Coll [27 Nov. 1820][2]

My dear Ricardo

I was just thinking of writing to you when I received your letter. I saw Miss Sims at the Hertford Ball the other night who said that Mrs. Ricardo had been very ill. I trust from your silence on that subject she is now quite well.

I quite agree with you in your opinion of the foolish and insulting conduct of ministers with regard to the Queen. If things go on in their present train, I shall think it the greatest proof I have yet seen of the want of a reform in Parliament. There is however still a great body of the higher classes against the Queen; but it is one of the specific evils of the whole proceeding that it has tended so much to increase the separation of the higher and middle classes, as well as lower.

I cannot but congratulate you on your liberty of staying at Gatcomb, though personally I am sorry to miss seeing you in Town during any part of our vacation which commences next week. I had deferred answering regularly your former letter[3] till I could see you in Town, and now I am quite thrown back. We had intended to go into Surrey to my brothers, but his younger son[4] is not well, and our visit will be deferred. As I should like much to see your remarks upon my book before I publish another edition, I am half inclined to propose calling upon you at Gatcomb for a week, if it will be convenient and agreeable to you and Mrs. Ricardo, to receive me sometime before Xmas. Mrs. Malthus of course cannot leave her children, and the journey for the

---

[1] Addressed: 'D. Ricardo Esq[r] / Gatcomb Park / Minchinhampton / Gloucestershire'.
    MS in *R.P.*

[2] London postmark, 27 Nov. 1820.

[3] Letter 392.

[4] Charles (1807–1821), son of Sydenham Malthus.

whole party would not suit us, even if we could suppose it would suit Mrs. Ricardo; so let me know whether you can receive me as a batchelor, and when it will be most convenient to you that I should come. Perhaps you could tell me also at the same time what coach goes the nearest to you.

The case you mention in your book is expressly stated to be *temporary;* but this makes all the difference. If the taste for luxuries and conveniences, or unproductive labour be absolutely necessary to the existence of a neat surplus from the land, permanently nothing can be more clear than that saving may be carried too far with a view to such neat surplus, and the general principle is obviously impugned.

I answer your question most readily, that I never believed you thought that fifty oak trees would cost as much labour as the stone wall; but it was precisely because I was sure you could not think so that I stated the question, conceiving it a most fair and proper one to shew you, that a theory of exchangeable value which rejects rents, and considers labour almost exclusively, cannot be well founded.

Every day I am more and more convinced that I am right in what I have said of unproductive labour, in the latter part of my work, and I dont yet quite despair of seeing you of my opinion five years hence. Every thing that I have seen and heard since I wrote my book confirms me in my principles, though I feel confident that I am still open to conviction, and shall listen with a docile mind to your arguments. Mrs. M joins me in kind regards to Mrs. Ricardo

Ever truly Yours

T R MALTHUS

## 405. RICARDO TO MALTHUS [1]
*[Reply to 404.—Answered by 408]*

[Gatcomb Park, 29 Nov. 1820]

My Dear Malthus

As Miss Sims told you Mrs. Ricardo has been very unwell with a bilious complaint, to which she is every now and
then liable. This last attack was a very severe one, but she is
now only suffering from the weakness and debility which it
has occasioned.

I am very glad to hear of your intention of paying me a
visit here—I hope it will be for a longer time than you mention. I am desired by Mrs. Ricardo to say that it would give
her great pleasure to see Mrs. Malthus, and your three
children:—she can accommodate them all with the greatest
facility, and therefore unless really inconvenient to Mrs. Malthus to quit home, we hope she will accompany you to
Gatcomb. There is a coach which leaves London 3 times a
week at 5 oClock in the evening; on monday, wednesday
and friday This coach goes to Minchinhampton, one mile
from our house; it carries 4 inside, travels at a very good
pace, and sets off from The Angel Inn S.ᵗ Martin's-le-Grand.
There is also a morning coach which goes from Gerard's
Hall, Basing Lane Cheapside, 3 times a week, in the morning, at a quarter before 6. I believe this coach goes on Tuesday, thursday and saturday—it is a Stroud Coach, and does
not come nearer to our house than within 4 miles, on the
Cirencester Road. If you prefer this coach we will send for
you to the place where the roads diverge. This is of course in
case Mrs. Malthus does not accompany you. Now as for

---

[1] Addressed: 'The Rev.ᵈ T. R.
Malthus / East India College /
Hertford'. Franked by Ricardo:
'Minchinhampton       November

Twenty-nine 1820'.
    MS at Albury.—*Letters to Mal-
thus,* LXXV.

the time of coming, that I leave entirely to you. The sooner 29 Nov. 1820
the more agreeable to me.

It is true the case in my book is stated to be temporary and in my opinion it can only be temporary, because it cannot exist when the population has increased with the demand for people. When we meet we must agree upon the meaning to be attached to "a neat surplus from the land"—it may mean the whole material produce after deducting from it what is absolutely necessary to feed the men who obtained it, or it may mean the value of the produce which falls to the share of the capitalist, or to the share of the capitalist and landlord together. If the first be neat surplus it is equally so whether given to labourers, capitalists or landlords. If the second it may fall short of giving as great a value to the capitalist as he expended in obtaining it, and therefore for him there would be no neat produce. This term neat produce is used ambiguously in your book and is made the ground of an observation[1] on something [which I][2] said about neat and gross produce. The observation is j[ust] or not just, according to the meaning attached to the term neat produce; but more of this when we meet.

Knowing as I do how much we are influenced by taking a particular view of a subject, and how difficult it is to destroy a train of ideas which have long followed each other in the mind, I will not say I am right about the effects of unproductive demand, and therefore it is possible that five years hence I may think as you do on the subject, but at present I do not see the least probability of such a change for every renewed consideration of the question confirms me in the opinion which I have long held.

Ever Truly Y$^{rs}$
DAVID RICARDO

[1] See above, II, 381.  [2] MS torn here and below.

## 406. MᶜCULLOCH TO RICARDO [1]
### [*Reply to* 401.—*Answered by* 407]

Edinburgh 28ᵗʰ Nov 1820

My Dear Sir

Nothing I assure you could be more gratifying to me than a perusal of your observations on Mr. Malthus book— I have long been of opinion that Mr. Malthus merits as a Political Economist were very much exaggerated; but the reputation he has acquired renders his errors the more dangerous—and I congratulate myself on the certainty of the instruction and pleasure I shall derive from your remarks on his principles and conclusions—Do not fear that I shall have the least difficulty in reading your remarks; I am so much accustomed to interlineations and abbreviations of all kinds that I am quite sure I shall read them with the utmost facility. Have the goodness to get the parcel well wrapped up, and send it to me by the Mail—I shall be impatient for its arrival—

I do not know how Mr. Malthus book has sold in London, but I know it has not sold well here—It is the text book—the very gospel indeed—of a few landlords who have read it in order to find arguments to enable them to defend our factitious system; but otherwise it has not been in much demand—

I am tolerably well acquainted with the fourth Edition of Say, and I quite agree with you that the notions of value which pervade it are nearly as confused as in the previous ones—It is astonishing that he should still adhere to his old opinions on the subject of rent; and it is much to be lamented that so popular[2] a work should be erroneous in so important a particular—After all however the great merit of Says work seems to me to consist almost exclusively in the luminous arrangement of the parts and the perspicuity of the stile—

---

[1] MS in *R.P.*          [2] Replaces 'important'.

Excepting the Chapter Des Debouchés it contains no disquisition that can be said to be either original or ingenious— It is sensible and well written and that is all—I have just glanced at his Letters to Malthus, but have not read them through—They struck me as being decidedly inferior to his other work; and I cannot help thinking that your taking any very particular notice of them would be dooing them an honour to which they have no just title. Perhaps Jeffrey would have no objections to my reviewing them;[1] and if so the perusal of your remarks would be of the most essential service to me—

I am just about finishing an article on Interest for the Supp. to the E. Brittanica—I could not say any thing that was new in this; but I think it will contribute to the dissemination of sound opinions on a subject of considerable importance—I shall send you a copy—

Pray have you turned your attention to the subject of the Combination Laws? I have had some intentions of endeavouring to throw together a few observations on them, and if I were not ashamed to give you such an infinity of trouble I should like to know what you think of them—For my part I look on them as extremely pernicious—as totally incompetent to effect any good purpose—as rendering those combinations dangerous which would otherwise be harmless —and as tending to widen the breach, which is already by far too ample, between the labourers and the propertied classes.[2]

Pray do you know any thing of our friend Colonel Torrens?—I have not heard from him for a very long time —I presume he is not in London.

---

[1] They were not reviewed.

[2] See M<sup>c</sup>Culloch's articles on the subject in the *Scotsman*, 26 July 1823, and *Edinburgh Review,* Jan. 1824, Art. III.

28 Nov. 1820 I think the conduct of ministers to the Queen is as weak as it is base—Their policy was now to treat her with all possible respect to give her a Palace, to restore her name to the Liturgy, and to get her a handsome provision. The more they persecute her she will become the more popular—There is not, however, I am afraid the least prospect of a change of ministers. It is the policy of Cobbet and of all the ultra radical writers to hold out all public men as alike corrupt, or in other words to say that revolution is the only cure— Ministers know this and they will profit by it. The violence and the intemperance of the leaders of the mob will soon disgust the greater part of the middle classes who are now united with them, and with their support the ministers will be able to get on as well as ever—Excuse these remarks and believe me to be with the most unalterable sentiments of respect and esteem

Yours truly<br>
J. R. M<sup>c</sup>CULLOCH

## 407. RICARDO TO M<sup>c</sup>CULLOCH [1]
[*Reply to* 406.—*Answered by* 412]

Gatcomb Park Minchinhampton<br>
4 Dec.<sup>r</sup> 1820

My Dear Sir

4 Dec. 1820 After writing my last letter to you I received one from Mr. Malthus,[2] for the purpose of informing me that as the meeting of Parliament was put off, and my visit to London consequently deferred, he would, if convenient to me, pay me a visit here, for a few days, during his vacation. He says that he should much like to see my remarks on his work before he publishes another edition. I do not know precisely when

---

[1] MS in British Museum.—*Letters to M<sup>c</sup>Culloch*, XIX.      [2] Letter 404.

Mr. Malthus will come, but it probably will be at the latter    4 Dec. 1820
end of this week or the beginning of the next. This arrangement will prevent me from immediately availing myself of
the permission which you kindly gave me of sending my
MS to you, but will not probably delay it for more than a
fortnight, as I shall dispatch it directly after I have shewn it
to Mr. Malthus, trusting, most implicitly trusting, that you
will after you have read it give me your candid opinion of it,
with such remarks as may occur to you. The style you will
find miserably bad but that is a fault from which I cannot free
any performance of mine, and all I dare ask of you is to point
out to me any glaring error that may offer itself to your
notice.—

    I do not know that I should say any thing about Say if I
had not received a letter from him[1] with his book, in which
he rather invites me to declare my opinion of his sentiments
in the first work which I shall publish. I wish you may review
his book in the Edin. Rev.: the opportunity is favorable for
I perceive that a translation of it is just advertised by a
Mr. Prinsep.[2] I wish you may find any thing new in my
remarks.

    Before I left London Mr. Murray told me he should soon
wish to publish a new edition of my book. As M Say has left
out of his 4th Edition a part of the matter on which I before
animadverted, and has given his opinion of value in a new,
and as he thinks, an amended form, I think it right to omit
my former observations, and to insert others in their place.
These also I send you.[3]

---

[1] Letter 393.
[2] *A Treatise on Political Economy; or the Production, Distribution, and Consumption of Wealth,* trans-lated from the fourth edition of the French, by C. R. Prinsep, M.A.,
with Notes by the Translator, 2 vols., London, Longman, 1821. M<sup>c</sup>Culloch reviewed the trans-lation in the *Scotsman,* 21 April 1821; see below, p. 374.
[3] See above I, 279–88.

I am glad to hear that you are about finishing an article on Interest for the Supp.ᵗ to E. Brittanica. I am sure it will be well done and I shall read it with great interest.

I have never particularly turned my attention to the combination laws. From the little I do know of them they appear to me to be unjust and oppressive to the working classes, and of little real use to masters. In spite of these laws masters are frequently intimidated, and are obliged to comply with the unjust demands of their workmen. The true remedy for combinations is perfect liberty on both sides, and adequate protection against violence and outrage. Wages should be the result of a free compact, and the contracting parties should look to the law to protect them from force being employed on either side; competition would not, I think, fail to do all the rest. There is a bad practice prevailing in this manufacturing county (Gloucestershire). I am assured by the clothiers that the wages of their men hardly ever vary. When work is slack they cannot find constant employment for their men;—they pay the same for what is done, and employ them all, but perhaps for $\frac{3}{4}$, or $\frac{1}{2}$, of the day, instead of the whole day. This is in fact the same thing as a fall of the wages to the men, but it is unattended with the slightest advantage either to the master or to the public, and has the pernicious effect of inducing the men to linger in a trade which can no longer support them, and prevents the superfluous labour in one branch of trade from being removed so soon as it otherwise would be to another.

I have not heard of Col. Torrens for a long time. Mr. Mill who was here in September told me that the "Traveller" was succeeding very well.[1]

I fear with you that we shall not have a change of ministers. I wish much that the Whigs were to be tried,—they would

---

[1] See above, p. 185.

I think do something for us, although I confess I do not expect much from them. A Reform of the parliament is the only security we can have for a real reform of abuses, and any thing which shall be fairly entitled to that name, we shall not I think get from the Whigs. They may however do some little good and they would at any rate, if they did not reform the parliament, satisfy us that it could be obtained only by the energy and resolution of the people. Although I am very far from agreeing with Cobbett in most of his opinions, I have long been convinced that our security for good government must rest on the institutions themselves, and the influence under which those who govern us act, and not on the more or less virtue in the characters of our governors. The conduct of two different sets of men educated nearly in the same manner, acting under the same checks, and with the same objects in view, as far as their own personal interest is concerned, cannot be materially different.—With sentiments of great esteem I am most truly Y.ʳˢ

DAVID RICARDO

4 Dec. 1820

## 408. MALTHUS TO RICARDO [1]
[*Reply to* 405]

London Dec 7ᵗʰ 1820

My dear Ricardo,

I delayed thanking Mrs. Ricardo and you, on the part of Mrs. Malthus and myself for your very kind invitation to Gatcomb, till I could ascertain whether it was in our power to accept it. I found that as I should at any rate be wanted in Surrey in a very short time, and might be called upon suddenly at any time, Mrs. Malthus's journey with her children was out of the question; but I set out this morning with the inten-

7 Dec. 1820

---

[1] MS in *R.P.*

7 Dec. 1820    tion of paying you a visit myself, for a week at least. I found
however a letter in Town which obliges me to set off to-
morrow morning for Brighton. One of my sisters has been
ill there for some [time][1], and is now just about moving home-
wards, and my brother who had been with her, not being
able to accompany her on account of his son, my assistance
is wanted. How long I may stay at Brighton or in Surrey I
am unable to say; but I need hardly add that if I can find time
during the vacation from more pressing duties and feelings,
and you are disengaged, it will give me great pleasure to
accomplish what I had projected. I will write again when I
know more about my future movements.

Mrs. Malthus was much tempted to accept Mrs. Ricardo's
invitation. She begged to be kindly r[emembered to][2] her.

[Your]s

[T. R. MALTHU]S.

### 409. RICARDO TO McCULLOCH[3]
*[Answered by* 412]

My Dear Sir

13 Dec. 1820    Mr. Malthus had commenced his journey, to pay me his
promised visit, when he heard that his sister, who was ill at
Brighton, wanted him to escort her to London. It is now
doubtful whether he will come at all, and, therefore, I will
no longer delay sending you my papers. On casting my eye
over them, I almost regret having mentioned them to you,
for they are I am sure too insignificant to merit the employment of your time for so long a period, as will be requisite
for you to look them over. I send them to London, with

---

[1] Omitted in MS.
[2] MS torn here and below.
[3] Addressed: 'J. R. McCulloch

Esq[r] / Buccleugh Place / Edinburgh'.—MS in British Museum.
—*Letters to McCulloch*, XX.

directions to forward them to you, immediately, by the mail[1]; 13 Dec. 1820
when you have read them return them by the same convey-
ance to Brook Street, London.

I shall be in London about a week before the meeting of
Parliament: will you be kind enough to direct that the Scotsman be sent to me in London at that time? I hope your agent
will call on me for the payment of my subscription.

Ever truly Yours<br>DAVID RICARDO

Gatcomb Park
13 Dec.ʳ 1820


## 410. TROWER TO RICARDO [2]
*[Reply to 403.—Answered by 415]*

Unsted Wood. Godalming—<br>December 11—1820.

My Dear Ricardo

Many thanks for your Essay on the Funding System. 11 Dec. 1820
I like it very much. The historical part is clearly given; the
view of the subject extremely just, and the arguments by
which it is supported are ably and forcibly urged. I subscribe
to all its doctrines. You have clearly exposed, and justly
censured, the unwise and unwarrantable deviations, from the
original plan of Mr. Pitt, which have been made by Lord
Henry Petty, and Mr. Vansittart. Alterations to which, I feel
persuaded, that great Statesman never would have consented.
I perfectly agree with you, that a Sinking Fund, wisely
arranged, and religiously preserved, is a national benefit. The
powerful effect, which it has in silently converting Revenue

---

[1] Thomas Crosse, Ricardo's solicitor, writes to him from London,
19 Dec. 1820, that the 'parcel for
Edinburgh was forwarded by the
Mail as desired.' (MS in *R.P.*)

[2] Addressed: 'To / David Ricardo
Esqr / M.P. / Gatcomb Park /
Minchinhampton'. Redirected to
'Bromesborow Place near Ledbury
Herefordshire'.
MS in *R.P.*

into capital, is an important consideration. I dont think you have succeeded in answering *fully* the objections of Drs. Price and Hamilton to the raising of Loans in the *3* pCts.[1] I doubt, whether the difference of price and difference of interest, at which the Loans have been contracted in 3 pC., and might have been in *5* pC is nearly equivalent to the different terms on which the capital must be repaid. The contracted market of the 5 pC. would soon have become expanded by the operations of frequent funding in that Stock; and the expansion of market would probably have occasioned speculation to be carried on in that Fund, in preference to 3 pCt.—

I should like to see your Essay in the shape of a Pamphlet; in which form you might enlarge more than you have done, (or perhaps, than was consistent with the object in view, in writing the article,) upon the policy and practicability of discharging a large portion of the Funded Debt.—

I am glad to find you have been at work upon Malthus. It is quite necessary, that the falacies and inconsistencies in his Book should be detected and exposed. The Bulk of our Political Economists take their notions upon that subject, upon *trust;* and the deservedly high character Mr. Malthus holds in this branch of Science, gives a weight to his doctrines, which will command the assent of those, who will not take the trouble to think for themselves. His refutation, therefore, ought to go forth to the public. And, if I might venture to suggest, what appears to me the most expedient mode of publishing your Notes, I should recommend, that you publish a *new edition* of your Principles of Political Economy; and that you throw your Notes on Malthus into an *Appendix*— Perhaps, you may agree with me in thinking, that you might avail yourself of the criticisms which have been made upon your work, to new cast some of your arguments, and to

¹ See above, IV, 184–5.

remove the objections, which have been urged against them;
and which, in my mind, apply merely to their form, and not
to their substance.—There would be a peculiar propriety in
your answering Malthus' Book in this manner; because his
publication is avowedly an attack upon your new and important views of the subject. By printing the Appendix in a
smaller type than the Text, and by compressing your remarks
on his work as much as is consistent with perspicuity, I do
not think it would occupy too large a portion of the Volume.
And marginal references in the pages of those parts of your
work, which he has attacked, might direct the reader to those
parts of the Appendix where he would find Malthus' objections, and your reply to them.—

I quite agree with you in thinking, that your Notes,
published by themselves, would not assume a form sufficiently
popular to insure them an easy admission into the public
mind. Whereas if you publish them, together with your Book,
and thus enable the reader to see how your arguments stand,
after the objections to them have been considered, and
answered, you will not fail to accomplish your object compleatly, and to establish the soundness of your Principles.—
Do not let me hear you urge as an objection, that the new
modelling of your Book is a work of time and labor.
Recollect, that Malthus has disregarded these considerations
in his attack upon your Work; and that his elaborate performance is the fruits of *2 years exertions*. Your Book is
written for *Posterity*, as well as for the Economists of the
present day, and you must not grudge a few months to
render it more perfect; and to brush away the cobwebs with
which it has been attempted to surround it.—

I wish very much you would let me see these Notes of
yours. During my confinement I made some progress in an
abstract of Malthus' Book, which I have not been able to

touch for the last 2 Months; but to which I hope to return after Xmas. I should be glad to compare my comments with *yours,* and to detect and correct any errors into which I may have fallen; by applying to them the touchstone with which you can furnish me.—

I am afraid you think I am become a very idle fellow; as you think it necessary to apologise "for troubling me" with a quotation from your Notes; which you add, "you would not have done had it imposed upon me any heavier task than reading it"!!! The more you trouble me in this way the better. I delight in the subject; and my complaint is, that circumstanced as I am, I have no inducement to pursue it, and thus suffer myself to be led away to the idler pursuits of the Country.—One would gladly imagine, that the love of science is, of itself, a sufficient inducement to its cultivation. But, I fear such is not the fact. The natural byass of the mind is to idle occupation. Industry comes upon the most active, I believe, only by fits and starts. And we require some stronger stimulus, than the love of study, to impel us to exertion. The mere pleasure of existence, which a Country life affords, the various calls of domestic life, the example and solicitations of ones neighbours, the numerous little duties naturally devolving upon a Country Gentleman, all these occupations and interruptions, which fall in so readily with the natural indolence of the mind, are constantly crossing our love of science, and drawing us off from that steady pursuit of an object, which is essential to successful exertion.—To counteract these powerful adversaries, some strong stimulus is necessary; and among these a congeniality of pursuit among those with whom one lives, and moves, is most important. That stimulus I do not enjoy. If you charge me in this fanciful theory, with an attempt of finding an apology for my own individual indolence, I can refer you to some splendid authorities to justify my observations. But perhaps it will be sufficient to remind you, that that Intellectual Giant, the late Bishop of Landaff, tells us in his own life,[1] that influenced by these considerations he sold his Library when he retired into the Country, feeling no longer any adequate motives for those mental exertions, in which he had ardently engaged, as long as any inducements presented themselves!—

Your comments on page 128 of Malthus are quite satisfactory. You have exposed the fallacy of his argument compleatly. With equal propriety might he contend, that when two men are running a race, they are running in opposite directions, because one outruns the other; or because they run an equal pace, they dont run at all!—

I am going next week into Sussex to my brother in law Mr. Slater's,[2] at Newick Park, near Uckfield; where we shall pass our Christmas; and from thence I shall go to London for a few days; where I suppose I shall not have any chance of seeing you—

I have got Godwins attack upon Malthus; but I have not yet looked into it. It is somewhat curious, that after a lapse of more than 20 years the writer whose work originally suggested Malthus' Essay, should send forth to the public an attempted refutation of it. Godwin has a powerful and ingenious mind, but he has given no proofs of a sound judgment. The principle for which Malthus contends, is no doubt undeniable, but I think he has laid himself open to attack by the manner in which he has conducted his argument; I shall read Godwin, although Mr. Mills character of it, does not hold out much temptation.

Our indefatiguable friend Mr. Hume is now exerting himself, I see, in a new line. Pronouncing popular declamations from post to pillar; and occupying the few intervals,

---

[1] See above, VII, 258, n. 1.    [2] James Henry Slater (1793–1864).

that can be left him, in presenting ardent addresses to the exalted Lady at Brandeburgh House! What lasting obligations does her Majesty owe to Messrs. Noel, Moor, and Hume![1]

Adieu My Dear Ricardo. Mrs. Trower desires to join in kind remembrances to you and Mrs. Ricardo and believe me

Yrs very sincerely

HUTCHES TROWER.

### 411. MALTHUS TO RICARDO[2]

London Dec 12th 1820

My dear Ricardo,

12 Dec. 1820     I am just arrived in Town in time for the post, and am happy to say that I have left my sister at home in Surrey, very much better, and indeed quite in a satisfactory state compared with what I feared. I shall set out by the coach which goes through Minchinhampton either tomorrow or friday evening according to circumstances, and hope therefore to see you either thursday or saturday. I shall take the chance of finding you at home if I can start tomorrow, but for fear you should be otherwise engaged it might be worth while just to give me one line which I should receive if I do not leave Town till friday. Direct to me 57. Great Russel Street. The Bell rings

Ever truly Yours

T ROBT Malthus.

[1] Sir Gerald Noel, Peter Moore and Joseph Hume, members of Parliament.
[2] Addressed: 'D. Ricardo Esqr MP. / Gatcomb Park. / Minchin-hampton, / Gloucestershire.' Redirected to 'Bromesbrow Place near Ledbury Herefordshire'. MS in *R.P.*

## 412. M<sup>c</sup>CULLOCH TO RICARDO [1]
[*Reply to* 407 & 409.—*Answered by* 416]

Edinburgh 25<sup>th</sup> Dec<sup>r</sup> 1820

My Dear Sir

I am truly ashamed at my delay in acknowledging receipt     25 Dec. 1820
of your two letters and of the packet containing your notes
on Mr. Malthus late work—The truth is, however, that during
the last few days I have been exceedingly occupied; so much
so indeed that hitherto I have been able to read only a few
pages of your manuscript—But. in a few days I shall have
more leisure, and then I shall immediately set about studying
your notes with that attention to which everything coming
from your pen is so justly entitled—From what I have already
read I am certain I shall derive much instruction as well as
pleasure from their perusal.

Though Mr. Jeffrey would not allow me to review
Mr. Malthus book, he has requested me to write an article
on Accumulation which I have undertaken,[2] and where I shall
endeavour to refute the absurd and pernicious maxims which
Mr. Malthus has inculcated in that part of his work—

Party feeling is much more strongly excited in this city,
and throughout Scotland generally, at this moment than at
any former period in my recollection—The Tories have the
monopoly of power, but, on the other hand, the Whigs have
nearly a monopoly of talent, and possess the confidence of
a vast majority of the citizens—For my part I am exceedingly
anxious for the advancement of a liberal administration to
power, not because I think they would adopt many of those
measures which the circumstances of the country seem

---

[1] Addressed: 'David Ricardo Esq
M.P. / Gatcomb Park / Minchinhampton / Gloucestershire'.
    MS in *R.P.*—*Letters of M<sup>c</sup>Cul-
loch to Ricardo*, VII.

[2] *Edinburgh Review,* March 1821,
Art. VI, 'Effects of Machinery
and Accumulation'.

imperiously to demand, but because they would be more conciliatory in their conduct towards the people, and because they would certainly reform the Scots burgh system—You can have no idea how debasing an engine this is—And I am sure that if you were practically acquainted with the nature of our institutions, you would be astonished we have any independence at all—Cannings resignation will be a severe blow to ministers[1]; still however those amongst us here who are best informed about those matters are of opinion that they will still be able to keep their ground—

Have you seen Godwins work on Population?[2] I have looked into it, and I do not think I ever saw a more miserable performance—It would be dooing it far too much honour to take the least notice of it—

Wishing you many happy returns of this festive season, I am with the greatest esteem and regard

Yours most faithfully

J. R. M[c]CULLOCH

### 413. MILL TO RICARDO [3]
[*Answered by* 414]

East India House 28th Dec[r] 1820

My Dear Sir

I saw Brougham on sunday morning who entrusted me with a commission to you; as it was a thing which he thought that, situated as he was, it was better that he should not write about. It seems that certain propositions have been made to you about the means of increasing your securities in regard

---

[1] Canning had resigned the Presidency of the Board of Control in order to dissociate himself from the Government's proceedings against the Queen.

[2] See above, p. 291, n. 3.

[3] MS in *R.P.—Minor Papers,* p. 204.

to money which you have lent to a certain Irish Lord; and if I understand right about enlarging the loan.[1] However, that is not what I have to write about. That is as follows—A proposition will be made to you, to add immediately three years certain to the two which still remain unexpired of the duration of your seat; for this, however, £3000, (or perhaps guineas) will be asked of you immediately. The 1000 £ or guineas was the rate per annum before. This, therefore, is a demand of the interest upon £3000 for two years in addition.

I have had a touch of the gout in both my feet. The pain has not been much; but it has lamed me, and this is the first day I have been at this house since wednesday se'ennight. I was able, even now, to walk but a little part of the way.

During my confinement at home I have been making good progress with my School Book of Political Economy.[2] In fact I have got over all the knotty points; and, as I think, clearly; so that any body will understand them. Every thing, too, has come within a narrow compass, except money. So many different circumstances had to be noticed, on that subject, that it has been tedious to me in the writing; and occupies a considerable space. Of the whole subject, I have not much to consider, except the topic of *consumption,* including the doctrine of taxes.—I wish it may appear to you calculated to teach the science, easily and effectually. In that case I shall conclude that I have done a good service; as diffusing of knowledge is now the work of greatest importance.

There is to be in the next N.º of the Edin. Rev. a sort of official manifesto of the Whigs on the subject of parlia-

---

[1] The loan to Lord Portarlington, in connection with Ricardo's seat in Parliament.

[2] *Elements of Political Economy.*

mentary reform; so Brougham named it, when he told me of it on sunday. It is from the Mackintoshian pen.[1] You may therefore conceive what sort of a thing it will be. Brougham says the Whigs are too timid to do any thing that will be of any service, either to themselves or to the country.

They are always willing however to join in that cry of irreligion and sedition in the minds of the people, which they think the expedient best calculated for deterring a certain class of men from having recourse to the means of good government; and preserving to the aristocracy the power of doing what they please: that is carrying on an organized system of pillage upon the great body of the people; and as a necessary means to that end, preserving them in a state of as much ignorance, misery and vice, as they possibly can.

I am amused with the old-womanish imbecillity of the Whig addresses.[2] They wish the people, if possible, to clamour for a change of ministers. If we keep the present ministers, they say, we shall have nothing but mischief and misery; they will go on misgoverning as they have misgoverned; and they will either excite the people to rebellion and all the horrors of civil war, or they will land us in despotism. On the other hand, if we can throw them out, and have a new ministry, we shall have every thing as we could wish; we shall have delightful measures of government, and the utmost prosperity to the people. What is this, but saying, what they call other people radicals for saying, that the

---

[1] *Edinburgh Review*, Nov. 1820 [published at the end of Jan. 1821], Art. XII, 'Parliamentary Reform.' A reply, inspired by Mill and written by Grote, to this and the earlier article of Mackintosh (above, VII, 263) was published anonymously under the title *Statement of the Question of Parliamentary Reform; with a Reply to the Objections of the Edinburgh Review, No. LXI*, London, Baldwin, 1821.

[2] Addresses to the King praying for the removal of his Ministers were being adopted at public meetings all over the country.

parliament is good for nothing; that it is ready to do mischief in the hands of a bad minister, and does good only when it gets a minister to make it? That is to say, the parliament is a base, wicked tool, in the hands of ministers. This is the language of the addresses! This is the whig language for their own purposes! This they are very willing to applaud the government for sending Wooler[1] and others to jail for printing.

Mean, dirty set!

I beg to present my best regards to Mrs. Ricardo and the young ladies, whom I long to see

Ever truly Yours

J. MILL

## 414. RICARDO TO MILL[2]
### [*Reply to* 413]

Widcomb House Bath
Jan.ʸ 1 1821

My Dear Sir

I have been very active in my movements since I received your letter, for I have been to Gloucester to attend the County Meeting, and am now here at Bath with my daughter, and Mr. Clutterbuck, where I shall stay till saturday next. My two married daughters have each claimed visits from me lately on the score of having happily got over their confinements.—Sylla has, within little more than a month, presented me with a grandson, and Henrietta within fifteen days with a grand-daughter: so the world goes on, and all that I have to wish for, and which I firmly believe will be accomplished, is that these succeeding generations may be more wise than the present, and may be better able to avail

---

[1] T. J. Wooler, editor of the radical *Black Dwarf*.

[2] MS (in Ricardo's handwriting) in Mill-Ricardo papers.

themselves of the means of happiness which this world affords.——

I thank you for the communication you make to me, respecting the proposition which will be made to me of adding 3 years to the 2 which remain unexpired of the duration of my——. As I shall soon be in London I shall probably hear nothing of it till I get there, and it will not be necessary for me to make up my mind immediately as to the answer which I shall return. At the present moment I am not disposed to accede to it, unless I shall as in the former case have my chance for a longer period. Altho' it was understood that I should in my former agreement have four years certain I actually had a chance of sitting 7 years,—— therefore 7 years was the maximum and 4 the minimum—in the present proposal 3 is to be both maximum and minimum. Mr. Crosse my solicitor was with me at Gatcomb on saturday with a load of papers for me to sign. He had heard something of a wish to enlarge the loan, but he does not encourage me to comply with it.

Our Gloucester county meeting was tame and insipid, but was fully attended by the grandees of the county—many of them too usually to be found on the side of ministers. The speaking was wretchedly bad. I did not intend to say one word. I stoutly refused to second the address, but consented to move thanks to Lords Ducie and Sherborn for their conduct in the H of Lords.[1] I availed myself of this opportunity to utter half a dozen sentences in favor of Reform in Parliament, and endeavored to impress on the meeting that most of our grievances were occasioned by the bad constitution of the H of Commons, and the little sympathy which did or could exist between such a body and the people. I was listened to with attention, and was cheered by the

---

[1] See above, V, 469.

auditors below the upper classes, and even amongst the higher ranks I am sure there were many agreeing with me. One respectable man expressed his regret to me that I did not move a resolution embodying my sentiments he said he would have seconded it, and there is no doubt it would have been carried.

I hope you have got stout on your feet again, and can take your exercise with your usual activity. I am glad to hear that you have made great progress with your book on Polit. Economy. I have no doubt but that you will make it a very useful book, fixing the science on its right basis.

Malthus has been staying with me for a few days—he returned to London a week ago. We had plenty of discussion. In all those cases where he has advanced one proposition in which he says he differs with you, Say and me, and has actually endeavored to prove another, which we should not dispute, he appears to me to hold the proposition which he does prove to be identical with the one not proved; the error therefore is in his language, he appears to me not to be aware of the import of the words which he uses—they convey a totally different meaning to his mind, and to mine. Another of his great mistakes is I think this; Political Economy he says is not a strict science like the mathematics, and therefore he thinks he may use words in a vague way, sometimes attaching one meaning to them, sometimes another and quite different. No proposition can surely be more absurd.

[The last sheet is wanting.]

## 415. RICARDO TO TROWER [1]
[*Reply to* 410.—*Answered by* 419]

Gatcomb Park
Minchinhampton
Jan[y] 14—1821

My Dear Trower

I am sorry that so long a time has elapsed without my returning an answer to your last kind letter, but since I received it I have not only been a great deal employed at home, but I have been to Gloucester; to my sons[2] near Malvern; and to my daughter's[3] near Bath. You give me great pleasure by the favorable opinion you give of my Essay on the Funding System; I am glad to have your sanction to the view which I have taken of that subject, and that you condemn equally with myself the breach of faith to the Stockholder which is so hypocritically defended by our present Chancellor of the Exchequer, who really would have us imagine he performs all that was engaged to be done, by his nominal sinking fund of £16,000,000, while he is every year borrowing 12 millions and adding that sum with 2 or 3 more millions to the public debt. What you say about the market of 5 pc[ts] becoming more expanded by frequent repetition of funding large sums in that stock is most true, but as the capital of 3 pc[ts] was already so large at the commencement of the late war, I doubt whether it would not have been an exceedingly difficult thing to give the same currency to the 5 pc[t] Stock which has been so long possessed by the 3 pc[ts].—Probably Dr. Price and Dr. Hamilton have overrated the advantage one way, and I have underrated it the other. At some future time perhaps I may try whether I can say any thing worth publication in the shape of a pamphlet

---

[1] MS at University College, London.—*Letters to Trower*, XLIII.

[2] Osman.

[3] Henrietta (Mrs Clutterbuck).

on the subject of the policy and practicability of paying off
the Debt.

My remarks on Malthus's work have been sometime with
MCulloch,[1] who long ago requested me to shew him any
observations I might make on Malthus's book. I am desirous
of having his opinion on the remarks themselves, as well as
on the expediency of publishing them. I expect soon to hear
from him, and to have my papers returned to me. Although
they are in a very rough form you shall see them if they
possess the least interest in your estimation. Your opinion,
I perceive, is in favor of publishing them as an appendix to
a new edition of my "Principles of Political Economy."
That was the form in which I at first had an idea of giving
them to the public, but I was strongly dissuaded from it by
Mill, who thought I ought by all means to avoid giving too
controversial a character to my book, and indeed he advises
me not to notice any of the attacks which have been made
upon me, in my third edition, which will I apprehend be
printed soon after I get to London. I shall not urge the
objection which you appear to anticipate, that the new
modelling of my book is a work of time and labor—I should
not grudge however much of these [I][2] should be called upon
to bestow on it, if I thought I could give it a [be]tter chance
of success, either with the present race, or any future race of
Political Economists. I have carefully looked over every
part of it, and with my limited powers of composition I am
convinced I can do very little to improve it. When Mill,
MCulloch, Malthus, and you have seen these notes of mine,
and have given me your opinions of them, I shall know what
to resolve upon respecting the mode of disposing of them.
Perhaps the fire will be the proper place to which to consign
them.

[1] See above, p. 318–19.   [2] MS torn.

I have lately had a visit here from Malthus—he came with the expectation of seeing my notes and he would have seen them had he not after engaging to come to me, been detained in town by the illness of his sister, which made him think that his visit to me must be put off altogether.[1] Before I knew of his coming I had engaged to send the notes to MCulloch, and detained them when I had reason to expect him, but finally sent them off when I despaired of seeing him. While here, he was as good natured, and as agreeable as ever. We spent many hours of each day in discussion, the result of which was only to understand more clearly the points of difference between us.[2] He must be as well acquainted with my objections to his work as if he had read the notes themselves, for I believe there was not one which I forgot to urge, but he is still desirous of seeing the notes, and I have promised to pay him a visit, with them, as soon as they are returned to me.

You are mistaken in supposing that it is possible I may th[ink][3] you a very idle fellow, by the apology with which I accompanied the long quotation I sent to you. I know you are something very different from an idle fellow, and I insist that you had no right to come to any such conclusion because I hesitated about sending you a long winded performance of mine. If you never studied at all, I should not call you an idle

[1] See Letters 408 and 411.
[2] A witness of one of their discussions, the Rev. Benjamin Newton who was staying with the Smiths at Easton Grey, writes in his diary, 21 Dec. 1820: 'Mr Ricardo and Mr Malthus came and entertained us for two hours and upwards with an argument in defence of their respective theories on Political Economy. Mr Malthus contending that the present distress arose from unemployed capital and Ricardo from misemployed capital which would soon assume its proper channels.... Went to Chevenage to dine at Phelps',...it was a woeful falling off from the intellectual treat we had in the morning.' (Extract from the unpublished MS kindly supplied by Mr E. A. Crutchley.)
[3] MS torn.

fellow, I know that much of your time is very usefully em- 14 Jan. 1821
ployed. I hope now I have appeased your irascible spirit. It
was not one of the acts of the late Bishop of Landaff which
has contributed much to his fame, his selling his library when
he retired into the country; it surely must have arisen from
a sordid passion for money, for he could not fail to have
preserved his relish for books.

I leave the country on thursday next, and expect to feel
a great deal of interest in the approaching session of parliam$^t$.
I hear that Ministers are relaxing a little in their severe
measures respecting the Queen—I am told that they will
propose £50000 p$^r$ Ann. for her, and a suitable sum for the

[At the end of the sheet there is written, in red ink and by another
hand: 'The rest wanting. Ch. A. Sec$^y$ May 12/43.'[1]]

## 416. RICARDO TO M$^c$CULLOCH [2]
[*Reply to 412.—Answered by 417*]

Gatcomb Park
Jan$^y$ 17$^{th}$ 1821

My Dear Sir

I leave this place to morrow for London where I shall 17 Jan. 1821
remain in all probability for the next 6 months. I shall be
much disappointed if I do not witness many warm debates
in Parliament, in which all the talents of that assembly will
be called forth, and I am not without hopes that the ministers
may be obliged to quit the places which they so unworthily
fill. Lord Grey, Lord Holland, and several more of the
Whigs, have lately spoken a little of reform in the representation, at the public meetings; but I very much fear that
if they were possessed of power, they would not propose, or
sanction, such a reform as could, or ought to satisfy the

[1] Charles C. Atkinson was secretary of the Council of University
College in 1843–44.

[2] MS in British Museum.—*Letters to M$^c$Culloch*, XXI.

rational friends of freedom. The party are in possession of
a number of boroughs themselves, but what they would be
most loth to part with is the influence which they possess
over the electors in consequence of their being great proprietors of land and other property. They will not consent
to let the real unbiassed choice be in the people, or in that
part of the people which may be considered as having an
identity of interests with the whole.

Soon after I sent you my papers, Mr. Malthus, whom
I despaired of seeing here this season arrived, and stayed
with me a few days. He was sorry not to see my observations.—I told him how I had disposed of them, and promised to pay him a visit on my arrival in London, and to take
them with me. I hope therefore I shall not be hurrying you
too much if I request you to return them to me in the next
week. Mr. Malthus and I had a great deal of discussion, and
on some points understood each other's objections better
than before, but yet there remains the greatest difference
between us. He frequently I think advances one proposition
and endeavours to prove another, and afterwards refers to
the one advanced as settled beyond dispute; and argues from
it accordingly. I never knew a man more earnest on any
subject than Mr. Malthus is on Political Economy—I follow
him pretty closely—and yet after the many hours that we
have passed in trying to convince each other we appear to
have made very little progress. One or other of us must be
very much in fault.

I do not know whether I have ever told you that Mr. Mill
is engaged in writing an elementary work on political
economy.[1] You know I believe that he agrees with you and
me in the principles which we think the correct ones, and
consequently it is those principles which he will endeavor to

---

[1] *Elements of Political Economy,* published later in 1821.

explain and elucidate. When I last saw him it was his intention to steer clear if possible of the difficult word value, and
meant to shew the effect that would be produced on rents,
profits, and wages from the different proportions of the commodity produced which would under different circumstances
be allotted to the 3 classes of landlords, capitalists, and
labourers. I hope Mill will succeed.

There was a very good paper in the Scotsman on the
mistaken view which farmers take of their own interest in
their endeavors to keep the price of our corn so enormously
above the level of the price of other countries.¹ I wish I could
speak on that part of the subject in parliament.

The correct views on the bullion question, and on some
other points of the science of Polit. Economy are neatly
explained in a small work which the author has just sent to
me, but which in his letter to me he said he did not mean to
publish, though he had printed it. The author is quite unknown to me, but I have advised him to publish it in the
usual way, and from the answer which I have received from
him I think he will. His name is Bassett and his letter is dated
from the neighbourhood of Ilfracombe.²—

---

¹ 'Agricultural Distress—Causes and Remedies', leading article in the *Scotsman,* 6 Jan. 1821.
² *Elementary Thoughts on the Bullion Question, the National Debt, the Resources of Great Britain, and the Probable Duration of the Constitution* [Anon.], Barnstaple, printed by J. Avery, 1820, pp. 144. M⁣ᶜCulloch's copy (given to him by Ricardo, see below, IX, 156, 164) is in the Overstone Library of the University of Reading. M⁣ᶜCulloch in his *Literature of Political Economy,* pp. 177–8 reprints, slightly al-tered, the first two sentences of the above paragraph, citing 'Pri-vate Letter of Mr. Ricardo.'

Joseph Davie Bassett later pub-lished as a 2/6 pamphlet, under his own name, *Elementary Thoughts, on the Principles of Currency and Wealth; and, on the Means of Diminishing the Burdens of the People,* Exeter, printed by Trew-man and Co., pp. 75, iv, 1 (un-dated; most of this pamphlet might well have been written in 1820, but there is one reference to 1828, p. 66; in British Museum Cata-logue, '1830?').

Bassett had been a candidate for the borough of Barnstaple

I hope I shall soon hear from you. I am always glad to know that your pen is employed in the dissemination of just principles both on politics and political economy. I hope your article on accumulation is in progress. You are engaged to furnish one on Interest and an other on the Combination Laws,[1] this is as it should be. Believe me

Most sincerely Yours

DAVID RICARDO

### 417. McCULLOCH TO RICARDO[2]
*[Reply to 416.—Answered by 418]*

Edinburgh 22<sup>nd</sup> Jany 1821

My Dear Sir

I return you herewith your manuscripts which I have read with as much attention as was possible for me to bestow, and with equal advantage and pleasure—If Mr. Malthus can read over your remarks on his work without renouncing many of those positions on which he has laid the greatest stress, he can have but a very slender claim to the character of a candid reasoner or of a sincere lover of truth—Nothing I apprehend can be more complete and satisfactory than your remarks on accumulation and on the improvement of machinery[3]—Your argument is here quite unassailable—You have not in fact left a single loop-hole or cranny by which your adversary can escape—Nothing remains for him but to

---

(*Star*, 30 June 1819). Cp. a curious passage in a letter of William Dunn, an Owenite and writer on finance, to Ricardo: 'I see Mr Bassett has begun to harangue on opposition Topics at Barnstaple. Such opinions prevail in those parts and if distress *widens* I think you will be sooner in Downing Street than I anticipated.' (Undated but apparently of the summer 1819; MS in *R.P.*, unpublished.)

[1] For the three articles see above, pp. 313 and 325.

[2] Addressed: 'Mr Ricardo'—not passed through the post, being enclosed with the MS of Ricardo's *Notes on Malthus*.

MS in *R.P.*—*Letters of M<sup>c</sup>Culloch to Ricardo*, VIII.

[3] The notes on Malthus's Ch. VII, Secs. III and V.

surrender unconditionally—I do not, however, think that
you are either so perspicuous or so successful in what you
have said about value—This in my humble opinion is the least
valuable part of your notes—You say that Mr. Malthus "is
quite right in asserting that many commodities in which
labour chiefly enters, and which can be quickly brought to
market will rise with a rise in the value of labour,"[1] meaning
I presume with a rise of real wages, that is, with an increase
in the proportion of the produce of the labourers exertions
given to him—I confess I was not prepared for this proposition, and I should like to have seen you devote three or four
pages to explain it—You do not I am sure mean to say that
a rise of wages can raise the *real* value of any class of commodities—It can only raise their relative value, and it does
this not in consequence of their rising in absolute value, but
of others falling in a still greater ratio—Suppose that the
durability of the different capitals employed in production
are as 1, 2, 3, 4, 5, 6, 7, 8, 9, 10, &c, and that 1 is the least and
10 the most durable—When wages rise they are all affected
in the same way but in different degrees. 10 is less affected
than 9, 9 than 8 and so on; they must, therefore, all sink in
relative value except the first, 2 will fall but a very little,
3 a little more and so on—As any standard with which they
can be compared must itself be produced by the employment
of capital returnable in a certain period, when wages rise
those commodities which are produced by less durable
capitals will appear to rise and those which are produced by
more durable capitals will appear to fall—In truth, however,
the whole would have fallen; and if the standard had been
produced by capital whose durability was equal to 1 they
would almost all have fallen as compared with this standard
while it is plain none could have risen—If I am right in this

[1] Note 25; above, II, 64.

reasoning it is conclusive as to Mr. Malthus objections, and it shews that no commodities, however rapidly returnable the capital employed in their production may be[,] can be raised by a rise in the wages of labour. I hope you will have the goodness to state to me your opinion on this point, for it is one on which of all others I most wish to have sound opinions.

This, however, is a point which if it be really involved in any degree of obscurity you can very easily clear up, but I have other objections to your publishing your notes in their present shape—They are by far too controversial; and the plan you have adopted has necessarily involved you in what seems to me to be a good deal of tedious and unnecessary repetition—The better way in my humble opinion would have been to have briefly stated the leading objections of Mr. Malthus to your theory, and then to have refuted him, without following him like a commentator from page to page—This is the plan, or nearly so which you adopted in your reply to Mr. Bosanquet, and it is the only one that can be satisfactory to the reader—Satisfied as I truly am of the very great value of your Notes, and of the benefit which their publication would confer on the science, still I should be extremely sorry were you to give them to the world in their present state—If you consider it as too great a sacrifice to recast them in the shape of answers to propositions, you might at least shorten the previous part of them—all before accumulation—with very great advantage—The first economist of the age ought not to waste his time in writing a refutation of every error into which another economist may have fallen, but only to set him right on those great principles which affect the foundations of the science—

I throw myself on your goodness to excuse the freedom of my remarks—It is alone to my anxiety for your

reputation as an economist that you must ascribe them—
Had my respect and attachment for you been less sincere I
should not certainly have troubled you with the previous
remarks—

Your observations on Say are excellent, but is there not
a little repetition in the first part of the one of what is said in
the first part of the other?[1]—

I am heartily glad to see a third edition of your work
advertised—Though I am of opinion that it is nearly perfect
still I think it may be improved a little—I think you might
recast the chapter on Accumulation and make it a good deal
more complete; there are also one or two other points on
which I think you might make some alterations with advantage—I see Malthus is taking to his old trick of book-
making[2]—His book instead of being lengthened ought to
have been curtailed one third[3]—

I have enclosed you a copy of my article on Interest[4]—
I am afraid you will hardly reckon it worth sending—The
subject was so hacknied that I had little or nothing new to
bring forward—

I am glad you approved of the paper on the Corn laws in
the Scotsman; and I wish heartily you would when the
subject comes before Parliament make a speech shewing the
injurious effects of the Corn Laws on the farmers—This

---

[1] Ricardo had sent to McCulloch both the Notes on Say's *Lettres à M. Malthus* and the revised passage of the *Principles* criticising Say's *Traité*. See above, p. 315, and below, p. 344–5.

[2] Cp. above, VII, 383.

[3] Murray's list of 'works preparing for immediate publication' (*Monthly Literary Advertiser*, 10 Jan. 1821) included Ricardo's *Principles*, 'The Third Edition, corrected, 8vo.' and Malthus's *Principles of Political Economy*, 'A New Edition, corrected and enlarged, 2 vol. 8vo.', described as 'similar to the last Edition of the Essay on Population'. Malthus's 2nd ed. did not, however, appear in his lifetime.

[4] *Supplement to the Encyclopaedia Britannica*; the article is mostly on the subject of the Usury Laws.

22 Jan. 1821

would be a great practical good—I am with the greatest respect and regard

Yours most faithfully
J. R. McCULLOCH

### 418. RICARDO TO McCULLOCH[1]
[*Reply to 417.—Answered by 421*]

London Jan.ʸ 25—1821

My Dear Sir

25 Jan. 1821

There being no business in the House of Commons this evening, I cannot more agreeably employ my time than in returning you my sincere thanks for the very candid and friendly manner in which you have given me your opinion of my papers. You may be assured that it has the greatest weight with me, and confirms the view which I myself took of the inexpediency[2] of publishing my notes on Mr. Malthus's work. For the present I shall do nothing with them. I cannot spare time to try to extract what may be most useful in them, and put it in the form which you advise, and I fear the same reason may prevent me from recasting the chapter on accumulation in my former work, which is now actually in the printers hands for the purpose of printing a 3d. edition. If however before he comes to that chapter I find that I have time and talent sufficient to improve it I shall not fail to attempt it.[3] I have made some alterations in the first chapter "on value" which I fear from the remarks in your letter will not meet with your approbation.—I wish I had sent you the chapter, as it is now printing, with the other papers, that I

[1] Addressed: 'J. R. M'Culloch Esqᵣ / Buccleugh Place / Edinburgh'. Franked by Ricardo 'January Twenty six 1821'.

MS in British Museum.—*Letters to McCulloch*, XXII.
[2] Replaces 'expediency'.
[3] *Principles*, Ch. XXI, unchanged in ed. 3.

might have profited by your opinion of it, before I had
proceeded so far towards its publication. I agree in every
thing you say respecting the variations which would take
place in the relative value of commodities on the supposition
that they were produced with capitals of degrees of durability, as 1, 2, 3, 4, 5, 6, 7, 8, 9, 10 "as any standard with
which they can be compared must itself be produced by the
employment of capital returnable in a certain period, when
wages rise those commodities which are produced by less
durable capitals will appear to rise and those which are
produced by more durable capitals will appear to fall—In
truth, however, the whole would have fallen; and if the
standard had been produced by capital whose durability was
equal to 1 they would almost all have fallen as compared with
this standard while it is plain none could have risen." These
are my opinions expressed only in language ten times more
clear than I could have expressed them in. But here is I think
the difficulty. You say "if the standard had been produced
by capital whose durability was equal to 1 they would almost
all have fallen as compared with this standard, while it is
plain that none could have risen" true, if the standard were
so produced, but Mr. Malthus and our adversaries say that
the standard shall be produced with labour without any
capital at all, or at most the capital only that is necessary to
support a man a single day. In this standard your No. 1
would fall with a rise of food and necessaries, and labour
never could rise at all. Malthus has supposed a case of a
man by a day's labour being enabled to pick up a certain
number of grains of gold or silver on the sea shore[1];—suppose
he could pick up as much silver as we coin into a shilling,
labour never could fall below a shilling a day, and if corn
rose in silver labour could not rise and all commodities,

[1] See above, II, 81.

produced with capital, which could not be brought to market for a year, a month or even for two days, would fall in such a standard with every rise in the price of food and necessaries. If we could take our stand at No. 1 we should do very well but we are driven from it, and it is proved that a thing which is produced and brought to market in one day by ten mens labour, is not so valuable as another commodity produced and brought to market at the end of ten days, after one mans labour has for that time been employed upon it. Are you prepared to adopt this standard of daily labour? It may possibly be the correct one, but the circumstances under which it is produced agree so little with the circumstances under which most other commodities are produced, that by adopting it we introduce a cause of variation of price, which we avoid if we chuse a standard produced under the ordinary circumstances that other commodities are produced. I am not satisfied, as I have often told you, with the account I have given of value, because I do not know exactly where to fix my standard. I am fully persuaded that in fixing on the quantity of labour realised in commodities as the rule which governs their relative value we are in the right course, but when I want to fix a standard of absolute value I am undetermined whether to chuse labour for a year, a month, a week, or a day. I should not so soon after the receipt of your letter, for I received it and the parcel this morning, have given you my thoughts on this difficult subject, if I had flattered myself that by more consideration I could have arrived at more satisfactory conclusions, but I am sure I could not, for I have reflected so much upon it that I despair of becoming more enlightened upon it by my own unassisted efforts.

There is a great deal of repetition in the two parts of the observations on Say and they should not both have been sent to you, one part was intended for the 3$^{\text{d}}$ edition of my work

—the other for the notes on Malthus—if I published one 25 Jan. 1821
I should not have published the same matter in the other.

If the House will listen to me, and my courage do not fail
me, I will take the first good opportunity of saying something on the injurious effects of the corn laws on the farmers.

I thank you for your article on Interest, I shall read it with
much satisfaction. With sentiments of the greatest regard and
esteem I am

My dear Sir<br>
Very truly Yours<br>
DAVID RICARDO

### 419. TROWER TO RICARDO [1]
[*Reply to 415.—Answered by 420*]

Unsted Wood. Feb. 16—1821

My Dear Ricardo—

It was a very great disappointment to me, not to have 16 Feb. 1821
the pleasure of seeing you during the few days we were in
London last week. I fully intended surprising you one
morning at breakfast; but the violent cough and cold from
which I suffered, whilst in London, and which still torment
me, prevented my getting out at an hour sufficiently early
for *you;*[2] and as our Nursery was left *here,* Mrs. Trower was
anxious to return home as soon as possible.—I shall be much
obliged by your favoring me with a sight of your Notes on
Malthus; which I cannot for a moment admit should not go
forth to the public, in some shape or other. Malthus' reputation and influence with those, who *talk* upon political
economy, more than they *think,* requires that his attack upon
your Book should be answered by *some*body; and who so

---

[1] MS (in Trower's handwriting) in *R.P.*
[2] Ricardo's breakfast hour was half past nine; see above, p. 19.

capable of answering him as *yourself.* His work is vulnerable, in many points; and the inconsistencies into which he has frequently fallen, if properly pointed out, would have the effect of strengthening those opinions, which it was the main object of his Book to attack. Your great candor and liberality afford Mr. Malthus a considerable advantage over you. You, at all times, place before him, without reserve, your views of the subject in dispute between you, and thus enable him to anticipate *your* objections in his *own* publications, and to prepare his *own* objections before *your* publications are ready for the press. I do not condemn this liberality, on the contrary I commend it. It is the true spirit in which the search after truth ought to be conducted. But, at the same time, we ought not to shut our eyes, to the advantages you thus give to your antagonists. I believe, Mr. Malthus is, himself, too liberal a man, to take any undue advantage of your candor: but it is obvious, that such a benefit could not be safely granted to every controversialist.—

I bow with reverence to Mr. Mills better judgment; but I confess I do not see how you can publish a new edition of your Book, without taking *some notice* of the answer to it which has been published by the Professor of Political Economy ! And if you take *any,* then the question arises as to the best mode of doing it. No doubt, if you determine upon a separate publication, your new edition may, then, go forth in silence; but will you be able to place your objections in a tangible shape, to give them a fair chance with the public, or to grapple thoroughly with your antagonist, without embodying in your publication the sum and substance of your original work. And, if so, had they not better be united?

I agree with you in what you said in your reply to Mr. Baring the other night.[1] The two standards for currency would be

---

[1] On 8 February; see above, V, 71–8.

objectionable on many accounts. And the fall in the prices of commodities is too great to be attributed solely to the late rise in the value of the currency. Mr. Barings opinions, however, (and deservedly too upon most commercial points) have great weight with men of business, on account of his extensive practical experience. The observations, I have heard made upon what passed the other night, have been to this effect. That Mr. Barings speech was *practical,* yours *theoretical.* Now *your theory* is founded on *practice* as much as his *practise* is; and if you were to throw into your observations some of the leading *facts* upon which your views are founded, it would have an excellent effect. These subjects are likely to be much handled during the Sessions, and I rejoice to see you fight for the cause of sound principles, so strenuously, and so ably.—

Thank God the subject of the Queen is losing its interest with the public quickly; and it will be no easy matter to rouse again the enthusiasm which so long existed; even if any body should be mad enough to attempt it. Ministers have done wrong, I think, in not replacing her name in the Litturgy, but she is I am persuaded, what I wont soil my paper by expressing, and may congratulate herself in having so well escaped the dangers she so rashly encountered.—

On the 27. I shall resign my Office[1] into the hands of Mr. Spicer, who is to give his dinner on that day at Esher place, to which I find the Prince of Coburg is invited.

I am sorry, Ministers have granted an Agricultural Committee. It cannot do any good. All the facts of the case are before the public. And an enquiry will have the effect of raising hopes and expectations, that it can never satisfy.—We ought to rejoice and not lament at the evidences which present themselves! Things are now taking their natural

---

[1] The Shrievalty of Surrey.

course, and will, I am persuaded, ere long, place matters on their proper level. It is impossible to regain our right position without much severe pressure. Landlords are loud in their calls for a robbery on the public creditor; but they take care never to admit to the *only true* remedy; a fall in Rents, a fall in Tithes, and a fall in the *expences* of Husbandry. These, however, will come, in spite of the left handed honesty of these clamorous landlords; who silently fattened upon the distresses of the annuitants and the consumers, for many years; and who now call out, lustily, when forced to disgorge a portion of their unnatural acquirements!

[The conclusion is wanting.]

## 420. RICARDO TO TROWER [1]
### [*Reply to* 419]

London 2 March 1821

My Dear Trower

Before I address you on any other subject, I must express the great pleasure I have felt, from hearing from all quarters, and from all parties, commendations of your impartiality and talents, on the occasion of the County meeting in Surrey, at which you presided.[2] Before the meeting I was sure that the part you had to perform would be done in a way to reflect credit on you, but I confess I did not expect that the opportunity would have been so favourable for the display of the good temper, moderation and talents which so certainly belong to you.

I was disappointed in not seeing you on your late short

[1] MS at University College, London.—*Letters to Trower*, XLIV.
[2] The meeting of the freeholders of Surrey, held on 2 Feb. 1821 at Epsom, had adopted resolutions deprecating the proceedings against the Queen and urging economy in public expenditure. Trower, as Sheriff of the county, presided. (*The Times*, 3 Feb. 1821.)

visit to London. I hope that you will soon be disposed to take another trip to this busy scene, and that then you will not forget the satisfaction you will afford me by giving me your company as often as you may find it convenient.

Mr. Malthus has now had my notes for 5 weeks,—he has been interrupted in the examination of them by the death of Mr. Dalton, a friend of his in Lincolnshire, to whose funeral he was obliged to go.[1] I expect to see him in London next week at which time he will no doubt return me my MS. I am glad that you speak with approbation of the spirit in which I carry on the contest with Mr. Malthus—I always wish him to see what I have to say against his opinions before I publish them, that I may be sure that I have not misunderstood him, and therefore not misrepresented him. He certainly has not done the same thing to me, and has, I am sure, without intending it, misrepresented me in many important particulars.

A writer in the Times of this morning[2] appears to have adopted some of Malthus' principles, and the conclusions he draws from them are so wild and extravagant, that if we had no other reason for suspecting their fallacy, these would afford them. This writer recommends that we should raise loans now instead of the taxes with which we are burthened, and for this sagacious reason, because it will promote expenditure and take off the superfluity of our productions.

In my dispute with Baring the House listened to me with great attention. The subject of the two standards will again come under discussion, and I shall be prepared to shew from Baring's evidence that there are insuperable objections to the alteration which he proposes.[3] He, I am sure, ascribes too

[1] Cp. above, VI, 35, n. 1.
[2] The fourth of a series of letters 'On the Revenue and Taxation', signed 'Abraham Tudela.'
[3] See above, V, 93, n. 3 and 106.

much to the rise in the value of money and I am prepared to shew that even measured by silver, that is, to say by the exchange with France, or Hamburgh, the rise in our currency has not been more than 10 pc. in five years,— he may answer that silver itself has risen in value,—that may be, but then it is common to all countries that use silver as a standard, and I should be glad to know what security we can have against such an inconvenience, whilst we use the metals as a standard, and by what means he would guard us against it. Would he give us the paper system again unchecked by a fixed standard?

I am sorry that no security can be found against the forgery of Bank notes,—the recalling of the one pound notes cannot fail to enhance the value of the currency.[1]

You speak of the landholder most justly—he is an interested being seeking unjustly to load the other classes of the community with his share of the public burthens. I am however disposed to concede that if we are to have restrictions on the importation of foreign corn the most eligible mode would be by a fixed duty, not more operative in excluding corn than the present restrictions; for I think it is better to have a steady price of corn, rather than one which must alternate from low to high and then from high prices to low ones again. On the present plan we are either overwhelmed with foreign corn, or totally deprived of it.

Mr. Plunkett's speech the other evening was a very fine one[2]—I thought Peel tame and feeble. Surely no reasonable

---

[1] On 20 February it was stated in the House of Commons that the Commissioners appointed to inquire into the means of preventing the forgery of Bank Notes had so far failed to discover a process which would produce an inimitable Bank Note. Vansittart on 19 March pointed to these disappointing results as a circumstance which justified the anticipation of the period in which the Bank should resume the issue of gold coins. (*Hansard*, N.S., IV, 804 and 1316.)

[2] On his own Motion for a Committee on the Claims of the Roman Catholics of Ireland, 28 February;

man can apprehend danger to the United Kingdom from according the catholic claims in Ireland—I believe that the church establishment in Ireland would be more secure, but I should not see much to regret if Ireland had a catholic establishment, in the same way as Scotland has a presbyterian one. If there be an established religion it should be that of the greatest number. In this I do not expect you to agree with me. Fare you well my dear Trower, and believe me ever $Y^{rs}$

DAVID RICARDO

Mrs. Ricardo begs to join with me in kind remembrances to Mrs. Trower.

421. McCULLOCH TO RICARDO [1]

[*Reply to* 418.—*Answered by* 422]

Edinburgh 13 March 1821

My Dear Sir

I am quite ashamed at my having been so long in replying to your friendly and excellent letter of the 25$^{th}$ of January—The truth is that I intended to have written to you long ago; but as Mr. Jeffrey intended leaving this place for London very soon, and as I wished to have my article on machinery and accumulation [2] printed before his departure, I was induced to delay troubling you with any communication—When you read over the article in question you will be

---

*Hansard,* N.S., IV, 961 ff. Peel opposed the motion which was carried by 227 votes to 221; accordingly, on 2 March a bill was ordered to be brought in. *Hansard* gives the lists of majority and minority and it is curious that Ricardo's name should not be included, although from this letter he appears to have been present in the House. Cp. above, V, xxii–xxiii.

[1] Addressed: 'David Ricardo Esq / M.P. / Upper Brook Street / London'.

MS in *R.P.—Letters of McCulloch to Ricardo*, IX.

[2] See below, p. 366, n. 2.

at no loss to discover the source from whence I have borrowed the greater part of my principles—I have been quite
as much indebted to you on this as on other occasions—The
letters you have honoured me with, and the perusal of your
notes on Mr. Malthus work have furnished me with a sufficient
knowledge of the principles regulating the decision of this
question, and it must be my own fault if I have not turned
them to good account—

I have been so much engaged otherwise that I have not
yet had time to consider the subject of value under the view
given by you in your letter to me—I shall, however, take
an early opportunity of doing so—I should feel considerable
reluctance in being obliged to relinquish the stand on capital
of the durability of No 1; but although this position were
not tenable still it appears to me, on a very hasty consideration of the subject, that the difficulty might be obviated by
making a proportional allowance for the different times during
which capital is employed in the work of production—When
I have reflected more maturely on the subject, I shall take
the liberty to lay my opinions respecting it before you—

I read your speech on the agricultural question,[1] as
reported in the Courier, with great interest—I confess, however, that I was extremely staggered with some of the positions
you are reported to have laid down—Such, for example, as
that it was imperative to impose some shackles on the corn
trade[2]—and that the country had nearly got the better of all
her difficulties[3]—It is impossible you can be accurately
reported in what you say about the corn trade, and it is of
great importance that you should get the error rectified—If
you admit that the trade in corn ought to be shackled to any
greater extent than the imposition of a duty on importation

---

[1] On 7 March; see V, 81 ff. above.     [3] *ib.* p. 91.
[2] *ib.* p. 87.

equal to the burdens which can be shewn to fall exclusively on the agriculturists, you give up the whole principle of the question—It is impossible to say where interference ought to stop; and a proposal to increase the importation price to 100*l* would be quite as reasonable as a proposal to reduce it to 60*l*—Whenever you give up the principle of free trade you are quite at sea, and one duty may be just as good as another— Since your speech came down the monopolists have been quite in high spirits; and I, therefore, entreat of you to take some effectual method of obviating the erroneous impression which the report of it in the Courier is so well calculated to produce—

If in stating that the country has nearly got the better of *all her difficulties* you mean that the supply of manufactured goods will in future be more nearly adjusted according to the effective demand, and that capital will be better distributed, I should entirely agree with you—But the faulty distribution of capital does not make a tithe of the real and substantial difficulties of the country—Our taxation and our corn laws have lowered, and must continue to lower, the profits of stock in this country—They have brought us into the condition of a snow ball in a furnace—And unless we were surrounded with Bishop Berkeleys wall of brass,[1] our stock will be gradually transferred to other countries—I hold this to be the real difficulty with which the country has to contend, and I have yet to learn that there is the shadow of a ground for saying that it is nearly gone by—I admit that with prudent management the burdens which sink the rate of profit and stimulate the transfer of stock to other countries might be easily reduced; but we have no such management, and in

---

[1] 'Whether, if there was a Wall of Brass a thousand Cubits high, round this Kingdom, our Natives might not nevertheless live cleanly and comfortably, till the Land, and reap the fruits of it?' *The Querist,* [Part I,] Qu. 140.

arguing this question we must take things as they are—
a bad government—an oppressive system of taxation—and
an average price of corn twice as high as the average price of
any other country—For a time it may be possible to dam up
water or capital to a comparatively high level, but ultimately
and in spite of every obstacle it must fall to the general level
—Besides is it not absolutely certain that while the corn
law system is persevered in we shall continue to experience
excessive fluctuations in prices? Why I beg to know should
the next five years differ in this respect from the last five?
I thought you had admitted that fluctuations at one time had
the effect of entailing famine on the consumer and at another
time of entailing ruin on the farmer—I may be wrong in this
supposition—I suppose I am so—But if I am right it humbly
appears to me that nothing could be more completely at
variance with this principle than the opinion expressed by
you in the Courier—If Political Economy be worth one
straw as a science—if there be one principle which may be
said to be ascertained—if it is not a mere holyday bauble—
we are entitled boldly and confidently to affirm that so long
as the present taxation and corn law system is kept up the
country never can rise superior to the difficulties—To maintain the contrary is to countenance and propagate a most
dangerous delusion—Why ask the minister to abolish taxes,
or to relax the barbarous restraints on trade, if we have
already nearly got the better of all our difficulties, and are
about to enter the haven of prosperity?

You will forgive me for saying so, but it is my honest and
sincere conviction that your speech is calculated to do infinite
mischief—The opinions of the great mass of those who
address the House are not entitled to the least consideration,
and do not meet with it—But when we find the first Political
Economist of the age stating that the corn trade ought to

be shackled—and that in spite of the distresses of the agri-13 March 1821
culturists, of the pressure of the poor rates, and of taxation
that we have nearly got the better of all our difficulties—
what are we to think?

I cannot for my own part express to you the concern I feel
on this occasion—And did I not flatter myself that your
speech had been altogether misrepresented, I should feel as
if I had been deprived of my firmest support, and that there
was very little in common between my opinions and the
person from whom I believed I had derived them all—
I am with great regard

Yours most faithfully<br>J. R. M<sup>c</sup>CULLOCH

422. RICARDO TO M<sup>c</sup>CULLOCH <sup>1</sup><br>[Reply to 421.—Answered by 424]

London 23 March 1821

My Dear Sir

I have been impatient for an opportunity to answer23 March 1821
your last letter ever since I received it, but have never had
one till this time, having been incessantly occupied either in
the Agricultural Committee,<sup>2</sup> or by my attendance in the
House of Commons.

I must in the first place thank you for the frankness with
which you express your opinion to me of the sentiments
which you suppose me to have uttered in the debate on the
appointment of the Agricultural Committee. I should estimate your letters much less highly than I do, if you did not

<hr>

[1] Addressed: 'J. R. M'Culloch Esq<sup>r</sup> / Buccleugh Place / Edinburgh'.
MS in British Museum.—*Letters to M<sup>c</sup>Culloch,* XXIII.

[2] The Select Committee on the Distressed State of the Agriculture of the United Kingdom, appointed on 7 March 1821, of which Ricardo was a member.

freely animadvert on every part of my public conduct which you may think questionable, and particularly that part of it which should appear to you to compromise those principles of Political Economy for the maintaining of which I first entitled myself to your notice. If I should ever change my opinion I will manfully avow it, and trust I shall be able to give such reasons for the change as shall at least satisfy all candid men that I do so from a conviction of my error. In the present instance no such change has taken place, and in the speech, to which your letter alludes, I, boldly, and without any equivocation, defended all the doctrines on the corn trade which I have advanced in my book. It was my object to[1] shew the absurdity of Mr. Curwen's notions of a protecting or countervailing duty on the importation of corn, and I thought I did it successfully by my allusion to the manufacture of sugar from beet root in France during the war[2]—I shewed that on his system the French Governm:[t] should have imposed a duty on the importation of West India sugar, after the peace, equal to the difference of the cost of manufacturing sugar in the West Indies and France. My argument appeared to make a great impression even on those who were absurd enough to be bewildered by such a doctrine as that of Mr. Curwen. I laid down my own principle of a countervailing duty, and which has been misrepresented in all the papers[3]—I contended that it should not amount to more than the peculiar taxes to which the Agriculturist was subject, and on the same principle he should be allowed a bounty equal to those taxes on the exportation of corn—that thus the prices abroad, and at home, would be always nearly alike, and if we had an abundant harvest the farmer might export it without a great and destructive fall of price. I cer-

---

[1] 'ridicule' is del. here.
[2] See V, 90–1, above.
[3] See V, 87, above.

tainly did admit that we could not immediately adopt such
a plan, but contended that all our measures should have that
object in view. This I have always said and so have you—we
have both agreed that we should not, immediately, and at
once, jump from a bad system to a good one,—what we have
contended for is that the good system should be never absent
from our view, and that all our measures should enable us
gradually to approach it. The newspapers have, and always
do, misrepresent me,—I dare say the fault is mine in a great
degree, for I speak very badly, and always hurry on too fast.
In many parts of my speech I have been best reported by the
British Press which I have endeavored to get to send to you
but without success. With respect to the opinion I gave of
our situation I have not been incorrectly reported—I uttered
what I thought. I was answering Mr. Whitmore who represented our situation as almost desperate from the magnitude
of our taxation, and the effects of the alteration in our
currency. I said only what I thought, when I expressed an
opinion that it would not be long before we saw a marked
improvement in our condition. I do not attribute the distressed state of Agriculture to taxation, I believe that it might
have been as bad, with the present corn laws, if we had not
had a single tax to pay—abundance without a vent cannot fail
to produce distress, but must it be lasting? I think not. You
think otherwise because you are of opinion that capital will
be constantly drawn away from this country whilst the corn
laws are in force. I acknowledge the tendency of capital to
flow from us, but I think you very much overrate it. I have
always said that the desire to stay in our own country is a
great obstacle to be overcome. You infer too strongly I think
that profits abroad exceed profits here by the whole difference
in the money price of corn. My opinion is this—if we were
allowed to get corn as cheap as we could get it, by importa-

tion, profits would be very considerably higher than they now are; but this is a very different thing from saying that profits are very considerably lower here than abroad. It is quite possible (tho I do not believe it is true) that profits may be higher here than abroad. It is possible that the labour price of corn may be cheaper here than in the countries from which we should import corn if the trade were free and open. I have put the case in my book of a country having a very little superiority over its neighbours in the production of corn but a very great one in the production of manufactured goods.[1] In such a country, notwithstanding a corn law, profits would be higher than in the neighbouring countries, and consequently no capital would flow from it, although it should refuse to import cheap corn. I beg you to observe that I do not say this is our case, I only say it might be our case, and I mention it to shew you that the rate of profits may not be so enormously different here and elsewhere as you are disposed to think. I acknowledge the tendency of the corn laws to send capital from the country—I acknowledge that our immense taxation has a tendency to produce the same effects, and I believe in my conscience that no measures could so much contribute towards our wealth and prosperity as repealing the corn laws, and paying off our debt, but though this is my opinion I am by no means ready to admit that we may not have a more limited measure of prosperity notwithstanding the continued operation of our corn laws, and the continued existence of our debt. In nothing that I have now said am I conscious of maintaining any opinion at variance with those principles which it has been my pride to advocate, and which I can assure you I am strenuously supporting against a host of adversaries, in the shape of witnesses, as well as members, in the Agricultural Committee.—I pray you not

---

[1] See above, I, 136, note.

to judge me by the newspapers—my last speech[1] as detailed by them on the currency is so unlike any thing I delivered that I scarcely recognise a sentiment of mine in it—I am sorry for this, but I know no remedy for it.—

In my speech on the corn laws I recommended an open trade on the principle I have already stated, and I further said that whilst any corn law existed it should not be on the present footing, which had the effect of alternately giving us a glut of corn, and then a scarcity and high prices—that next to an open trade a fixed and permanent duty was desirable provided it were only moderately higher than the limit I had pointed out. Such a regulation would at least give us steady prices, but in adopting it we should never lose sight of the principle that free trade was our true policy. If the opinion of so humble an individual as myself can be of any importance to any one, you have my free consent to state in your paper as from authority that the sentiments which I have already expressed are those which I endeavored to convince the house were the correct ones.[2] You may possibly be startled at the idea of giving a bounty on the exportation of corn, I have not now time to give you my reasons for such an opinion but shall only say that no protecting duty can at any time be justifiable unless it be allowed to draw it back on exportation:—the freedom of trade in fact requires a bounty to such an amount. You ask ["Why][3] ask the minister to abolish taxes or to relax the barbarous restraints on trade, if we have already nearly got the better of all our difficulties, and are about to enter the haven of prosperity"? I answer, because I am not contented with a little prosperity if I can obtain a great deal for my country. My opinion was given

---

[1] Of 19 March; above, V, 91 ff.  [3] MS torn.
[2] The *Scotsman* did not publish this statement.

23 March 1821 also[1] in reference to the currency question, to which all our misfortunes are frequently referred, and I held responsible, as if I was the sole author of that measure.[2]

I have a great deal to say on the different effects which follow from a taxation to support expenditure and a taxation to pay the interest of debt, but on which I cannot now write. I hope after this explanation you will relinquish the idea that there is very little in common between your opinions and mine. I shall be always at my post advocating the good cause, which I never have nor never will compromise—it has always appeared to me that the generality of people very much undervalue the resources of a great nation: if the language of the opposition in the house of Commons be sincere they undervalue them, and I think they do no good by making the picture more dismal than the reality

Ever My dear Sir Truly Y$^{rs}$

DAVID RICARDO

### 423. TROWER TO RICARDO [3]
[*Answered by* 426]

Unsted Wood—
1. April. 1821.

My Dear Hunter[4]

1 April 1821 Since I had the pleasure of seeing you I have met with an accident that has confined me to the Sofa, and very near cost me my life. This day 3 weeks I went into the stable to look at one of my Carriage Horses, which was unwell; and whilst I was in the Stall he was siezed with a fit of mad

---

[1] 'also' in ins.
[2] Peel's Bill of 1819.
[3] MS in *R.P.*
[4] Notwithstanding this curious slip (or is Trower teasing Ricardo for his aversion to hunting? cp.

above, VII, 308–9 and 318–19) the contents and the conclusion of the letter show that it was intended for, as well as sent to, Ricardo.

staggers, broke his halter, reared up, and before I could get out of the stall, fell down, and, in falling, struck my leg very violently with his head. The injury is on the tendons of the leg, which though very painful, will not, eventually, be of any serious consequence—Had I been a foot or two nearer the Horse I must have been smashed in pieces. In justice to my *prudence,* I must tell you, that when I went into the Stall the Horse was quiet, and the Coachman with him. I can hobble about with a stick, and I hope soon to be able to resume my usual exercise.—

It gave me great pleasure to observe, that justice was done to the "Ricardo System," in the debate the other night.[1] Upon the whole Mr. Baring's appeared to be a very able speech; and that part of it which was faulty I think you answered very triumphantly. No theory was ever more compleatly established by facts, than the doctrines, you have taught, have been by the evidence of the last few years. We are now in the right course, and all that is requisite is *patience* to give time for the natural development of the causes in operation. I have been reading Godwin's attack upon Malthus.[2] It is not written in the true spirit of philosophick enquiry. It is intemperate and abusive; and with all the *pretence* of systematick investigation, it is a rambling disjointed performance. It proceeds upon a gross misconception of Malthus' system, and is supported by scandalous misrepresentations of his opinions. As an attack upon the great principle inculcated in the Essay it is perfectly impotent. Whether population will double itself in *25* or in *50* years is of no moment as far as the *principle* is concerned; and Godwin himself is forced to admit the tendency of population to increase. I have always thought Malthus did not place his doctrine upon its proper *basis.* It is not the more rapid

---

[1] See above, V, 92.  [2] See above, p. 291, n. 3.

multiplication of animal life, than vegetable life, which occasions population to out run food, but it is the *limited extent of land,* and the rate at which it can be encreased—that is to say, at which fresh land can be taken into cultivation. The mere increase of vegetable life is infinitely more rapid than that of vegetable[1] life; and the industry of every man, properly directed, is capable of producing much more food than is necessary for his own existence. But, the *quantity of land* from which that produce can be obtained is *limited,* whilst the growth of population is not affected by that limit, consequently this growth will have a tendency to run on till it is stopped by the *want of subsistence.* Of course, this is what Malthus *means,* but it is not what he has *said;* and therefore he has laid himself open to the attacks of those, who object to the *litteral terms* in which his doctrine is delivered.—

Pray let me know what is *your* opinion of Godwins Book, as I recollect you said you were reading it, when I was in London.—

When is Mr. Mill's Work[2] to make its appearance? What is its *object?* A new digested system? Or an answer to Malthus? Or new views of any part of the system? I am very impatient to see it. Of course his opinions are identified with your own?—

I begin to hope the Catholick question will succeed *in both Houses.* Lord Castleregh's[3] language does not appear to me to anticipate any difficulties in the *Lords.* Is this the case? I dont know how to respect the opinion of any man, who seriously entertains the apprehensions, that have been expressed by the opponents of the measure. But, in fact I dont believe they *do* entertain them. The *real fear* is the *ultimate*

---

[1] Should be 'animal'.
[2] *Elements of Political Economy.*
[3] Castlereagh had spoken and voted in the House of Commons in favour of Plunket's motion for the Catholics, see above, p. 350, n. 2.

1 April 1821

*consequences* of that spirit of *concession* in which the measure originates. Test, and Corporation Acts, Tithes, Church Establishment, these are the real foundation of the alarms attributed to "the Old Whore of Babylon"! Dont forget to let me have your Notes upon Malthus. How does your Agricultural Committee come on? What is to be done? Shall you collect any important evidence? Perhaps, as a Member of the Committee, you will be able to procure me a Copy of your Report? I should like to see it very much.—

The Catastrophy in Italy[1] disappoints me very much— I had hoped better things from the people. But, if they have really acted in the dastardly manner that is represented, it proves, that they are not deserving a better state of things; or perhaps, it would be more just to them to say, they are not yet *ripe for it.* To be sure, one good may arise out of the result that has occurred; it will prevent the lighting up of a general war in Europe, which a successful resistance on the part of the Italians might, ultimately, have occasioned. And, I think there can be no doubt, that the general prosperity of Europe, and, perhaps, under all the circumstances, even of Italy itself, will be more essentially promoted by the preservation of *peace,* than by the benefits of a more liberal government, encumbered, as it would have been, by the evils of war. *Rest, Rest* is what we want; leave nature to herself and she will work her own cure.

Let me hear from you soon. Mrs. Trower begs to join with me in kind remembrances to you and Mrs. Ricardo, and believe me

Yrs very truly—
HUTCHES TROWER

[1] The suppression, by the Austrian army, of the revolution in Naples and in Piedmont, and the restoration of absolute government.

## 424. McCULLOCH TO RICARDO [1]
*[Reply to 422.—Answered by 428]*

Edinburgh 2 April 1821

**My Dear Sir**

2 April 1821     Your letter of the 23$^{rd}$ ulto gave me great satisfaction—
I never doubted that you had been grossly misrepresented
on the subject of the Corn laws; still however I am not sorry
that I took the liberty of calling your attention to the subject
—I knew you were not one of those who would take offence
at any fair animadversion on their public conduct, and the
ingenuous manner in which you have been pleased to reply
to my hasty remarks would, had that been possible, have
sufficed to have given you a higher place in my estimation—
     Still, however, I must acknowledge that I am not a convert
to your opinion respecting the prospects of the country—
I admit that a considerable relative reduction in the price of
manufactured goods might sustain the rate of profit in a
country which had high corn prices—But, in point of fact,
we can never be in this situation—Our corn, which is the
main regulator of wages, may be double or triple its price in
other countries but owing to the facility of transport, and
their great value in small bulk, it is next to impossible that
our manufactured goods can be from 15 to 20 per cent
cheaper—The opposing forces do not, therefore, balance each
other, and there must be a drain of capital from the country
with low profits—You appear to me to lay far too much stress
on the love of country—This passion is, I believe, strongest
in low states of society—There is no reason why the capitalists
of Great Britain should be more disposed to remain satisfied
with comparatively small profits than the capitalists of
Holland—Indeed I feel a firm conviction that it is owing
infinitely more to the unsettled state of the Continent and

---

[1] MS in *R.P.—Letters of McCulloch to Ricardo*, X.

the distance of America than to any other circumstance that an infinitely greater quantity of British capital has not been transferred to other countries—Were the United States as near us as France the love of country, I am afraid, would be found to be a very small restraint indeed upon the desire to get larger profits by sending capital across the channel—

It has frequently occurred to me that it would be of the greatest importance to have accurate accounts of the prices of corn in other countries, for as long a period as possible such as at the markets of Amsterdam, Dantzick, Archangel, Paris, Medina de Rio Sico in Spain, New York, &c.—By comparing the prices in England with these prices many curious conclusions might be deduced, and much light might be thrown on the provision made by nature for regulating the differences of climate and of seasons—May I, therefore, be allowed to suggest to you either to move in the House or in the Agricultural Committee that instructions be sent to our Consuls in foreign countries to procure accurate, and well authenticated, lists of the prices at these or such other places as may be judged proper—I presume that such a motion would be at once acceded to; and I am sure that the information it would furnish, particularly the Amsterdam prices, would be of the greatest service—It would be necessary that precise instructions should be sent out to have the prices at each place calculated in the same measure and carefully converted into so many grains of gold, or into coins of a known weight and fineness—They might be obtained at Paris for a space of 200 years—Permit me, from *selfish* as well as from public motives, to entreat of you to submit a proposition to this effect to the House—Our information respecting the state of the corn trade is quite incomplete without these lists— I have, during the course of the winter, given a course of instruction in Political Economy[1] to a few young gentlemen attending the University here—The greater part of them were foreigners—I hope I have been of some use to them—At least it is not from any want of attention on my part if they are not well acquainted with the principles explained in your great work—

I shall send you in a few days the sheets of my article on Machinery and Accumulation—It will not I am well aware communicate any information to you; but I hope it will have a good effect in counteracting the influence of the poisonous nostrums, for they can be called nothing else, of Messrs. Sismondi and Malthus[2]—Believe me to be with the greatest esteem and regard

Yours most faithfully<br>J. R. M<sup>c</sup>CULLOCH

## 425. TOOKE TO RICARDO[3]

Russell sq<sup>re</sup><br>Thursday morn: [19 April 1821]

My dear Sir

If you have got my evidence of Friday last[4] printed, have the goodness to send it to me under cover and I will return it to you as soon as I have looked it over.

I sent back the minutes of my evidence of last Monday[5]

---

[1] Cp. below, IX, 134, n. 1.

[2] *Edinburgh Review*, March 1821 [published late in May], Art. VI, 'Effects of Machinery and Accumulation'. M<sup>c</sup>Culloch, convinced by Ricardo's arguments, had reversed his former opinions (see above, p. 171, n. 1) and now maintained that 'no improvement of machinery can possibly diminish the demand for labour, or reduce the rate of wages' (p. 115). Ricardo, however, had now changed his own views (see below, p. 373).

[3] MS in *R.P.*—For dating, see following footnotes.

[4] 13 April 1821; see 'Report from Committee on the Agriculture of the U.K.' (*Parliamentary Papers*, vol. IX, 1821), pp. 287–94.

[5] 9 April; see *ib.*, pp. 233–40.

with many alterations altho still with many imperfections on their head:—the only alteration however upon the propriety of which there can be any question as doing any thing more than making sense of the answers, is the addition to my answer to the question relative to the connection between the harvest and the revenue:[1] at the same time I think that addition so essential to my view of the question that I shall be much obliged to you if you will see to its being printed as part of my answers.

I was sorry not to meet you at dinner yesterday, but knowing before I went the importance of what was going forward in the house[2] I did not expect you.—The institution of a society for promoting the knowledge of political economy was determined upon under tolerably favorable auspices; and you will in due time learn the particulars I presume from Col Torrens.[3]—

Most truly Yrs

THO[s] TOOKE

[1] The question and answer are not to be found in the published minutes of Tooke's evidence.

[2] Lambton's motion for the Reform of Parliament; lost in the House of Commons by a majority of 12 against it, on 18 April 1821.

[3] The preliminary meeting for the foundation of the Political Economy Club had been held on Wednesday, 18 April 1821, at the house of Swinton Holland, 13, Russell Square. Holland, Tooke, Torrens, Larpent, Norman, Mill, Mallet, Mushet and Cowell were present. It was decided to hold the first meeting of the Club on 30 April at the Freemasons' Tavern; Mill was requested to prepare the draft Regulations, while Holland and Torrens were entrusted with the preparations for the meeting. (See *Political Economy Club, Minutes of Proceedings, 1821–1882,* London, 1882, p. 35.)

## 426. RICARDO TO TROWER [1]
### [*Reply to 423*]

Upper Brook Street
21 April 1821

My Dear Trower

21 April 1821      I was very much concerned to hear of the accident you had met with; and yet considering how very near you were to a result much more serious I ought rather to congratulate you on your narrow escape, than condole with you on the slight injury you have received. Since receiving your letter I have heard of you twice; once from Mr. Turner, when you were in town for a day, and another time from your brother, whom I accidentally met in the street. I am glad to find that you are getting well.

Our discussions in the House on the currency question, are I hope now closed—I trust that we shall have no more proposals to deviate from the course which after due consideration has been determined on.

Your view of Godwin's book exactly agrees with mine. The real question at issue is not whether under favorable circumstances population will double in 25 or in 50 years, but whether it has not a tendency to increase faster than the capital which is to employ it, and if so what measures of legislation should be pursued. It must be manifest that the principle of population is strong enough for human happiness, and it neither wants poor laws nor any other laws to encourage it.

Mr. Mill's book is not yet quite finished, though in a state of great forwardness. His object is to give a clear exposition of all the elementary principles of Political Economy as they are at present understood. He does not mean to notice any other writer, nor to attempt to controvert the errors into

---

[1] MS at University College, London.—*Letters to Trower,* XLV.

which he may think they have fallen. It may probably be a month or two before his book will be published.

The catholic bill is lost.[1] I am sorry for it, though I cannot but think that it is only delayed. You are undoubtedly right, "the real fear is the ultimate consequences of that spirit of cession in which the measure originates. Test and Corporation Acts, Tithes, Church Establishments these are the real foundation of the alarms." If by good legislation the resources of Ireland were fairly brought forth, they would contribute greatly to the wealth of the United Kingdom. What a quantity of capital might be advantageously employed in that country, and no doubt would be, if there were not fears for its security in so disturbed a region. This resource is however in store for us. We landholders have formidable rivals in the landholders of that country. Our alarm is excited by the rivalship and competition of Poland, Russia and America, but we never think of Ireland the most formidable of them all. The tillage of Ireland continues uniformly to increase and will I have no doubt for many years to come. When the improvements in husbandry so well followed in England are introduced into that country the effects must be very marked on the price of corn, and on the interests of English landlords.

I have worked very hard in the Agricultural Committee and I hope not without effect in correcting mistaken principles. We have had many farmers before us who have given a sad but I believe a true picture of the great prevalence of distress. These farmers were questioned as to remedies, and were all for protecting duties, amounting almost to the prohibition of foreign corn. It was my business to shew how little they were qualified to be advisers on this important

---

[1] It was defeated in the House of Lords on 17 April. Cp. above p. 350, n. 2

question, by exposing their ignorance of the first principles which should guide our judgments.

Mr. Attwood, a great publisher of Essays on the currency, was called before us, and if he were to be believed, there is no other cause for a fall of prices but an increase in the value of money. His claims to infallibility have been sifted by Huskisson and myself, and I believe it will appear that he is no great master of the science.[1] Mr. Hodgson and Mr. Tooke have been our best informed witnesses. Mr. Hodgson is a merchant and corn dealer of Liverpool, who expends annually a large sum of money in sending people about the country to examine into the state of the crop just before it is reaped. They do so by going from field to field at 2 or 3 miles distance from each other, and actually counting the ears, and weighing the grains in a square foot or yard; by which means they are enabled to compare it with the crops of former years.[2] The last appears to have been an unusually abundant crop, greater than for many years before. This evidence is confirmed by more than one land surveyor. Mr. Tooke who is a good political economist gave us some valuable information of the effect of abundance on price, particularly with such a corn law as is now established, when we are deprived of the markets of other countries, until our prices are below theirs.

[1] Thomas Attwood, the Birmingham banker and currency reformer, after being examined wrote to his wife on 11 April: 'I answered all the objections of Ricardo and Huskisson, I believe most completely, and very evidently to their deep mortification.' And on 13 April: 'The stupid landholders...are like sheep under the butcher's knife.... The misfortune is that they are all as dull as beetles, whilst Huskisson and Ricardo are as sharp as *needles* and as active as bees' (C. M. Wakefield, *Life of Thomas Attwood*, London, privately printed, 1885, p. 81).
[2] David Hodgson (on whom see below, IX, 182, n. 1) had disclosed these details of the method for the use of the Committee only, requesting that they should not be made public; accordingly, they were withheld from the printed Minutes of Evidence, p. 263.

This is in fact the present cause of the great depression 21 April 1821
in the price of corn. A little effect may be ascribed to the
currency; but abundance is the great operating cause.

You will have seen that we made a stand for good
principles on the question of the Timber duties, without
success at the present moment, but not I hope without
making some impression.[1] The debate was very briefly and
very badly reported.

Mrs. Ricardo joins with me in kind remembrances to
Mrs. Trower.

Ever Y<sup>rs</sup>

DAVID RICARDO

## 427. TOOKE TO RICARDO[2]

Russell square
Sunday [? 22 April 1821][3]

My dear Sir

I return the accompanying papers with thanks. 22 April 1821

Mr. Attwoods evidence in point of absurdity exceeds my
utmost expectations.—

The information given by Mr. Hodgson is in many
respects valuable.—

The falling off which he proves in the slaughter of Cattle
and Sheep seems to be confined to a comparison of the two
last years with 1817 and 1818, for there is no diminution
worth mentioning on a comparison of 1819 and 20 with any
of the years preceding 1817.—And I think that the extra

---

[1] See above, V, 102 and 110.
[2] MS in *R.P.*
[3] The dating is doubtful: it is assumed that the papers returned by Tooke were the minutes of his own evidence to the Agricultural Committee on 13 April 1821, which he had asked for in his letter of 19 April; and that with them Ricardo had sent the evidence given by Thomas Attwood on 10 and 11 April and by David Hodgson on 12 and 13 April.

slaughter in 1817 and 1818, supposing a general increase to be deducible from the increase in the places named,[1] may be referred to the foll$^g$ causes.

1   The very high price of Wheat in those years.—

2   The very high price of Tallow which was in 1818 nearly double of what it now is

3   The extraordinary drought and consequent deficiency and high price of provender which prevailed till late in the Autumn of 1818, and added to the other inducements to bring Cattle even half fatted to market.

4   There was an extensive rot among the Sheep in 1817 and 18, which rendered it desireable to kill a larger proportion than usual to prevent their being destroyed by the disorder.—

5   Our ports were open for the importation of Corn, and the consequent increased demand for manufactures naturally admitted of an extended consumption of the more expensive article of Meat.

The nearly opposite state to all those circumstances, may account for the diminution in the two last years, but whether such diminution bears out Mr. Hodgson's inference[2] I am not quite clear.

Believe me always

Most truly Yrs

Tho$^s$ Tooke

D$^d$ Ricardo Esq$^r$

---

[1] Liverpool, Manchester, Leeds, Sheffield and Birmingham; see Hodgson's evidence, in 'Report from Committee on the Agriculture of the U.K.', 1821, p. 266.

[2] 'Is your inference this; that owing to the scarcity of live stock (of which you consider the high price under a diminished consumption to be evidence) a considerable part of the land, formerly appropriated to pasture, must have been brought into tillage?—Yes.' (Hodgson's evidence, *ib.*, p. 267.)

## 428. RICARDO TO M^cCULLOCH [1]
*[Reply to 424.—Answered by 431]*

London 25^th April 1821

My Dear Sir

Col! Torrens sent me your article on accumulation, and on the effects of the use of machinery,[2] which I think very good, although there are parts of the article which do not quite accord with my present opinions. I think that I informed you, in a former letter, of a change in my sentiments respecting the advantages of machinery, and that it was my intention to write a chapter on that subject in the new edition of my book.[3] As you have probably read the chapter by this time, as I requested Mr. Murray to send you a copy last week, it will not be necessary for me to explain my views here— I should be glad however to hear from you whether I have satisfied you of the correctness of the opinions which I have ventured to give. You will not find much of novelty in the new edition; all that is new is pointed out in the advertisement at the beginning of the volume.

Mr. Malthus second edition will not appear for the present, he has had my notes ever since you returned them to me, but I fear they have made very little impression on him.

The labours of our Agricultural Committee are suspended during the holidays.—I have called two merchants before it, whose evidence I think valuable. Mr. Tooke is one, and from him I have got sound opinions to appear on our minutes. I do not entirely agree with him, nor will you. He thinks that

25 April 1821

---

[1] MS in British Museum.—*Letters to M^cCulloch*, XXIV.—Written before receiving M^cCulloch's letter 429.
[2] See above, p. 366, n. 2.
[3] Ch. XXXI, 'On Machinery'. That in fact Ricardo had not in-

formed M^cCulloch of the change in his views on machinery is evident from M^cCulloch's reply to this letter. He had, however, told Malthus, as appears from Malthus's letter to Sismondi, printed below, p. 375.

the Corn laws have no effect whatever in raising the average price of corn, and consequently that they are of no use to the landed interest—he thinks further that the United Kingdom would if no corn laws existed grow on an average the quantity of corn which she annually consumes, as in his opinion we can compete with other countries in the growth of corn.[1] I do not believe this. If our ports were regularly open at all times I am confident that we should be an importing country. You will read his evidence with interest. Mr. Solly, the other merchant I called, gave some valuable information respecting the price of corn in Poland, and in the Prussian Ports, and also regarding the expences of conveying corn from the interior, to the Ports of Embarkation, and from those Ports to London.[2]

The character of the evidence generally is bad;—farmers are very bad legislators, and ought not to have been asked their opinions on the policy of laws. As they were asked however, I thought it right to endeavor to shew their ignorance of the subject—and I flatter myself that I have been of a little use in making them talk nonsense and having it on record.—

Mr. Huskisson tells me that Lord Castlereagh has written to all our consuls and ambassadors abroad for an account of the prices of corn in foreign countries for a series of years which will be laid before Parliament as soon as it arrives.[3]

The criticism on Say in the last number of the Scotsman[4] is I think very just—he is certainly very far behind in his knowledge of the present state of the science.

---

[1] See Tooke's evidence on 6 April, 'Report from Committee on the Agriculture of the U.K.', 1821, pp. 229–30.

[2] See the evidence of Edward Solly, a London merchant, formerly of Danzig, on 17 April, *ib.* p. 319 ff.

[3] These accounts were not published till 1824; see *Parliamentary Papers,* 1824, vol. XVIII, p. 103.

[4] A review of Prinsep's translation of the *Traité;* see above, p. 315, n. 2.

Mill's book on Political Economy is nearly finished—he          25 April 1821
recognizes all the principles which you deem the correct
ones, and I have no doubt you will think his work well
calculated to disseminate useful information.—

On tuesday my labours recommence—I hope it will not
be long before we shall make our report. I know that there
is a slight difference in our opinions on the corn laws, but
I am not conscious of having deviated in the slightest degree
from those which I expressed in my book.

Ever truly Y<sup>rs</sup>

DAVID RICARDO

[The following letter contains the earliest statement we have that
Ricardo had changed his views on the effects of machinery.

MALTHUS TO SISMONDI [1]

E I Coll March 12<sup>th</sup> 1821.

Dear Sir

If you knew the inveterate habits of indolence which frequently          12 March 1821
overcome my best intentions towards my correspondents, and how
much in consequence, I am in arrear to my friends in Paris, America,
and the East Indies, at this moment I might perhaps indulge in some
hope of forgiveness for my delay in answering your very kind communications. As it is, I must appear to you quite inexcusable, and I
have only to throw myself on your mercy for pardon: I at first waited
for an opportunity of sending a letter to Geneva by a friend and I have
often observed that, when the opportunity does not readily occur, there
is no knowing how long such a plea for indolence may last.

I can assure you most sincerely that your letter gave me great
pleasure. It was very gratifying to me to find that you thought me on
the whole successful in my controversy with Mr Ricardo, and that the
points on which you differed from me were fewer than I had supposed.
I was aware however from the conversations I had the pleasure of
having with you at Sir James Mackintosh's that there were many points

---

[1] Addressed: 'A Mons<sup>r</sup> / Mons<sup>r</sup> nale, Pescia (Tuscany). [Published
Simonde de Sismondi / Geneve / by P. Jannaccone in *Rivista di*
Suisse'.—MS in Biblioteca Comu- *Storia Economica*, 1942, p. 104–5.]

of the subject on which we should not disagree, and on that account perhaps I was the more surprised at some observations which I found in your work on the subject of population. But you have explained the source of them. So many misconceptions have been in circulation respecting what I have said in my work on population, that without referring to it, it is very easy to receive impressions, that it contains opinions and doctrines which are not to be found in it.

I have lately been attacked, after a delay of twenty years, by my old antagonist Mr Godwin; but it is a very poor and feeble performance, and the only semblance of an argument in it is founded upon a miscalculation.

The Edinburgh Review has so entirely adopted Mr Ricardo's system of Political Economy that it is probable neither you nor I shall be mentioned in it. I know indeed that a review of your work was written and sent, but it appears to have been rejected through the influence of the gentleman[1] who is the principal writer in the department of Political Economy, and who is known to have adopted fully and entirely all Mr Ricardo's views. The article however which you have so ably controverted in the sheet you were so good as to send me was written by another convert of the name of Torrens.[2] In general however I should say that though Mr Ricardo's doctrines have certainly captivated some very able men, they are not [? spread][3] very much among the great body of political Economists[4] and I am inclined to

[1] McCulloch.
[2] The article on Owen in the *Edinburgh Review* (see above, p. 159, n. 2) contained also a lengthy criticism of Sismondi's views. Sismondi replied with an article entitled 'Examen de cette question: Le pouvoir de consommer s'accroit-il toujours dans la société, avec le pouvoir de produire?' in *Annales de Législation et de Jurisprudence*, tome I, 1820, pp. 111–144. He refers to the author of the *Edinburgh Review* article as 'le disciple de M. Ricardo' and remarks: 'On dit, que le maître lui-même l'a approuvé, et que les autres disciples y reconnaissent leur profession de foi la plus claire.' (p. 112.) It is curious, in view of Malthus' statement, that in reprinting his article in the 2nd ed. of his *Nouveaux principes,* 1827, under the new title 'Examen d'une réfutation des *Nouveaux principes d'économie politique,* publié dans la *Revue d'Edinburgh,* par un disciple de M. Ricardo', he added a footnote identifying the author with McCulloch. ('J'ai appris depuis que c'était M. Macculloch, qu'on peut regarder désormais comme le chef de l'école fondée par M. Ricardo.' Vol. II, p. 376.)
[3] Covered by seal.
[4] In the article in the *Annales* referred to above, n. 2, Sismondi had written: 'Le chef de la nouvelle école, M. Ricardo, a, dit-on,

think that many of them will not stand the tests of examination and experience.

You will be rather pleased to hear that he has altered his opinions on the subject of the effect of machinery on the labouring classes of society, and in a new edition which he is about to publish of his work, will I believe go so far as to say that it may not only for a time, but permanently injure the labourer, although it may increase the neat produce. This is going just as far or perhaps a little farther than I should go, but the view which he takes of the subject is somewhat different.

I am glad to hear that you are preparing a new edition.[1] I am engaged in a similar occupation.

I hope you are right respecting the effects of the equal division of landed property among children, as it seems to be the tendency of Europe at present. It may be excusable in an Englishman to be prejudiced in favour of a different system of property which for so long a time has appeared to be productive of favourable results. There is one part of the economy of Italy which I cannot understand. How does it happen that so many farms are let at half produce, when the difference of their fertility must be very great. The half of the produce which might be easily paid from a rich soil, I should think impossible to be paid from a poor soil.

I am sorry you are not likely to settle in Paris, as I should have had a better chance of seeing you.

> Believe me dear Sir
> with great respect and esteem
> truly Yours,
> T. R. Malthus]

déclaré lui-même qu'il n'y avait pas plus de vingt-cinq personnes en Angleterre qui eussent entendu son livre. Peut-être de ce qu'il a fait profession d'obscurité, est-il résulté que ceux qui l'ont entendu, ou qui ont cru l'entendre, se sont déjà regardés comme des adeptes, et ont apporté un esprit de secte plus obstiné à soutenir, presque exclusivement avec ses propres paroles, tout l'ensemble de son système.' (p. 112.)

[1] Of the *Nouveaux principes;* the second edition was not published till 1827.

## 429. McCULLOCH TO RICARDO [1]

Edinburgh 23 April 1821

My dear Sir

23 April 1821 Eight or ten days since I forwarded to Colonel Torrens a copy of my article on Machinery[2] which I desired him to hand over to you—I hope my manner of stating the argument has met with your approbation—Are you aware whether Mr. Malthus means to alter any of his conclusions in his new Edition?[3] If he does not he will deserve a much severer castigation than any he has hitherto met with—What he says about accumulation is absolutely disgraceful—He has it so mixed up, involved, and diluted that it is not easy for an ordinary reader to know what he would be at, but when attentively examined its rottenness is quite apparent—A very stupid book has lately appeared here in which some parts of your great work are attacked[4]—I would have answered it had I not thought it might perhaps have disturbed the quiet transit of the work to the pastry and the snuff shop—I hope you approved of the greater part of the article in the Scotsman on the reduction of the standard[5]—Excuse the liberty

---

[1] Addressed: 'David Ricardo Esquire / M.P. / Upper Brook Street / London'. London postmark, 26 April 1821.
    MS in *R.P.*
[2] See above, p. 366, n. 2.
[3] See above, p. 373.
[4] Probably John Craig, *Remarks on some Fundamental Doctrines in Political Economy; Illustrated by a Brief Inquiry into the Commercial State of Britain, since the Year 1815,* Edinburgh, Constable, 1821. Advertised by the publisher in the *Scotsman,* 21 April 1821. There is in *R.P.* a bill of Geo. Greenland, bookseller, charging Ricardo 7*s.,*

on 11 June 1821, for 'Craig's Pol! Econmy'.
[5] 'The Proposed Reduction of the Standard of the Currency considered as a Means of Relieving the Public Distresses', *Scotsman,* 14 April 1821. McCulloch in this article attacks Baring as 'the great patron of the scheme for degrading the standard of the currency' and rejects this proposal as involving 'the robbery of…the *private* creditors'; but he still advocates his own plan for reducing the interest on the National Debt (see above, VII, 93, n. 2).

I take in sending you the enclosed[1] and believe me to be with
the greatest regard

Yours most faithfully

J. R. M<sup>c</sup>CULLOCH

## 430. RICARDO TO SAY[2]
*[Reply to 393.—Answered by 446]*

London 8 May 1821

Dear Sir

I should have written to you immediately after I received your present of the "Letters" which you addressed
to Mr. Malthus, had I not expected, that by delaying it for
a short time, I should have been able to send you a copy of
the 3<sup>d</sup> edition of my book. Owing to the delay of Bookseller, and Printer, the time has been protracted far beyond
my expectation, but at length I am able to send you herewith
one of the first published copies of this last edition. In it,
I have pointed out the particular difference which exists
between us, respecting the meaning which should be attached
to the word "value". You use it in the same sense as "riches"
and as "utility" and it is this part of your valuable work
which I am very anxious should have the benefit of your
further consideration.

In your doctrine of productive services I almost fully
agree, but I submit to you, whether, as rent is the effect of
high price, and not the cause of it, it should not be rejected
when we estimate the comparative value of commodities.
I have two loaves of bread before me, one raised on the very
best land in the country, for which there is probably paid
£3 or £4 p<sup>r</sup> acre for rent; the other raised on land for which

---

[1] Probably a letter to be franked.
[2] MS in the possession of M.
Raoul-Duval.—*Mélanges*, pp. 108–

11; *Œuvres diverses*, pp. 416–17 (in
French translation).

there is not paid p.$^r$ acre as many shillings for rent, and yet both loaves are precisely of the same value, and are equally good. You would say that in one the productive service of land was highly paid, while comparatively little was paid for the productive services of capital and labour; while in the other much was paid for the productive services of capital and labour, and little for that of the land. This is no doubt true, but the information is not useful and can lead to no inference whatever that can guide our future practice. What we wish to know is what the general law is that regulates the value of bread, as compared with the value of other things, and I think we find that one description of bread, namely, that for the raising of which little or no rent is paid, regulates the value of all bread; and that its value in relation to other things depends on the comparative quantity of labour bestowed on *its* production, and the quantity of labour bestowed on the production of those other things.

Allow me also to remark that your work would be much more valuable if you entered more fully into the laws which regulate rent and profit. It certainly was a great mistake of Adam Smith to suppose that profits depended on the degree of accumulation of capital, without reference to the question of population, and the means of providing for that population.

I have read your letter to Mr. Malthus with great interest. In much of what you say in it I fully agree, but I cannot give my assent to all the doctrines which it advocates,—particularly to those on which I have already spoken, and which are substantially the same as the doctrines contained in your more important work. Mr. Malthus and I frequently see each other—we talk incessantly on the points we differ about, but without convincing each other. I am happy to say that the science of Political Economy is more and more studied by the young men of this country. We have lately formed a society, or rather a club of Political Economists,[1] in which we can boast of the names of Torrens, Malthus, and Mill— we have many others who are anxious for the establishment of the principles of a liberal policy in trade, but whose names have not been so much before the public as those I have mentioned.

You, I know, always exert yourself in the good cause, and have no other object in view but the diffusion of knowledge, and the triumph of truth.

> Believe me to be Dear Sir
> Very sincerely Yours
> DAVID RICARDO

## 431. McCULLOCH TO RICARDO[2]
### [*Reply to 428.*—*Answered by 433*]

Edinburgh 5 June 1821

My Dear Sir

I have to apologise for being so long in returning you my best thanks for the valuable present of the third Edition of your great work—I congratulate you on its success—It is the best proof that can be given of the growing attention now paid to this important science; and it must have a powerful influence in furthering the dissemination of sound principles—

At the same time I must say (and I say it with that regret which I ever must feel in differing widely from one to whom I shall always be proud to look up as to my master) that in my humble opinion the Chapter on Machinery in this

---

[1] See above, p. 367, n. 3.
[2] Addressed: 'David Ricardo Esq / M.P. / Upper Brook Street / London'.—MS in *R.P.*

Edition is a very material deduction from the value of the work—Little did I expect after reading your triumphant answer to the arguments of Mr. Malthus that you were so soon to shake hands with him, and to give up all—for that is what you have really done—which you had contended for a month or two before[1]—Excess of candour has in this instance occasioned your doing a very serious injury to your favourite science—It was certainly proper that you should have renounced your previous opinions the moment you were satisfied of their fallacy; but this may be done in various ways, and I do not think it was at all necessary for you to make a formal recantation—Your object never has been and never can be any other than to endeavour to promote the real interests of the science; but I apprehend you will agree with me in thinking that nothing can be more injurious to these interests than to see an Economist of the highest reputation strenuously defending one set of opinions one day, and unconditionally surrendering them the next—The fundamental differences that formerly existed (for I am sorry to think they have now nearly disappeared) between you and Messrs. Malthus and Sismondi induced many to believe that Political Economy was a thing of fudge, a fabric without a foundation—And I certainly think that those who were formerly of that opinion have a good deal better ground for entertaining it now—

However the manner in which you have published your change of opinion is of comparatively little consequence—It is what I consider the extreme erroneousness of the principles to which you have incautiously lent the sanction of your name that has excited my principal regret—It is impossible to fritter away your argument by fencing it about with conditions—If it is good for any thing at all it is con-

[1] In the *Notes on Malthus*.

clusive against all employment of machinery—It is not with
greater or less gross or nett produce[1] that we have the
smallest concern in considering this question; but simply
whether does machinery produce commodities cheaper or
not? If it does *not* produce them cheaper it will not be
erected, and if it does produce them cheaper its erection must
be profitable to every class of persons—The example which
you have given does not, as far as I can perceive, by any
means warrant a single one of the extraordinary conclusions
you have drawn from it—You have not said whether the
machine worth £7,500 is to last one, ten, or one hundred
years[2]—But, it is as plain as any proposition in geometry
that if it lasted only one year there could be no diminution
of the manufacturers capital, for the goods produced by it
at the end of the year would have to sell for £8,250; and the
capitalist would have this capital to lay out in the construction
of another machine, or in the employment of some sort
of labour—If the machine lasts more than one year then
the price of the commodities produced by it must sink;
and although the proprietor of the machine would not then
have an equally large capital wherewith to employ labour,
its deficiency will be fully compensated by the increased
revenues, or capitals of the purchasers of his goods—Your
example differs in no respect from that of Sismondi which
I analyzed in the last Number of the Review[3]—And in my
apprehension far from affording the shadow of a reason for
doubting of the constant advantages attending the employment of machinery, ought to be quoted in proof of it—

I deny that less cloth would be produced by this machine
of which you speak at the bottom of page 472[4]—Such a sup-

---

[1] 'produce' replaces 'profit'.
[2] Above, I, 389.
[3] *Edinburgh Review*, March 1821, Art. VI, pp. 113–15; cp. Sismondi, *Nouveaux principes*, 1819, vol. II, pp. 324–6.
[4] Above I, 390–1.

5 June 1821 position is totally out of the question. If the machine only lasted one year it must produce *more* cloth; and for this sufficient reason that if it did not there could be no motive for its erection—But, enduing the machine with greater durability will not lessen its productive power; it will only sink the prices of the commodities produced by it, and render its erection supremely advantageous—

I admit that if machinery were to become less productive according to the increase of its durability, there might be some force in your reasoning—But here you are completely silent[1]. You have neglected to establish[2] this fundamental position; and have not advanced a single word to shew why that should be the case of which the reverse appears obvious— For example an iron plough does not diminish gross produce, or to speak more intelligibly it does not execute less work than one that is constructed of wood: A Dock that is built of granite does not hold fewer ships than one that is built of brick—Nor would the productiveness of the steam engine be at all impaired though the fiat of almighty power were to confer indestructibility on the materials of which it is composed—Before you began to describe to your readers the disadvantages attending the diminution of gross produce by the introduction of machinery, it would have been well had you inquired whether in point of fact such diminution ever did actually take place, or whether it was at all likely that it could take place—Your argument is to be sure hypothetical; but the hypothesis will be thrown aside, and all those who raise a yell against the extension of machinery, and ascribe to it that misery which is[3] a mere necessary consequence of the oppressiveness of taxation, and of the restraints on commerce will fortify themselves by your authority! If your

[1] Replaces 'you are at a complete stand'.
[2] Replaces 'strengthen'.
[3] 'justly' is del. here.

reasoning and that of Mr. Malthus be well founded, the laws   5 June 1821
against the Luddites are a disgrace to the Statute book—

Let me beg of you to reconsider this subject—A heresy
on a mere doctrinal point is of no moment; but really I could
not recommend to any of my friends to bestow the least
attention on the study of this science, if I was satisfied that
it remained yet to be settled whether the reducing of the
price of commodities was advantageous or not—Truly if we
are not got this length, our disputes about profits and our
other remote conclusions ought to afford infinite amusement
to the scoffers—But, I, at least, am not in this quandary—
I will take my stand with the Mr. Burke of the American war
not with the Mr. Burke of the French revolution—with the
Mr. Ricardo of the first not of the third edition—Were there
nothing else to allege on the subject I should be perfectly
satisfied with what I consider the inherent fallacy involved
in all the arguments which have been advanced against
machinery—To maintain that a reduction of the price of
commodities can in any circumstances be disadvantageous,
appears to me to contradict every idea of the nature of wealth,
and to be in fact absurd—Such opinions are besides in complete contradiction to the universal consent of mankind—It
is the object of every individual—a law implanted in him by
Providence which compels him to endeavour to produce
with the least possible expence—I go a good way when I
admit the bare possibility that this general principle may
occasionally be productive of bad consequences—But nothing
but the clearest and most convincing reasoning will suffice
to establish an instance of what is so much at variance with
all preconceived opinions, and I will also add with all the
sound notions of Political Economy—

Were I not aware that in all your speculations you are
actuated solely by a desire to contribute to the improvement

of the science, I should not have presumed to address to you this hasty and ill-digested letter—But I am satisfied that opinions dictated equally by a regard to the interests of the science, and coming from one who is not the least sincere of your admirers, though they may seem erroneous, will claim and meet with your attentive perusal—I am with the greatest regard and esteem

ever faithfully yours

J. R. M<sup>c</sup>Culloch

## 432. RICARDO TO SINCLAIR [1]

56, Upper Brook Street, 15th June 1821.

Dear Sir,

Your plan is neither more nor less than a proposal to depreciate the currency 20 *per cent.* If I could consent to such a measure, I should propose to do it openly, without disguise; but I do not think such a plan necessary or expedient, and confidently expect, that in no long time, we shall surmount all our difficulties. I remain your obedient servant,

David Ricardo.

## 433. RICARDO TO M<sup>c</sup>CULLOCH [2]
### [*Reply to* 431.—*Answered by* 434]

London 18 June 1821

My dear Sir

Although I am not disposed to defend the manner in which I have acknowledged the change of my opinion, on the subject of machinery, in the third edition of my book,

---

[1] *Correspondence of Sir John Sinclair,* vol. i, pp. 374–5; *Letters to Trower,* XLVI.

[2] MS in British Museum.—*Letters to M<sup>c</sup>Culloch,* XXV.

I cannot agree with you that it will arm those, who have contended that Political Economy is a fabric without a foundation, with any additional arguments in favor of that opinion. The whole change of my opinion is simply this, I formerly thought that machinery enabled a country to add annually[1] to the gross produce of its commodities, and I now think that the use of it rather tends to the diminution of the gross produce. I have stated my reasons for thinking so, and I am willing again to acknowledge my error if I should be proved wrong. There are so many faults of manner in my book which I cannot defend, that I must submit to have this one added to their number.

There is on this part of the subject one expression of yours which I confess surprises me, and appears to me so great a misapprehension of my present opinion, that I cannot but flatter myself, when that opinion is more clearly explained to you, you will yourself embrace it as sound doctrine. You say, "little did I expect after reading your triumphant answer to the arguments of Mr. Malthus that you were so soon to shake hands with him, and to give up all." Mr. Malthus does not think that I have given up any thing to him, and no one who has read the chapter has supposed me to have approached one step nearer to Mr. Malthus's doctrine than I was before. You surely must forget that Mr. Malthus' objection to machinery is that it adds so much to the gross produce of the country that the commodities produced cannot be consumed —that there is no demand for them: mine, on the contrary, is that the use of machinery often diminishes the quantity of gross produce, and although the inclination to consume is unlimited, the demand will be diminished, by the want of means of purchasing. Can any two doctrines be more different? and yet you speak of them as identically the same.

---

[1] 'annually' is ins.

I will now proceed to the consideration of the doctrine itself, and I am not without hopes that I shall convince you of its being a correct one; as demonstrable as any in the science of Political Economy. I acknowledge that machinery would not be erected if it did not produce commodities cheaper than they were produced before its erection, but I deny "that if it does produce them cheaper its erection must be profitable to every class of persons". Its erection must be profitable to every class of buyers as buyers[1], but the question between us, is whether it will or not diminish the number of the class of buyers. I say it will, because it will diminish the quantity of gross produce; and therefore the observation in your letter that it is not with the greater or less gross or nett produce that we have the smallest concern, cannot be well founded, for the whole question rests on the truth of this proposition. Diminish the quantity of exchangeable articles, and you diminish the demand for commodities;—you diminish the means of enjoyment of some one, or more, of the classes of the community. If I have not said whether the machine was to last one, ten, or a hundred years I have not been so explicit as I ought to have been. I admit too that it is as plain as any proposition in geometry that if it lasted only one year there could be no diminution in the demand for labour, but I do not admit that the same result would necessarily take place if the machine lasted for ten years. If the machine was to last one year only, the cloth produced must be of as great a value at least[2] as before, but if it were to last 10 years, a value much less than that, would afford the ordinary profits of stock, because although the same amount of capital would be employed, less of that capital would be employed in the maintenance of labour, and consequently a less deduction would be annually made from the gross value

---

[1] 'as buyers' is ins.          [2] 'at least' is ins.

of the commodity produced. It is what remains after this
deduction that invariably constitutes profits. A manufacturer
of cloth produces 10,000 yards of cloth, at £2 p$^r$ yard, or
£20,000, of which he pays 9000 yards, or £18,000, for labour.
By the assistance of machinery, and with the same amount of
capital, he can produce only 3000 yards annually, but of these
3000 he is able to retain 1500 yards for his share as profit, and
by the economy in the means of production, cloth we will
suppose falls to £1. 10 – p$^r$ yard, does not the manufacturer
get £2250 – on the same amount of capital, instead of £2000,
which he got before? Are there not motives enough for him
to substitute the fixed for the circulating capital, and can he
do so without displacing labour? Here then we have a case
of a commodity becoming cheaper, because its cost of production is reduced, although its aggregate quantity is
diminished. Give to the machine greater durability, and a
less return than 3000 yards will be sufficient to compensate
the manufacturer, because he must sacrifice fewer yards for
the purpose of keeping his fixed capital in its original efficient
state. If with greater durability you suppose the machine
still to produce 3000 yards of cloth, the price of cloth will fall,
for its cost of production will still further diminish. It is only
in the case of the machine affording 10000 yards of cloth that
you could employ the same quantity of labour, for it is only
in that case that you would have the same quantity of food,
cloth, and all other commodities annually.[1] You say the
productiveness of the steam engine would not be impaired
though the fiat of Almighty[2] power were to confer indestructibility on the materials of which it is composed. True,
but then the steam engine would be of less value, because
nature would do more for it, and labour less. To obtain an
indestructible steam engine now, we are obliged annually to

[1] 'annually' is ins.   [2] Replaces 'almighty'.

bestow a quantity of labour upon it, and therefore it is of great value. I have not said that if Almighty power would give us steam engines ready made, and capable of doing work for us without the assistance of human labour, that such a present would be injurious to any class—it would be far otherwise; but I have said that when a manufacturer is in possession of a circulating capital he can employ with it a greater number of men, and if it should suit his purposes to substitute a fixed capital of an equal value for this circulating capital, it will be inevitably followed by a necessity for dismissing a part of his workmen, for a fixed capital cannot employ all the labour which it is calculated to supersede. I confess that these truths appear to me to be as demonstrable as any of the truths of geometry, and I am only astonished that I should so long have failed to see them. I pray you, in my turn, to give an unprejudiced attention to them; if you do I think you will agree with me.

The Report of the Agricultural Committee will be delivered to the House to-morrow. Considering the composition of the committee it is better than could be expected, and I flatter myself there is enough of good about it to shew the fallacies which we could not expunge from it. Mr. Huskisson drew it up, and it is but justice to him to say that he is for establishing the trade on the most free and liberal foundation.

Mushet wishes I believe that his tables[1] should be noticed in the Scotsman. I have not examined them very accurately, but I observe that he reckons the whole debt as a capital bearing 5 pc$^t$, whereas a great part only bears an interest of 3 pc$^t$. Whether this leading error is compensated for by

---

[1] *A Series of Tables, exhibiting the Gain and Loss to the Fundholders arising from the late Fluctuations in the Value of the Currency from* *1800 to 1821,* by Robert Mushet, London, Baldwin, 1821. For a summary see below, pp. 396–8 and cp. IX, 39.

18 June 1821

reckoning the debt created since the depreciation in 1800 in the same manner I do not know—if it is the result will probably be correct. He was bound I think to make all his calculations at compound interest—he has made them at simple interest.

I request you will be kind enough to give directions that the Scotsman be sent to me at Gatcomb to which place I am going on tuesday sen'-night.

Ever faithfully Y<sup>rs</sup>

DAVID RICARDO

### 434. McCULLOCH TO RICARDO [1]
[*Reply to 433.—Answered by 436*]

Edinburgh 21 June 1821

My Dear Sir

21 June 1821

I had this morning the pleasure to receive your valuable letter of the 18<sup>th</sup>—I beg to apologise for my mistake in saying that you had joined with Malthus—What I meant to state was that "I did not expect you would so soon have joined him in considering that the employment of machinery might, in certain cases, be disadvantageous"—

You state in your letter that you acknowledge that "machinery would not be erected if it did not produce commodities cheaper than they were produced before its erection"—Now, I confess it appears to me to be quite impossible to hold this sound opinion and at the same time to arrive at your other conclusions—Suppose a manufacturer employs labourers who produce him 100,000 yards of cotton, of which his profit amounts to 10,000, and that he constructs a machine with his capital which will last for ever and which yields him the same profit or 10,000 yards—There would

---

[1] MS in *R.P.*

here be a diminution of gross produce; but is it possible that such a diminution could take place without the price of cottons rising? I think it is not—The reasoning in your book (p 473)[1] on this subject does not satisfy me—You have fallen into an error of the same kind that a mechanician would fall into who should neglect to make any allowance for friction—Men do not change employments with the same ease that they walk from a drawing into a dining room— The farmers would unquestionably offer a higher price for their cottons rather than produce them themselves—It does not therefore appear to me to be possible to diminish gross produce without raising prices, without dooing that which you admit a machine never does; and consequently it must result that the hypothesis on which your reasoning is founded can never really occur—

It was not, however, my object in writing you this letter to enter at large on this question, but to inform you that I intend sending an Article to the forthcoming Number of the Review deprecating in the strongest manner the efforts that have been made to induce government again to tamper with the standard of our currency[2]—In this article I would notice Mr. Mushets Tables; but as I am not very familiar with the subject, I would consider your sending me such remarks as occur regarding their accuracy, and the principles on which they are constructed, as would enable an ordinary reader to judge of their value as a most particular favour— I hope you will forgive my taking the liberty to make this request; and as I have but little time to spare I have further to request that you will allow me to hear from you at your earliest convenience—

I hope you will endeavour to come down to Scotland this

[1] Above I, 391.
[2] *Edinburgh Review,* July 1821,     Art. XI, 'Pernicious Effects of De-grading the Standard of Money'.

summer—I think you would not regret dooing so; and, 21 June 1821 although I am aware that can be no inducement to you, permit me to say that nothing could give me so much pleasure as to have the satisfaction of seeing one to the study of whose works I owe any little success in life I have ever had—

Yours most sincerely<br>J. R. MᶜCULLOCH

435. TROWER TO RICARDO [1]<br>[Answered by 437]

Unsted Wood—June 24. 1821

My Dear Ricardo

I am much obliged to you for the Agricultural Report; 24 June 1821 a very interesting part of which, viz the Evidence, I observe is not included.—

I intended myself the pleasure of writing to you to day, to say, that you will receive by tomorrow's Coach your very elaborate Notes on Malthus, which I have read with great interest, and much attention.—

I think you have succeeded in compleatly vindicating your Book from the charges he brought against it; and in exposing many of his numerous errors and inconsistencies. After all, it appears to me, that when the question is stripped of the ambiguities and misconceptions, which he has mixed up with it, there is no very essential difference between you, at least with regard to *Principles.* With regard to many of his *conclusions,* they are very erroneous, and no less mischievous; and you have forcibly exposed their fallacies and their contradictions. He is incessantly puzzling and perplexing himself with undefined notions of *value.* Not that I can entirely agree with You in *your definition* of *exchangeable value*—No

<hr>

[1] MS in *R.P.*

doubt, the *labor expended* upon a commodity is the *measure* by which the accuracy of its exchangeable value, is ascertained, and eventually regulated; but I confess I think, that the labor, which a commodity can *command* is what actually constitutes its *exchangeable* value.

The term *value* is employed to designate the *relative value* of Commodities; which is necessary to be ascertained in exchanging them for each other. It refers to *exchangeable*, and not to *positive* value. It is intended to express how much of one thing is worth, or can procure, so much of another thing. If there were *no exchange* of Commodities they would have no *value*. They would, of course, retain their *use;* but they could not be said to possess *value;* which implies the *worth* of one thing estimated in some other things. There are no means of estimating what is the *value* of Commodities in *use*. If they had no *use* they would possess no *value*, because they would not pass in exchange, and because therefore there would not be any thing with which they could be compared. I submit therefore, that the only proper use of the term *value* is in *exchange*. And value in *exchange* will signify the relative or comparative value of two commodities, which are exchanged for each other. If so, I doubt whether the term exchangeable value can be applied to signify the quantity of labor necessary to acquire or *produce* a commodity; but the quantity of labor that commodity can *command* when exchanged: The quantity of labor necessary to acquire or produce a commodity is the expence of acquiring it, and is very properly termed its *cost,* but this *cost* may be very different from, and is rarely exactly the same as, the *value* it can command in exchange. It is nevertheless the central point to which exchangeable value is constantly gravitating and from which any violent aberrations are neither frequent nor lasting. It would be a great pity, that your criticism on

Malthus should not meet the public eye. But I confess I do not think, that in their present shape they would answer the purpose. Very few persons are sufficiently interested in the Science of Political Economy, especially in the controversies respecting to its abstruser points, to go through the labor of continually turning from the text to the comment, and examining the reasoning by which the opposite opinions are supported:—If Malthus is to be answered *effectually*, it must be by mixing up with the comments such an abstract of his work as shall put the reader into possession of the arguments, which are combatted, so as to enable him to follow out the reasoning without the labor of constant reference to the original works. But, perhaps such a work is unnecessary; and you may safely trust, that the Principles you have so ably developed in your Book, will silently win their way, and force the proper conviction on the minds of those, whose right understanding of the subject is likely to produce any practical effects upon the Public.

From Mr. Mill's Book,[1] too, I expect very essential assistance. No doubt, he must propose to throw some *new light* upon the subject, or to treat it in a manner which he conceives more likely to procure his doctrines a ready admission into his readers mind. I am looking impatiently for this performance.

I have already run my letter to such a length as to leave little room for any other subject. What say you to Continental affairs? The political horizon is clouded and stormy; but whatever may be the inclination of that frightful mass of people, who, in all Countries, are ever ready for War, I hope and trust, that the mere necessity of the case, the deranged finances, and distressed circumstances of every Country in Europe, will prevent the renewal of hostilities.—

[1] *Elements of Political Economy.*

24 June 1821
When will your labors in the Senate end, and when shall you spread your wings for the Country? Pray make our united Comps to Mrs. Ricardo, and believe me

Yrs most truly

HUTCHES TROWER

## 436. RICARDO TO McCULLOCH [1]
### [*Reply to 434.—Answered by 474*]

Gatcomb Park, Minchinhampton<br>30 June 1821

My Dear Sir

30 June 1821
I am glad that you are going to write an article in the Review on the importance of adhering to the standard of currency fixed in 1819. It is singular that those who have usually maintained sound principles on this important question are, or rather have been, amongst the most vehement to call for[2] such modifications of the standard, as would be equivalent to an alteration of it,[3] while the ministers, who were the last to see the question in its true light, are now found amongst the firmest supporters of an unvarying and fixed standard. I am in hopes that all chance of a repeal of the law of 1819 is now gone by, and that we shall so far profit by our past experience as never to venture on the repetition of so dangerous a measure as that of 1797.

You wish to have my opinion of Mr. Mushet's tables which I will give to you most freely, and only hope that I may be sufficiently clear to be easily understood. His plan was to shew, by a debtor and credit account, what the fund-holders, had, on the whole, gained or lost, by the successive measures

---

[1] Addressed: 'J. R. M'Culloch Esq! / Buccleugh Place / Edinburgh.'
    MS in British Museum.—*Letters to M^cCulloch*, XXVI.

[2] 'call for' replaces 'admit'.
[3] The allusion is to Alexander Baring; cp. above, p. 378, n. 5, and V, 91 ff. and 105 ff.

of first depreciating the currency, and then restoring it to its    30 June 1821
ancient standard. During the period that the currency was
depreciated, the stockholder lost a portion of his annual
dividends, on that portion of the debt which existed prior to
the depreciation. But as during the same period he advanced
loans to the State in the depreciated currency, on which he
should have received dividends, for ever, in a medium of the
same value, he is a gainer by being now paid in a medium
raised in value. Mr. Mushet proposed to compare these gains
and losses, and to determine which on the whole prepon-
derated, but he has committed some very grave errors. In
the first table, his calculation is made on a capital of
£471,335,923, on the supposition that such was the amount
of the unredeemed debt;—in 1800, in point of fact that was
the amount of the whole debt, redeemed as well as unredeemed—he should have confined himself to the unredeemed
debt. Secondly, in the same table, he calculates the interest
at 5 pc! on the nominal capital, and therefore supposes the
public creditor entitled to a dividend of 23 millions, but as
the greatest part of the capital consisted of 3 pc!s the real
dividends did not amount to more than about    [1]. The
same observation applies to the last column, which consists of
the capital Stock created, not the money value of that stock.
Mr. Mushet himself thinks that this is not a matter of much
consequence, as it tells one way as well as the other;—it
certainly does so, but I very much doubt whether it tells as
much one way as the other. Thirdly; In the first table he sets
out with his money at par, and therefore if his dividends were
correct in amount the result would be as he has stated, a loss
to the stock holder of £40,099,891, in money of our present
standard; but in table 3, and in most of the others, the market

[1] Blank in MS. Should be £15,611,864, as in the 2nd ed. of Mushet's
*Series of Tables.*

price of gold differs from the standard price, and therefore the gain at bottom of £69,457 is not a gain in our standard money, but in a depreciated money, valued by a standard of gold at £4. 5 – p.$^{r}$ oz. To make this amount correct he ought to make a further calculation, and say, as £4. 5 is to £3. 17. 10$\frac{1}{2}$, £69,457 is to $x$, the correct sum. In table 4 the standard is £4. 4; 5, £4 16, £5 4 &c.$^{a}$, &c.$^{a}$ His results, which are finally added together, instead of being in one standard common to all, are in standards almost as various as the sums, and must lead to the most false conclusions. In all his calculations for interest from table 21 to 226 he has been satisfied with simple interest—I contend he should have taken compound interest. If I had been an old stock holder, and if for 20 years, in consequence of the depreciation of the currency, I had been deprived of £100 p.$^{r}$ Ann.$^{m}$, my loss would have been £3300; for £100 p.$^{r}$ Ann.$^{m}$, accumulated for 20 years at compound interest, would amount to that sum; according to Mr. Mushet my loss would only be £2950, or £2000 for loss of dividends, and £950 for the simple interest on them. These which appear to me to be errors, I have pointed out to Mr. Mushet himself, and I believe it is his intention to cast his tables anew and make them more correct in another edition.[1]

I believe I have entered more particularly into the details of these tables than is necessary—I have done so for the purpose of shewing you how totally inadequate they are to satisfy us respecting the real loss or gain to the Stock holder from the various tamperings with the currency during 20 years.

Now for a few words respecting machinery. You state a

[1] In the 'second edition, corrected' of Mushet's *Series of Tables*, 1821, most of these corrections are made. See below, IX, 7.

very fair case of a manufacturer getting 10,000 yards of cotton out of 100,000. If his 10,000 yards were wholly produced by machinery, which is to last for ever, and to be of the same value as the capital previously employed in labour and in producing 100,000 yards, you say cottons would rise, because capital cannot move from one employment to another with the rapidity which a contrary supposition would require. I admit every thing you contend for on this point, and I ask what will be the condition of the labourers in consequence of the application of machinery to this trade. Whatever may be the price of the cottons there will be a diminution in the quantity produced, and no more of any other commodity will be produced in its stead. Is it possible to conceive so great a diminution of production without suffering to some of the classes of society. The effective demand for cottons cannot be so great as before, because that demand depended on the demand for corn and cloth, the commodities consumed by the labourers, whose wages were really paid in cottons. Labour will fall because there will be a diminished demand for it—Corn and cloth will fall because the demand for them depended on the demand for labour. Cottons may rise a little but the high price can only last till additional capital is attracted by high profits to that trade. There will be every motive to quit that employment which does not yield the ordinary profits, for the purpose of engaging in that which yields more than the ordinary profits. I ask for no greater concession than this. In admitting that by the use of machinery the gross annual[1] produce of the industry of the country will be diminished you give up the argument, for the gross annual produce cannot be diminished in any other way but by a diminished employment of the industrious classes. If machinery could

---

[1] 'annual' is ins.

do all the work that labour now does, there would be no demand for labour. Nobody would be entitled to consume any thing who was not a capitalist, and who could not buy or hire a machine.

I wish much that I could pay a visit to Scotland this summer, but my engagements with my family will I fear prevent me. I have three children married, and they all live within the distance of 28 miles from my residence in the country,[1] besides which Mrs. Ricardo would not consent to my going without her, and she could not go without my two youngest girls, and if they went the governess must go:— she in her turn would make it necessary to take others, and thus the undertaking would become a serious one. It would I assure you give me great pleasure to be personally known to you, and I do not despair on some future occasion of surmounting the obstacles which at present oppose them- selves to our meeting. If you were at all inclined to a little journey I should be most happy to see you here. Perhaps you could spare a little time from your labours, if so, pray come.

Most truly Yours<br>DAVID RICARDO

[1] Osman, at Bromesberrow Place, Ledbury; Henrietta (Mrs. Clutter-buck), at Widcomb, Bath; and Priscilla (Mrs. Anthony Austin), at Bradley, Wootonunderedge.

# INDEX OF CORRESPONDENTS
## 1819 – June 1821

*denotes letters not previously published*